"Our mission is to improve decision making, stimulate research and inform debate within government and the wider community by providing a quality statistical service"

Social Trends 25

1995 Edition

Editor: JENNY CHURCH

Associate Editor: CAROL SUMMERFIELD

Production team: DAVID FRY
ALYSON WHITMARSH
ANDREW LEDGER
GAVIN HALES
DAVID PENNY
DAVID SHARP
TONY SYMMONDS
STEVE WHYMAN
AMANDA HUGHES
CATHY WYKES
CLAIRE MERRICK

London: HMSO

Contents

Introduction

Social Trends draws together statistics from a wide range of government departments and other organisations to paint a broad picture of British society today, and how it has been changing. The 13 chapters each focus on a different social policy area, described in tables, charts and explanatory text. *Social Trends* is aimed at a very wide audience: policy-makers in the public and private sectors; marketing and advertising professionals; market researchers; journalists and commentators; academics and students; schools; and the general public. In this Silver Jubilee edition, comparisons with 1971 are provided wherever possible.

The editorial team always welcomes readers' views on how *Social Trends* could be improved. Please write to the Editor at the address shown below.

New material and sources

To preserve topicality, over half of the 367 tables and charts in *Social Trends 25* are new compared with the previous edition. In all chapters, the source of the data is given below each table and chart. *Social Trends 25* also includes at the end of each chapter a list of references directing readers to other published sources of data (both government and non government) and a list of contact telephone numbers. Those using *Social Trends* as a first point of reference should find this particularly useful. Regional and local authority analyses of much of the information in *Social Trends* may be found in the CSO's publication *Regional Trends*, available from HMSO bookshops.

In this edition of *Social Trends* there has been some reorganisation of chapters. The Health chapter now concentrates on the health status of the population. Material on health service provision is included in a new chapter on Social Protection together with provision of social services and of financial benefits. This chapter also includes material on the activities of the voluntary sector including charities, previously covered in the Participation chapter. The Participation chapter no longer appears in the book: other material from it has now been re-allocated to other chapters, for example information on trade union membership can now be found in the Employment chapter.

Availability on electronic media

The data contained in the tables and charts in *Social Trends 25* are available on diskette to any reader returning the order form enclosed in this copy of *Social Trends 25*. Just complete the few questions on the form and your diskette will be sent to you free of charge. Mail order customers who completed the questions on their order form or provided the details when ordering by phone will have been sent their diskette directly. Please let us know if you have been unable to obtain yours by calling us on 0171 270 6081.

The first 25 editions of *Social Trends* will be available on CD-ROM towards the end of February 1995. For details on how to order a copy please again contact us on 0171 270 6081.

Contributors

The Editor and Associate Editor wish to thank all colleagues in the Government Statistical Service and contributors in other organisations without whose help this publication would not be possible. Thanks also go to the CSO Graphic Design Unit.

Appendix

The Appendix gives definitions and general background information, particularly on administrative structures and legal frameworks. Anyone seeking to understand the tables and charts in detail will find it helpful to read the corresponding entries in the Appendix in addition to the footnotes relevant to each table and chart. A full index to this edition is included following the Appendix.

Social Statistics Section
Central Statistical Office
PO Box 1333
Millbank Tower
Millbank
LONDON SW1P 4QQ

List of tables and charts

Numbers in brackets refer to similar items appearing in *Social Trends 24*

Page

Page

Page

Chapter 1 Population

Population structure and changes

In mid-1993, the population of the United Kingdom was 58.2 million, 4 per cent higher than in 1971. (Table 1.3)

Over 20 per cent of the United Kingdom population were aged 60 or over in 1993. The Irish Republic had the lowest proportion in the EC at just over 15 per cent. (Chart 1.5)

Greater London had a population density of over 4 thousand people per square kilometre in 1993. By contrast, the Highland region of Scotland had only 8 people per square kilometre. (Chart 1.7)

Births and deaths

The number of deaths in the United Kingdom is projected to rise from 658 thousand deaths in 1993 to peak at 830 thousand in 2051, when those born in the 1960s baby boom will be in their 80s. (Chart 1.10)

The number of births each year in the United Kingdom is projected to exceed the number of deaths until the year 2027. (Chart 1.10)

The mean age at which mothers gave birth in England and Wales rose to 28.1 years in 1993, from 26.2 years in 1971. (Chart 1.12)

Migration

Just under half of applications for asylum in 1993 were made by people from Africa. (Table 1.16)

World population

By the year 2000, half of the world's population is expected to live in cities, compared with only a quarter in 1975. (Page 26)

1.1

Dependent population: by age

United Kingdom

Millions

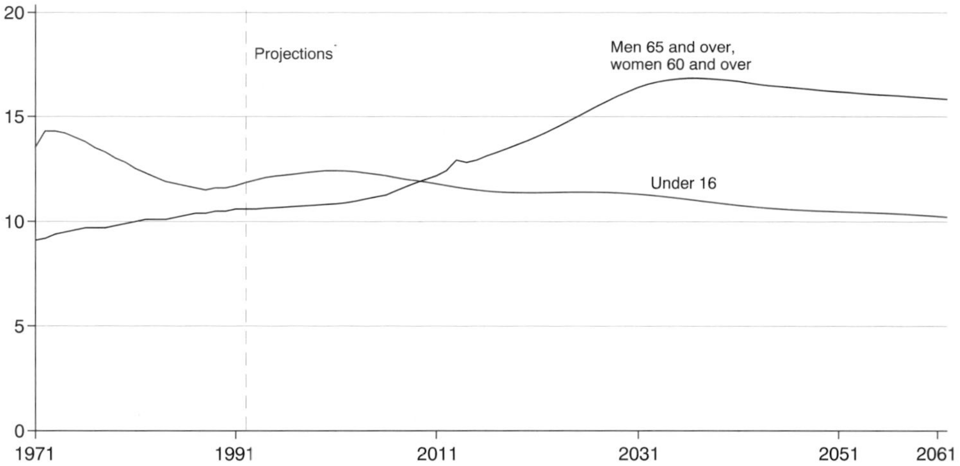

1 1992-based projections.

Source: Office of Population Censuses and Surveys; Government Actuary's Department; General Register Office (Scotland); General Register Office (Northern Ireland)

1.2

Population[1] of the United Kingdom

United Kingdom							Thousands
	1961	1971	1981	1991	1992	1993	2031
England	43,561	46,412	46,821	48,208	48,378	48,533	52,435
Wales	2,635	2,740	2,813	2,891	2,899	2,906	2,977
Scotland	5,184	5,236	5,180	5,107	5,111	5,120	4,998
Northern Ireland	1,427	1,540	1,538	1,601	1,618	1,632	1,831
United Kingdom	52,807	55,928	56,352	57,808	58,006	58,191	62,241

1 Data are mid-year estimates for 1961 to 1991 and 1992-based projections for 2031. See Appendix, Part 1: Population and population projections.

Source: Office of Population Censuses and Surveys; Government Actuary's Department; General Register Office (Scotland); General Register Office (Northern Ireland)

1.3

Population change[1]

United Kingdom						Thousands
		Average annual change				
	Population at start of period	Live births	Deaths	Net natural change	Other[2]	Overall annual change
Census enumerated						
1901-1911	38,237	1,091	624	467	-82	385
1911-1921	42,082	975	689	286	-92	194
1921-1931	44,027	824	555	268	-67	201
1931-1951	46,038	785	598	188	25	213
Mid-year estimates						
1951-1961	50,287	839	593	246	6	252
1961-1971	52,807	963	639	324	-12	312
1971-1981	55,928	736	666	69	-27	42
1981-1991	56,352	757	655	103	42	145
1991-1993	57,808	779	637	142	49	192
Mid-year projections[3]						
1993-2001	58,179	776	623	153	50	203
2001-2011	59,800	716	614	102	44	146
2011-2021	61,257	718	635	83	6	89
2021-2031	62,146	703	693	9	0	9
2031-2041	62,241	666	767	-102	0	-102
2041-2051	61,223	656	819	-163	0	-163

1 See Appendix, Part 1: Population and population projections.
2 Includes net civilian migration and other adjustments.
3 1992-based projections. The 1992-based projection for mid-1993 was 58,179 compared with the actual figure of 58,191 thousand.

Source: Office of Population Censuses and Surveys; Government Actuary's Department; General Register Office (Scotland); General Register Office (Northern Ireland)

Population structure and changes

Since the first British Census was carried out in 1801, they have been conducted on a decennial basis, with the exception of 1941 (during the Second World War). The latest population censuses for Great Britain and Northern Ireland were carried out on 21 April 1991. As well as providing a count of the population, information was collected on the economic and demographic characteristics of the population, housing and household characteristics and, for the first time, the ethnic origin of the population.

The population of the United Kingdom was 58.2 million in 1993, a rise of just over 10 per cent since 1961 (Table 1.2). Over the same period, there was a wide variation between the constituent countries within the United Kingdom. With the exception of Scotland, they all experienced increases in population; the biggest rise occurred in Northern Ireland at nearly 15 per cent. In contrast, the population in Scotland was just over 1 per cent lower in 1993 than in 1961, although it has shown small increases in each of the last five years. The United Kingdom population as a whole is projected to peak at 62.3 million in 2027.

The rate at which the population changes is dependent upon the number of births and deaths (ie the net natural change) and the net effect of people moving into, and out of, the country. Table 1.3 illustrates how these different factors have affected the United Kingdom's population since 1901, as well as giving projections up to 2051. In mid 1993 the population of the United Kingdom was projected to be 58.2 million; this was 4 per cent higher than in 1971 and 52 per cent higher than at the turn of the century. The highest average annual growth in the population, of around 385 thousand per year, occurred during the first decade of the century when the number of births was high. Growth in the population was again high during the 'baby boom' of the 1960s, but low in the 1970s due to a combination of a small number of births and a large number of deaths giving the smallest overall annual increase this century - 42 thousand per year. However, an even smaller net average increase of 9 thousand per year is projected for the period from 2021 to 2031; and thereafter the population is projected to fall.

The United Kingdom continues to have an ageing population. In 1971, just over 13 per cent of the United Kingdom population were 65 or over; this proportion is projected to rise to around 24 per cent in the year 2051 (Table 1.4). More noticeable, within this group, is that the proportion of people aged 80 or over in the population is projected to more than double between 1993 and 2051, from just under 4 per cent to just over 9 per cent. This is mainly attributable to those born in the 1960s baby boom entering their 80s, as well as increases in longevity (see Table 7.2). The 16 to 39 age group, which accounted for 31 per cent of the population in 1971, peaked at 36 per cent in 1986, and is projected to fall to 28 per cent in 2051.

1.4

Population[1]: by age and gender

United Kingdom — Percentages

	Under 16	16-39	40-64	65-79	80 and over	All ages (= 100%) (millions)
Mid-year estimates						
1971	*25.5*	*31.3*	*29.9*	*10.9*	*2.3*	55.9
1981	*22.3*	*34.9*	*27.8*	*12.2*	*2.8*	56.4
1991	*20.3*	*35.3*	*28.6*	*12.0*	*3.7*	57.8
1993	*20.6*	*34.9*	*28.8*	*11.9*	*3.9*	58.2
Males	*21.6*	*36.3*	*29.2*	*10.6*	*2.4*	28.5
Females	*19.6*	*33.5*	*28.4*	*13.1*	*5.4*	29.7
Mid-year projections[2]						
2001	*20.7*	*32.9*	*30.6*	*11.4*	*4.3*	59.8
2011	*19.2*	*30.0*	*34.1*	*11.9*	*4.7*	61.3
2021	*18.3*	*29.7*	*32.7*	*14.3*	*5.1*	62.1
2031	*18.2*	*28.4*	*30.5*	*16.3*	*6.6*	62.2
2041	*17.6*	*27.8*	*30.1*	*16.8*	*7.8*	61.2
2051	*17.6*	*28.0*	*30.3*	*14.9*	*9.2*	59.6
Males	*18.2*	*28.9*	*30.9*	*14.5*	*7.5*	30.9
Females	*17.0*	*27.2*	*29.7*	*15.2*	*10.9*	30.1

1 See Appendix, Part 1: Population and population projections.
2 1992-based projections.
Source: Office of Population Censuses and Surveys; Government Actuary's Department; General Register Office (Scotland); General Register Office (Northern Ireland)

Chart 1.1 shows the number of people aged under 16 and those over the current pensionable age in the United Kingdom. These two age groups together constitute the dependent population: a crude estimate of that population which is supported economically by those of working age. The number of children under 16 fell from 14.3 million in 1971 to 11.5 million in 1988. Since then the number has risen again but is projected to fall after the beginning of the next century.

There has been a great deal of recent attention focused on the population over pensionable age, largely due to the increased share of national budgets that pensions will take and the increasing cost of health care for the elderly. As the baby boom generation reaches retirement, so the numbers over the current pensionable age are projected to reach a peak at just under 17 million in 2036. The combined number of children and pensioners for every 100 people of working age is termed the dependency ratio. This ratio fell from 68 in 1971 to 63 in 1992; it is projected to peak in 2036 at 82, fall and then rise to reach 83 in 2062.

1.5

Percentage of the population aged 60 and over: EC comparison, 1993

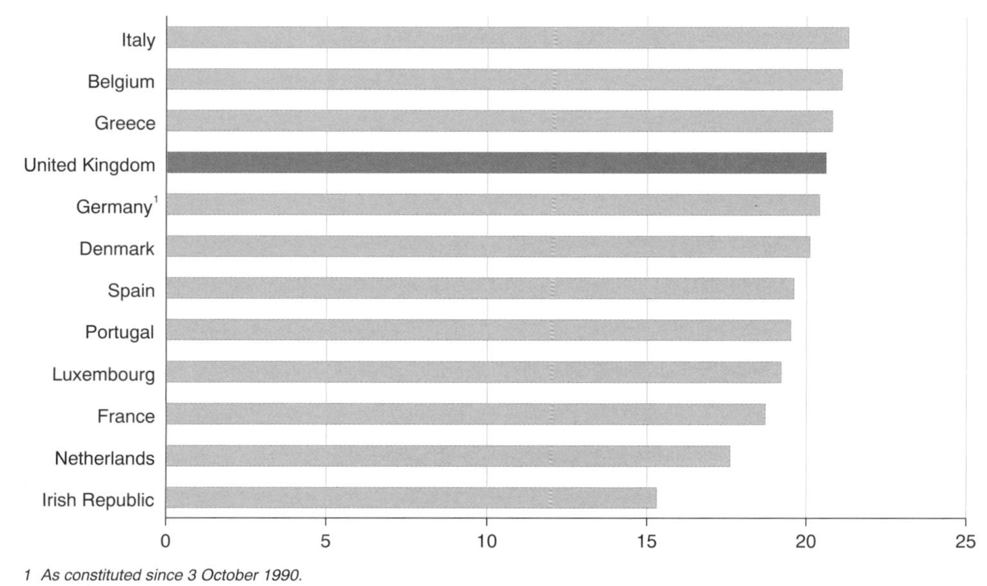

1 As constituted since 3 October 1990.

Source: Eurostat

Chart 1.5 illustrates how an elderly population is not just a concern for the United Kingdom, but for Western Europe as a whole. Although the United Kingdom had a relatively high proportion of its population aged 60 or over in 1993 (nearly 21 per cent), three other countries in the European Community (EC) had slightly higher proportions; Italy had the highest with just over 21 per cent of its population being aged 60 or over. The Irish Republic had the lowest proportion at just over 15 per cent. The proportion is projected to increase in all EC countries. In 2020, Italy is projected to still have the highest proportion of between 27 and 28 per cent; a 6 to 7 percentage point increase since 1993. The largest percentage point increase is projected in the Netherlands. In 1993, nearly 18 per cent of its population was aged 60 or over; this is projected to be between 24 and 26 per cent by 2020, a percentage point rise of between 6 and 8 per cent.

1.6

Population: by type of area, 1971 and 1993

England & Wales		Thousands
	1971	1993
London		
Inner London	3,060	2,647
Outer London	4,470	4,286
Greater London	7,529	6,933
Metropolitan districts		
Principal cities	3,910	3,463
Others	7,952	7,736
All metroplitan districts	11,862	11,199
Non-metropolitan districts		
Cities	4,715	4,710
Industrial	6,486	6,882
With new towns	1,895	2,391
Resort and retirement	3,184	3,662
Mixed urban-rural	8,821	10,069
Remoter largely rural	4,661	5,592
All non-metropolitan districts	29,761	33,307
All areas	49,152	51,439

Source: Office of Population Censuses and Surveys

Table 1.6 shows the change in the size of the population in the different types of areas in England and Wales. Overall, the population of remoter largely rural areas generally grew faster between 1971 and 1993 than urban areas, by around 20 per cent. The population of Inner London fell by 13 per cent between these two years; the trough was actually in 1983, since when there has been a small increase. Together with the fall in population in Outer London, which hit a trough in 1988, this led to a decrease in the city's population of 8 per cent to just under 7 million. Metropolitan districts also experienced a fall in population, of nearly 6 per cent, over the same period. However, the population grew in non-metropolitan areas, from 29.8 million to 33.3 million, a rise of almost 12 per cent. Within this group, the largest increase in percentage terms was in those areas which include new towns, with a rise of nearly 26 per cent. The population in resort and retirement areas increased by 15 per cent, to 3.7 million - reflecting the general ageing of the population.

The density of the United Kingdom population in 1993 is shown in Chart 1.7. Not surprisingly, Greater London had by far the greatest concentration of population of any area in the United Kingdom, with 4.4 thousand people per square kilometre, more than 500 times the density in the Highland Region of Scotland, which at 8 people per square kilometre had the lowest density. Urban areas are predicted to see the biggest falls in population over the next ten years, particularly areas in Scotland such as Inverclyde (10 per cent), Glasgow (6 per cent), Dundee (5 per cent) and Monklands (7 per cent).

The Labour Force Survey collects information on the ethnicity of the population. Table 1.8 shows a breakdown of the population aged 16 and over in Great Britain by ethnic origin and country of birth in Spring 1994. There were 616 thousand adults in the Indian ethnic group, 1.4 per cent of the adult population. Within this group, 20 per cent were born in the United Kingdom. The Black ethnic group was only slightly smaller; at 583 thousand it accounted for 1.3 per cent of the adult population, but over one third were born in the United Kingdom. Overall, the ethnic minority population constituted 4.9 per cent of the total population of Great Britain aged 16 or over, at 2.1 million; just over a quarter were born in the United Kingdom. However, the table only shows the population aged over 16. Results from the 1991 Census contained in *Social Trends 24* showed that 33 per cent of the ethnic minority population in Great Britain was under 16 compared with 19 per cent of the White population. Overall, just over 3 million people, 5.5 per cent of the population of Great Britain, described themselves as belonging to an ethnic minority group in the 1991 Census.

1.7

Population density: by area, 1993

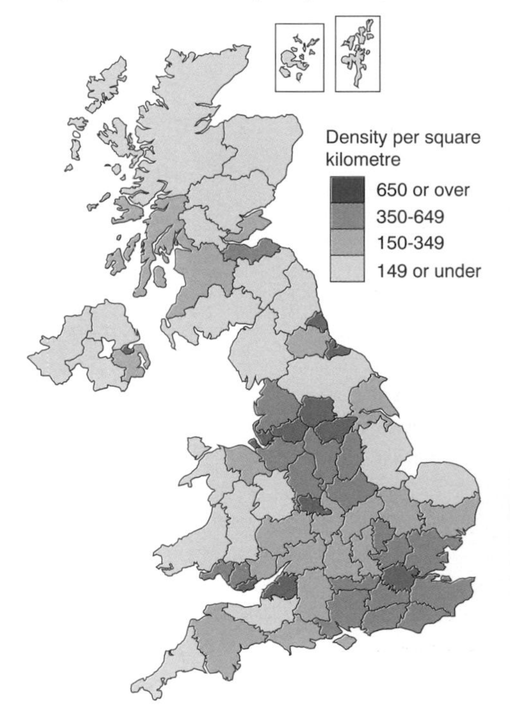

Source: Office of Population Censuses and Surveys; General Register Office (Scotland); General Register Office (Northern Ireland)

1.8

Adult population[1]: by ethnic group and country of birth, Spring 1994

Great Britain — Thousands

	United Kingdom	Irish Republic	Other EC countries[2]	Rest of World	All countries
Ethnic minority group					
Black	216	0	..	366	583
Indian	125	0	..	491	616
Pakistani / Bangladeshi	93	0	..	363	456
Other[3]	110	..	..	375	489
All ethnic minority groups	544	..	..	1,596	2,145
White	40,078	522	464	980	42,046
All ethnic groups[4]	40,627	523	469	2,580	44,206

1 Aged 16 and over.
2 As currently constituted - excluding United Kingdom and Irish Republic.
3 Includes Chinese, other ethnic groups of non-mixed origin and people of mixed origin.
4 Includes people of Northern Ireland who are not asked the ethnic origin question and ethnic group not stated.

Source: Employment Department.

1.9

People in employment[1] by ethnic group, socio-economic group[2] and gender, Spring 1994

Great Britain | Percentages

	Ethnic group						
	Black	Indian	Pakistani or Bangladeshi	Other ethnic minority groups	All ethnic minority groups	White	All persons
Males							
Professional	..	13.7	..	19.5	11.7	8.2	8.4
Intermediate	25.2	30.5	18.3	28.2	26.3	31.1	30.9
Skilled non-manual	13.7	13.5	15.7	16.8	14.7	11.6	11.8
Skilled manual	28.6	22.3	33.5	19.2	25.3	31.6	31.3
Partly skilled	17.2	17.0	22.9	11.1	16.9	13.4	13.5
Unskilled	9.4	..	..	..	5.1	4.1	4.1
All males (=100%) (thousands)[3]	144	190	110	126	571	12,887	13,458
Females							
Professional	..	7.0	..	..	4.8	2.6	2.6
Intermediate	35.1	23.2	28.7	30.9	29.4	30.3	30.3
Skilled non-manual	28.8	34.2	40.7	35.9	33.5	37.0	36.8
Skilled manual	9.6	..	..	..	8.1	8.1	8.1
Partly skilled	14.2	26.7	..	13.0	18.7	15.5	15.7
Unskilled	9.7	..	..	..	5.5	6.6	6.5
All females (thousands) (=100%)[3]	147	152	45	103	443	10,272	10,715

1 Males aged 16 to 64, females aged 16 to 59.
2 Based on occupation.
3 Includes members of the armed forces and those who did not give ethnic group or occupation.
Source: Employment Department

Employment patterns within the various ethnic groups and by gender are given in Table 1.9 Three in ten men from the Indian ethnic group were in intermediate occupations in Spring 1994 - this was the only one of the clearly definable ethnic groups not to have the largest proportion of male workers in skilled manual employment. The Pakistani and Bangladeshi ethnic groups had the largest proportion in the skilled manual group with around 33 per cent. Indians had the highest proportion of professional males, at around 14 per cent, compared with only around 8 per cent in the White population. Among females, those from the Black ethnic group had the largest percentage in the intermediate occupations at 35 per cent, whereas all other groups had their largest percentage in skilled non-manual occupations. Again, the highest proportion of professionals was within the Indian community at 7 per cent, compared with under 3 per cent of the White population.

Births and deaths

The annual number of births in the United Kingdom has only exceeded 1 million twice since 1931 - in the post-war baby boom of 1947, and again in 1964 (Chart 1.10). Since the mid 1980s, the number of births each year has remained at around three quarters of a million, although there was a mini peak in 1990; the next minor peak is projected for 1996 at around 790 thousand. Births are then projected to start falling so that, when combined with the projected increase in the number of deaths from the turn of the century, in 2027 deaths should exceed births for the first time since 1976. The projected peak for deaths is in 2051, at around 830 thousand. This is when the baby boomers of the 1960s will be in their 80s.

The minor peak in the number of births in 1990 did not reflect rising fertility rates; it was caused by the generation born in the 1960s baby boom reaching their most fertile time of life. The Total Period Fertility Rate (TPFR), which gives the average number of children born per woman if current age-specific rates remained the same throughout her childbearing life, has fallen in the United Kingdom since 1990 - to 1.76 in 1993 (Table 1.11)

There has been a downward trend in fertility rates for women in their 20s and a rise for older women, as women continued to defer childbearing. In 1992, for the first time, women in their early 30s were more likely to have a baby than those in their early 20s: a fertility rate of 87 births per thousand women was recorded among women aged 30 to 34, compared with a rate of 86 among 20 to 24 year olds. As recently as 1981, the rate for the 20 to 24 age group was some 50 per cent higher than that for women aged 30 to 34.

1.10

Births and deaths

United Kingdom

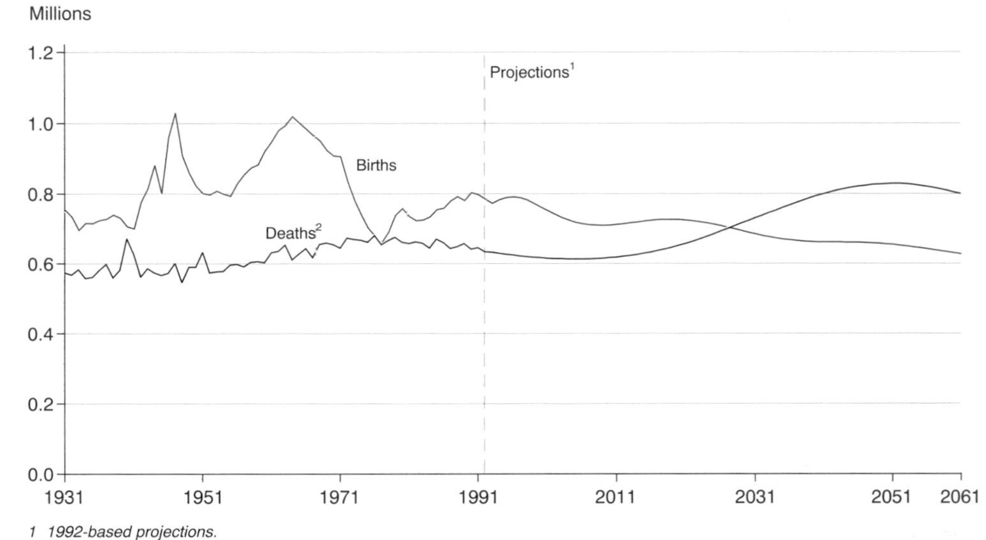

1 1992-based projections.
2 Includes deaths of non-civilians and merchant seamen who died outside the country.

Source: Office of Population Censuses and Surveys; Government Actuary's Department; General Register Office (Scotland); General Register Office (Northern Ireland)

1.11

Fertility rates: by age

United Kingdom — Rates

	Births per thousand women in each age group							Total period fertility rate[1]
	Under 20	20-24	25-29	30-34	35-39	40 and over	All ages	
1981	28	107	130	70	22	5	62	1.81
1986	30	93	125	78	25	5	61	1.78
1987	31	94	125	81	27	5	62	1.81
1988	32	95	125	82	28	5	63	1.83
1989	32	91	121	83	29	5	62	1.80
1990	33	91	123	87	31	5	64	1.85
1991	33	89	120	87	32	5	64	1.83
1992	32	86	118	87	33	6	63	1.81
1993	31	82	114	87	34	6	62	1.76

1 The average number of children which would be born per woman if women experienced the age specific fertility rates of the period in question throughout their child-bearing lifespan.

Source: Office of Population Censuses and Surveys

1.12

Mean age of mother at all births

England & Wales

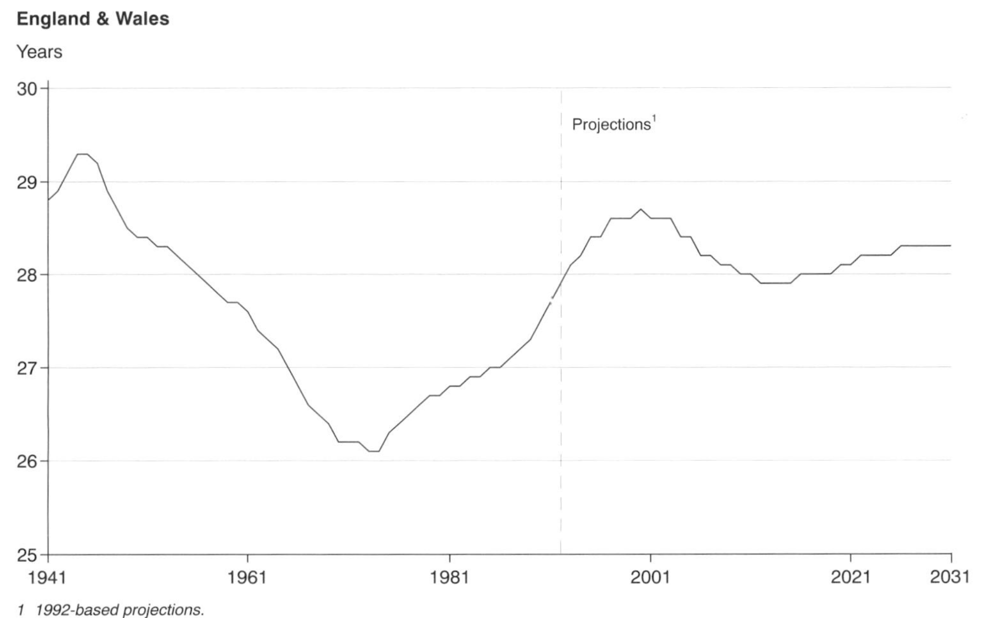

1 1992-based projections.

Source: Office of Population Censuses and Surveys; Government Actuary's Department

As a result of the trend towards child-bearing at older ages, the mean age of mothers at birth in England and Wales has risen, from 26.2 in 1971 to 28.1 in 1993 - the highest since 1955 (Chart 1.12). It is projected that the age will peak in 2000, at 28.7, fall back and then rise again to 28.3 years in 2026. There has also been a steady rise in the number of women who have never had a child; 11 per cent of women born in 1945 were childless at the age of 35, but this proportion had almost doubled among women born ten years later and the signs are that it will continue to rise. (Further information is given in Chapter 2: Households and Families.)

The other end of the life cycle is shown in Table 1.13 which looks at deaths in the United Kingdom. There were 658 thousand deaths in 1993, 4 per cent more than in 1992. Among men the crude death rate, which takes no account of the age structure of the population, fell from 12.6 per thousand population in 1961 to 11.1 in 1993. In 1961, the female crude death rate was 11.4. Since then, the male and female rates have been converging and, since 1991, the female rate has exceeded that for males. However, in 1993 the rates for males were higher than those for females for all age groups shown in the table. This apparent anomaly is due to the different age structures for men and women. Further information on causes of death is given in Chapter 7: Health.

1.13

Deaths: by gender and age

United Kingdom Rates

	Death rates per 1,000 in each age group							Total deaths (thousands)
	Under 1[1]	1-15	16-39	40-64	65-79	80 and over	All ages	
Males								
1961	26.3	0.6	1.3	11.7	65.7	193.5	12.6	322.0
1971	20.2	0.5	1.1	11.4	59.9	174.0	12.1	328.5
1981	12.7	0.4	1.0	10.1	56.1	167.5	12.0	329.1
1991	8.3	0.3	1.0	7.3	48.2	148.2	11.1	314.4
1993	7.8	0.2	1.0	7.0	47.5	149.8	11.1	317.3
Females								
1961	18.2	0.7	0.8	6.5	41.0	156.8	11.4	309.8
1971	15.5	0.4	0.6	6.3	35.3	138.0	11.0	316.5
1981	9.6	0.3	0.5	5.8	32.1	126.2	11.4	328.8
1991	6.3	0.2	0.5	4.5	29.1	112.2	11.2	331.8
1993	6.2	0.2	0.5	4.3	29.0	115.3	11.5	340.4

1 Rate per 1,000 live births.

Source: Office of Population Censuses and Surveys; General Register Office (Scotland); General Register Office (Northern Ireland)

Migration

Migration between the United Kingdom and other countries of the world is estimated from the International Passenger Survey. However, the survey does not cover movements between the United Kingdom and the Irish Republic. Over the period 1988 to 1992, an average of 243 thousand people entered the country each year to stay for at least a year - a third more than in the same period ten years previously (Table 1.14). The number of British citizens leaving the country to live abroad in 1988 to 1992 was, on average, 134 thousand a year - 11 per cent lower than in the same period ten years previously. The average net loss of 31 thousand British citizens in 1988 to 1992 was smaller than the net average gain of 46 thousand non-British citizens. In 1988 to 1992, 58 per cent of immigrants were non-British

1.14

Average annual international migration into, and out of, the United Kingdom[1]: by country of last or next residence[2]

United Kingdom Thousands

	1974-1980			1981-1987			1988-1992		
	Inflow	Outflow	Balance	Inflow	Outflow	Balance	Inflow	Outflow	Balance
Country of last or next residence									
Commonwealth countries									
Australia	13.3	35.2	-21.9	15.3	27.4	-12.0	25.8	37.8	-12.0
Canada	5.8	18.9	-13.1	6.1	7.5	-1.4	5.9	9.9	-4.0
New Zealand	6.6	9.6	-3.0	8.8	7.4	1.3	12.6	6.9	5.7
African Commonwealth	13.6	10.5	3.1	13.8	7.0	6.8	12.8	6.5	6.3
Bangladesh, India, Sri Lanka	17.5	3.9	13.6	14.2	3.7	10.5	12.2	3.8	8.4
Pakistan	12.9	1.5	11.4	10.3	1.8	8.5	9.5	3.0	6.5
Caribbean	4.1	3.2	0.9	3.6	2.8	0.8	3.6	3.2	0.4
Other	15.6	12.9	2.7	16.6	14.9	1.7	17.9	16.3	1.6
All Commonwealth	89.4	95.8	-6.4	88.6	72.6	16.1	100.4	87.4	13.0
Non-Commonwealth countries									
European Community	33.7	36.8	-3.0	51.9	44.6	7.3	62.5	58.3	4.2
Rest of Europe	13.1	11.8	1.3	8.4	8.0	0.4	14.2	12.0	2.2
United States of America	16.2	26.8	-10.6	25.3	30.3	-5.0	25.3	34.3	-9.0
Rest of America	3.6	4.8	-1.2	2.6	2.3	0.3	3.0	3.5	-0.5
Republic of South Africa	7.6	14.4	-6.8	11.6	5.4	6.1	8.0	6.2	1.8
Middle East	12.6	24.8	-12.2	15.6	17.4	-1.7	10.6	12.5	-1.9
Other	5.9	5.2	0.7	15.4	8.6	6.8	19.0	13.6	5.3
All Non-Commonwealth	92.7	124.6	-31.9	130.9	116.6	14.3	142.6	140.4	2.1
All countries, of which	182.1	220.4	-38.3	219.6	189.2	30.4	243	227.9	15.1
British citizens	75.3	150.8	-75.6	103.8	119.0	-15.3	103.1	134.2	-31.0
Non-British citizens	106.8	69.6	37.3	115.8	70.2	45.7	139.9	93.7	46.1

1 Excludes the Channel Islands and the Isle of Man from 1988.
2 Data are from the International Passenger Survey and exclude migration with the Irish Republic and other categories. See Appendix, Part 1: International Passenger Survey migration estimates.
Source: Office of Population Censuses and Surveys

citizens, much the same proportion as in 1978 to 1982; just under half of these were from the EC compared with under a third in 1978 to 1982.

Migration within the United Kingdom (Table 1.15) is estimated using information on registrations with General Practitioners recorded by the National Health Service Central Registers based in Southport (for England and Wales) and in Edinburgh (for Scotland). The Central Services Agency in Belfast monitors Northern Ireland.

England continued to experience a small net loss of population in 1993 of 9 thousand; Northern Ireland also showed a net loss, of 1 thousand. Conversely, Scotland and Wales both gained population, by 7 thousand and 4 thousand respectively. The biggest increase

1.15

Migration[1] within the United Kingdom: inter-regional movements, 1993

Thousands

	Region of origin												
	United Kingdom	North	Yorkshire & Humberside	East Midlands	East Anglia	South East	South West	West Midlands	North West	England	Wales	Scotland	Northern Ireland
Region of destination													
United Kingdom	.	50	87	83	49	252	101	92	101	108	48	47	12
North	47	.	9	3	2	12	3	3	8	40	1	5	1
Yorkshire & Humberside	88	11	.	14	4	24	6	8	15	80	3	4	1
East Midlands	93	4	16	.	7	30	7	13	9	87	3	3	1
East Anglia	57	2	4	7	.	31	4	3	3	53	1	2	-
South East	224	12	22	26	23	.	51	28	27	190	14	17	3
South West	121	3	6	7	4	64	.	14	9	108	9	4	1
West Midlands	83	3	7	11	3	26	11	.	11	72	7	3	1
North West	92	8	14	8	3	26	7	11	.	77	8	6	2
England	99	43	79	76	45	213	88	80	83	.	46	44	9
Wales	52	1	3	3	1	16	8	8	9	49	.	2	-
Scotland	54	6	5	3	2	19	4	3	7	50	2	.	2
Northern Ireland	11	-	1	-	-	5	1	1	1	9	-	1	.

1 Data are based on patient movements recorded by the National Health Service Central Registers at Southport and Edinburgh and the Central Services Agency in Belfast.

Source: Office of Population Censuses and Surveys; General Register Office (Scotland); General Register Office (Northern Ireland)

within the English regions was in the South West; the population increased by 20 thousand. The East Midlands also experienced a substantial rise, of 10 thousand. The South East however, continued to lose population: 28 thousand in 1993 compared with 36 thousand in 1992. Net losses were also experienced by the North (3 thousand), the West Midlands (9 thousand) and the North West (9 thousand).

In 1992, Europe provided the majority of applications for asylum in the United Kingdom, most of whom were from people from the former Yugoslavia. At the end of 1992, just under 6 thousand former Yugoslavs had applied for asylum.

The total number of applications for asylum (excluding dependants) received in the United Kingdom fell by about 9 per cent from around 25 thousand in 1992 to 22 thousand in 1993. By far the largest proportion of applications in 1993 came from Africa, at 46 per cent (Table 1.16). This was nearly twice as many as from Europe and Americas (24 per cent of all applications) and Asia (23 per cent). Africa accounted for over 60 per cent of all refusals of asylum and exceptional leave, more than double the proportion refused from Asia (23 per cent). Similarly, Africa represents about 60 per cent of all grants of exceptional leave to remain compared with 23 per cent from Asia.

1.16

Applications received for asylum (excluding dependants) and decisions[1]: by main geographical area of origin, 1993

United Kingdom — Numbers

	Europe and Americas	Africa	Middle East	Asia	Nationality not known	All applications
Applications received	5,280	10,295	1,520	5,175	100	22,370
Decisions[1] taken						
Recognised as a refugee and granted asylum	350	865	340	35	-	1,590
Not recognised as a refugee but granted exceptional leave	925	6,825	800	2,575	-	11,125
Refused asylum and exceptional leave	1,275	6,675	310	2,405	25	10,690
Applications withdrawn	470	470	160	805	15	1,925
Applications outstanding at end of year	13,275	20,675	2,550	9,195	15	45,805

1. Excludes South East Asia Refugees. Information is of initial determination decisions, excluding the outcome of appeals or other subsequent decisions. Decisions figures do not necessarily relate to applications made in 1993. See Appendix Part 1: Asylum.

Source: Home Office

In 1993, 54 per cent of those recognised as refugees and granted asylum were Africans compared with only 2 per cent from Asia, 22 per cent from Europe and Americas and 21 per cent from the Middle East.

In 1993, around 56 thousand people were accepted for settlement in the United Kingdom (Table 1.17), some 3 thousand more than in 1992. The number of wives and children accepted from the New Commonwealth continued to fall, by 2 per cent and 13 per cent respectively between 1992 and 1993, while the number of husbands accepted for settlement increased by 18 per cent to more than twice the number in 1981. The total number of acceptances for settlement from the New Commonwealth fell by nearly 12 per cent between 1981 and 1993. Applications from the Rest of the World rose by 12 per cent between 1992 and 1993 with own right, wives and children acceptances all rising from the previous year.

1.17

Acceptances for settlement: by category of acceptance

United Kingdom					Thousands
	1981	1986	1991	1992	1993
New Commonwealth[1]					
Own right	4.1	2.4	1.7	1.6	1.6
Husbands	3.2	3.2	6.3	6.0	7.1
Wives	10.0	7.4	9.7	9.6	9.4
Children	10.7	6.4	4.5	4.5	3.9
Others	3.4	3.3	5.8	6.1	5.6
All New Commonwealth	31.4	22.7	28.0	27.7	27.7
Rest of the world					
Own right	11.6	8.6	3.7	4.0	5.4
Husbands	3.4	3.6	5.4	4.9	4.9
Wives	6.8	6.8	9.3	9.0	9.8
Children	3.7	3.9	4.5	3.9	4.7
Others	2.3	2.4	3.1	3.2	3.1
All rest of the world	27.7	25.2	25.9	24.9	28.0
All acceptances	59.1	47.8	53.9	52.6	55.6

1 Includes Pakistan.

Source: Home Office

World population

World population indicators, compiled by the United Nations, are given in Table 1.18. In mid 1994, the world population was 5.7 billion, projected to rise to 6 billion by 1998, 8.5 billion in 2025 and 10 billion in 2050. Although fertility rates worldwide have fallen, the annual population increase stands at 94 million a year, the highest increase on record; after peaking in 1997, the rate is projected to decline to around 85 million a year by 2020. Africa and south Asia are projected to account for half of the growth in the world's population between 1997 and 2020. The current annual growth rate in Africa of 2.9 per cent means that it is the world's fastest growing region. Asia and Latin America have the next highest growth rates at 1.8 per cent compared with 1.1 per cent in North America, 0.5 per cent in the former Soviet Union and 0.3 per cent in Europe. Africa is projected to account for 19 per cent of the world's population by 2015 compared with around 18 per cent in 1994. The world is steadily becoming more urbanised. In 1992, 44 per cent of the world's population lived in cities. By 2000, 50 per cent of the world will be urbanised with 300 cities in developing countries having populations over 1 million.

1.18

World population indicators

	Population (millions)		Growth rate (percentages)	1990-1995				
	1994	2025	1990-1995	Birth rate[1]	Death rate[1]	Infant mortality[2]	Fertility rate per woman[3]	Life expectancy
Selected countries/areas								
Europe	512	541.8	0.3	13	11	10	1.7	75
European Community								
Belgium	10.0	9.9	0.1	12	11	8	1.7	76
Denmark	5.2	5.1	0.2	12	12	7	1.7	76
France	57.4	60.8	0.4	13	10	7	1.8	77
Irish Republic	3.5	3.6	-0.2	14	9	7	2.1	75
Germany	80.6	83.9	0.4	11	11	7	1.5	76
Greece	10.2	10.1	0.3	10	10	8	1.5	78
Italy	57.8	56.2	0.1	10	10	8	1.3	77
Netherlands	15.3	17.7	0.7	14	9	7	1.7	77
Portugal	9.9	10.1	0.0	12	10	12	1.5	75
Spain	39.2	40.6	0.2	11	9	7	1.4	78
United Kingdom	58.2	60.3	0.2	14	11	7	1.9	76
Other Western Europe								
Austria	7.8	8.3	0.4	12	11	8	1.5	76
Switzerland	6.9	7.7	0.7	13	10	7	1.7	78
Other Southern Europe								
Albania	3.3	4.5	0.8	23	5	23	2.7	73
Yugoslavia (former)	20.8	22.6	0.3	14	10	23	1.9	72
Other Northern Europe								
Estonia	1.6	1.7	-0.2	14	12	14	2.0	71
Finland	5.0	5.2	0.3	13	10	6	1.8	76
Latvia	2.7	2.8	-0.3	14	12	10	2	71
Lithuania	3.8	4.1	0.2	15	10	10	2.0	73
Norway	4.3	4.9	0.5	15	11	8	2.0	77
Sweden	8.7	9.5	0.5	14	11	6	2.1	78
Eastern Europe	96.9	107.2	0.2	14	11	16	2.0	71
Union of Soviet Socialist Republics (former)	284.5	344.5	0.5	16	10	21	2.3	70
North America	282.7	360.5	1.1	16	9	8	2.0	76
Canada	27.8	38.4	1.4	14	8	7	1.8	77
United States of America	257.8	322.0	1.0	16	9	8	2.1	76
Africa	681.7	1582.5	2.9	43	14	95	6.0	53
Asia	3233	4900.3	1.8	26	8	62	3.2	65
Of which: China	1205.2	1539.8	1.4	21	7	27	2.2	71
India	896.6	1393.9	1.9	29	10	88	3.9	60
Japan	125.0	127.0	0.4	11	7	5	1.7	79
Latin America	457.7	701.6	1.8	26	7	47	3.1	68
Oceania	27.5	41.3	1.5	19	8	22	2.5	73
Of which: Australia	17.8	25.2	1.4	15	8	7	1.9	77
New Zealand	3.5	4.3	0.9	17	8	8	2.1	76
World	5665.5	8472.4	1.7	26	9	62	3.3	65
Developed regions[4]	1237.6	1403.3	0.5	14	10	12	1.9	75
Developing regions	4427.9	7069.2	2.0	29	9	69	3.6	62

1 Per thousand population.
2 Per thousand live births.
3 Total period fertility rate. The average number of children which would be born per woman if women experienced the age specific fertility rates of the period in question throughout their child-bearing span.
4 Europe, Northern America, Australia, New Zealand, Japan and the former Union of Soviet Socialist Republics.

Source: United Nations

References and further reading

The following list contains selected publications relevant to **Chapter 1: Population**. Those published by HMSO are available from the addresses shown on the inside back cover of *Social Trends*.

Annual Report of the Registrar General for Northern Ireland, HMSO
Annual Report of the Registrar General for Scotland, General Register Office (Scotland)
Asylum Statistics, Home Office
Birth Statistics (Series FM1), HMSO
Control of Immigration: Statistics - United Kingdom, HMSO
Demographic Statistics, Eurostat
Demographic Yearbook, United Nations
International Migration Statistics (Series MN), HMSO
Key Population and Vital Statistics (Series VS/PP1), HMSO
Labour Force Survey, HMSO
Mortality Statistics for England and Wales (Series DH1, 2, 3, 4, 5, 6), HMSO
OPCS Monitors, Office of Population Censuses and Surveys
Population Estimates, Scotland, HMSO
National Population Projections (Series PP2), HMSO
Population Projections for the Counties and District Health Authorities of Wales (1989 based), Welsh Office
Population Projections, Scotland (for Standard Areas), General Register Office (Scotland)
Population Trends, HMSO
Regional Trends, HMSO
Subnational Population Projections - England (Series PP3), HMSO
The State of World Population, 1993, UNFPA

Contacts

Telephone contact points for further information relating to **Chapter 1: Population.**

Office of Population Censuses and Surveys	0171 396 2828
General Register Office (Northern Ireland)	01232 252031
General Register Office (Scotland)	0131 314 4301
Government Actuary's Department	0171 242 6828 extn 318
Employment Department	0171 273 5585
Eurostat	00 352 4301 34567

Chapter 2 Households and Families

Households

In 1993 only 7 per cent of households had 5 or more members compared with 16 per cent in 1961. (Table 2.2)

In Spring 1994 nearly 30 per cent of White households were people living alone compared with about a tenth of Indian and Pakistani/Bangladeshi households. (Chart 2.5)

Families

If 1988-89 divorce rates were to continue, 24 per cent of children would experience divorce in their family by age 16. (Page 34)

The proportion of lone mothers increased gradually until 1987, but since then has increased rapidly, so that almost one in five mothers with dependent children was a lone mother in 1992. (Chart 2.11)

Marriage and divorce

For every two marriages in Great Britain in 1992 there was one divorce. (Chart 2.14)

August and September are the favourite months for a wedding: five times as many couples marry in August as in January (the least popular month).(Page 37)

Family building

Of women born in 1947, about one fifth were still childless by the time they were 30, but for women born in 1967, indications are that nearly two fifths will still be childless at 30. (Chart 2.22).

Merseyside had the highest percentage of births outside marriage in 1992 at 42 per cent, while Surrey had the lowest at 20 per cent. (Chart 2.28)

2.1

Live births outside marriage as a percentage of all births

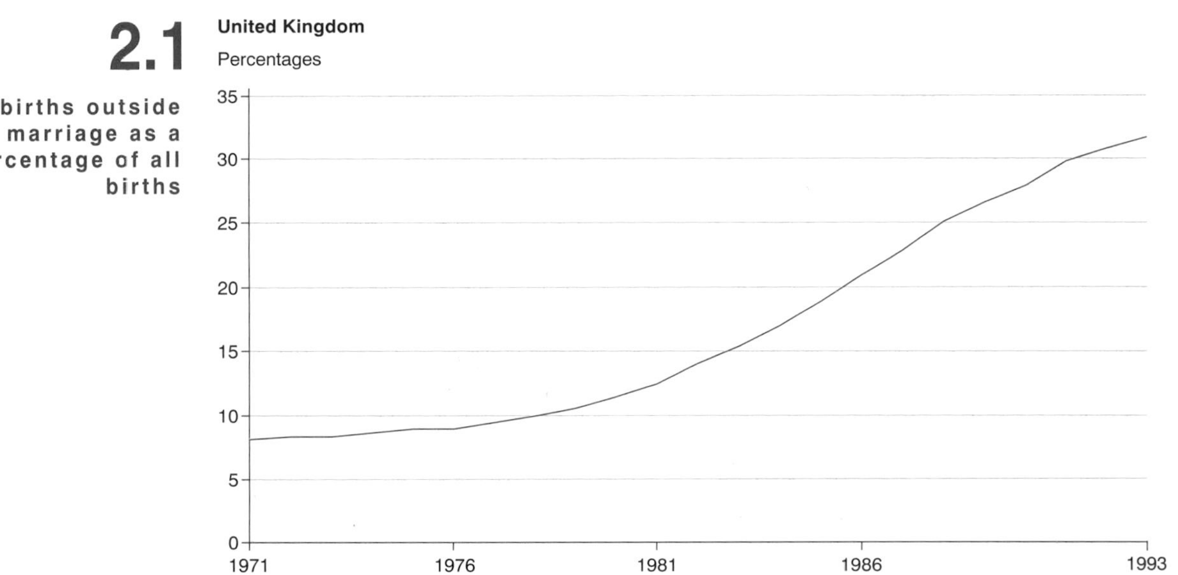

Source: Office of Population Censuses and Surveys; General Register Office (Scotland); General Register Office (Northern Ireland)

2.2

Households[1]: by size

Great Britain					Percentages
	1961	1971	1981	1991	1993
Household size					
1 person	*14*	*18*	*22*	*27*	*27*
2 people	*30*	*32*	*32*	*34*	*35*
3 people	*23*	*19*	*17*	*16*	*16*
4 people	*18*	*17*	*18*	*16*	*15*
5 people	*9*	*8*	*7*	*5*	*5*
6 or more people	*7*	*6*	*4*	*2*	*2*
Number of households (= 100%) (millions)	16.2	18.2	19.5	21.9	22.9
Average household size (number of people)	3.1	2.9	2.7	2.5	2.4

1 See Appendix, Part 2: Households.

Source: Office of Population Censuses and Surveys; Department of the Environment; The Scottish Office Environment Department; General Register Office (Scotland)

This chapter looks at the trends in the size and make up of households and families. Households comprise either people living alone or groups of people living together as a unit. Most households consist of one family, but sometimes two or more families live together in a single household (for example, grandparents, mother and daughter living together would be one household but two families) and sometimes people live together who are not related, such as in student households. The population living in institutions is generally excluded from this chapter.

Households

The number of households has been increasing since the Second World War, partly because households now contain fewer people (Table 2.2). In 1993 there were 22.9 million households in Great Britain, over two fifths more than in 1961. However, the average household size fell from 3.1 in 1961 to 2.4 in 1993. In 1993 only 7 per cent of households had five or more members compared with 16 per cent in 1961. There has been a particularly large increase in the number of people living alone. In 1993, more than a quarter of the households in Great Britain were one person households, almost double the proportion in 1961. Households in Northern Ireland tend to be larger than those in Great Britain: in 1991 around 18 per cent had five or more members which was two and a half times greater than the proportion in Great Britain.

The growth in the proportion of one person households in England and Wales is examined in more detail in Chart 2.3. The chart shows that women over pensionable age are the largest group of people living alone, but that they have formed a relatively stable proportion of the total since 1971, at between 10 and 12 per cent. The growth in the proportion of one person households has been among people under pensionable age living alone, particularly men. By 2001, nearly one in ten households in Great Britain are projected to comprise a man under pensionable age living alone compared with only one in thirty in 1971.

2.3

One-person households as a percentage of all households: by gender and whether under or over pensionable age[1]

England & Wales

Percentages

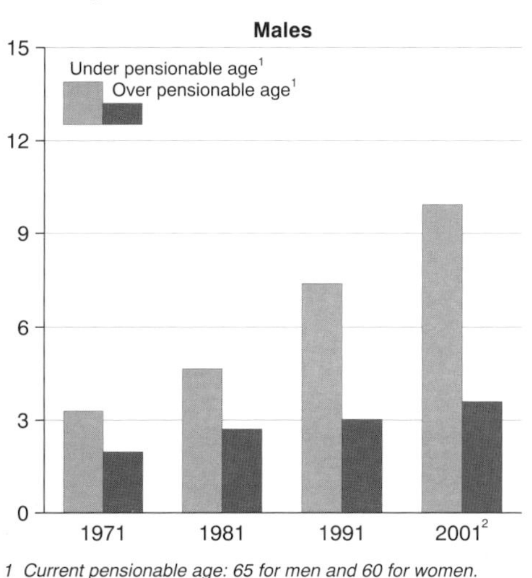

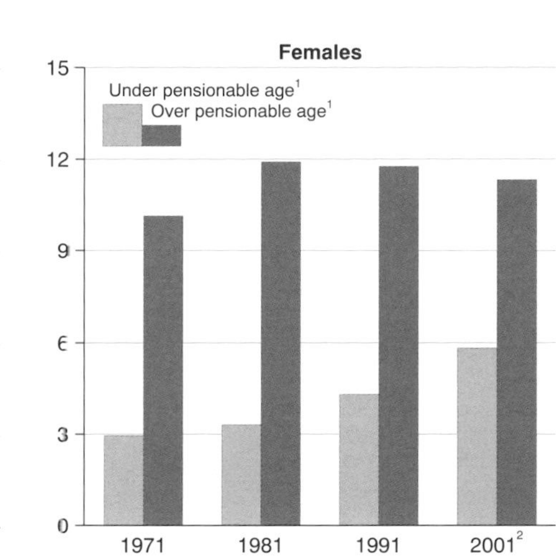

1 Current pensionable age: 65 for men and 60 for women.
2 Projections.

Source: Department of the Environment

While the proportion of one person households has been growing, the proportion of 'traditional' one family households with children has been declining (Table 2.4). Households consisting of a married couple with no children have formed a relatively stable proportion of all households over the last 30 years, at around 26 to 28 per cent. In 1961 there were more households consisting of a married couple with dependent children (38 per cent), but this proportion declined to 25 per cent in 1993. Lone parents with dependent children form a smaller but growing proportion of households; around seven per cent of households in 1993.

The proportion of different types of households varies between ethnic groups. Chart 2.5 highlights the differences in the proportion of single person households and the proportion of households with dependent children. In Spring 1994, 29 per cent of White households were single person households; this compares with 31 per cent of Black households but only 7 per cent of Pakistani/Bangladeshi households. Households headed by a Pakistani/ Bangladeshi, on the other hand, were most likely to contain dependent children. These differences are influenced by variations in the age structure of the ethnic groups. For example, the high proportion of White single person households is attributable to elderly people being more likely to live alone and the White population having an older age distribution than that for ethnic minority groups. Similarly the proportion of households with dependent children is related to the number of women of child bearing age. There are also cultural differences. For example, over half West Indian mothers were lone mothers in 1989-1991 compared with just over one in ten Pakistani/Bangladeshi mothers.

2.4

Households[1]: by type of household and family

Great Britain — Percentages

	1961	1971	1981	1991	1993
One person households					
Under pensionable age	*4*	*6*	*8*	*11*	*11*
Over pensionable age	*7*	*12*	*14*	*16*	*16*
Two or more unrelated adults	*5*	*4*	*5*	*3*	*3*
One family households					
Married couple[2] with:					
No children	*26*	*27*	*26*	*28*	*28*
1-2 dependent children[3]	*30*	*26*	*25*	*20*	*20*
3 or more dependent children	*8*	*9*	*6*	*5*	*5*
Non-dependent children only	*10*	*8*	*8*	*8*	*7*
Lone parent[2] with:					
Dependent children[3]	*2*	*3*	*5*	*6*	*7*
Non-dependent children only	*4*	*4*	*4*	*4*	*3*
Two or more families	*3*	*1*	*1*	*1*	*1*
Number of households (=100%)(millions)	16.2	18.2	19.5	21.9	22.9

1 See Appendix, Part 2: Households.
2 Other individuals who were not family members may also have been included.
3 May also include non-dependent children.

Source: Office of Population Censuses and Surveys; Department of the Environment; The Scottish Office Environment Department

2.5

Households: by ethnic group of head of household[1], Spring 1994

Great Britain

Percentages

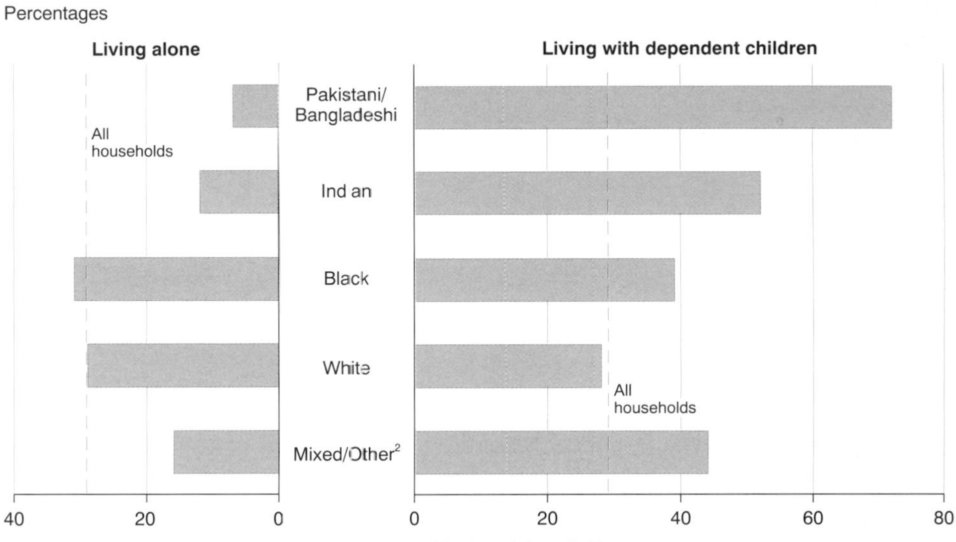

1 Percentage of heads of households in each ethnic group living in each household type.
2 Includes Chinese, other ethnic groups of non-mixed origin and people of mixed origin.

Source: Employment Department

2.6

People in households and communal establishments[1]: by type of household and family in which they live

Great Britain — Percentages

	1961	1971	1981	1991	1993
One family households					
Living alone	*3.9*	*6.3*	*8.0*	*10.7*	*11.1*
Married couple with:					
No children	*17.8*	*19.3*	*19.5*	*23.0*	*23.4*
Dependent children[2]	*52.2*	*51.7*	*47.4*	*41.1*	*40.8*
With non-dependent children only	*11.6*	*10.0*	*10.3*	*10.8*	*9.5*
Lone parent with:					
Dependent children[2]	*2.5*	*3.5*	*5.8*	*10.0*	*7.7*
Non-dependent children					*2.9*
Other households	*12.0*	*9.2*	*9.0*	*4.3*	*4.7*
All people in private households (=100%)(millions)	..	53.4	53.9	55.4	55.7
People not in private households (millions)	..	0.9	0.8	0.8	0.8
Total population (millions)	51.4	54.4	54.8	56.2	56.6

1 See Appendix, Part 2: Families.
2 These family types may also include non-dependent children.
Source: Office of Population Censuses and Surveys; Department of the Environment; The Scottish Office Environment Department; General Register Office (Scotland)

Between 1971 and 1993 the number of people living in households grew by about 4 per cent to 55.7 million (Table 2.6). This table is similar to Table 2.4 but the unit of analysis is persons rather than households. Thus 11 per cent of people lived alone in 1993, but they formed 27 per cent of all households.

The British Social Attitudes Survey which is carried out in Great Britain by Social and Community Planning Research asked married couples, and people who live as married, questions about who does certain household tasks. The survey found that men had greater involvement in certain household tasks in 1991 than they did in 1983 although the division of tasks is less equal than people think it should be (Table 2.7). The percentage of men who mainly did the evening dishes increased from 17 per cent in 1983 to 28 per cent in 1991, but they are still much less likely than their partners to do the household cleaning and washing and ironing. These were mainly the man's job

2.7

Division of household tasks[1], 1983 and 1991

Great Britain — Percentages

	Actual allocation of tasks						How tasks should be allocated		
	1983			1991			1991		
	Mainly man	Mainly woman	Shared equally	Mainly man	Mainly woman	Shared equally	Mainly man	Mainly woman	Shared equally
Household shopping	*5*	*51*	*44*	*8*	*45*	*47*	*1*	*22*	*76*
Makes evening meal	*5*	*77*	*17*	*9*	*70*	*20*	*1*	*39*	*58*
Does evening dishes	*17*	*40*	*40*	*28*	*33*	*37*	*12*	*11*	*76*
Does household cleaning	*3*	*72*	*24*	*4*	*68*	*27*	*1*	*36*	*62*
Does washing and ironing	*1*	*89*	*10*	*3*	*84*	*12*	-	*58*	*40*
Repairs household equipment	*82*	*6*	*10*	*82*	*6*	*10*	*66*	*1*	*31*
Organises household money and bills	*29*	*39*	*32*	*31*	*40*	*28*	*17*	*14*	*66*
Child rearing[2]									
Looks after sick children	*1*	*63*	*35*	*1*	*60*	*39*	-	*37*	*60*
Teaches children discipline	*10*	*12*	*77*	*9*	*17*	*73*	*8*	*4*	*85*

1 By married couples or couples living as married.
2 Data for 1983 relate to 1984.
Source: Social & Community Planning Research

in 4 per cent and 3 per cent of cases respectively. However the cleaning was shared equally in 27 per cent of households in 1991, slightly more than in 1983 (24 per cent), but 62 per cent of couples thought it ought to be shared equally.

Families

A family is defined as a married or cohabiting couple with or without children, or a lone parent with children. People living alone are not normally considered a family.

As children we are nearly all members of families (either couple families with children or lone parent families). As young adults we either remain with our parent(s) as part of the family or move away. Overall more than 80 per cent of males and females aged under 20 were members of couple families with children in 1991 and 17 per cent were members of lone parent families (Table 2.8). People in their 20s are more likely to live as couples without children than as single people. Men in their 20s are more likely than women to be on their own, at 20 and 14 per cent respectively. The remaining three fifths of men and women in their 20s are either living with their parent(s) or have children of their own. Women are more likely than men to be lone parents in this, and most other, age groups. Fewer people in their 30s and early 40s are part of a lone parent family while 69 per cent were part of a couple family with children in 1991. The tendency for women to marry older men and for women to live longer explains, at least in part, the high proportion of elderly women who are on their own; 69 per cent of women aged 75 and over were on their own in 1991 compared with 35 per cent of men of the same age.

2.8

People in households: by gender, age and family type, 1991

Great Britain Percentages

		Couple		Lone parent		
	One person	No children	With children	Dependent children	Non-dependent children	All persons (millions) (=100%)
Males						
0-19	*1*	*0*	*82*	*16*	*1*	7.1
20-29	*20*	*21*	*51*	*1*	*7*	4.2
30-44	*12*	*15*	*69*	*1*	*3*	5.8
45-59	*11*	*35*	*50*	*1*	*3*	4.6
60-74	*18*	*67*	*13*	*0*	*2*	3.6
75 and over	*35*	*59*	*4*	*0*	*2*	1.3
Females						
0-19	*1*	*1*	*81*	*16*	*1*	6.8
20-29	*14*	*25*	*47*	*11*	*4*	4.3
30-44	*6*	*13*	*69*	*10*	*2*	5.8
45-59	*12*	*41*	*39*	*2*	*6*	4.6
60-74	*36*	*53*	*6*	*0*	*5*	4.2
75 and over	*69*	*24*	*1*	-	*6*	2.5

Source: Office of Population Censuses and Surveys; Employment Department

During the 1980s there have been some marked changes in these patterns: women have delayed having children or chosen to remain childless. There were also more lone parent families and fewer couple families with children in 1992 compared with 1981. The number of couple families without children is higher, particularly for people in their twenties. This is because people have delayed having children or even chosen to remain childless.

Not all married couple families with dependent children contain children from that marriage only, but this was still the most common type of family with children in Great Britain in 1991 at 71 per cent (Chart 2.9). Lone parent families accounted for 19 per cent of families with dependent children; of the remaining family types, either the parents were not married or the family included step children of one or both

2.9

Families with dependent children: by family type, 1991

Great Britain
Percentages

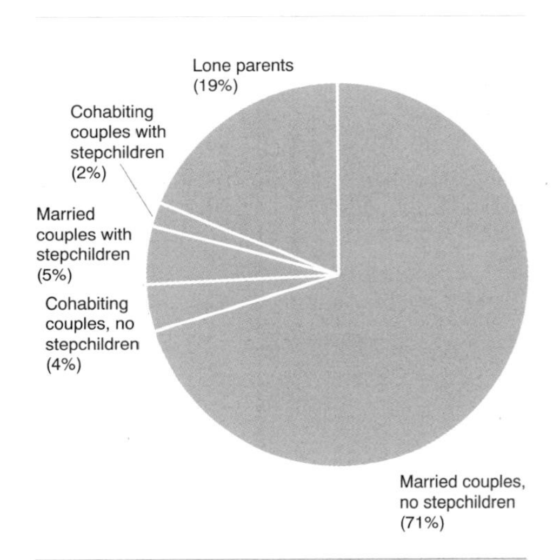

Source: Office of Population Censuses and Surveys

2.10

Dependent children: by family type, 1991

Great Britain — Percentages

	Couple families			Lone parent families	All families
	Married	Cohabiting	All		
Children living in families with their natural mother and natural father with:					
No step brothers/sisters	*72.8*	*2.7*	*75.5*	-	*75.5*
Step brothers/sisters[1]	*1.8*	*0.3*	*2.1*	-	*2.1*
Children living with one natural parent					
Mother	*2.9*	*1.5*	*4.4*	*14.8*	*19.2*
Father	*1.0*	*0.4*	*1.4*	*1.8*	*3.2*
All dependent children	*78.5*	*4.9*	*83.4*	*16.6*	*100.0*

1 Of either or both parents.

Source: Office of Population Censuses and Surveys

2.11

Families headed by lone parents as a percentage[1] of all families with dependent children

Great Britain

Percentages

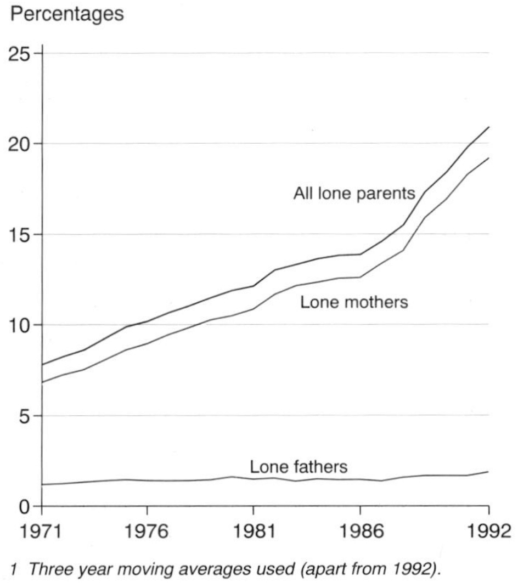

1 Three year moving averages used (apart from 1992).

Source: Office of Population Censuses and Surveys

parents. The relative size of these groups indicates that parents with step children are more likely to be cohabiting than other parents.

The proportion of children in different family types, rather than the proportion of families, is given in Table 2.10. This shows that in 1991 three quarters of children lived in married couple families with both their natural parents although some will have step brothers and sisters living with them. Of the remainder, another 3 per cent lived with both natural but unmarried parents and a further 6 per cent were step children in a couple family. The remaining 17 per cent lived in lone parent families.

Children who live with only one of their natural parents are more likely to live with their mother: in 1991, 19 per cent of all dependent children lived with their natural mother but not their natural father while only 3 per cent lived with their natural father, but not their natural mother. These children were very likely to be in a lone parent family if they lived with their mother, but those who lived with their natural father were almost as likely to live as step children in a couple family.

Altogether just over 1 million, 8 per cent, of dependent children lived in step families in 1991. However, if 1988-89 divorce and remarriage rates continued, 24 per cent of children would experience divorce in their family by the age of 16 and 13 per cent would become step children in a married or cohabiting couple family.

The proportion of families headed by a lone parent increased from nearly 8 per cent in 1971 to 21 per cent in 1992 (Chart 2.11). The proportion of lone mothers increased gradually until 1987, but has since increased rapidly, so that in 1992 one in five mothers with dependent children was a lone mother. The proportion of lone fathers, on the other hand, has changed very little at under 2 per cent of all families with dependent children.

The gradual increase in the proportion of lone mothers until the mid 1980s was caused mainly by increasing numbers of divorced mothers (Table 2.12). Since then the proportion of divorced lone mothers has stabilised, but the proportion of single, never married, mothers has more than doubled. Despite this increase in the proportion of single mothers, marital breakdown is still the most common reason for the formation of a lone parent family; 11 per cent of all families with dependent children were headed by a divorced or separated mother and 7 per cent by a single, never married, mother in 1992.

The age of the youngest child in lone mother families tends to be slightly younger on average than those in married couple families. However, lone fathers are far less

2.12

Families with dependent children: by family type

Great Britain								Percentages
	Couple families	Lone mothers					Lone fathers	All families with dependent children
		Single	Divorced	Separated	Widowed	All		
Percentage of families in each family type								
1971	*91*	*1*	*2*	*2*	*2*	*7*	*1*	*100*
1981	*88*	*2*	*4*	*2*	*2*	*11*	*1*	*100*
1986	*86*	*3*	*6*	*3*	*1*	*13*	*1*	*100*
1991	*80*	*7*	*6*	*4*	*1*	*18*	*2*	*100*
1992	*79*	*7*	*6*	*5*	*1*	*19*	*2*	*100*
Median age of family head								
1992	..	26	37	32	42	..	44	..

Source: Office of Population Censuses and Surveys

likely to have very young children and twice as likely as married fathers with dependent children to have a teenager as their youngest child. In 1991-1992 the youngest dependent child was 10 or older in two thirds of lone father families compared with a third of couple families and over a quarter for lone mother families.

Marriage and divorce

There has been a considerable social change across Europe in the experience of, and attitudes to, marriage. People are choosing to cohabit before marriage, as a 'trial' marriage, or perhaps instead of marriage. These changes have tended to reduce marriage rates overall and increase the age at first marriage. In addition, couples may well place less emphasis on the unconditional commitment of marriage and consider divorce more readily than twenty or thirty years ago. Still most men and women eventually marry.

European marriage and divorce data in Table 2.13 show that the number of marriages per thousand population has decreased in most countries while the number of divorces per thousand population has generally increased. However there are some interesting exceptions. In Denmark and Luxembourg marriage rates were low in 1981, but they had increased by 1992; the Netherlands and Spain reported slight increases. In Denmark and Germany divorce rates fell between 1981 and 1992, but from a relatively high level. Consequently there is now less variation in marriage and divorce rates across the European Community (EC) than 10 years ago. The variations that do exist can be attributed to the effects of religion, cultural and social differences and legal requirements. The divorce rates are very low in Italy, Greece and Spain. The United Kingdom had the highest divorce rate in the EC in 1992, at almost twice the average.

2.13

Marriage and divorce rates: EC comparison, 1981 and 1992

				Rates per 1,000 population
	Marriages		Divorces	
	1981	1992	1981	1992
United Kingdom[1]	7.1	5.4	2.8	3.0
Belgium	6.5	5.8	1.6	2.2
Denmark	5.0	6.2	2.8	2.5
France[1]	5.8	4.7	1.6	1.9
Germany (Fed Rep.)	5.8	5.6	2.0	1.7
Greece	7.3	4.7	0.7	0.6
Irish Republic	6.0	4.5	.	.
Italy	5.6	5.3	0.2	0.5
Luxembourg	5.5	6.4	1.4	1.8
Netherlands	6.0	6.2	2.0	2.0
Portugal	7.7	7.1	0.7	1.3
Spain[1]	5.4	5.5	0.3	0.7
EC average[1]	6.0	5.4	1.5	1.6

1 Data in 1992 column for divorces relate to 1991.

Source: Eurostat

2.14

Marriages and divorces

Great Britain

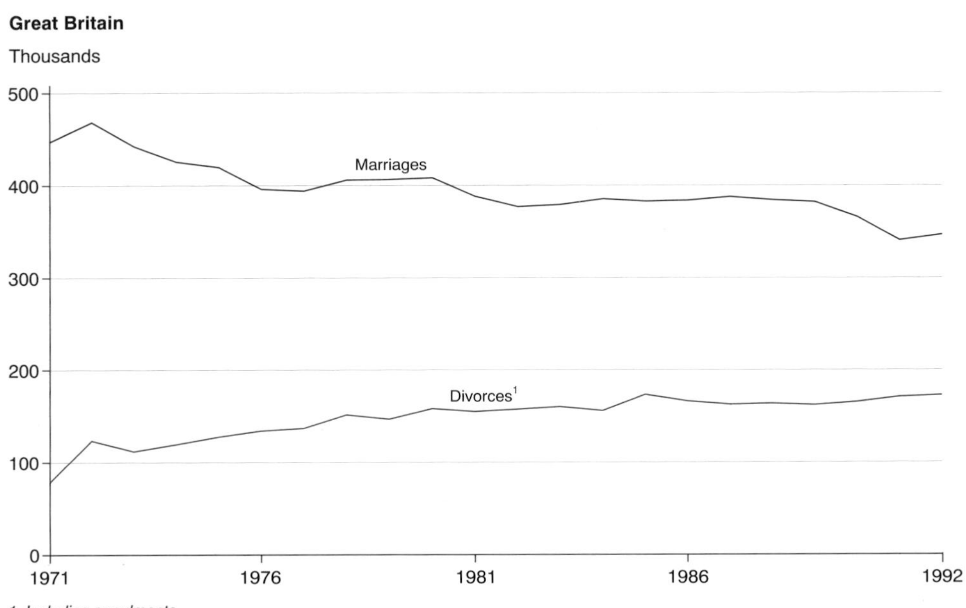

1 Including annulments.

Source: Office of Population Censuses and Surveys; General Register Office (Scotland)

Chart 2.14 looks at marriage and divorce in Great Britain over the past twenty years. The number of marriages fell by 24 per cent between 1971 and 1991 to 340 thousand and then rose slightly to 347 thousand in 1992. Divorces, on the other hand, increased sharply to 173 thousand in 1992 - more than double the number in 1971.

Nearly two thirds of marriages in 1992 were first marriages for both partners (Table 2.15). Remarriages grew rapidly in the 1960s and 1970s from 14 per cent of all marriages in 1961 to 34 per cent in 1981. However, the proportion then changed very little in the

2.15

Marriages: by type

United Kingdom Thousands

	1961	1971	1981	1991	1992
First marriage for both partners	340	369	263	222	222
First marriage for one partner only					
Bachelor/divorced woman	11	21	32	32	35
Bachelor/widow	5	4	3	2	2
Spinster/divorced man	12	24	36	35	36
Spinster/widower	8	5	3	2	2
Second (or subsequent) marriage for both partners					
Both divorced	5	17	44	45	47
Both widowed	10	10	7	4	4
Divorced man/widow	3	4	5	4	4
Divorced woman/widower	3	5	5	4	4
All marriages	397	459	398	350	356
Remarriages[1] as a percentage of all marriages	*14*	*20*	*34*	*36*	*38*
Remarriages[1] of the divorced as a percentage of all marriages	*9*	*15*	*31*	*34*	*35*

1 Remarriage for one or both partners.

Source: Office of Population Censuses and Surveys; General Register Office (Scotland);General Register Office (Northern Ireland)

1980s; in 1992, 38 per cent of marriages were remarriages. August and September are the favourite months for a wedding: five times as many people marry in August as in January (the least popular month).

Two points about age at marriage emerge clearly from Chart 2.16: women marry younger than men and the age at which people first get married has increased in the last 30 years. In 1992 the median (ie most common) age for first marriage was 26 for women; for men it was two years older.

The median age for remarriage for those who had been divorced, was 37 for women and 41 for men - much the same as in 1961 although higher than in 1971 and 1981. The proportion of teenagers marrying has fallen dramatically. In 1971, 9 per cent of teenage girls got married compared with less than 1 per cent in 1992.

Between 1977 and 1992 both the number of divorces and the number of children aged under 16 of couples divorced increase by a sixth (Chart 2.17). However, divorce of couples with young children is more common; the number of children aged under 5 affected by divorce in 1992 was 57 thousand, almost two thirds higher than in 1977.

The number of divorces nearly trebled between 1961 and 1971 and doubled between 1971 and 1981. Between 1981 and 1992 the increase was just 11 per cent. Legal changes over the period have made it easier to get a divorce, as well as allowing couples to divorce earlier in marriage. These changes came into effect in January 1971 and October 1984 and their effect can be seen in the statistics. Thus in

2.16

Average age at first marriage and remarriage following divorce: by gender

England & Wales

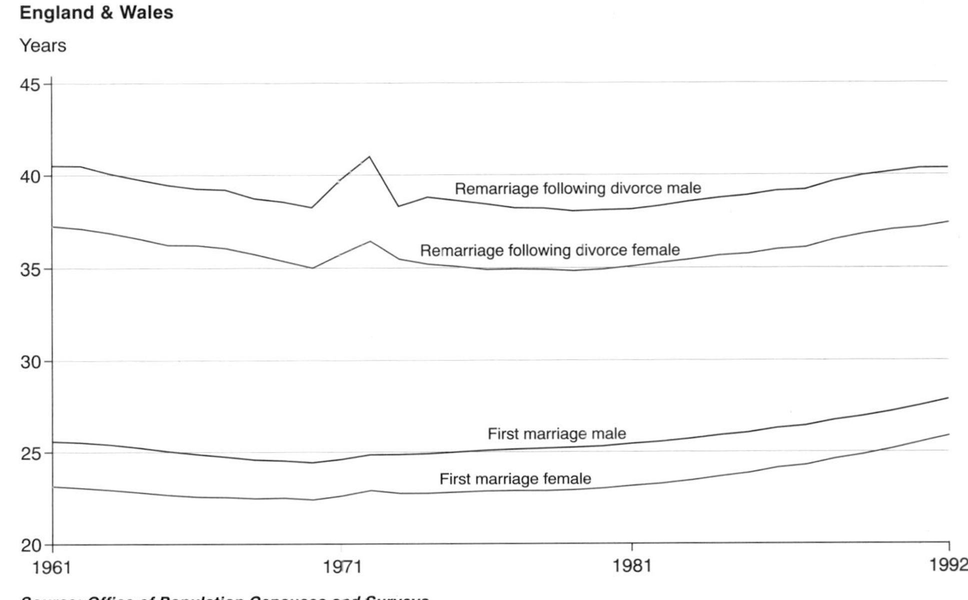

Source: Office of Population Censuses and Surveys

2.17

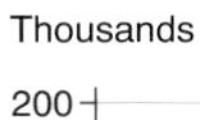

Divorces[1] and children of couples divorced

Great Britain

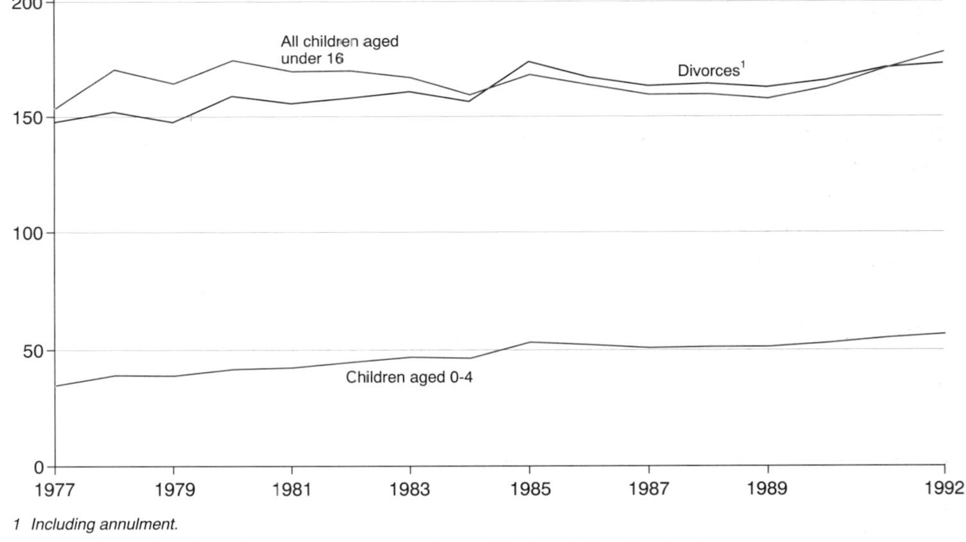

1 Including annulment.

Source: Office of Population Censuses and Surveys; General Register Office (Scotland)

2.18

Divorce: by duration of marriage

United Kingdom | Percentages

	1961	1971	1981	1991	1992
0 - 2 years	*1*	*1*	*2*	*9*	*9*
3 - 4 years	*10*	*12*	*19*	*14*	*14*
5 - 9 years	*31*	*31*	*29*	*27*	*27*
10 - 14 years	*23*	*19*	*20*	*18*	*18*
15 - 19 years	*14*	*13*	*13*	*13*	*13*
20 - 24 years		*10*	*9*	*10*	*10*
25 - 29 years	*21*	*6*	*5*	*5*	*5*
30 years and over		*9*	*5*	*4*	*4*
All durations (=100%)(thousands)	27.0	79.2	155.6	171.1	175.1

Source: Office of Population Censuses and Surveys; General Register Office (Scotland); General Register Office (Northern Ireland)

2.19

Divorces granted: by ground, 1992

England & Wales and Northern Ireland

Thousands

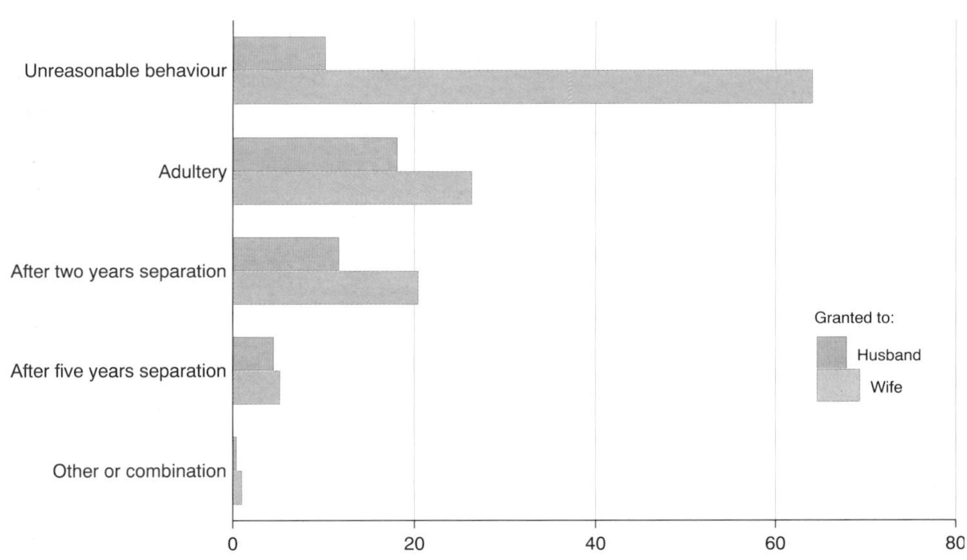

Source: Office of Population Censuses and Surveys; General Register Office (Northern Ireland)

1992, 9 per cent of divorces were of marriages which had lasted up to 2 years compared with only 2 per cent in 1981 (Table 2.18) before the *Matrimonial and Family Proceedings Act 1984*. At the other extreme only 9 per cent of divorces in 1992 were after 25 years of marriage, compared with 21 per cent in 1961. Over a quarter of divorces took place between the fifth and ninth years of marriage.

More than two and a half times as many divorces were granted to women as men in England, Wales and Northern Ireland in 1992 (Chart 2.19). Where a divorce was granted to the husband, adultery was the most common ground given. Where the divorce was granted to the wife, the most common ground was unreasonable behaviour by the husband; unreasonable behaviour accounted for 46 per cent of all divorces in 1992.

Divorced women are more likely to cohabit than single women who have never married. This may reflect an inability or unwillingness to remarry, perhaps in the light of their previous experience of marriage and divorce. There is also some evidence that divorced men and women who cohabit tend to have been cohabiting for longer periods than their younger, single counterparts. In 1991-1992 around 7 per cent of non-married women aged 16-59 cohabited (Table 2.20). Just over a quarter of divorced women aged 16-59 were cohabiting together with almost a fifth of those who had never married. The proportion of single women cohabiting varies markedly according to age; in 1991-1992 almost 30 per cent of those in the 25 to 34 age group were cohabiting compared with just 4 per cent of those aged 50 to 59.

Family building

Estimates of the number of children women will have and the size of families are an important part of the population projections which are discussed in Chapter 1. However an EC comparison of fertility rates is given in Table 2.21. The number of children born per woman fell in every country shown between 1970 and 1992. The fall was greatest in the Irish Republic, Spain and Portugal where the fertility rates were highest in 1970. There is now less variation in fertility rates between EC countries compared with 20 years ago. As well as having fewer children, women are delaying starting a family and the average age of a woman at the birth of her first child has generally increased.

The birth rate among teenage mothers has fallen particularly sharply, but the United Kingdom still had the highest teenage birth rate in the EC in 1992 at 32 births per thousand women aged 15 to 19, almost six times the Dutch rate. On the other hand, women also tend to complete their family earlier in life; there are now fewer than 8 births per thousand women aged 40 to 44 in every country in the EC except the Irish Republic where the rate is nearly twice as high. Overall, in Europe today, a higher proportion of women have never had a child than ever before.

2.20

Percentage of women cohabiting: by age, 1991-1992

Great Britain — Percentages

	Single[1]	Separated	Divorced	Widowed	All non-married women
16-24	*14*	*3*	..	..	*12*
25-34	*30*	*11*	*29*	..	*11*
35-49	*17*	*15*	*29*	*4*	*5*
50-59	*4*	*12*	*14*	*4*	*2*
All aged 16 to 59	*18*	*12*	*26*	*4*	*7*

1 Never married.

Source: Office of Population Censuses and Surveys

2.21

Fertility rates: EC comparison, 1970 and 1992

	Total fertility rate		Births per 1,000 women			
			1970		1992	
	1970	1992	Aged 15-19	Aged 40-44	Aged 15-19	Aged 40-44
Irish Republic	3.9	2.1	..	..	17.0	14.5
United Kingdom	2.4	1.8	49.1	9.2	31.8	5.5
Denmark	2.0	1.8	24.6	6.5	6.9	5.5
France	2.5	1.7	26.7	13.6	8.6	7.6
Luxembourg	2.0	1.7	20.2	11.5	9.0	6
Netherlands	2.6	1.6	17.0	16.8	5.5	5.7
Belgium[1]	2.3	1.6	22.9	12.1	8.8	3.5
Portugal	2.8	1.5	..	..	17.8	6.7
Greece	2.4	1.4	..	..	14.2	5.1
Germany[2,3]	2.0	1.3	37.4	9.7	13.4	4.5
Italy[2]	2.4	1.3	20.9	19.5	6.1	6.3
Spain[2]	2.9	1.2	..	..	8.8	6.9
EC average	2.4	1.5	..	..	..	..

1 1992 data for births per 1,000 women relate to 1989.
2 1992 data for births per 1,000 women relate to 1991.
3 As constituted since 3 October 1990.

Source: Eurostat; Office of Population Censuses and Surveys

2.22

Percentage of women childless at age 30 and 40

England & Wales

Percentages[1]

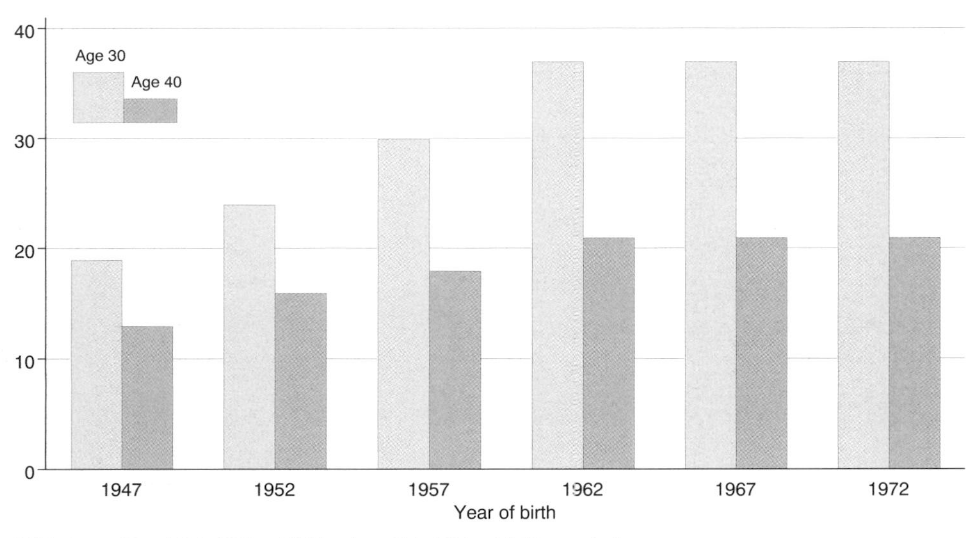

1 Data for age 30 and 40 in 1967 and 1972 and age 40 in 1957 and 1962 are projections.

Source: Office of Population Censuses and Surveys

Many more women now delay starting their families until their 30s. In England and Wales, only 19 per cent of women born in 1947 were still childless at the age of 30 (Chart 2.22). This proportion has increased sharply over time and it is expected that over a third of women born in 1967 will still be childless at 30. Most women do eventually have children and indications are that only one in five of women born between 1947 and 1957 were, or will be, still childless at 40. Evidence from the General Household Survey suggests, however, that the proportion of women who never have children may be increasing. Twice as many women said that they expected to remain childless in the 1991 survey as in the 1986 survey. The survey also shows that women with no qualifications started childbearing at an earlier age and had larger families than women with qualifications. They also expected to have more children.

2.23

Contraception: by method used

Great Britain — Percentages

	1976	1986	1991	1993
Pill	*29*	*23*	*23*	*25*
Male condom	*14*	*13*	*16*	*17*
Hysterectomy	*7*	*12*	*12*	*12*
Vasectomy	*6*	*11*	*13*	*12*
IUD	*6*	*7*	*5*	*5*
Withdrawal	*5*	*4*	*3*	*3*
Safe period	*1*	*1*	*1*	*1*
Cap/Diaphram	*2*	*2*	*1*	*1*
Other	*1*	*1*	*1*	*1*
At least one method	*68*	*71*	*70*	*72*

Source: Office of Population Censuses and Surveys

In 1993 around seven in ten women aged 16 to 49 still practised some form of contraception - a proportion which has remained broadly unchanged since the mid 1970s (Table 2.23). The pill is the most popular method overall and about 39 per cent of women under 35 were on the pill in 1993. Women over 35 were more likely to have had a hysterectomy or to have a partner who had had a vasectomy - only 9 per cent were on the pill. The male condom was a more popular choice in 1991 than 1986 and was used by all age groups to much the same extent. Seventeen per cent of women aged 16 to 49 said this was the method of contraception they used in 1993.

In 1971, 836 thousand women in England and Wales became pregnant; three quarters of these conceptions were inside marriage

(Table 2.24). Over the past twenty years the number of conceptions fell and then rose again to 854 thousand in 1991, but the proportion within marriage has fallen and in 1991 only 56 per cent of all conceptions were inside marriage. Married women who conceive are far less likely to have an abortion than unmarried women. Within marriage almost one in thirteen conceptions led to an abortion in 1991 compared with more than one in three conceptions outside marriage. As the number of conceptions outside marriage has increased, fewer people get married before the baby arrives, but they are far more likely to register the birth jointly than twenty years ago.

The proportion of teenage girls (aged 13 to 19) becoming pregnant fell sharply in the early 1970s, but started rising again in the early 1980s and in 1990 there were 69 conceptions per thousand teenage women in England and Wales. In 1991 teenage pregnancies fell sharply to 65 conceptions per thousand 15 to 19 year olds (Table 2.25), but it is too early to tell if this indicates a change in trend. The rate for under 16s was 9 conceptions per thousand girls aged 13 to 15 in 1991 and reducing this is one of the *Health of the Nation* targets. The target for England implies a rate of 4.8 conceptions per thousand girls under 16 in the year 2000. About half those who conceived before they were 16 had an abortion in 1991. For older teenagers maternities outnumbered abortions and altogether two thirds of teenagers who conceived had the baby. Unmarried teenagers becoming pregnant are far less likely to get married than twenty years ago. In 1971 one in three pregnant unmarried teenagers had their baby inside marriage compared with one in eleven in 1991.

2.24

Conceptions: by marital status and outcome

England & Wales — Percentages

	1971	1981	1990	1991
Inside marriage				
Maternities	*72.6*	*65.9*	*52.3*	*51.9*
Legal abortions[1]	*5.2*	*5.6*	*4.4*	*4.4*
Outside marriage				
Maternities inside marriage	*8.1*	*5.5*	*3.9*	*3.7*
Maternities outside marriage[2]				
- joint registration	*3.5*	*6.8*	*17.6*	*18.9*
- sole registration	*4.1*	*4.8*	*6.2*	*6.1*
Legal abortions[1]	*6.7*	*11.4*	*15.5*	*15.0*
All conceptions (= 100%)(thousands)	835.5	752.3	871.5	853.7

1 Legal terminations under the 1967 Abortion Act.
2 Births outside marriage can be registered by the mother only (sole registrations) or by both parents (joint registrations).
Source: Office of Population Censuses and Surveys

2.25

Teenage conception rates: by type of area, 1991

England & Wales — Rate per 1,000 women

	All conceptions		Leading to maternities	
	Aged under 16[1]	Aged under 20[2]	Aged under 16[1]	Aged under 20[2]
Inner London	12.5	90.4	6.3	51.1
Principal cities	13.3	83.2	7.5	58.4
Other metropolitan districts	12.2	79.1	6.5	55.9
Other cities	12.4	76.6	6.9	54.1
Industrial non-metropolitan districts	10.7	72.1	5.4	50.4
New towns	10.3	71.1	5.0	49.1
Outer London	7.2	59.9	3.2	33.3
Resort and retirement	7.8	59.1	3.5	37.9
Remoter largely rural	6.3	48.9	2.5	30.9
Mixed urban/rural	5.7	43.7	2.2	24.7
All areas	9.3	65.1	4.6	42.7

1 As a proportion of girls aged 13-15.
2 As a proportion of girls aged 15-19.
Source: Office of Population Censuses and Surveys

2.26

Abortions to single and married women: by age

Great Britain					Percentages
	1971	1981	1986	1991	1993
Single women					
Under 16	*4.3*	*5.6*	*4.3*	*2.8*	*3.0*
16-19	*36.1*	*40.6*	*38.7*	*27.3*	*24.2*
20-34	*55.9*	*50.5*	*54.6*	*67.1*	*69.3*
35-44	*1.9*	*1.9*	*2.0*	*2.7*	*3.5*
45 and over	-	-	-	-	*0.1*
Age not known	*1.6*	*1.4*	*0.4*	-	-
All abortions (= 100%)(thousands)	63.4	71.9	96.4	127.6	119.6
Married women					
16-19	*1.4*	*2.4*	*2.0*	*1.2*	*0.9*
20-34	*63.9*	*65.8*	*66.8*	*69.7*	*68.4*
35-44	*31.9*	*29.0*	*29.8*	*28.2*	*29.7*
45 and over	*0.9*	*1.0*	*1.0*	*0.9*	*0.9*
Age not known	*1.9*	*1.8*	*0.4*	-	-
All abortions (= 100%)(thousands)	58.6	51.9	55.5	42.0	39.3

Source: Office of Population Censuses and Surveys; The Scottish Office Home and Health Department

The number of abortions increased by 43 per cent between 1971 and 1991 to over 190 thousand but has since fallen to 180 thousand in 1993. The number of single women having an abortion has roughly doubled over the past twenty years, but there are fewer abortions among married women (Table 2.26). In 1993 two thirds of abortions were performed on single women. Nearly 70 per cent of abortions involved women aged 20 to 34, whether single or married. However, whereas the other 30 per cent of single women having an abortion were nearly all younger than this, the other 30 per cent of married women having abortions were nearly all over 35.

Abortions tend to be carried out earlier in pregnancy these days. In 1993 only 12 per cent of abortions were carried out on women more than 12 weeks pregnant, compared with 22 per cent in 1971; in 1993, 39 per cent were on women under nine weeks pregnant compared with 19 per cent in 1971.

The increasing number of conceptions outside marriage has led to a big increase in the proportion of births outside marriage. Over the past thirty years the percentage of births outside marriage has increased from about one in twenty to almost one in three in 1993 (Chart 2.1). Despite the increase, there is evidence that most births outside marriage now occur within stable relationships. Around three quarters of such births in 1993 were registered jointly by both parents, though not necessarily giving the same address. In 1971 more than half the births resulting from conceptions outside of marriage were registered by the mother only.

2.27

Live births outside marriage: EC comparison, 1992

Percentages

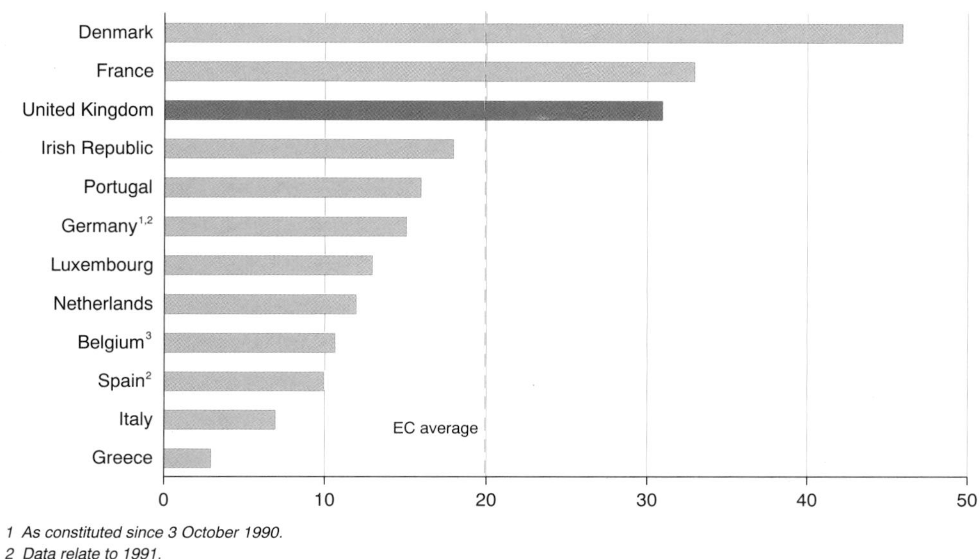

1 As constituted since 3 October 1990.
2 Data relate to 1991.
3 Data relate to 1988.

Source: Eurostat

Although the proportion of births outside marriage varies considerably between countries, it is increasing throughout the western Europe (Chart 2.27). The United Kingdom had a relatively high proportion of births outside marriage, at 31 per cent in 1992, but the rate is higher still in Denmark and France at 46 per cent and 33 per cent respectively. On the other hand, the rate is still very low in Greece and Italy (3 per cent and 7 per cent respectively).

There is also a great deal of variation within the United Kingdom in the percentage of births outside marriage. Within England and Wales in 1992, the highest percentages were in the urban counties of northern England and the Midlands and lowest in central and southern English counties (Chart 2.28). Merseyside had the highest percentage of births outside marriage in 1992, at 42 per cent; Surrey had the lowest rate at 20 per cent. There were also considerable variations in the percentage of births outside marriage in Northern Ireland; Belfast had the highest proportion - 35 per cent while the Southern Board had the lowest - 15 per cent.

As births outside marriage have become more common and the number of lone parents has increased, the number of adoptions has fallen. In 1992 there were only 8 thousand adoptions in the United Kingdom compared with 27 thousand in the peak year of 1968 (Chart 2.29). There has been a gradual trend towards the adoption of older children. The proportion of children under 1 adopted fell from 21 per cent in 1975 to 12 per cent in 1992, while the proportion aged 10 or over rose from 19 per cent to 25 per cent.

2.28

Percentage of births outside marriage: by area,1992

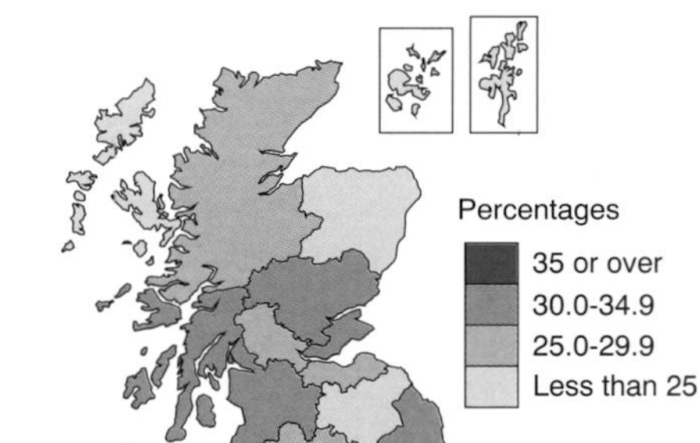

Source: Office of Population Censuses and Surveys; General Register Office (Scotland); General Register Office (Northern Ireland)

2.29

Adoption orders

United Kingdom

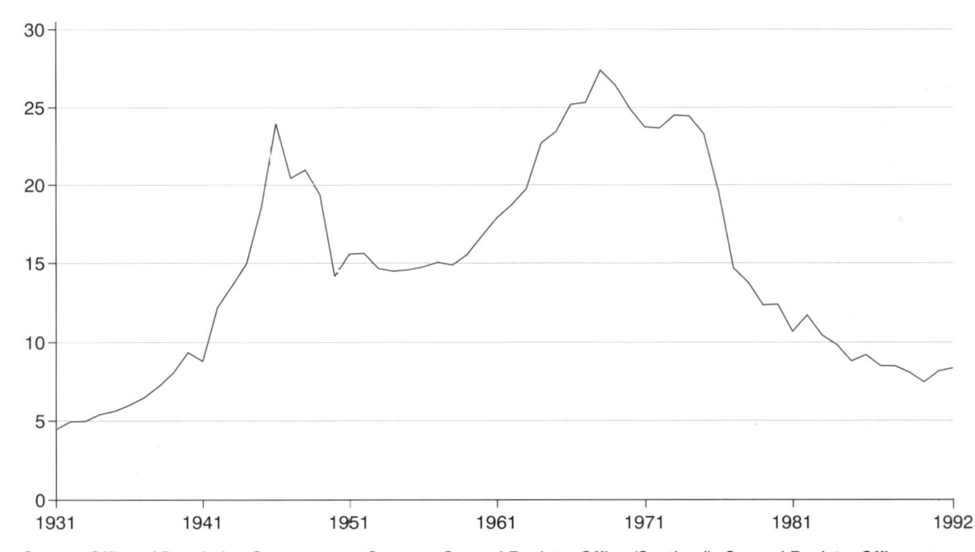

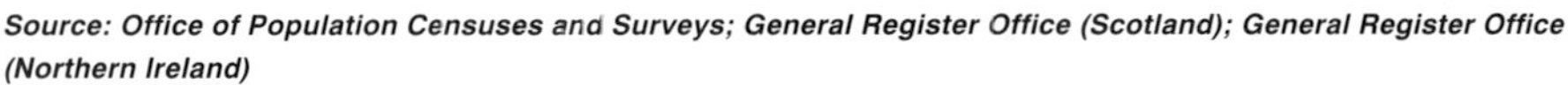

Source: Office of Population Censuses and Surveys; General Register Office (Scotland); General Register Office (Northern Ireland)

References and further reading

The following list contains selected publications relevant to **Chapter 2: Households and Families**. Those published by HMSO are available from the addresses shown on the inside back cover of *Social Trends*.

Annual Report of the Registrar General for Northern Ireland, HMSO
Annual Report of the Registrar General for Scotland, General Registrar Office (Scotland)
Birth Statistics (Series FM1), HMSO
British Social Attitudes: The 9th Report, Dartmouth Publishing
Demographic Statistics, Eurostat
Family Expenditure Survey Report, HMSO
General Household Survey, HMSO
Household Projections, England, 1989-2011, HMSO
Household Projections for the Counties and District Health Authorities of Wales, Welsh Office
Key Population and Vital Statistics (Series VS/PP1), HMSO
Labour Force Survey, HMSO
Marriage and Divorce Statistics (Series FM2), HMSO
Population Trends, HMSO
Regional Trends, HMSO
Scottish Household Projections 1987 based The Scottish Office
Social Focus on Children, HMSO
Welsh Social Trends, Welsh Office

Contacts

Telephone contact points for further information relating to **Chapter 2: Households and Families.**

Office of Population Censuses and Surveys	
General Household Survey	0171 396 2327
Other inquiries	0171 396 2828
Department of the Environment	0171 276 3496
General Register Office, Northern Ireland	01232 252031
Eurostat	00 352 4301 34567
Social & Community Planning Research	0171 250 1866

Chapter 3 Education

Education and day care of children under 5

An increasing proportion of under fives are attending school - over half in 1992/93, compared with only a fifth in 1970/71. (Chart 3.1)

Schools and their pupils

Just over 1 million children in primary schools in England were in classes of more than 30 pupils in January 1992. (Page 49)

There were 102 thousand pupils with statements of special needs in the United Kingdom in ordinary public sector schools in 1992/93. (Table 3.11)

Educational qualifications and attainments

Overall, girls outperform boys. In 1991/92 just under a third of girls left school with one or more A levels or Highers compared with around a quarter of males. (Table 3.15)

Further and higher education

In 1992/93, 460 thousand women were enrolled on full-time further education courses in the United Kingdom, compared with 182 thousand in 1970/71. (Table 3.18)

Educational standards of adults

In 1992-93, 12 per cent of the population aged between 25 and 69 had a degree. (Table 3.24)

In 1992, two fifths of 21 year olds reported difficulties with writing and spelling. (Chart 3.25)

Resources

Total government expenditure on education increased by just over half in real terms between 1970-71 and 1992-93. (Table 3.27)

3.1

Children under 5 in schools as a percentage of all children aged 3 or 4

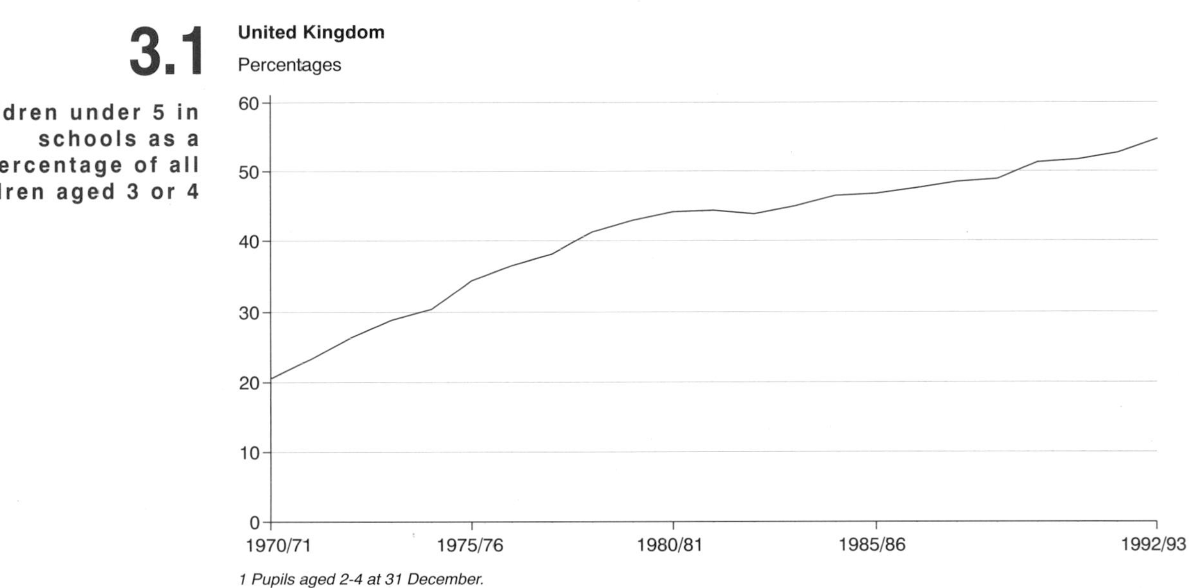

1 Pupils aged 2-4 at 31 December.

Source: Department of Education; Welsh Office; The Scottish Office Education Department; Department for Education, Northern Ireland

3.2

Education of children under 5

United Kingdom									Thousands
		1965/66	1970/71	1975/76	1980/81	1985/86[1]	1990/91	1991/92	1992/93
Children under 5 in schools[2]									
Public sector schools									
Nursery schools	- full-time	26	20	20	22	19	16	16	15
	- part-time	9	29	54	67	77	68	69	70
Primary schools	- full-time	220	263	350	281	306	357	359	376
	- part-time	-	38	117	167	228	303	318	329
Non-maintained schools	- full-time	21	19	19	19	20	28	29	29
	- part-time	2	14	12	12	15	20	20	21
Special schools	- full-time	2	2	4	4	4	4	4	4
	- part-time	-	-	1	1	2	2	3	3
All public sector schools		280	384	576	573	671	799	817	848

1 Data for Scotland relate to 1984/85.
2 Pupils aged under 5 at December/January of academic year.
Source: Department for Education; Welsh Office; The Scottish Office Education Department; Department of Education, Northern Ireland

This chapter looks at the various stages of education, from pre-school provision to further and higher education. It also covers academic and vocational qualifications and standards, as well as the resources that are devoted to education.

3.3

Day care places[1,2] for children under five

United Kingdom						Thousands
	1971	1981	1986	1991	1992	1993
Local authority day nurseries	23	32	33	33	30	28
Local authority playgroups		5	5	3	5	3
Registered day nurseries[3]	296	23	29	88	105	127
Registered playgroups		433	473	502	496	475
Registered child minders[4]	90	110	157	273	297	352
Total	409	603	698	899	932	985

1 Figures for 1971 cover England and Wales at end-March 1972. From 1976 data are at end-March except for the Northern Ireland component which is at end-December of the preceding year up to 1989.
2 See Appendix, Part 3: Day care.
3 No figures are available for registered nurseries in Scotland for 1988 and later. Estimates have been made for the purpose of obtaining a United Kingdom total.
4 Because of a different method of collection of data relating to registered child minders between 1979 and 1982, these figures are less reliable. Includes child minders provided by local authorities. English and Welsh data include places for children under 8 in 1992 and 1993.
Source: Department of Health; Welsh Office; The Scottish Office Social Work Services Group; Department of Health and Social Services, Northern Ireland;

Education and day care of children under 5

Chart 3.1 illustrates the number of children under 5 in schools as a percentage of all 3 and 4 year olds. In 1970/71, around a fifth attended school but by 1992/93, this had risen to over half. This was mainly due to the increase in the number of under 5s attending primary schools on a part-time basis: in 1992/93, nearly 9 times more children went to a maintained primary school part-time than in 1970/71.

In 1992/93 nearly 850 thousand children under 5 attended school (either full or part-time) in the United Kingdom - more than double the number in 1970/71 (Table 3.2). In 1992/93, the number in public sector nursery schools remained the same as in 1991/92, at 85 thousand, although this is still three quarters more than in 1970/71. The number in public sector primary schools rose by 4 per cent between 1991/92 and 1992/93 to 705 thousand, while the number in non-maintained schools increased marginally to 50 thousand.

As well as the increase in the number of under 5s attending school, a growing number of day care places are available (Table 3.3). In March 1993, nearly 1 million places were available, almost 6 per cent more than in the previous year and more than double the number available in 1971. Within this total, by far the largest increases were in places with registered child minders and day nurseries; there were over 350 thousand places with registered child minders in 1993, over three times the number in 1981, and over 120 thousand places in registered day nurseries - almost six times as many as in 1981.

An international comparison of participation of 3 to 5 year olds in pre-primary school education is given in Table 3.4. Compulsory primary education starts at the age of 6 in most countries shown in the table. However, the percentage of under 5s in education varies considerably between countries. For example, in France 98 per cent of 3 year olds and all 4 year olds are provided for in the 'écoles maternelles'. These institutions are usually open from 8.30 am to 4.30 pm with supervision and meals during a two hour lunch break. In contrast, there is no provision for 3 year olds in Canada and the Netherlands, while Japan provides for only a fifth of 3 year olds and three fifths of 4 year olds. The United Kingdom provides for just under one third of 3 year olds and nearly three quarters of 4 year olds; full-time primary education is started at the age of 5.

Table 3.5 gives a more detailed breakdown of where pre-school children spend their time when they are not being cared for by their mother. The data are taken from the Day Care Services for Children survey which was carried out by the Office of Population Censuses and Surveys on behalf of the Department of Health in 1990. The survey found that the mothers of about a fifth of pre-school children did not use any form of day care and a further one in five only received care on domestic premises in their mother's absence (mainly those aged under 3). The remainder attended non-domestic facilities such as parent and toddler

3.4

Participation of 3 to 5 year olds in pre-primary education[1]: by age, international comparison, 1991

Percentages

	Age at which compulsory schooling starts	Age 3	4	5
Belgium	6	*97*	*99*	*98*
Canada	6	-	*48*	*70*
France	6	*98*	*100*	*99*
Germany[2]	6	*35*	*71*	*84*
Japan	6	*21*	*58*	*65*
Netherlands	5	-	*98*	*99*
Spain	6	*28*	*94*	*100*
United Kingdom[3]	5	*32*	*72*	*100*
United States[4]	6-8	*33*	*57*	*90*

1 Full-time and part-time combined.
2 Former Federal Republic.
3 Age 3 includes some children aged 2. Participation rates of those in school at start of calendar year (1 January 1991) with age at that point (31 December 1990).
4 Varies between states.
Source: Department for Education

3.5

Use of day care[1] services by pre-school children[2]: by age and type of provision, 1990

England Percentages

	Age of child 0	1	2	3	4	All pre-school children
Domestic premises[3]						
Father	*19*	*18*	*24*	*24*	*24*	*21*
Grandparent	*22*	*24*	*25*	*22*	*18*	*23*
Non-domestic premises						
Parent and toddler group	*12*	*36*	*31*	*13*	*7*	*21*
Day nursery	*2*	*6*	*8*	*13*	*9*	*8*
Playgroup	-	*1*	*18*	*50*	*42*	*21*
Nursery class or school	-	-	*4*	*30*	*54*	*15*

1 See Appendix, Part 3: Day care.
2 Children may receive day care from more than one source. Children attending school full-time are not included.
3 Others providing regular day care in the mother's absence included friends, neighbours, childminders, nannies, au pairs, brothers, sisters and other relatives.
Source: Office of Population Censuses and Surveys

3.6

Use of day care[1] services by pre-school children[2]: by mother's employment status and type of provision, 1990

England			Percentages
	Mother working	Mother not working	All pre-school children
Child's own home	*51*	*17*	*33*
Other home	*44*	*14*	*28*
Non-domestic premises	*62*	*54*	*58*
No service used	*8*	*34*	*22*

1 See Appendix, Part 3: Day care.
2 Children may receive day care from more than one source. Children attending school full-time are not included.
Source: Office of Population Censuses and Surveys

groups, day nurseries, playgroups and nursery schools. Not surprisingly, the proportion of children attending these day care and educational facilities on non-domestic premises increased with age, from 14 per cent of under 1s to 96 per cent of 4 year olds not yet at school full-time. Around a third of children aged 1 or 2 attended parent and toddler groups, whereas playgroups and nursery schools or classes were used extensively by 3 and 4 year olds.

As a child grows older, the form of its education changes. Of all 4 year olds in the survey, a third were attending school full-time (they are excluded from Tables 3.5 and 3.6) and, of the remainder, over half were going to a nursery class or school and about two-fifths to a playgroup.

About half of all pre-school children attending non-domestic facilities were also regularly cared for on domestic premises while their mother was absent. In all, 21 per cent of pre-school children were looked after regularly by their father and 23 per cent by a grandparent. A smaller proportion were looked after by friends and neighbours (7 per cent), registered childminders (6 per cent), nannies or au pairs (3 per cent), brothers or sisters (2 per cent) or other relatives (4 per cent).

More than nine in ten pre-school children with working mothers used some form of day care, compared with only two thirds of those with non-working mothers (Table 3.6). Much of this difference is associated with the proportions receiving care on domestic premises (in their own or another person's home).

Schools and their pupils

The number of pupils in schools is directly affected by the birth rate in previous years (see Chapter 1: Population) and the age at which children start and leave school. The total number of school pupils in the United Kingdom peaked in 1977 when it reached 11.3 million; it then fell to 9.2 million in 1989/90. Since then the number has climbed again to reach 9.5 million in 1992/93 (Table 3.7). Between 1970/71 and 1992/93, the number of pupils in public sector nursery schools more than doubled from 50 to 109

3.7

School pupils[1]: by type of school[2]

United Kingdom				Thousands
	1970/71	1980/81	1990/91	1992/93
Public sector schools				
Nursery	50	89	105	109
Primary	5,902	5,171	4,955	5,077
Secondary	3,555	4,606	3,473	3,606
All public sector schools[3]	9,507	9,866	8,533	8,791
Non-maintained schools	621	619	613	607
Special schools[4]	103	148	114	115
All schools	10,230	10,633	9,260	9,513

1 Full and part-time pupils are counted as one.
2 See Appendix, Part 3: Main categories of educational establishments and Stages of education.
3 Excludes public sector special schools.
4 Includes maintained and non-maintained sector.
Source: Department for Education; Welsh Office; The Scottish Office Education Department; Department of Education, Northern Ireland

thousand. Overall, the total number of pupils in public sector schools (excluding special schools) fell by around 8 per cent between 1970/71 and 1992/93. Over the same time period, the number of pupils in non-maintained schools fell by 2 per cent to 607 thousand.

In 1992/93 nearly two thirds of public sector primary school classes in England contained 21 to 30 pupils (Table 3.8). Since 1980/81, the number of classes has fallen by 7 per cent to 149 thousand, but the average number of pupils in a class has increased from 26 to 27. In public sector secondary schools, the number of classes fell by 24 per cent over the same period, to 133 thousand in 1992/93, when the average number in a class was 21. The average class size in Scotland was slightly smaller than in England in both primary and secondary schools, at 25 and 19 respectively.

After falling during the 1970s, pupil/teacher ratios for public sector nursery and primary schools in the United Kingdom have remained fairly static (Table 3.9) as the fall in pupil numbers was matched by a fall in teacher numbers. However, in non-maintained schools the ratio continued to fall to 10.4 in 1992/93; this was just over half of the ratio for public sector schools. For primary schools in England, there were just over 1 million children in classes of more than 30 in January 1992; this rose to just over 1.1 million in January 1993, a rise of 10 per cent.

3.8

Class sizes[1]: by type of school

England — Percentages

	1980/81	1985/86	1990/91	1992/93
Primary schools				
One teacher				
1 - 20 pupils	*20*	*17*	*12*	*10*
21 - 30 pupils	*55*	*58*	*62*	*63*
31 or more pupils	*22*	*19*	*19*	*20*
Two or more teachers	*3*	*6*	*7*	*7*
Number of classes (thousands)	161	142	147	149
Average number in class	26	26	27	27
Secondary schools				
One teacher				
1 - 20 pupils	*44*	*46*	*44*	*40*
21 - 30 pupils	*45*	*45*	*47*	*50*
31 or more pupils	*8*	*6*	*4*	*4*
Two or more teachers	*2*	*3*	*5*	*5*
Number of classes (thousands)	174	155	130	133
Average number in class	22	21	21	21

1 Class size related to one selected period in each public sector school on the day of the count in January.

Source: Department for Education

3.9

Pupil/teacher ratios[1]: by type of school

United Kingdom — Ratios[1]

	1970/71	1980/81	1990/91	1992/93
Public sector schools				
Nursery	26.6	21.5	21.5	21.5
Primary	27.1	22.3	21.8	21.9
Secondary[2]	17.8	16.4	15.0	15.4
All public sector schools[3]	22.6	19.0	18.3	18.6
Non-maintained schools[4]	14.0	13.1	10.7	10.4
Special schools[5]	10.5	7.4	5.7	5.8
All schools	22.0	18.2	17.0	17.3

1 See Appendix, Part 3: Pupil/teacher ratios.
2 Includes voluntary grammar schools in Northern Ireland from1989/90 (formerly allocated to the non-maintained sector).
3 Excludes maintained special schools.
4 Excludes independent schools in Scotland in 1970/71 and in Northern Ireland in 1980/81.
5 Includes maintained and non-maintained special schools.

Source: Department for Education

3.10

Boarding pupils: by type of school[1]

England				Thousands
	1975/76	1980/81	1985/86	1992/93
Public sector schools[2]	10	8	7	4
Independent schools[2]	131	131	117	94
Special schools	21	18	15	11
All schools	162	157	138	109

1 At January of latest year
2 Excludes special schools
Source: Department for Education.

The number of pupils who board at schools in England has fallen quite considerably since 1980/81 to stand at 109 thousand in 1992/93, a drop of a third (Table 3.10). Public sector schools, although only ever having small numbers boarding, have seen numbers more than halved over the same period. In 1992/93, 94 thousand children, nearly nine in ten boarders in England, boarded at an independent school. The reasons for the fall in boarding pupils may be partly due to the recession, the fall in the number of children of school age and cutbacks in the Armed Services and the allowances payable to service families.

3.11

Pupils with special needs: by type of establishment

	1970/71	1975/76	1980/81	1985/86	1990/91	1992/93
Hospital schools						
England, Wales and Northern Ireland						
Schools (numbers)	86	159	136	91	48	41
Full time pupils (thousands)	3.6	9.5	7.1	4.4	0.9	0.5
Full time teachers (thousands)	0.5	1.2	1.2	0.7	0.4	0.3
Other special schools or departments[1]						
United Kingdom						
Schools (numbers)	1113	1747	1875	1821	1782	1734
Full time pupils (thousands)	99.6	139.5	139.2	126	110.8	111.7
Full time equivalent number of teachers (thousands)	9.3	15.8	18.4	18.5	19.1	19.2
Pupils with statements of special needs in other public sector schools[2]						
United Kingdom (thousands)	.	.	.	38.2	75.2	102.5

1 Includes all Scottish special schools. 1984/85 data for Scotland have been used for 1985/86. Figures from 1987 onwards include schools and pupils which were previously the responsibility of the Department of Health and Social Services, Northern Ireland.
2 Includes preparatory and secondary departments of grammar schools for Northern Ireland in 1992/93.
Source: Department for Education; Welsh Office; The Scottish Office Education Department; Department of Education, Northern Ireland

Table 3.11 shows that the number of full-time pupils with special needs in special schools in the United Kingdom increased by around two fifths between 1970/71 and 1975/76. This was mainly due to the *Education (Handicapped Children) Act 1970* and the *Education (Mentally Handicapped Children) (Scotland) Act 1974*. Under these Acts the local education authorities, rather than the health authorities, assumed responsibility for all establishments catering for physically and mentally disabled children, including the provision of an assessment and statement of special needs. Since 1975/76, the number has fallen back by a fifth, to 112 thousand in 1992/93. Over the same period, the number of hospital schools fell by three quarters, while the number of other special schools or departments remained fairly constant. The number of pupils with statements of special needs was just over 102 thousand in 1992/93.

Authorised and unauthorised absence from school is illustrated in England in Table 3.12. Unauthorised absence is a serious problem for schools. It cuts down the child's chances of gaining a proper education and is a contributory factor in juvenile crime.

For all types of school the average number of half days missed per absent pupil fell between 1992/93 and 1993/94. Special schools have the highest number of unauthorised half days missed per absent pupil - at 28 it is four times that of independent schools. However, there is a smaller gap between authorised and unauthorised absences for special schools than for any other type of school (only 1 half day).

Care should be taken with the unauthorised absence figures, however, as they measure failure to register at the start of the morning and afternoon sessions without good reason; sometimes late arrivers may be recorded as absent and some who register may then go absent.

3.12

Authorised and unauthorised absence: by type of school, 1993/94

England

	Authorised absence		Unauthorised absence	
	Average number of half days missed per absent pupil	Percentage of half days missed by all pupils	Average number of half days missed per absent pupil	Percentage of half days missed by all pupils
Maintained primary	19	*5.6*	11	*0.5*
Maintained secondary	27	*8.1*	22	*0.9*
Special schools	29	*8.0*	28	*2.4*
City technology colleges	22	*6.7*	13	*0.4*
Independent schools	13	*3.2*	7	.
All schools	22	*6.5*	16	*0.7*

Source: Department for Education

In 1993, 45 per cent of children in public sector schools had school lunches (Table 3.13). One in six of all children received free school meals. Just under a third of children had packed lunches, while 'other arrangements' such as chip shops and cafes comprised just under a quarter of lunchtime meals.

3.13

Lunchtime meals of pupils[1], 1991 and 1993

Great Britain Percentages[2]

	1991	1993
Packed lunch[3]	*31*	*32*
Paid school meal	*31*	*29*
Free school meal	*12*	*16*
Other	*25*	*23*
All pupils	*100*	*100*

1 In maintained schools excluding boarders.
2 Data as at January for England and Scotland and September 1991 and 1992 for Wales.
3 Packed lunches for Wales are included in 'Other'.

Source: Department for Education

3.14

Adults[1] with qualifications at or above GCSE grades A-C or equivalent: by gender

Great Britain

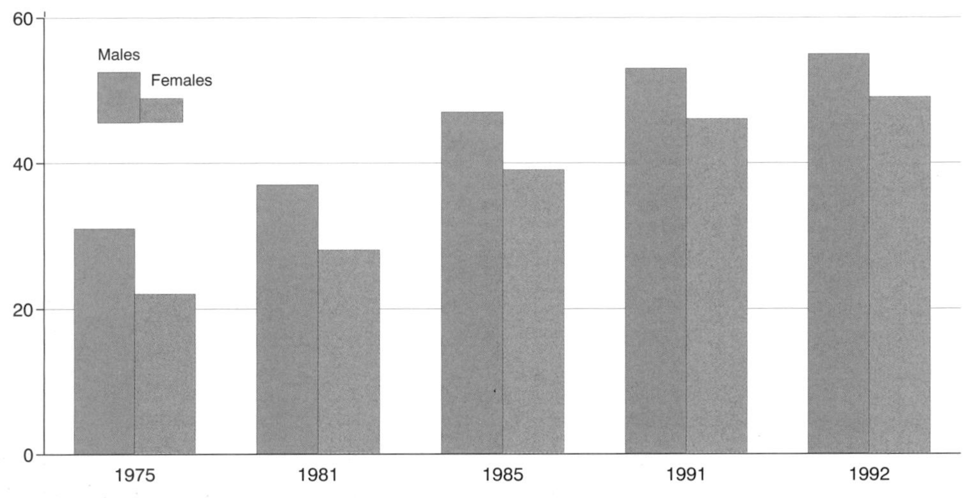

1 People aged 16-69, not in full time education.

Source: Office of Population Censuses and Surveys

Educational qualifications and attainments

Chart 3.14 shows the proportion of adults in Great Britain with qualifications at or above GCSE grades A-C or equivalent. Since 1975, the proportion has nearly doubled from 27 per cent to 53 per cent in 1992. Men are more likely than women to be qualified to at least this level. However, the gap is narrowing. In 1975, 31 per cent of men, compared with 22 per cent of women had a qualification at or above GCSE grades A-C or equivalent; by 1992 the proportions had risen to 55 and 49 per cent respectively.

3.15

School leavers' examination achievements[1]: by gender and region, 1991/92

Percentages

	1 or more A levels[2] (or SCE highers)		GCSEs[3] or SCE O/standard (no A levels or SCE highers)		No graded results[4]		All leavers (= 100%) (thousands)	
	Males	Females	Males	Females	Males	Females	Males	Females
United Kingdom	27.8	31.4	65.2	62.6	7.1	6.0	323.9	312.0
North	17.6	24.7	74.7	69.4	7.7	5.9	18.2	18.0
Yorkshire & Humberside	23.5	26.6	68.6	65.9	7.9	7.5	28.2	25.5
East Midlands	22.8	26.7	72.5	69.0	4.6	4.3	21.2	20.7
East Anglia	33.1	26.2	62.0	67.9	5.0	5.9	9.3	7.6
South East	31.5	35.5	63.3	59.5	5.3	5.0	92.7	89.5
South West	27.1	23.2	69.4	68.5	3.4	2.3	27.8	25.5
West Midlands	25.7	27.2	67.8	68.1	6.5	4.7	31.9	30.3
North West	24.8	24.4	68.2	68.5	7.0	7.0	35.0	37.8
England	27.0	29.6	67.1	65.1	5.8	5.3	264.3	254.8
Wales[5]	22.8	28.3	63.0	61.4	14.2	10.4	16.7	15.9
Scotland	36.9	47.2	51.9	44.2	11.2	8.7	30.8	29.8
Northern Ireland	28.0	36.7	57.2	54.9	14.7	8.5	12.0	11.4

1 Excludes results in further education.
2 Two AS levels are counted as equivalent to one A level.
3 Includes equivalent grades at GCE and CSE and leavers with 1 AS level.
4 Some of these pupils will have achieved passes in other examinations, eg BTEC, RSA, Certificate of Education (in Wales) and SCOTVEC (in Scotland).
5 Includes leavers from maintained and independent schools but not special schools.

Source: Department for Education; Welsh Office; The Scottish Office Education Department; Department of Education, Northern Ireland

The educational attainments of 1991/92 school leavers are analysed in Table 3.15. Overall in the United Kingdom, girls outperform boys. This is particularly marked in Scotland, where over 47 per cent of girls achieve 1 or more Scottish Certificate of Education highers compared with only 37 per cent of boys. However, figures for Scotland are not directly comparable with figures for the rest of the United Kingdom because of the different education system and examination structures.

Overall, in all regions except East Anglia, a higher proportion of girls than boys obtained graded results; in all regions except East Anglia, a higher proportion of girls than boys obtained 1 or more A levels or equivalent. The highest proportion of girls with passes at A level was in Northern Ireland at 37 per cent while the lowest was in the North West at 24 per cent.

Chart 3.16 shows that the proportions of both boys and girls who left school without a GCSE or equivalent has steadily declined since 1975/76, although the proportion for girls has always remained below that for boys.

A higher proportion of boys than girls used to leave school with 1 or more A level (18 and 16 per cent respectively in 1975/76) but since 1981/82 the proportion for boys has only been the same or lower, never greater than that for girls. In 1991/92, the proportion of girls with 1 or more A levels was 31 per cent compared with only 28 per cent for boys.

3.16

School leavers with no GCSE or equivalent qualifications[1]

Great Britain

Percentages

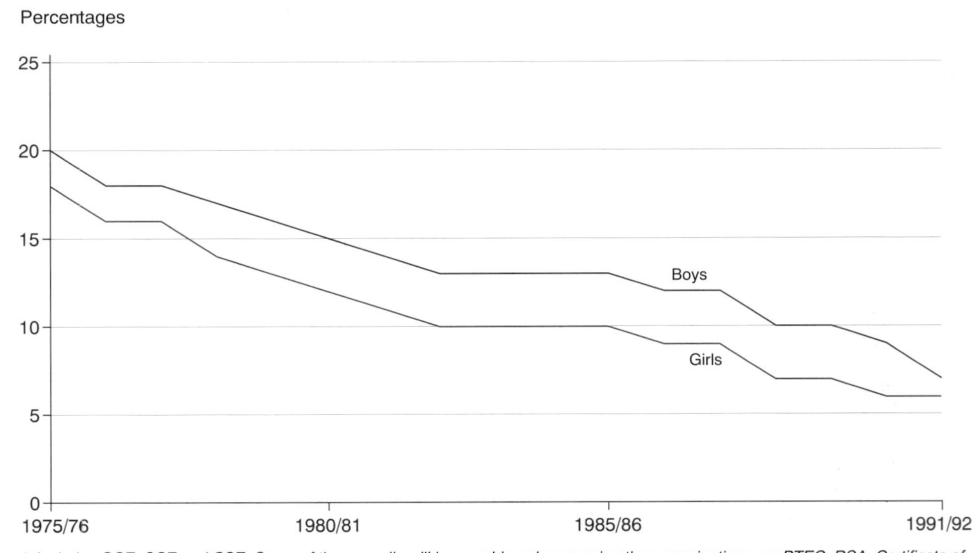

1 Includes GCE, SCE and CSE. Some of these pupils will have achieved passes in other examinations, eg BTEC, RSA, Certificate of Education (in Wales) and SCOTVEC (in Scotland).

Source: Department for Education; Welsh Office; The Scottish Office Education Department

Table 3.17 shows the destination of school leavers in Scotland which is the only country in the United Kingdom to collect this type of information at present. The last English School Leavers Survey was in 1991/92. The proportion of school leavers entering full-time education in Scotland increased by 9 percentage points between 1987/88 and 1991/92 whereas the proportion entering full-time employment fell by 4 percentage points. The proportion in Scotland who became unemployed doubled between 1987/88 and 1991/92 to 12 per cent. Wales and Northern Ireland collect information on the intended destination of school leavers; in 1991/92 56 per cent of school leavers in Wales, and just over 58 per cent in Northern Ireland, stated that they intended to go into further or higher education.

3.17

Actual destination of school leavers

Scotland — Percentages

	1987/88	1989/90	1991/92
Full-time education	*28*	*29*	*37*
Full-time employment	*31*	*32*	*27*
Youth training	*28*	*24*	*18*
Unemployed	*6*	*9*	*12*
Other/no reply	*6*	*5*	*7*
All leavers[1] (=100%)(thousands)	74.8	66.5	59.1

1 Excludes leavers with special educational needs.

Source: The Scottish Office Education Department

3.18

Full and part-time enrolments in higher education[1]: by gender and type of establishment

United Kingdom Thousands

	Males 1970/71	Males 1975/76	Males 1980/81	Males 1985/86	Males 1992/93	Females 1970/71	Females 1975/76	Females 1980/81	Females 1985/86	Females 1992/93
Full-time and sandwich enrolments										
Universities										
Undergraduates	134	141	157	148	191	59	77	101	108	166
Postgraduates	33	37	34	37	48	10	13	15	17	31
Other[2]										
Undergraduates	107	123	120	146	245	114	123	95	129	250
Postgraduates			7	7	13			6	7	13
All full-time enrolments	274	301	318	339	496	182	214	217	261	460
Part-time enrolments										
Universities										
Undergraduates	3	2	2	5	6	2	2	2	5	9
Postgraduates	15	17	20	22	35	3	5	8	11	26
Open University[3]	14	34	38	43	53	5	22	29	36	52
Other[2]										
Undergraduates	110	115	138	142	144	12	21	42	68	116
Postgraduates			9	12	24			3	6	21
All part-time enrolments	142	168	207	224	262	23	50	86	125	224
All enrolments	416	470	524	563	759	205	264	303	386	685

Note: for 1970/71 and 1975/76, "Other" undergraduates and postgraduates are bracketed together; the combined figure is shown in the Undergraduates row.

1 See Appendix, Part 3: Stages of education. Excludes students enrolled on nursing and paramedic courses at Department of Health establishments.
2 Polytechnics, new universities and other higher education establishments.
3 Calendar years beginning in second year shown. Excludes short course students up to 1982/83.

Source: Department for Education

Further and higher education

Among both males and females, the number of students in higher education rose dramatically between 1970/71 and 1992/93. The greatest increases were among females. Total female full-time student numbers increased two and a half times from 180 thousand to 460 thousand. The number of female part-time students was nearly ten times higher in 1992/93 than in 1970/71 and the number of female Open University students rose from 5 to 52 thousand.

In particular, the number of female post-graduate students has risen sharply since 1980/81. Since 1970/71 male numbers have shown dramatic rises too with the number of both full-time and part-time students increasing by over 80 per cent. In 1970/71, there were twice as many male students as female. By 1992/93 there were only 11 per cent more male than female students (Table 3.18).

Table 3.19 gives a breakdown of student enrolments in higher education by subject in 1992/93. Arts courses were more popular with women than men; women accounted for around two thirds of enrolments on these courses. Men outnumbered women on science courses: nearly twice as many men as women enrolled to study science. In social studies there was a greater parity in the numbers. Overall though, student enrolments for science courses were 45 per cent higher than for arts and 69 per cent higher than for social sciences. While the number of men who enrolled in universities and polytechnics and colleges was similar, 26 per cent more women enrolled in polytechnics and colleges than universities. The 'new universities' came into being officially in April 1993.

In 1990/91, over 1 million national vocational qualifications (NVQs) were awarded to students in the United Kingdom (Table 3.20). Of these, 86 per cent were awarded in England, around 5 per cent in both Wales and Northern Ireland and around 1 per cent in Scotland. However, figures for Scotland exclude the SCOTVEC National Certificate which is the predominant vocational qualification there. Among students whose ages were known, the 19 and over age group accounted for over 40 per cent of the total. Of the 3 levels available within NVQs, level 1 had the largest number of awards, with around half of the total for all levels.

3.19

Home full-time[1] first degree student enrolments: by subject and type of institution, 1992/93

United Kingdom Thousands

	Arts	Science	Social studies	Other	All Subjects
Universities					
Males	26	92	30	20	167
Females	44	54	27	21	145
Polytechnics and colleges					
Males	29	66	41	26	162
Females	68	31	46	38	182
All higher education					
Males	55	158	70	46	330
Females	112	85	72	58	328
All	167	242	143	104	657

1 Includes sandwich students.

Source: Department for Education; Welsh Office; The Scottish Office Education Department; Department of Education, Northern Ireland

3.20

Students[1] awarded vocational qualifications: by age and NVQ level, 1990/91

United Kingdom Thousands

	Under 16	16	17	18	19 and over	All ages[2]
NVQ level 1	34	71	90	42	180	538
NVQ level 2	3	17	56	51	142	345
NVQ level 3	-	1	12	45	126	210
All levels	36	89	157	137	448	1,093

1 Awards shown are estimated to represent 75 per cent of all awards. Excludes all SCOTVEC National Certificate qualifications (approximately 245 thousand students were enrolled on courses leading to this qualification). It is possible to obtain more than one qualification, so double counting may occur.
2 Includes age unknown.

Source: Department for Education

3.21

BTEC awards on certain types of vocational course, 1992/93[1]

England & Wales — Percentages

	Full awards	Part awards	No awards[2]
First Diploma[3]			
Engineering	49	24	27
Service Industries	71	14	16
Science and Caring	66	17	17
Business and finance	74	13	13
National Diploma[3]			
Engineering	58	19	23
Service Industries	73	13	14
Science and Caring	71	12	17
Business and finance	75	14	11

1 As at January 1994. Students who enrolled for the 1992/93 session may receive part or full awards at a later date but these awards will always be included in the data for the year in which they enrolled.
2 Includes both fail and refer. Refer means that to pass, students must submit extra work.
3 Diplomas are full-time courses.

Source: Business & Technology Education Council

In 1992, the government brought in General National Vocational Qualifications (GNVQs). The difference between GNVQs and NVQs is that NVQs are job related and measure competence to certain standards set by employers whereas GNVQs are designed for young people in full-time education and provide a broad programme of study designed to prepare students for higher education. They are aimed at 16 to 19 year olds. GNVQs cover such subjects as art and design, business, health and social care and manufacturing; the advanced GNVQs are seen as equivalent to two A levels.

Success and failure rates for certain BTEC GNVQ courses in 1993 are shown in Table 3.21. For a First Diploma, the course with the highest proportion of full awards was business and finance where 74 per cent of students successfully completed the course; this compares with only 49 per cent for engineering; over a quarter of students taking engineering failed to achieve an award - the highest failure rate for a First Diploma course. On National Diploma in business and finance (as for First Diploma), three quarters of students obtained a full award while just under three fifths obtained a diploma in engineering.

Chart 3.22 illustrates how the United Kingdom compares with other industrialised nations in participation rates for 18 to 21 year olds in higher education in 1991. Of all the countries shown in the table, Denmark has the lowest rate at 8 per cent. The United Kingdom has 18 per cent of 18 to 21 year olds in higher education, either full or part-time, almost twice as many as Germany. The highest rate occurs in the United States, where the participation rate of 36 per cent is double that for the United Kingdom and more than 4 times the rate in Denmark. However, it must be remembered that the number of places and the variety of subjects available can also determine participation rates, as can entry criteria.

Table 3.23 shows the destination of first degree graduates. Since 1988, the proportion of first degree graduates who entered employment in the United Kingdom has fallen from 55 per cent to 42 per cent in 1992. However, an increasing proportion have entered further education or training: in the academic year 1991/92, nearly 9 thousand post graduate students in the former University Funding Council funded universities successfully completed their doctorates - nearly a fifth more than in 1987/88.

3.22

Percentage of 18-21 year olds in higher education[1]: international comparison, 1991

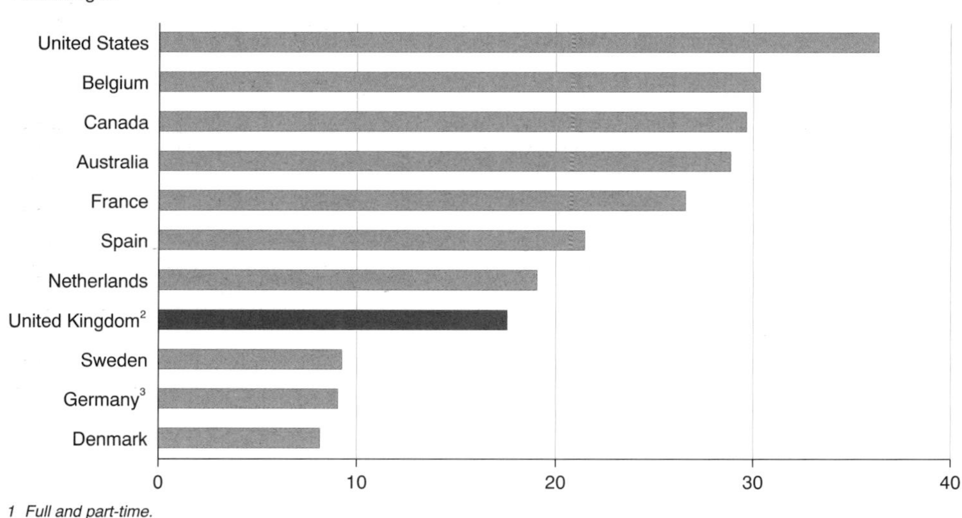

1 Full and part-time.
2 Excludes pupils in private further and higher education.
3 Former Federal Republic.

Source: Department for Education

Educational standards of adults

This section looks at educational standards among the adult population. Table 3.24 illustrates how the highest qualification attained by people aged 25 to 69 who have left full-time education varies for the different socio-economic groups in 1992-93. Not surprisingly, the majority of professionals (61 per cent) had a degree, but 3 per cent of them had no formal qualifications at all. The situation is almost completely reversed for unskilled manual workers where less than 1 per cent had a degree and 70 per cent had no qualification at all.

Chart 3.25 overleaf illustrates the numeracy and literacy difficulties experienced by a sample of 21 year olds. The sample was taken from the British Cohort Study which is a longitudinal study of all individuals born between April 5 and 11 1970; they were followed up at ages 5, 10, 16 and 21.

3.23

Destination of first degree graduates

Great Britain — Percentages

	Year of graduation				
	1983	1986	1988	1991	1992
United Kingdom employment[1]	*48*	*53*	*55*	*44*	*42*
Further education or training	*21*	*19*	*18*	*20*	*21*
Believed unemployed	*10*	*7*	*5*	*10*	*11*
Overseas graduates leaving United Kingdom	*4*	*3*	*4*	*6*	*6*
Not available for employment	*2*	*2*	*3*	*4*	*4*
Overseas employment[2]	*2*	*2*	*2*	*3*	*2*
Destination not known	*13*	*14*	*12*	*13*	*13*
All first degree graduates (= 100%) (thousands)	105	112	117	131	144

1 Permanent and temporary.
2 Home students.
Source: Department for Education

3.24

Highest qualification held[1]: by socio-economic group, 1992-1993

Great Britain — Percentages

	Professional	Employers and managers	Intermediate non-manual	Junior non-manual	Skilled manual and own account non-professional	Semi-skilled manual and personal service	Unskilled manual	All persons
Degree	*61*	*19*	*21*	*3*	*2*	*1*	-	*12*
Higher education	*16*	*19*	*29*	*6*	*9*	*4*	*2*	*13*
GCE A level[2]	*7*	*16*	*12*	*13*	*14*	*7*	*3*	*12*
GCSE, grades A-C[2]	*7*	*21*	*20*	*35*	*23*	*21*	*12*	*22*
GCSE, grades D-G[2,3]	*1*	*7*	*5*	*16*	*15*	*12*	*10*	*10*
Foreign	*4*	*3*	*3*	*3*	*2*	*4*	*3*	*3*
No qualifications	*3*	*15*	*10*	*24*	*36*	*51*	*70*	*28*

1 Persons aged 25-69 not in full-time education. See Appendix, Part 3: Education.
2 Or equivalent.
3 Includes commercial qualifications and apprenticeships.
Source: Office of Population Censuses and Surveys

3.25

Literacy and numeracy problems among 21 year olds, 1992

England & Wales

Percentages

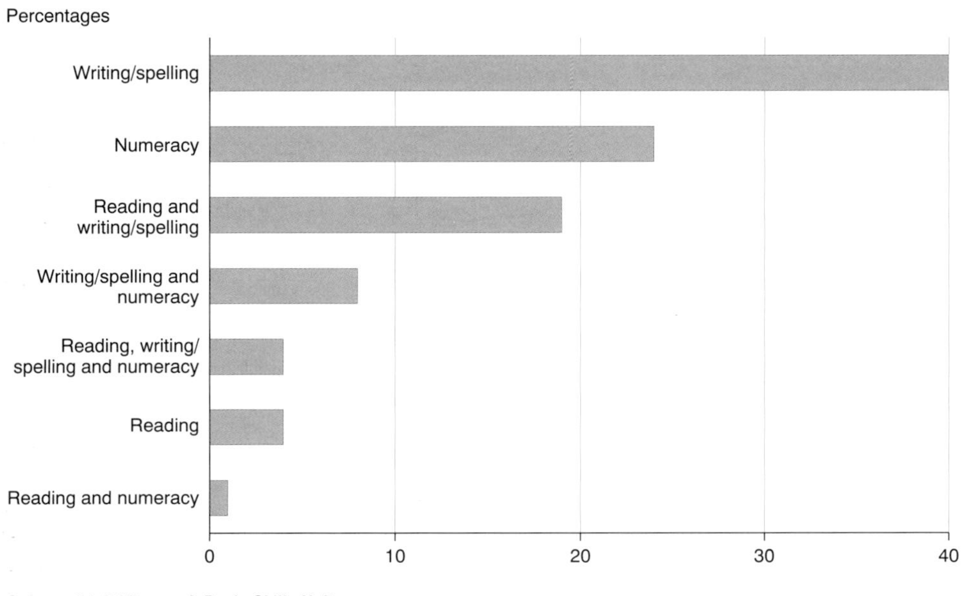

Source: Adult Literacy & Basic Skills Unit

The biggest area of self-reported difficulty was writing/spelling where 40 per cent had problems. Only 4 per cent reported difficulty with just reading, which suggests that reading problems are invariably accompanied by other kinds of problems. Nearly a quarter reported some difficulty with numeracy. The National Child Development Study carried out in 1981 on a group of 23 year olds, produced very similar results: 40 per cent reported problems with writing/spelling and 26 per cent reported problems with numeracy. This suggests that, despite efforts through schools and specific programmes to improve literacy and numeracy skills in young adults, the prevalence of problems has changed little.

The previous chart illustrated self-reported basic literacy and numeracy problems encountered by 21 year olds. Table 3.26 shows how the basic problems translate into coping with everyday experiences. Various tests to ascertain the levels of numeracy and literacy problems were set. Among both males and females, around nine in ten experienced difficulty in working out the discount offered on two items of clothing in sales, and thereby ascertaining which was the cheapest. The problem involved two jackets, one advertised with the price of £200 and offering a 12.5 per cent discount on this price, and the other advertised at £250 and offering a third off this price. An average 14 year old should be able to solve this problem. Among the literacy problems, the highest failure rate (77 per cent) was for understanding a complex literary passage which should have been a task that a bright 16 year old could have completed.

3.26

Percentage of 21 year olds failing numeracy and literacy tests: by gender, 1992

England and Wales Percentages

	Age expected[1] (years)	Males	Females	Total
Numeracy				
Calculating change in a shop	7	*14*	*16*	*15*
Working out the area of a geometric shape	11	*59*	*73*	*67*
Working out discount prices of clothes in a sale	14	*87*	*93*	*90*
Literacy				
Extracting information from a graph	11	*9*	*12*	*10*
Interpreting video recorder instruction manual	14	*21*	*27*	*24*
Understanding a complex literacy passage	bright 16	*77*	*77*	*77*

1 Age at which an average school pupil could be expected to answer the questions

Source: Adult Literacy & Basic Skills Unit

Perhaps less surprising, only about a quarter failed to interpret a video recorder instruction manual. A lower proportion of males than females failed the tests, with the exception of the literary passage where the proportion was the same. The greatest difference was in working out the area of a geometric shape: 73 per cent of females failed the test, compared with only 59 per cent of males.

Resources

Total government expenditure on education reached £31.5 billion in 1992-93, 52 per cent higher in real terms than in 1970-71 (Table 3.27). Spending on special schools showed the largest percentage increase over the same period: it tripled in real terms, although still only amounted to 4 per cent of total expenditure on education in 1992/93. Secondary schools accounted for around 28 per cent of the budget in 1992-93 at £8.9 billion, while nursery and primary together accounted for 27 per cent, at £8.6 billion. In 1992-93, education expenditure amounted to 5.2 per cent of GDP, which is marginally higher than in 1991-92 but lower than the level of 5.5 per cent in 1980-81.

An international comparison of public expenditure on education in 1991, again expressed as a percentage of GDP, is given in Chart 3.28. Japan spends the least of all the countries shown, devoting only 3.7 per cent of GDP to government spending on education. The United Kingdom spent 5.3 per cent. The biggest spender of the European countries

3.27

Government expenditure on education in real terms: by type

United Kingdom — £ million at 1992-93 prices[1]

	1970-71	1980-81	1992-93[2]
Schools			
Nursery	60	117	8,636 (Nursery and Primary)
Primary	4,858	6,067	
Secondary	5,692	7,991	8,876
Special	455	945	1,386
Higher, further and adult education[2]	2,972	3,625	3,385
Polytechnics and Colleges Funding Council	.	.	1,036
Universities	2,396	2,781	3,597
Other education expenditure	727	1,059	1,026
Total	17,161	22,585	27,940
Related education expenditure	2,811	3,087	2,971
VAT incurred on above expenditure	694	381	603
Total expenditure	20,666	26,053	31,515
Total expenditure as a percentage of GDP	*5.2*	*5.5*	*5.2*

1 Adjusted to real terms using the GDP market prices deflator.
2 Includes teacher training tuition fees for Northern Ireland. In April 1989 fees for polytechnics and colleges transferred to the Polytechnics and Colleges Funding Council.
Source: Department for Education

3.28

Public expenditure[1] on education as a percentage of GDP: international comparison, 1991

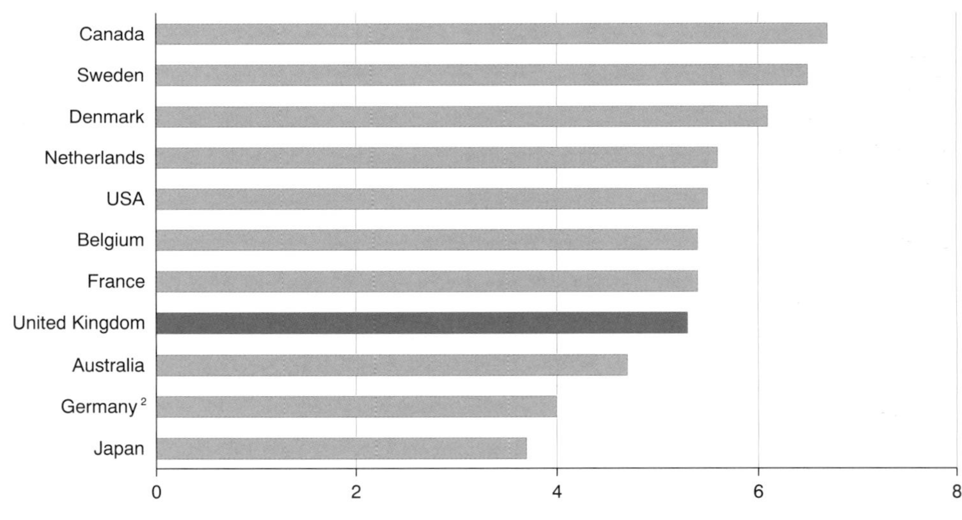

1 Includes loan charge expenditure and subsidies to the private sector.
2 The former Federal Republic.
Source: Department for Education

3.29

Percentage of schools with links with local businesses, 1991/92

England		Percentages
	Primary	Secondary
Involvement in curriculum development	*27*	*75*
Donations of cash	*26*	*62*
Donations of equipment	*28*	*58*
Technical advice	*15*	*57*
Provision of specialist equipment	*13*	*37*
Management training	*6*	*25*
Staff appraisal	*2*	*12*

Source: Department for Education

3.30

Average real annual income of higher education students[1]

United Kingdom			£ at 1992/93 prices[2]
	1986/87	1988/89	1992/93
Grants/awards	1,604	1,592	1,715
Parents	1,757	1,573	1,277
Earnings	138	240	230
Loans/overdrafts	141	139	147
Other income	372	527	293
All sources	4,010	4,071	3,662

1 Students aged under 26 at the start of their course.
2 Adjusted to 1992/93 prices using the retail prices index.

Source: Department for Education

shown is Sweden at 6.5 per cent but overall, the Canadians apportion more than any other country shown with 6.7 per cent of GDP going on education.

Table 3.29 shows the contribution made to our schools (both in cash and non-cash terms) by local businesses in 1991-92. Just over nine in ten secondary schools, and nearly six in ten primary schools, had links or contacts with local business. Of the practical help offered to schools, the most common among secondary schools was involvement in curriculum development (75 per cent). Three fifths of secondary schools received donations of money from local business compared with a quarter of primary schools. Nearly six in ten primary schools reported that representatives from local business had been seconded onto the school governing body; eight in ten secondary schools had a business secondment, with half having three or more representatives on the governing body. In addition, 91 per cent of pupils in their last year of compulsory schooling were involved in work experience placements.

The Student Income and Expenditure Survey, commissioned by the Department for Education, was carried out in 1992/93. It found that the average total income for non-mature students (ie under the age of 26 at the start of their course) in higher education was £3,662, a fall of around 10 per cent in real terms since 1988/89 (Table 3.30). The main reason for the decrease was due to a fall-off in support from family and friends. However, the level of state support rose by around 8 per cent in real terms to reach £1,715. These students spent around £120 less a year on food in 1992/93, at £627, compared with 1988/89, and £35 less on clothing at £157 in 1992/93. The survey found that less than half of students had taken up loans.

3.31

Having been through the education system, some students decide to make their careers helping others through the system. Chart 3.31 shows the numbers of people successfully completing initial teacher training. Since 1971, the number of graduates has risen by nearly three quarters, from 9 thousand to over 15 thousand. However, non-graduate numbers have fallen dramatically; in 1992 just over 8 thousand successfully completed the course compared with 38 thousand in 1971.

Successful completions on teacher training courses[1]

United Kingdom

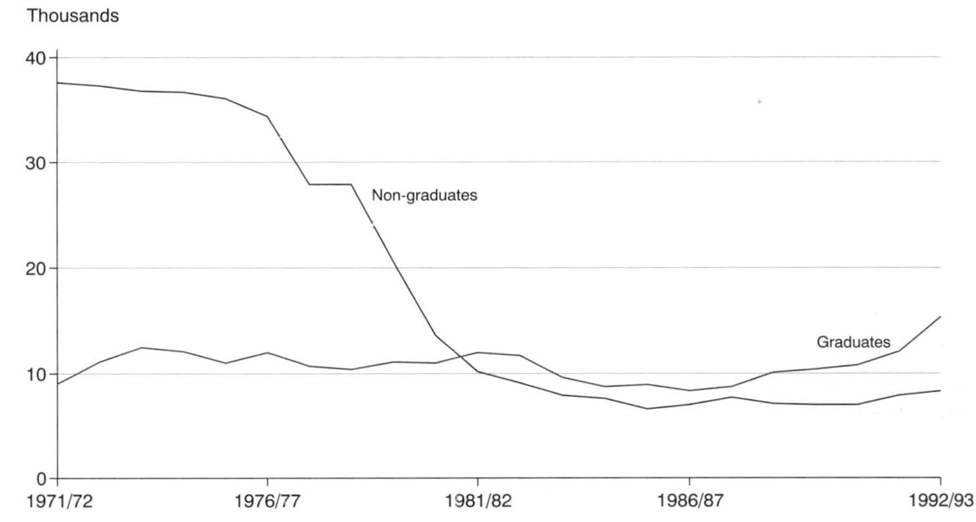

1 Includes students in England and Wales who failed their BEd degree course but have received qualified teacher status on the basis of a non-degree qualification obtained in an earlier year.

Source: Department for Education; Welsh Office; The Scottish Office Education Department; Department of Education, Northern Ireland

References and further reading

The following list contains selected publications relevant to **Chapter 3: Education**. Those published by HMSO are available from the addresses shown on the inside back cover of *Social Trends*.

Committee of Directors of Polytechnics: First Destination of Students, A Statistical Report
Day Care Services for Children, HMSO
Education Statistics Actual, CIPFA
Education Statistics Estimates, CIPFA
Education Statistics for the United Kingdom, HMSO
Employment Gazette, HMSO
Further and Higher Education and Training Statistics in Wales, Welsh Office
Northern Ireland Education Department Statistical Bulletins, HMSO
Regional Trends, HMSO
Social Focus on Children, HMSO
Statistical Bulletins, Department for Education
Statistical Bulletins, The Scottish Office Education Department
Statistical Bulletins, The Scottish Office Social Work Services Group
Statistics of Education, Finance and Awards England and Wales, HMSO
Statistics of Education, Further Education, Department for Education
Statistics of Education, Schools, Department for Education
Statistics of Education, Schools Examination Survey, HMSO
Statistics of Education, Teachers in Service, HMSO
Statistics of Education and Training in Wales: Schools, Welsh Office
Statistics of Education in Wales, Welsh Office
Statistics of Finance and Awards, Department for Education
Staying The Course, BTEC
The Basic Skills of Young Adults, ALBSU
The Handbook of Education Unit Costs, CIPFA
Training Statistics, Employment Department
Unfinished Business, Full-time Educational Courses for 16-19 Year Olds, Audit Commission and OFSTED
United Kingdom National Accounts (CSO Blue Book), HMSO
Universities Statistics Series, Universities' Statistical Record
Youth Cohort Study, Social and Community Planning Research

Contacts

Telephone contact points for further information relating to **Chapter 3: Education.**

Department for Education	01325 392658
Department of Education, Northern Ireland	01247 279677
Department of Health and Social Services, Northern Ireland	01232 522521
Office of Population Censuses and Surveys	0171 396 2327
The Scottish Office	
Education Department	0131 244 5362/5367
Social Work Services Group	0131 244 5431
Welsh Office	01222 825041
Adult Literacy and Basic Skills Unit	0171 405 4017

Chapter 4 Employment

The labour force

There were 4.9 million people under the age of 25 in the civilian labour force in Great Britain in 1993, a decrease of over a million since 1986; it is projected to fall by a further half million by 2006. (Table 4.2)

The United Kingdom had the second highest economic activity rates in the European Community in 1992 for both men and women. (Table 4.7)

Type of employment

More than one in eight of all workers was self-employed in Spring 1994. (Chart 4.10)

Time at work

In 1992 men in the United Kingdom worked an average of 43 hours a week - more than in any other country in the EC. (Table 4.15)

Around 12 per cent of full-time employees worked flexi-time in Spring 1994. (Table 4.16)

Trade unions and industrial tribunals

Union membership in 1993 was highest for those in professional occupations: nearly half belonged to a union. (Table 4.22)

Unemployment

The long-term unemployed accounted for about 45 per cent of all ILO unemployed in Spring 1994, up from 28 per cent in 1991, but lower than 1984 (48 per cent). (Chart 4.28)

Employment and training measures

The proportion of employees receiving job-related training in Spring 1994 was over 15 per cent compared with 9 per cent a decade earlier, with women now more likely than men to have received training. (Table 4.32)

4.1

Claimant unemployment: by gender

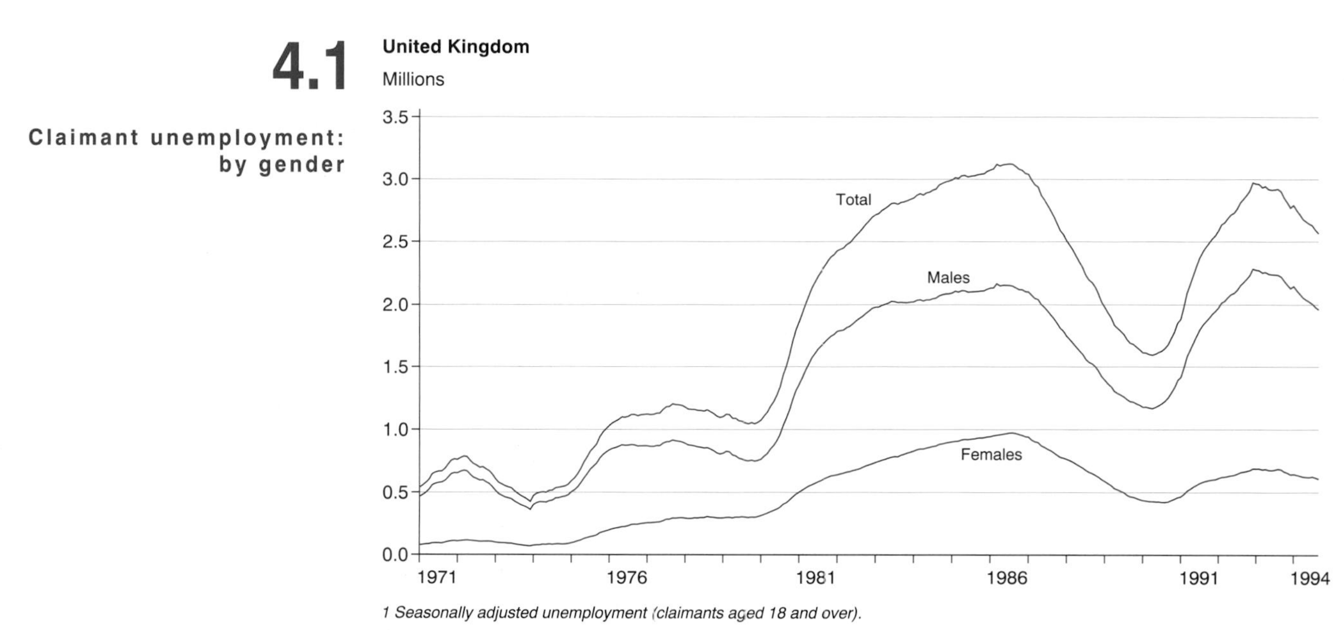

1 Seasonally adjusted unemployment (claimants aged 18 and over).

Source: Employment Department

Glossary of terms

Employees (Labour Force Survey measure) - a count, obtained from household surveys, of persons aged 16 and over who regard themselves as paid employees. People with two or more jobs are counted only once.

Employees in employment (employer survey based measure) - a count, obtained from surveys of employers, of jobs held by civilians who are paid by an employer who runs a PAYE tax scheme. People with more than one job are therefore counted more than once.

The self-employed - a count, mainly obtained from household surveys, of persons aged 16 and over who regard themselves as self-employed, ie who in their main employment work on their own account, whether or not they have only employees.

Government employment and training programmes - a count, obtained from household surveys, of those who said they were participants on Youth Training, Employment Training, Employment Action or Community Industry or a programme organised by a TEC/LEC.

Work-related government training programmes - a count, obtained from administrative returns, of all participants who receive some form of work experience in the course of their placement but who do not have a contract of employment and are not self-employed.

The labour force in employment - a count, obtained from household surveys and censuses, of employees in employment, self-employed persons, participants in government employment and training programmes, and persons doing unpaid family work.

The workforce in employment - a count of employees in employment (from employer survey based measure), self-employed persons, all HM forces and participants in government employment and training programmes.

The claimant unemployed - a measure, known as the claimant count, and derived from administrative sources, which counts as unemployed those people who are claiming unemployment related benefits at Employment Service local offices (formerly Unemployment Benefit Offices).

The ILO unemployed - an International Labour Organisation (ILO) recommended measure, used in household surveys such as the Labour Force Survey, which counts as unemployed those aged 16 and over who are without a job, are available to start work in the next two weeks and who have been seeking a job in the last four weeks or are waiting to start a job already obtained.

The workforce - the **workforce in employment** plus the **claimant unemployed.**

The economically active - the **labour force in employment** plus the **ILO unemployed.**

The civilian labour force - the **labour force in employment** plus the **ILO unemployed** less **HM forces.**

Claimant unemployment rate - the percentage of the **workforce** who are **claimant unemployed.**

ILO unemployment rate - the percentage of the **economically active** who are **ILO unemployed.**

The economically inactive - people who are neither part of the labour force in employment nor ILO unemployed. For example, all people under 16, those looking after a home or retired, or those permanently unable to work.

The population of working age - males aged 16 to 64 years and females aged 16 to 59 years.

Civilian economic activity rate - the percentage of the population in a given age group which is in the civilian labour force.

Some of these terms are covered in more detail in the appendix.

This chapter follows on naturally from the previous one by covering all aspects of people's economic activity once they have left full-time education.

The labour force

Table 4.2 shows how the age structure of the civilian labour force in Great Britain has changed over the last 25 years, and how it is projected to change in the future. Changes in the age structure are largely dependent on demographic factors: for example, the increase in the size of the labour force aged 25-44 years in the late 1980s reflects the high birth rates of the late 1960s. Conversely the civilian labour force aged under 24 fell by 1.2 million between 1986 and 1993, reflecting increasing participation in education as well as a falling population base, and is projected to fall by a further half a million between 1993 and 2006. The size of the labour force aged 45 and over has been rising since the mid 1980s and is projected to continue increasing as the population ages. In 1993 people in this age group formed 33 per cent of the labour force; by 2006 this proportion is projected to rise to 36 per cent.

The proportion of the resident population above the minimum school leaving age who are in the civilian labour force is referred to as the economic activity rate. Table 4.3 shows that economic activity rates vary between ethnic groups. In Spring 1994, 95 per cent of White men aged between 25 and 44 were economically active compared with only 86 per cent of men of this age from the Black ethnic group. Among women of the same age the difference between these two ethnic groups was much smaller, at 75 per cent and 71 per cent respectively. However, just under one in four Pakistani/Bangladeshi women were economically active.

4.2

Civilian labour force: by age

Great Britain — Thousands

	16-24	25-44	45 and over	All aged 16 and over
Estimates				
1971	5,082	9,725	10,096	24,903
1976	5,095	10,824	9,782	25,700
1981	5,832	11,358	9,052	26,242
1986	6,173	12,455	8,310	26,938
1991	5,536	13,879	8,714	28,129
1993	4,932	13,863	9,094	27,890
Projections				
1996	4,339	14,346	9,477	28,162
2001	4,206	14,678	9,951	28,835
2006	4,434	14,389	10,587	29,409

Source: Employment Department

4.3

Population of working age economic activity rates: by ethnic group, gender, and age, Spring 1994

Great Britain — Percentages

	Males			Females		
	16-24	25-44	45-64	16-24	25-44	45-59
White	*77*	*95*	*79*	*67*	*75*	*70*
Black[1]	*62*	*86*	*77*	*51*	*71*	*72*
Indian	*55*	*93*	*76*	*51*	*69*	*53*
Pakistani/Bangladeshi	*57*	*92*	*63*	*35*	*24*	..
Other[2]	*45*	*82*	*80*	*34*	*57*	*54*
All ethnic groups[3]	*75*	*94*	*79*	*65*	*74*	*70*

1 Includes Caribbean, African and other Black people of non-mixed origin.
2 Includes Chinese, other ethnic minority groups of non-mixed origin and people of mixed origin.
3 Includes ethnic group not stated.

Source: Employment Department

4.4

Civilian labour force economic activity rates[1]: by gender and age

Great Britain								Percentages
	16-19	20-24	25-34	35-44	45-54	55-59	60-64	All aged 16 and over[2]
Males								
Estimates								
1971	*69.4*	*87.7*	*94.6*	*96.2*	*95.7*	*93.0*	*82.9*	*80.5*
1976	*70.5*	*85.9*	*95.1*	*96.4*	*96.1*	*92.4*	*80.4*	*78.9*
1981	*72.4*	*85.1*	*95.4*	*96.0*	*94.8*	*89.4*	*69.3*	*76.5*
1986	*73.2*	*86.2*	*93.7*	*94.8*	*91.8*	*81.1*	*53.8*	*73.8*
1991	*70.4*	*85.6*	*94.0*	*94.7*	*91.0*	*80.3*	*54.1*	*73.7*
1993	*63.9*	*83.8*	*92.5*	*93.6*	*90.3*	*75.4*	*52.2*	*71.9*
Projections								
1996	*58.3*	*81.0*	*92.7*	*93.7*	*89.9*	*74.0*	*50.0*	*71.1*
2001	*56.7*	*78.0*	*92.6*	*93.9*	*89.5*	*74.0*	*46.9*	*70.1*
2006	*55.7*	*77.9*	*92.6*	*93.9*	*89.1*	*74.0*	*45.5*	*69.0*
Females								
Estimates								
1971	*65.0*	*60.2*	*45.5*	*59.7*	*62.0*	*50.9*	*28.8*	*43.9*
1976	*68.2*	*64.8*	*54.0*	*67.4*	*66.5*	*54.3*	*26.9*	*46.8*
1981	*70.4*	*68.8*	*56.4*	*68.0*	*68.0*	*53.4*	*23.3*	*47.6*
1986	*70.3*	*70.7*	*63.5*	*72.1*	*70.5*	*51.8*	*19.1*	*49.6*
1991	*69.1*	*72.7*	*69.7*	*76.7*	*72.7*	*54.5*	*24.1*	*52.4*
1993	*63.8*	*70.7*	*70.7*	*77.0*	*74.8*	*54.6*	*24.8*	*52.6*
Projections								
1996	*60.1*	*68.8*	*73.4*	*79.1*	*75.9*	*55.3*	*25.6*	*53.6*
2001	*59.8*	*68.1*	*77.4*	*82.1*	*77.2*	*56.0*	*25.8*	*55.2*
2006	*59.2*	*68.8*	*80.6*	*85.2*	*78.1*	*56.7*	*27.0*	*56.0*

1 The percentage of the resident population, or any sub-group of the population who are in the civilian labour force.
2 Includes those aged 65 and over.

Source: Employment Department

Women in Great Britain have become increasingly economically active, and this is projected to continue (Table 4.4). This increase is partly due to the increased availability of part time jobs, and is associated with economic and social changes such as falling birth rates. The economic activity rate for women aged 25 to 34 years rose by 25 percentage points between 1971 and 1993, a greater increase than for any other group. This increase may be partly attributable to an increase in the average age at which women have children (see Chapter 1: Population). The proportion of men who are economically active has decreased in every age group over the same period; this fall was particularly large for men aged 55 and over. The average economic activity rate for men is projected to continue falling but at a slower rate; for the 25 to 34 and 35 to 44 age groups it is actually projected to be higher in 2006 than in 1993. As a result women are projected to make up 46 per cent of the civilian labour force in 2006, compared to 44 per cent in 1993 and 37 per cent in 1971.

Whether or not a woman is economically active is dependent, to some extent on the number and ages of her children (Table 4.5). In Spring 1994 women whose youngest dependent child was over 5 years old were most likely to be working part-time; women with no dependent children were most likely to be working full time. In addition, the more children a woman has, the more likely she is to be economically inactive. For example, in Spring 1994, 66 per cent of women with four or more dependent children were economically inactive, compared with only 32 per cent of women with one child.

4.5

Economic activity status of women: by age of youngest dependent child, Spring 1994

United Kingdom					Percentages
	Age of youngest dependent child				
	0-4	5-10	11-15	No dependent children	All women aged 16-59
Working full-time	*16*	*20*	*34*	*46*	*36*
Working part-time	*30*	*45*	*40*	*23*	*29*
Unemployed	*6*	*6*	*4*	*5*	*5*
Inactive	*48*	*29*	*22*	*25*	*30*
All women (=100%) (thousands)	3,414	2,085	1,497	9,817	16,813

Source: Employment Department

Variations in economic activity rates among the counties of England and Wales and the regions of Scotland in Spring 1994 are shown in Chart 4.6. The Shetland Islands had the highest rate, at 76.6 per cent, while West Glamorgan had the lowest at only 51.7 per cent. The other counties with high rates, of 69 per cent or more, were Buckinghamshire, Northamptonshire, Wiltshire and Powys. Six of the ten counties with the lowest rates were in Wales.

The United Kingdom had the second highest economic activity rate in the European Community (EC) for both men and women in 1992, at 74.0 and 52.8 per cent respectively (Table 4.7); only Denmark had higher rates. For women, the difference between the rate in Denmark and the United Kingdom was nearly 10 percentage points while for men it was only half a percentage point. Denmark also had the smallest difference between the rates for men and women, at just under 12 percentage points, whereas the Irish Republic had the greatest difference, of 33 percentage points. However, high rates for Danish women reflect, in part, the fact that mothers have a legal right of return to work for three years, and are therefore counted as economically active during this period. The overall rate in the United Kingdom was 28 per cent higher than the lowest rate in the EC, which was in Spain.

Type of employment

In Spring 1994 there were over 25 million employed or self-employed people in the United Kingdom, 55 per cent of whom were male. Nearly one in five men, but only just over one in ten women, worked as a manager or administrator (Chart 4.8). A further one in five men worked in craft or related occupations compared with less than 1 in 30 women. Women comprised three quarters of people working in clerical or secretarial jobs.

4.6

Economic activity rates[1]: by county, Spring 1994

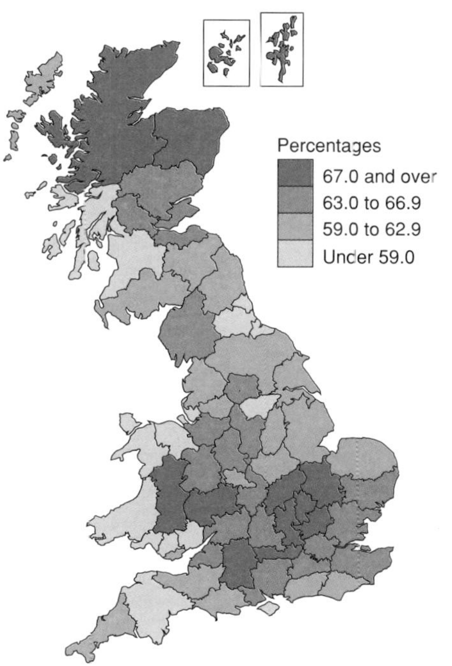

1 The percentage of people aged 16 and over who are either in employment or ILO unemployed.

Source: Employment Department

4.7

Economic activity rates[1]: by gender, EC comparison, 1992

Percentages

	Males	Females	All persons
Denmark	74.5	62.7	68.5
United Kingdom	74.0	52.8	63.0
Portugal	71.9	50.2	60.3
Germany[2]	71.5	48.4	59.4
Netherlands	71.1	46.5	58.6
France	65.7	48.0	56.4
Irish Republic	70.6	37.7	53.9
Luxembourg	69.7	39.5	54.2
Italy	65.4	34.9	49.5
Belgium	62.1	39.5	50.4
Spain	65.6	34.1	49.2
Greece	65.5	34.8	49.4
EC average	68.9	44.6	56.2

1 The civilian labour force aged 16 years and over as a percentage of the population aged 16 and over.
2 As constituted since 3 October 1990.

Source : Eurostat

4.8

Employees and self-employed: by gender and occupation, Spring 1994

United Kingdom

Percentages

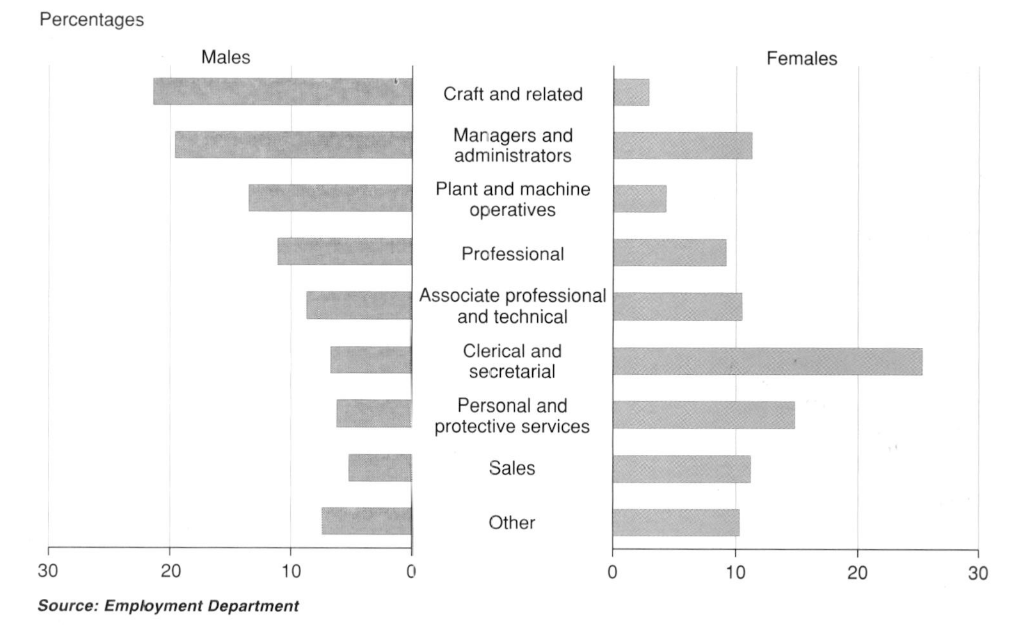

Source: Employment Department

4.9

Employees: by industry and gender

Great Britain Percentages

	Males				Females			
	1971	1981	1991	1994	1971	1981	1991	1994
Agriculture	*2*	*2*	*2*	*2*	*1*	*1*	*1*	*1*
Energy and water supply	*5*	*5*	*3*	*2*	*1*	*1*	*1*	*1*
Manufacturing	*41*	*35*	*29*	*28*	*29*	*19*	*13*	*12*
Construction	*8*	*8*	*7*	*6*	*1*	*1*	*1*	*1*
Distribution, hotels, catering and repairs	*13*	*15*	*19*	*20*	*23*	*24*	*25*	*24*
Transport and communication	*10*	*9*	*9*	*9*	*3*	*3*	*3*	*3*
Financial and business services	*5*	*7*	*11*	*13*	*7*	*9*	*13*	*13*
Other services	*15*	*18*	*20*	*21*	*35*	*41*	*44*	*45*
All employees (=100%)(thousands)	13,425	12,277	11,254	10,539	8,224	9,107	10,467	10,363

Source: Employment Department

4.10

Self-employed as a percentage of all in employment: by county, Spring 1994

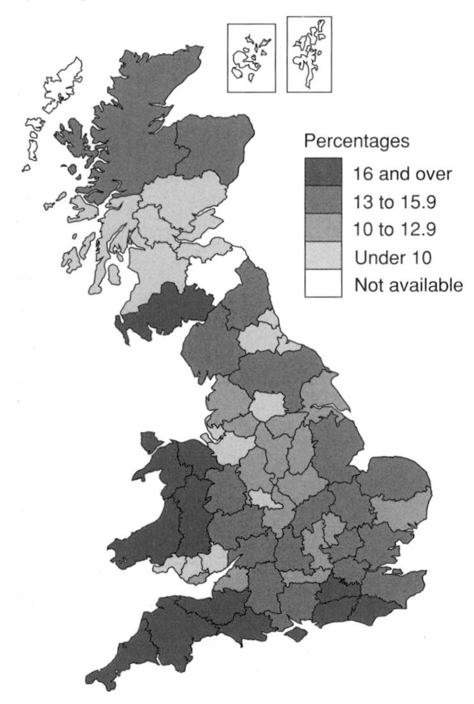

Source: Employment Department

Table 4.9 shows how employment in the different industries has changed since 1971. Overall, women accounted for 38 per cent of employees in 1971, compared with almost 50 per cent in 1994. Since 1971 there has been a switch in the number of both male and female employees away from manufacturing industries, towards the services sector: 41 per cent of men and 29 per cent of women were employed in the manufacturing industries in 1971 compared with only 28 per cent and 12 per cent respectively in 1994. The proportions of both men and women employed in financial and business services have increased since 1971; they stood at 13 per cent in 1994.

The Labour Force Survey (LFS) estimates that there were almost 3.3 million self-employed people in Great Britain in Spring 1994. This represents 12.9 per cent of all those in employment, compared with 11.3 per cent ten years previously. The rate varies among the counties of England and Wales and the regions of Scotland (Chart 4.10). The more rural areas tended to have the highest rates. The highest rate, of 36 per cent, was in Powys which was over five times the rate in Cleveland, the county with the lowest rate, where less than 7 per cent of those in employment were self-employed. Counties with major urban centres, such as those in Scotland, South Wales, the Midlands and the North, tended to have lower percentages of self-employed people.

Among those people in employment, people from the Pakistani or Bangladeshi ethnic groups are more likely to be self-employed than those from the other main ethnic groups (Chart 4.11); in Spring 1994 they were three times as likely to be self-employed as those from the Black ethnic group where less than 7 per cent of those in employment were self-employed.

Part-time working has become much more common in the last decade for both men and women (Table 4.12). Over the same period, the number of men working full-time has fallen by 3 per cent, while the number of women who work full-time has risen by 13 per cent. Over twice as many men as women work full-time, while more than five times as many women as men work part-time. In 1994 there were one and a half million more women working, either full or part-time, than there were ten years earlier.

4.11

Self-employed as a percentage of all in employment: by ethnic group, Spring 1994

Great Britain

Percentages

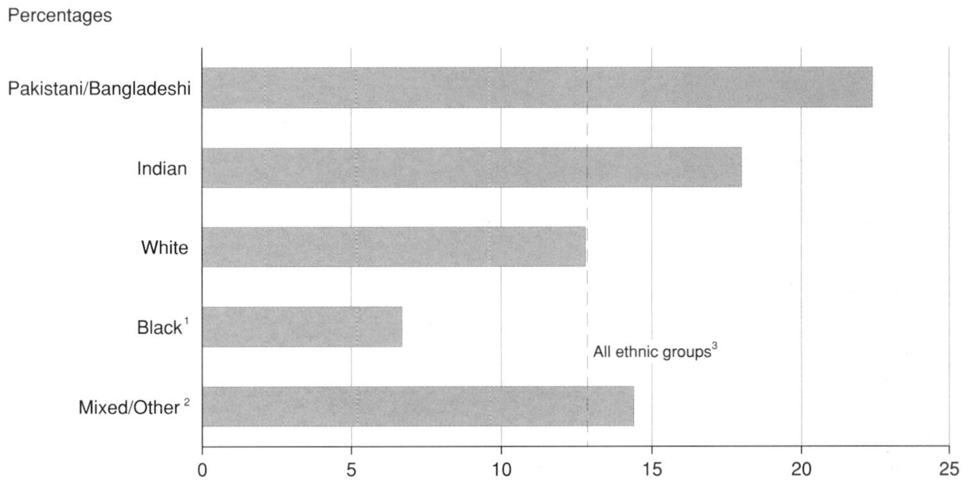

1 Includes Caribbean, African and other black people of non-mixed origin.
2 Includes Chinese, other ethnic minority groups of non-mixed origin and people of mixed origin.
3 Includes ethnic group not stated.
Source: Employment Department

4.12

Full and part-time[1] employment[2]: by gender

United Kingdom Thousands

	Males		Females	
	Full-time	Part-time	Full-time	Part-time
1984	13,240	570	5,422	4,343
1985	13,336	575	5,503	4,457
1986	13,430	647	5,662	4,566
1987	13,472	750	5,795	4,696
1988	13,881	801	6,069	4,808
1989	14,071	734	6,336	4,907
1990	14,109	789	6,479	4,928
1991	13,686	799	6,350	4,933
1992	13,141	885	6,244	5,081
1993	12,769	886	6,165	5,045
1994	12,875	998	6,131	5,257

1 Full/part-time is based on respondents self-assessment. Excludes those who did not state whether they were full or part-time.
2 At Spring each year. Includes employees, self-employed, those on government training schemes and unpaid family workers.
Source: Employment Department

4.13

Reasons for taking a part-time[1] job: by gender and marital status, Spring 1994

United Kingdom Percentages

	Males	Females			All persons
		Married	Not married	All females	
Did not want a full-time job	*40.1*	*89.5*	*66.2*	*87.0*	*82.5*
Could not find a full-time job	*42.5*	*8.8*	*21.2*	*10.1*	*13.2*
Students/still at school	*11.7*	*0.8*	*10.2*	*1.8*	*2.8*
Ill or disabled	*5.7*	*0.9*	*2.3*	*1.1*	*1.5*
All part-time workers[2] (=100%) (thousands)	477	3,965	481	4,445	4,923

1 Based on respondents self assessment.
2 Includes those not stating a reason for taking a part-time job.
Source: Employment Department

People take part-time work for a variety of reasons but the majority do so because they do not want a full time job (Table 4.13). Married women with young children were especially likely to work part-time by choice in Spring 1994: almost 94 per cent for those with children aged under 5. Almost 90 per cent of married women who worked part time did so because they did not want a full-time job. Men were more likely than women to be working part-time because they were unable to find a full-time job, although two fifths worked part-time by choice. Among men and single women, one in ten took a part-time job because they were a student or still at school.

Some people who have severe disabilities are given extra help by the Employment Service to obtain and keep jobs. This is known as supported employment: the Employment Service makes up the balance of the workers wages after the host firm has paid for the contribution made by the employee. Remploy, a private company sponsored by the government, accounted for over 40 per cent of sheltered employment in 1993-94 (Chart 4.14). Local authorities, sponsored by the Employment Service in the form of capital grants and provision for training places, employed a further 35 per cent, with the rest being employed by voluntary bodies. In total, over 20 thousand workers were in sheltered employment in Great Britain in 1993-94.

4.14

Workers in supported employment: by type of employer, 1993-94

Great Britain

Percentages

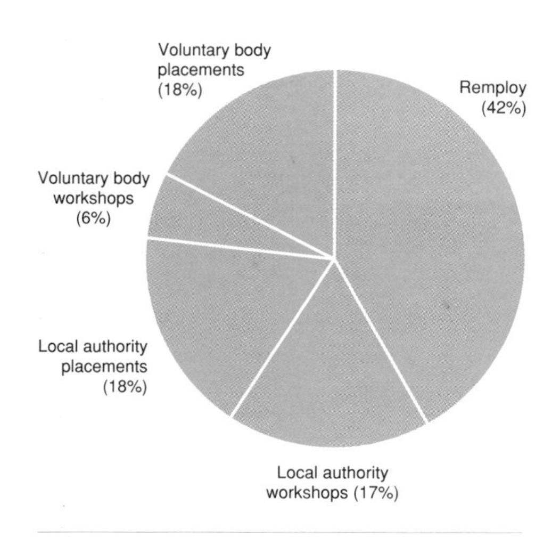

Source: Employment Department

Time at work

On average, male employees in the United Kingdom worked longer hours than their EC counterparts in 1992 (Table 4.15). In comparison, men in the Netherlands worked the shortest week, at just over 36 hours; less than the average hours worked by women in Portugal, Greece and Spain. Women in the United Kingdom, however, worked shorter hours than any other EC country with the exception of the Netherlands; this is due to the high proportion of women in the United Kingdom working part-time. Women in Portugal worked the longest hours. In all countries in the EC men work more hours than women.

Flexible working hours (or flexi-time) was worked by around 10 per cent of male and 15 per cent of female full-time employees in Spring 1994 (Table 4.16). Annualised hours is the next most common flexible arrangement for those working full time. This is where a set number of hours is to be worked over the course of a year. Flexible working patterns vary between the different industries; for example 18 per cent of people working in banking, financial and business services work flexitime, compared with 6 per cent in the distribution, hotels and catering and repairs industries, while a four and a half day week is more common in metal goods, engineering and vehicles than in any other industry. Almost 10 per cent of part-time workers, mainly women, work during term time only.

4.15

Average hours usually worked[1] per week[2]: by gender, EC comparison, 1992

Hours

	Males	Females	All persons
Portugal	42.6	38.2	40.6
Greece	41.0	38.1	40.0
Spain	40.7	37.0	39.5
Luxembourg	40.3	35.0	38.4
Irish Republic	41.1	34.4	38.2
Italy	39.4	35.0	37.8
France	39.8	34.6	37.4
United Kingdom	43.3	30.2	37.1
Germany[3]	39.6	33.6	37.1
Belgium	38.3	31.8	35.7
Denmark	36.7	31.3	34.1
Netherlands	36.3	25.8	32.1
EC average	40.2	33.1	37.2

1 Employees only.
2 Excludes meal breaks but includes paid and unpaid overtime.
3 As constituted since 3 October 1990.
Source: Eurostat

4.16

Employees with flexible working patterns[1]: by gender, Spring 1994

United Kingdom Percentages

	Male	Female	All persons
Full-time			
Flexible working hours	*9.7*	*15.4*	*11.7*
Annualised working hours	*5.6*	*6.4*	*5.8*
Term-time working	*1.1*	*4.7*	*2.4*
Job sharing	-	*0.2*	*0.1*
Nine day fortnight	*0.7*	*0.4*	*0.6*
Four and a half day week	*3.2*	*3.1*	*3.1*
All full-time employees (=100%)(thousands)	10,573	5,681	16,254
Part-time			
Flexible working hours	*7.3*	*9.1*	*8.8*
Annualised working hours	*3.1*	*5.3*	*5.0*
Term-time working	*4.9*	*10.3*	*9.6*
Job sharing	*1.8*	*2.5*	*2.4*
Nine day fortnight	-	-	-
Four and a half day week	-	*0.3*	*0.3*
All part-time employees (=100%)(thousands)	745	4,760	5,506

1 It is possible for respondents to appear in more than one category.
Source: Employment Department

4.17

People working at home as a percentage of those employed or self-employed: by occupation, Spring 1994

United Kingdom

Percentages

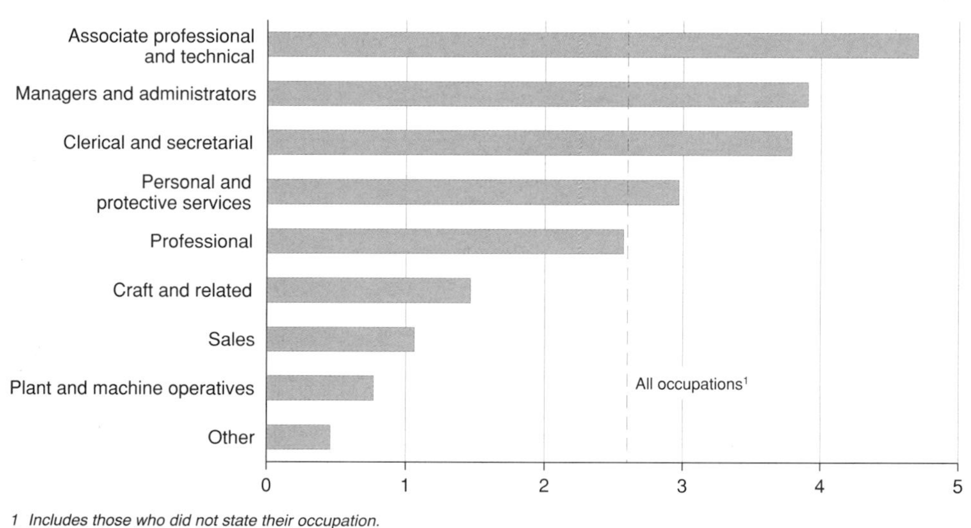

1 Includes those who did not state their occupation.

Source: Employment Department

Results from the LFS indicate that around one in forty of all those who were employed or self-employed in the United Kingdom in Spring 1994 (about 650 thousand) were working at home. Nearly 5 per cent of those in the associate professional and technical occupations work at home (Chart 4.17). In addition, over 150 thousand managers and administrators work at home; this is almost 4 per cent of their total number and represents nearly a quarter of all people working at home.

Some people regularly work so called 'unsocial' hours - weekends, nights or shift work. In Spring 1994 nearly a quarter of all in employment, over 6 million people, regularly worked on Saturdays whereas one in eight people regularly worked on Sundays (Table 4.18). It is not possible to calculate the total number of people working unsocial hours from the table as one person may well work more than one type of 'unsocial' hours.

4.18

People usually[1] engaged in weekend working, shift work and night work[2], Spring 1994

United Kingdom

	Total (thousands)	As a percentage of all in employment
Saturday working	6,289	*24.6*
Shift work[3]	4,138	*16.2*
Sunday working	3,110	*12.2*
Night work	1,577	*6.2*

1 Respondents were asked if they worked unsocial hours: usually, sometimes or never.
2 It is possible for respondents to appear in more than one category.
3 Includes both weekend and night shifts.

Source: Employment Department

Overall, nearly 4 per cent of men had some time off due to sickness in Spring 1994, compared with over 5 per cent of women (Table 4.19). The proportion of employees who had time off work due to sickness was highest for those approaching retirement and, in all age groups, was higher for women. The lowest rate, among both men and women, was for people over retirement age. However, it should be remembered that these results relate to sickness in the Spring, whereas sickness absence will vary according to the time of year. Other results from the LFS suggest that time off for sickness is highest among plant and machine operatives and lowest for managers and administrators.

Around 600 thousand working days were lost in the United Kingdom in 1993 as a result of labour disputes (Chart 4.20). This was slightly more than in 1992 when fewer days were lost than in any year since records began . The number of days lost due to industrial action fluctuates widely from year to year, although the peaks can be attributed to major disputes in large industries. In total in 1993, there were 211 stoppages - which was less than in any previous year since records began in 1891. There were just 18 prominent stoppages involving the loss of 5 thousand or more working days; these accounted for 83 per cent of the working days lost. The strike by civil servants over market testing, privatisation and cuts in service accounted for a quarter of all days lost and over 42 per cent of all workers on strike in 1993.

4.19

Employees absent[1] from work owing to sickness: by gender and age, 1986 and 1994[2]

United Kingdom Percentages

	Males		Females	
	1986	1994	1986	1994
16-19	*3.6*	*3.5*	*4.6*	*4.0*
20-29	*4.3*	*3.8*	*5.4*	*5.4*
30-39	*3.8*	*3.4*	*4.1*	*5.1*
40-49	*3.8*	*3.6*	*4.7*	*4.7*
Females 50-59/males 50-64	*5.1*	*4.7*	*6.0*	*5.9*
Females 60/males 65 and over	*1.5*	*2.9*	*3.6*	*3.1*
All aged 16 and over	*4.2*	*3.8*	*4.9*	*5.1*

1 At least one day away from work during the week before interview.
2 At Spring each year.
Source: Employment Department

4.20

Labour disputes: working days lost

United Kingdom

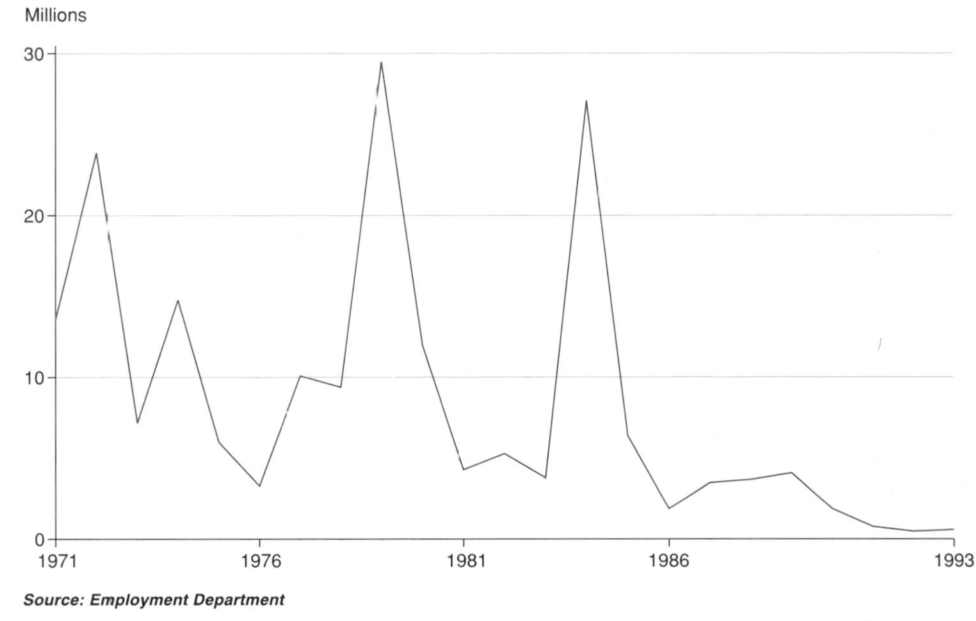

Source: Employment Department

4.21

Trade union membership[1] as a percentage of the civilian workforce in employment[2]

United Kingdom

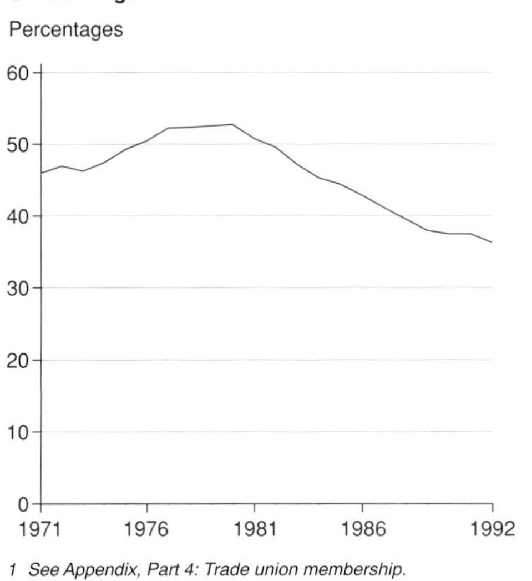

1 See Appendix, Part 4: Trade union membership.
2 Mid-year estimates up to 1977, end-year from 1978 onwards.
Source: Employment Department

Trade unions and industrial tribunals

Trade union membership in the United Kingdom fell by nearly 6 per cent in 1992, its sharpest fall since 1981 to reach its lowest level since 1946. Total membership, at just over 9 million, accounted for 36 per cent of the civilian labour force in employment (Chart 4.21). This was much lower than the rates of over 50 per cent experienced in the late 1970s. Although the proportion of employed women who were members of trade unions increased during the 1970s, it then fell so that the proportion in 1992 was the same as it was in 1971, at 31 per cent. Amongst men, the proportion also increased during the 1970s, but fell back more sharply to 40 per cent in 1992, 14 percentage points less than in 1971. At the end of 1992, there were 268 unions in United Kingdom, of which nine had a membership of over 250 thousand. Currently the largest union is UNISON with around 1.5 million members; it was created in July 1993 by the amalgamation of some public sector unions.

Overall, union membership in Great Britain is most common in professional occupations, although among men, plant and machine operatives are more likely to be union members (Table 4.22). Those in sales occupations are least likely to belong to unions: only 11 per cent of people employed in these occupations belonged to a union in Autumn 1993; while women in professional occupations are most likely to be union members. The data for this table comes from the LFS which gives a lower overall rate than the source used for Chart 4.21.

In 1993-94, there were over 70 thousand registered applications for industrial tribunals; these are independent judicial bodies set up to decide on matters relating to individual employment rights. Around 57 per cent of these applications were concerned with unfair dismissal, while a further 15 per cent were related to the Wages Act and 12 per cent were concerned with redundancy payments (Chart 4.23).

4.22

Trade union membership: by gender and occupation, Autumn 1993

Great Britain — Percentages

	Males	Females	All persons
Managers and administrators	*19.5*	*19.4*	*19.5*
Professional	*38.4*	*56.4*	*45.5*
Associate professional and technical	*33.6*	*52.9*	*43.1*
Clerical and secretarial	*35.9*	*24.7*	*27.4*
Craft and related	*28.7*	*27.8*	*28.6*
Personal and protective service	*39.6*	*22.2*	*27.9*
Sales	*11.9*	*11.2*	*11.5*
Plant and machine operatives	*42.5*	*33.1*	*40.6*
Other	*32.4*	*24.2*	*28.1*
All in employment[1]	*30.7*	*28.0*	*29.5*

1 Includes those who did not state their occupation.
Source: Employment Department

Unemployment

Unemployment is used as both an economic and a social indicator and can be defined in a number of different ways. In the United Kingdom there are two basic methods. The first, the claimant count, uses administrative systems to count those people recorded as unemployed at government offices. The advantage of this method is that timely statistics are available relatively easily. However, rules for unemployment and other benefits change from time to time, and this affects the claimant count. In order to provide a series free from distortions caused by changes in the coverage of the administrative systems, the Employment Department publishes a seasonally adjusted series which is consistent with the current coverage of the count. This is recalculated back to 1971 each time there is a significant change in coverage and this is the series given most prominence in the media.

Chart 4.1 shows the consistent series for the current claimant count. The number of claimant unemployed rose above 1 million for the first time in December 1975 and then to above 2 million in March 1981. The rate of increase then slowed slightly and 3 million unemployed was not reached until February 1985. After peaking in the middle of 1986, the number fell to just over one and a half million in mid 1990. There was then a sharp rise back up to nearly 3 million in January 1993, since when it has fallen. At September 1994, there were just over 2.5 million unemployed. The proportion of the unemployed who are women has risen fairly steadily since 1971 from around 14 per cent, to its current level of nearly 24 per cent in September 1994.

The main alternative method of measuring unemployment comes from the LFS which asks individuals whether they have a job and, if not, whether they would like work and what steps they have taken to find it. The LFS is the main source of survey data on the unemployed and uses the International Labour Organisation (ILO) definition (see the glossary of terms at the beginning of this chapter). LFS estimates, although not so timely as the claimant count, are now available quarterly, one and a half months after the end of the period to which they refer. On the other hand they have the advantage over the claimant count, of not being affected to the same extent by benefit rule changes.

Chart 4.24 shows how the two measures of unemployment compare. Even though the two measures differ markedly in coverage, with around a million people in each measure not included in the definition of the other, they both show broadly the same levels and trends. In both cases, unemployment fell in the late 1980s, rose again in the early 1990s and then fell in 1993, roughly a year after the economy had started to grow again. It is the ILO measure which is used for the rest of this chapter.

When making comparisons across countries or regions, it is much more meaningful to use an unemployment rate rather than an absolute level. Because different countries measure unemployment differently, the Organisation for Economic Co-operation and Development (OECD) uses a standard set of concepts to draw comparisons in a way which conforms as far as possible to ILO guidelines. The resulting figures are then calculated as percentages of the total labour force.

4.23

Applications to industrial tribunals: by jurisdiction, 1993-94

Great Britain

Percentages

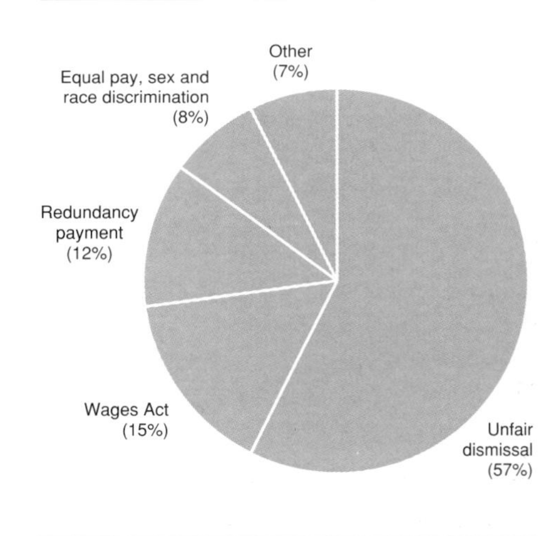

Source: Employment Department

Comparisons of alternative measures of unemployment

United Kingdom

Millions

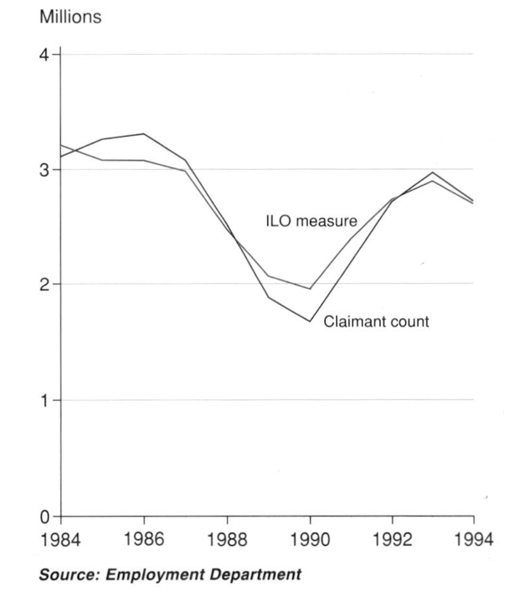

Source: Employment Department

4.25

Unemployment rates adjusted to OECD concepts[1]: international comparison

Percentages

	1976	1981	1986	1991	1993
Spain	4.6	13.9	21.0	16.0	22.4
Finland	3.8	4.8	5.3	7.5	11.7
France	4.4	7.4	10.4	9.4	11.7
Canada	7.1	7.5	9.5	10.2	11.1
Australia	4.7	5.7	8.0	9.5	10.8
United Kingdom	5.6	9.8	11.2	8.8	10.3
Italy	6.6	7.8	10.5	9.9	10.2
Belgium	6.4	10.8	11.2	7.2	9.6
Netherlands	5.5	8.5	9.9	7.0	8.3
Sweden	1.6	2.5	2.7	2.7	8.2
United States	7.6	7.5	6.9	6.6	6.7
Germany[2]	3.7	4.4	6.4	4.2	5.8
Portugal	..	..	8.4	4.1	5.5
Japan	2.0	2.2	2.8	2.1	2.5

1 See Appendix, Part 4: Definitions of unemployment - OECD concepts.
2 Former Federal Republic.
Source: OECD

Table 4.25 shows international unemployment rates according to these OECD/ILO concepts. The United Kingdom rate increased to 10.3 per cent in 1993, having previously peaked at 12.4 per cent in 1983. Japan and Sweden have both had the lowest unemployment rates historically, generally below 3 per cent, although by 1993 Sweden's rate had increased sharply to over 8 per cent. While in 1976 Spain's unemployment rate was similar to other OECD countries, by the 1980s it was significantly higher than the others - the only nation to have a rate above 20 per cent. Increasing world trade has resulted in more inter-dependence between countries. Consequently, many countries show a similar cycle to the United Kingdom's, with rates rising through the early 1980s and then falling until the early 1990s, before beginning to rise again.

ILO unemployment rates in the United Kingdom are higher for men than for women for all the age groups shown in Table 4.26. The gap grew for two years after 1991, following the low point of 1990, and narrowed in 1994, when the overall rate fell. Although the unemployment rate for women has remained relatively constant since 1991, at just over 7 per cent; the rate increased by 3 percentage points between 1991 and 1994 among 16 to 19 year olds, but fell by more than 1 percentage point among those over retirement age. Unemployment rates for men have shown much greater variation: with the exception of those over retirement age, the rate increased in all age groups between 1991 and 1993 with the largest increase, of 5.5 percentage points, occurring in the 16 to 19 age group. Between 1993 and 1994 the rates fell in all age groups.

4.26

Unemployment rates[1]: by gender and age

United Kingdom Percentages

	1991	1992	1993	1994
Males				
16-19	16.5	18.7	22.0	21.0
20-29	12.3	15.3	16.4	14.8
30-39	7.8	10.4	10.3	10.2
40-49	5.8	7.8	8.8	7.6
50-64	8.4	10.4	11.9	11.0
65 and over	5.9	4.9	4.6	3.7
All males aged 16 and over	9.2	11.5	12.4	11.4
Females				
16-19	13.2	13.8	16.0	16.1
20-29	9.4	9.4	10.2	9.3
30-39	6.9	7.2	7.0	7.0
40-49	4.9	5.0	4.7	4.7
50-59	5.1	5.0	5.6	5.6
60 and over	4.4	3.1	3.9	3.0
All females aged 16 and over	7.2	7.2	7.5	7.2

1 Unemployment based on the ILO definition as a percentage of all economically active. At Spring each year.
Source: Employment Department

Unemployment rates differ between the regions of the United Kingdom (Table 4.27). With the exception of the South West, the unemployment rate was higher in 1994 than in 1991 for all the regions in England, notwithstanding the general decline since 1993. The rate was also higher in 1994 in Wales and Scotland although lower in Northern Ireland. Northern Ireland had the highest unemployment rate between 1990 and 1993. However, in 1994 the rate in the North was marginally higher, at 11.7 per cent. The North was the only region with a larger unemployment rate in 1994 than in 1993.

In 1994 the long term unemployed accounted for 45 per cent of all unemployed people, up from 28 per cent in 1991, but a lower proportion than in the mid 1980s (Chart 4.28). Between 1991 and 1994 long term unemployment has increased by 84 per cent, compared with a rise of only 13 per cent in total unemployment.

Long term and total unemployment rates vary markedly between the ethnic groups in Great Britain (Chart 4.29 overleaf). In Spring 1994, Whites had the lowest rates for both long term and total unemployment. The long term unemployment rate is highest for those from the Black ethnic group at 15.8 per cent while Pakistanis and Bangladeshis have the highest overall unemployment rate of 27.9 per cent; this compares with 4.0 and 9.1 respectively for Whites.

4.27

Unemployment rates[1]: by region

Percentages

	1990	1991	1992	1993	1994
North	*8.6*	*10.6*	*11.2*	*11.2*	*11.7*
Yorkshire & Humberside	*6.8*	*9.1*	*9.9*	*9.8*	*9.8*
East Midlands	*5.1*	*7.8*	*8.7*	*9.0*	*8.3*
East Anglia	*3.8*	*6.2*	*7.1*	*8.3*	*7.4*
South East	*3.9*	*7.4*	*9.4*	*10.3*	*9.6*
South West	*4.5*	*7.7*	*9.1*	*9.2*	*7.5*
West Midlands	*5.9*	*9.0*	*10.7*	*11.6*	*9.9*
North West	*7.5*	*9.9*	*10.1*	*10.9*	*10.2*
Wales	*6.6*	*9.2*	*8.9*	*9.5*	*9.4*
Scotland	*8.0*	*9.2*	*9.5*	*10.1*	*9.9*
Northern Ireland	*13.7*	*14.1*	*12.1*	*12.5*	*11.5*

1 Unemployment based on the ILO definition as a percentage of all economically active. At Spring each year.

Source: Employment Department

4.28

Unemployment[1] and long-term unemployment

United Kingdom

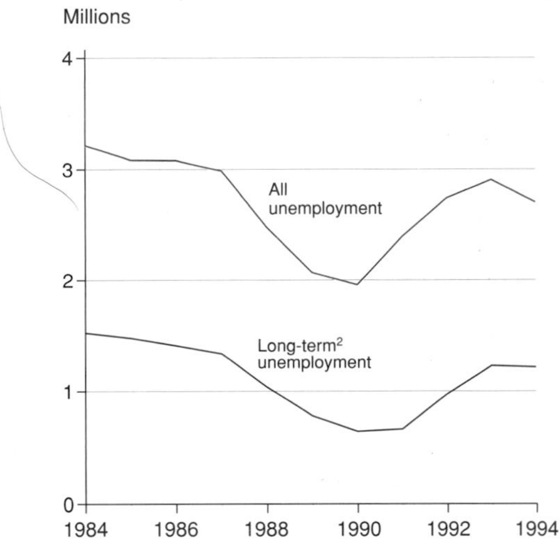

1 Unemployment based on the ILO definition.
2 Unemployed for at least a year.

Source: Employment Department

4.29

Unemployment rates[1]: by ethnic group, Spring 1994

Great Britain

Percentages

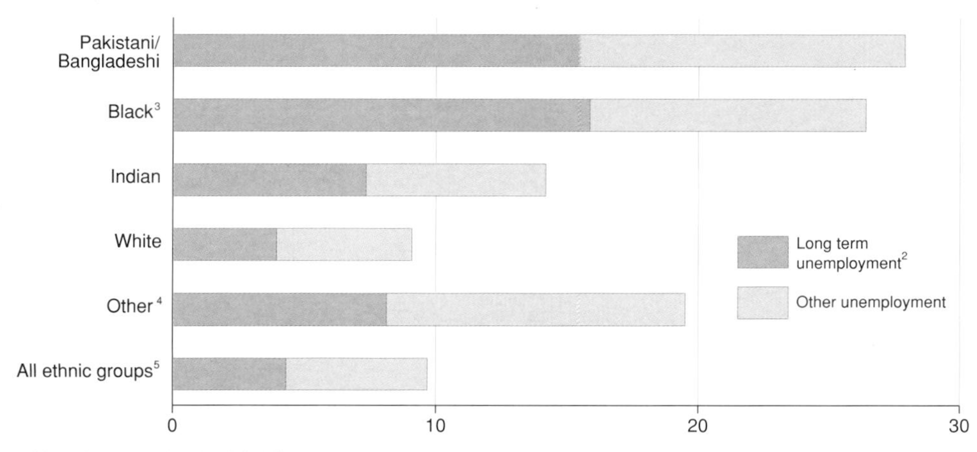

1 Unemployed based on the ILO definition as a percentage of all economically active.
2 Unemployed for more than 52 weeks.
3 Includes Caribbean, African and other black people of non-mixed origin.
4 Includes Chinese, other ethnic minority groups of non-mixed origin, and people of mixed origin.
5 Includes ethnic group not stated.
Source: Employment Department

4.30

Redundancy rates: by region.

Great Britain Rates[1]

	1990	1991	1992	1993	1994
Great Britain	8.1	17.8	15.1	12.4	9.7
North	..	18.4	16.6	16.5	13.0
Yorkshire & Humberside	10.1	15.5	16.2	13.0	10.8
East Midlands	10.3	19.4	19.9	13.9	10.0
East Anglia	..	14.1	17.8	..	..
South East	8.5	17.8	14.8	11.3	9.3
South West	6.0	14.7	14.3	12.5	8.7
West Midlands	8.1	21.2	16.1	13.9	10.5
North West	7.4	17.7	13.6	12.3	8.7
Wales	10.4	26.3	16.6	11.4	10.6
Scotland	6.1	14.4	9.7	11.5	9.4

1 Redundancy rates per 1,000 employees in the three months prior to interview in Spring each year.
Source: Employment Department

The LFS collects information about people who lose their job in the three months prior to their interview; redundancy rates are then calculated from this source and are shown for the regions of Great Britain in Table 4.30. This shows a sharp rise in redundancy rates between 1990 and 1991; the rate in many regions more than doubled. Since 1991 the rate has fallen in most of the regions; the average for Great Britain was lower in 1994 than in any year since 1990. In 1994 the South West and North West had the lowest redundancy rates, at 8.7 per cent, while the highest rate, of 13.0 per cent occurred in the North.

Table 4.31 shows the main methods used by the unemployed to look for work. Visiting job centres, employment or careers offices and answering advertisements were the most common methods used in Spring 1994. More than one in ten used personal contacts as their main method of seeking work. Women, particularly married women were the most likely to answer advertisements and study "situations vacant": over half of all women used this method compared with just over a third of men. Visits to the job centre were the most common method for those who previously held a manual job.

Employment and training measures

In Spring 1994, around one in seven employees in the United Kingdom had received job-related training in the four weeks prior to interview. On average younger employees were more likely to have received training than older employees (Table 4.32). Both men and women received more training in 1994 than they did a decade ago. The percentage of women receiving training is now greater than that for men, although young men are still more likely to have received training than young women. Job

4.31

Main method of seeking work: by gender, Spring 1994

United Kingdom						Percentages
	Visit job centre employment/career office etc	Answer adverts/ study situations vacant	Direct approach to employers	Personal contacts	Other methods	All ILO unemployed[1] (=100%) (thousands)
Men	*34*	*36*	*10*	*13*	*5*	1,808
Women	*26*	*53*	*7*	*9*	*4*	885
Married women	*23*	*58*	*6*	*8*	*3*	476
Non-married women	*29*	*46*	*9*	*9*	*4*	409
All persons	*32*	*41*	*9*	*12*	*5*	2,693

1 Includes those who did not indicate method of seeking work.

Source: Employment Department

4.32

Proportion of employees receiving job related training: by gender and age

United Kingdom									Percentages
	1984	1986	1988	1989	1990	1991	1992	1993	1994
Males									
16-19	*25.2*	*26.9*	*26.2*	*26.3*	*30.0*	*27.6*	*26.8*	*27.3*	*25.8*
20-24	*15.3*	*17.7*	*19.8*	*20.0*	*20.8*	*20.2*	*19.4*	*20.1*	*19.2*
25-29	*12.5*	*14.1*	*15.9*	*17.4*	*17.0*	*17.7*	*17.2*	*16.1*	*17.9*
30-39	*9.8*	*11.8*	*14.4*	*15.4*	*15.8*	*15.1*	*15.0*	*15.4*	*16.5*
40-49	*6.3*	*7.9*	*10.3*	*11.9*	*12.9*	*12.4*	*12.8*	*12.5*	*13.1*
50-59	*3.3*	*4.3*	*5.7*	*6.9*	*8.3*	*8.4*	*4.7*	*7.7*	*8.6*
60-64	*2.0*	*2.3*	*2.8*	*3.2*	*4.1*	*4.8*	*2.9*	*4.2*	*3.4*
All males aged 16 to 64	*9.7*	*11.5*	*13.4*	*14.4*	*15.3*	*14.8*	*14.4*	*14.3*	*14.9*
Females									
16-19	*16.4*	*17.8*	*19.8*	*19.8*	*20.5*	*20.6*	*19.9*	*20.6*	*24.1*
20-24	*11.7*	*14.3*	*17.4*	*18.7*	*20.3*	*17.6*	*18.9*	*18.8*	*21.5*
25-29	*10.2*	*12.7*	*16.0*	*15.9*	*18.6*	*17.0*	*16.1*	*17.4*	*18.9*
30-39	*8.9*	*9.8*	*13.5*	*15.3*	*15.8*	*16.1*	*15.2*	*15.1*	*16.4*
40-49	*6.1*	*6.9*	*10.8*	*12.4*	*14.1*	*14.0*	*13.8*	*15.0*	*14.8*
50-59	*3.5*	*4.3*	*6.4*	*8.3*	*8.4*	*8.4*	*8.4*	*8.1*	*9.5*
All females aged 16 to 59	*8.5*	*9.9*	*13.1*	*14.5*	*15.6*	*15.0*	*14.7*	*15.0*	*16.2*

Source: Employment Department

4.33

Perceived benefits[1] of training: by gender, 1991

Great Britain		Percentages
	Males	Females
To learn new sorts of skills	*25*	*23*
To improve chances of promotion	*13*	*7*
To make work more interesting	*6*	*11*
To improve chances of getting a better job	*7*	*5*
To earn more money	*5*	*2*

1 Respondents who stated that they would like more training were asked for their main reason.

Source: Social & Community Planning Research

related training also varies between the regions of Great Britain. In Spring 1994, 16 per cent of employees in the South East, including Greater London had received job-related training in the previous four weeks compared with only 13.2 per cent in the East Midlands.

Employees go on training courses for a variety of different reasons, the most common being to learn new skills (Table 4.33). Other reasons vary according to gender. For example, men are more likely than women to want to improve their chances of promotion, while women are more likely to want to make their work more interesting. A relatively small proportion of both men and women see training courses as a way of improving their chances of getting a better job or earning more money.

The Youth Cohort Study follows groups of 16 to 19 year olds in their transition from full-tme education into the labour market. It samples around 20 thousand young people and interviews them at three points in time, allowing a 'before and after' analysis. Table 4.34 shows how the labour market activities of the cohort of young people changed between 1991 and 1993. The majority of those in either full-time education or full-time employment in 1991 were doing the same two years later. In addition, more than four in ten of those who were out of work in 1991 were also out of work in 1993 (although not necessarily continuously). However, nearly a third of those who had been out of work in 1991 were in full-time employment in 1993. Of those who had been on Youth Training, or other government schemes in 1991, over half were in full-time employment two years later while one in five was unemployed.

4.34

Employment position of young people: by activity , in 1991, 1993[1]

England & Wales					Percentages
	1991 activity				
	Full-time education	Full-time employment	YT or government scheme	Out of work	Other
1993 activity					
Full-time education	*63*	*3*	*5*	*7*	*11*
Full-time employment	*20*	*76*	*55*	*29*	*39*
YT or government scheme	*2*	*3*	*11*	*5*	*2*
Out of work	*7*	*12*	*21*	*43*	*20*
Other	*8*	*4*	*8*	*16*	*28*
All young people	*100*	*100*	*100*	*100*	*100*

1 Young people in their first post-compulsory education year in 1991 (ie aged 16 or 17 in 1991 and aged 18 or 19 in 1993).

Source: Employment Department

In 1992-93, just 45 per cent of young people who left Youth Training (YT) were in full-time employment six months after leaving, down from 64 per cent in 1989-90 (Table 4.35). A higher proportion, 28 per cent, were unemployed after leaving YT in 1992-93 than in any of the other years shown in the table. Conversely, a higher proportion of YT leavers than in previous years entered full-time training or education.

In July 1991 the Confederation of British Industry (CBI) launched a list of targets for education and training to set standards for achievement for young people, working adults and employers. One target is for a half of all young people to reach National Vocational Qualification (NVQ) level 3 or equivalent by the year 2000 while another is for half of the workforce to be qualified to at least this level by the same date. NVQ level 3 is equivalent to two or more passes at GCE 'A' level. Levels of education and training inevitably vary according to the type of industry a person is employed in. Chart 4.36 shows the progress towards these targets for various industries. In Spring 1994, nearly 40 per cent of the employed workers in the United Kingdom had attained at least NVQ level 3. However, the target has already been exceeded in public administration and energy and water industries. While the agriculture and fishing and distribution industries are only around half way towards the target. Generally people in professional occupations were the most likely to have reached NVQ 3 or equivalent; over 80 per cent of people in these occupations are qualified to at least NVQ level 4.

4.35

Destination of Youth Training leavers[1]

Great Britain Percentages

	1987-88	1988-89	1989-90	1990-91	1991-92[2]	1992-93[2]
Full-time work						
Same employer	*23*	*32*	*34*	*29*	*28*	*28*
Different employer	*33*	*29*	*28*	*23*	*16*	*16*
Self-employed	*1*	*1*	*2*	*1*	*1*	*1*
Part-time work	*4*	*4*	*3*	*4*	*4*	*5*
Full-time course	*4*	*3*	*4*	*6*	*6*	*7*
Different YT Scheme	*12*	*12*	*11*	*10*	*9*	*9*
Other	*3*	*3*	*4*	*5*	*7*	*6*
Unemployed	*21*	*14*	*14*	*20*	*25*	*28*
All leavers (=100%) (thousands)	326	414	379	328	278	227

1 Until October 1990 leavers were surveyed three months after leaving; previously it was six months after leaving. Includes leavers from Youth Credits. Figures for 1989-90 onwards relate only to those for whom leaving certificates were returned - estimated to be around 85 per cent of leavers.
2 England and Wales only.

Source: Employment Department

4.36

Percentage of employed workforce achieving at least NVQ3 or equivalent: by industry, Spring 1994

United Kingdom

Percentages

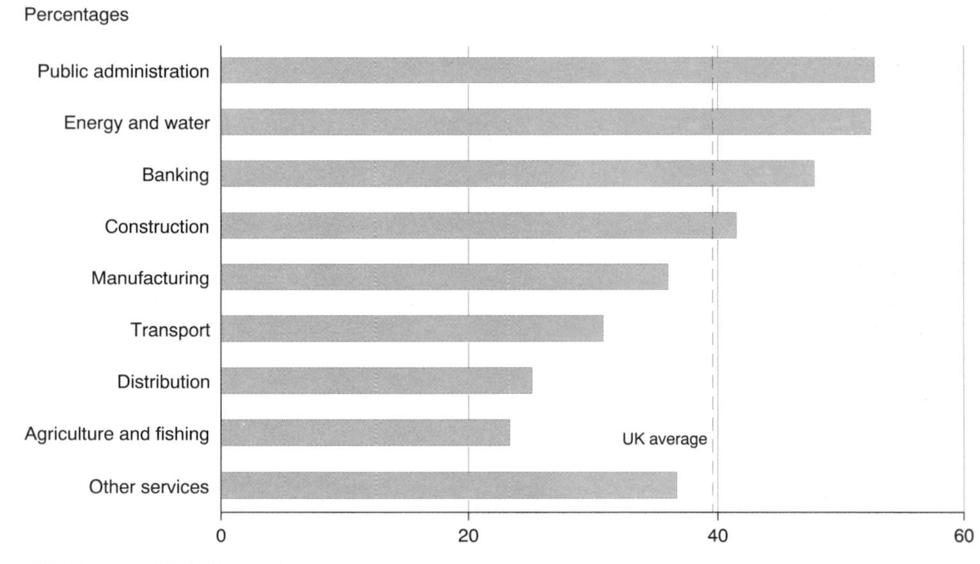

Source: Employment Department

References and further reading

The following list contains selected publications relevant to **Chapter 4: Employment**. Those published by HMSO are available from the addresses shown on the inside back cover of *Social Trends*.

British Social Attitudes, Gower

CBI Quarterly Industrial Trends Survey, CBI

Employment Gazette, Harrington Kilbride, for Employment Department

General Household Survey, HMSO

Labour Force Survey, HMSO

Labour Force Survey Quarterly Bulletin, Employment Department

Labour Market Quarterly Report, Employment Department

Main Economic Indicators, OECD

Northern Ireland Labour Force Survey Statistics Notice, HMSO

Regional Trends, HMSO

Scottish Economic Bulletin, HMSO

Skills Bulletin, Employment Department

Time Rates and Hours of Work, Employment Department

Training Statistics, HMSO

Youth Cohort Study, Employment Department

Contacts

Telephone contact points for further information relating to **Chapter 4: Employment.**

Employment Department	
Labour Force Survey	0171 273 5585
Other inquiries	0171 273 5582
Department of Economic Development, Northern Ireland	01232 529421
Eurostat	00 352 4301 34567

Chapter 5 Income and Wealth

Household income

Real weekly earnings for women in the top 10 per cent of earners more than doubled between 1971 and 1994 to £418, compared with an increase of just over two thirds for men. (Chart 5.6)

The average income of recently retired pensioners in 1992 in the United Kingdom was £225 per week, compared with £150 for other pensioners. (Chart 5.9)

Taxes

It is estimated that there will be nearly 26 million income taxpayers in the United Kingdom in 1994-95, with total income tax liabilities of about £69 billion. (Table 5.10)

A single man on half average earnings will pay over 11 per cent of his income in income tax in 1994-95, whereas a married man will pay just under 7 per cent. (Table 5.11)

Income distribution

In 1993, 85 per cent of income for those households in the top fifth of the income distribution came from employment earnings, compared with 21 per cent for those in the bottom fifth. (Chart 5.18)

Since 1971 the percentage of the population below half average income has increased from 11 per cent to 21 per cent. (Chart 5.21)

Wealth

The proportion of personal sector net wealth held in life assurance and pension funds was 33 per cent in 1993, compared with only 15 per cent in 1971. (Table 5.22)

National Income

GDP was higher in 1993 than in 1992 in volume terms, reversing the fall in the previous two years; it was 52 per cent higher in 1993 than in 1971. (Chart 5.27)

5.1

Real household disposable income

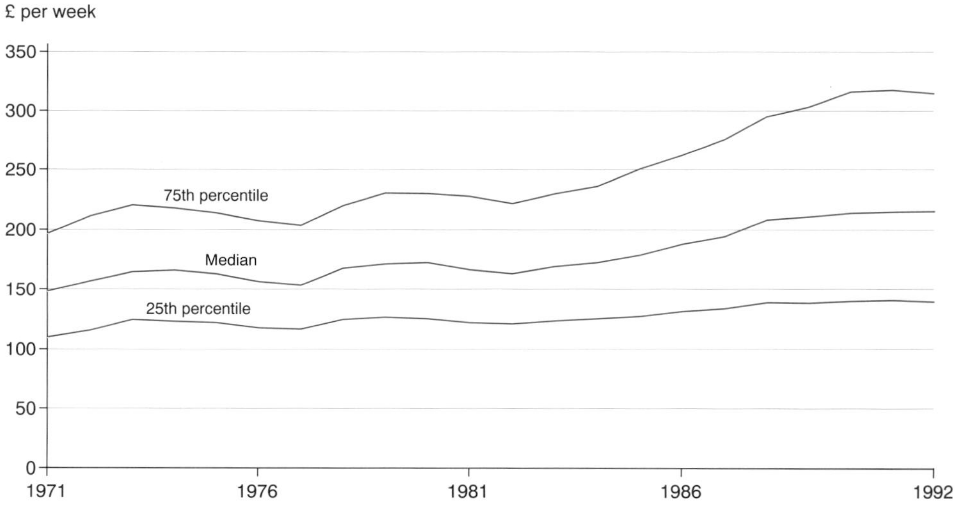

1 Before housing costs, at January 1994 prices deflated by the retail prices index.
2 Equivalised disposable income has been used for ranking the households. See Appendix, Part 5: Equivalisation scales.
Source: Institute for Fiscal Studies

Glossary of terms

Decile or quintile group - the main method of analysing income distribution used in this chapter is to rank units (households, individuals, etc) according to a given income measure, and then to divide the ranked units into groups of equal size. Groups comprising 20 per cent of units are known as 'quintile groups', those comprising 10 per cent of units are known as 'decile groups', and so on. Thus the 'bottom quintile group' is the 20 per cent of units with the lowest incomes.

Decile and quintile points - the term 'quintile point' is used to refer to that income which forms the maximum of one quintile group and the minimum of the next. Thus the 'bottom quintile point' is that income below which 20 per cent of units fall. The 'highest decile point' is that income above which 10 per cent of units fall.

This chapter looks at the composition and distribution of income and wealth in the United Kingdom today, and how it has been changing. It also examines the effects of changes in taxes and benefits and, finally, looks at national income.

Household income

Disposable income is the amount of money people have available to them to spend or invest. It is made up of income from all sources, less taxes on income, national insurance (NI) contributions and local taxes. Chart 5.1 shows trends in household equivalent disposable income, before housing costs such as rent and mortgage interest are taken into consideration. It is expressed in real terms to allow meaningful comparisons from year to year, by adjusting for the effect of inflation. It is also adjusted to an equivalised basis: this is to take account of household size and composition in order to recognise differing demands on resources. For example, to achieve the same living standard, a household of five people would need a higher income than a single person household.

The chart shows that real incomes have risen since 1971. However, the income of households at the 25th and 75th percentile points have diverged from the median over time. The income at the 75th percentile point has grown at a faster rate than the median, while that at the 25th percentile point has increased at a slower rate. Between 1971 and 1992 the income at the 25th percentile point increased by 28 per cent, the median by 46 per cent and the 75th percentile point by 60 per cent. Although the incomes of households at the different percentile points have diverged, they have followed the same general patterns; the rises and falls in the 1970s and the increases in the mid 1980s.

Chart 5.2, also expressed in real terms, shows how household disposable income per head has changed since 1971. This followed a general upward trend to reach its highest level ever in 1993, 80 per cent higher than in 1971. Increases were largest during the 1980s when the average year on year change was 4 per cent. There was a slight fall in 1991, the first since 1981; this was then reversed in 1992.

5.2

Real[1] household disposable income per head

United Kingdom

Index (1990 =100)

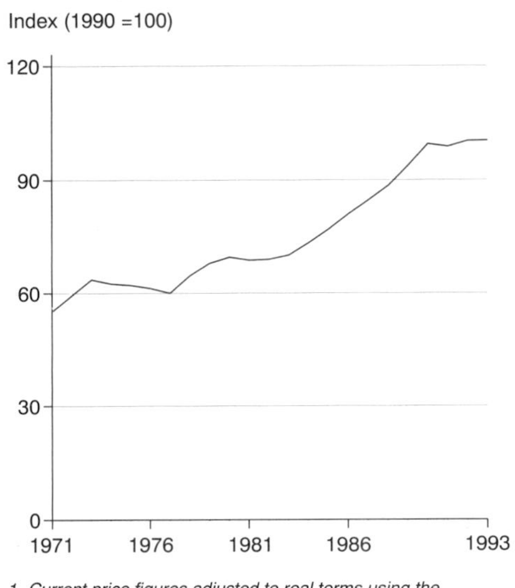

1 Current price figures adjusted to real terms using the consumers' expenditure deflator.

Source: Central Statistical Office

Households receive income from a number of sources, which are listed in Table 5.3. Wages and salaries are still by far the most important source of household income, accounting for 56 per cent in 1993, although their share of income has fallen by 12 percentage points since 1971. The proportion of household income from private pensions and annuities more than doubled between 1971 and 1993 to 11 per cent. This is partly explained by the growing numbers of elderly people in the United Kingdom (see Chapter 1), and by the fact that more and more people are entitled to occupational pensions. The share of income coming from other sources has remained fairly constant. The proportion of household income paid in income tax increased from 14 per cent to 17 per cent between 1971 and 1976 and then fell to 12 per cent in 1993. Chapter 6 gives details of how people spend their disposable incomes.

Earnings from employment change from year to year, according to the amount of overtime, bonuses, shift allowances, grade increments and other productivity and incentive payments. In addition, many workers have an annual pay settlement or review. One measure of the changes in earnings is the average earnings index. Chart 5.4 shows the annual percentage change in this index and compares it with the change in retail prices. For the majority of the period covered by the chart, increases in earnings have outpaced changes in retail prices which means that the real value of earnings has increased. Annual increases in average earnings peaked at 26 per cent in September 1980, dropped rapidly, along with the rate of inflation, and then fluctuated between 5 and 11 per cent for the next decade. During the early 1990s year on year growth in average earnings fell, reaching a low of 2.1 per cent in October 1993, the lowest level recorded since 1967.

5.3

Household income[1]

United Kingdom — Percentages

	1971	1976	1981	1986	1991	1992	1993
Source of income							
Wages and salaries[2]	68	67	63	58	58	56	56
Income from self-employment[3]	9	9	8	10	10	10	10
Rent, dividends, interest	6	6	7	8	9	8	7
Private pensions, annuities, etc	5	5	6	8	10	11	11
Social security benefits	10	11	13	13	11	12	13
Other current transfers[4]	2	2	2	3	2	3	3
Total household income (= 100%) (£ billion)	44.7	100.4	202.1	313.9	502.1	531.1	546.8
Direct taxes etc as a percentage of total household income							
Taxes on income	14	17	14	14	14	13	12
National insurance contributions[5]	3	3	3	4	3	3	3
Contributions to pension schemes	1	2	2	2	2	2	2
Total household disposable income (£ billion)	36.4	78.3	162.4	251.9	409.4	436.5	453.2

1 See Appendix, Part 5: The household sector.
2 Includes Forces' pay and income in kind.
3 After deducting interest payments, depreciation and stock appreciation.
4 Mostly other government grants, but including transfers from abroad and from non- profit-making bodies.
5 By employees and the self-employed.

Source: Central Statistical Office

5.4

Average earnings[1] and retail prices

United Kingdom

Percentage change over 12 months

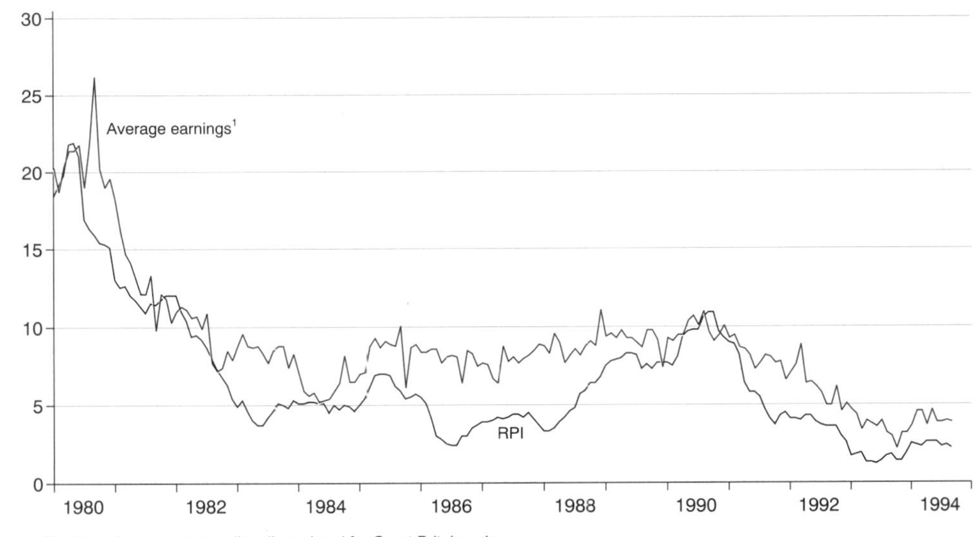

1 Earnings data are seasonally adjusted and for Great Britain only.

Source: Central Statistical Office; Employment Department

5.5

Average gross weekly earnings[1]: by area, April 1994

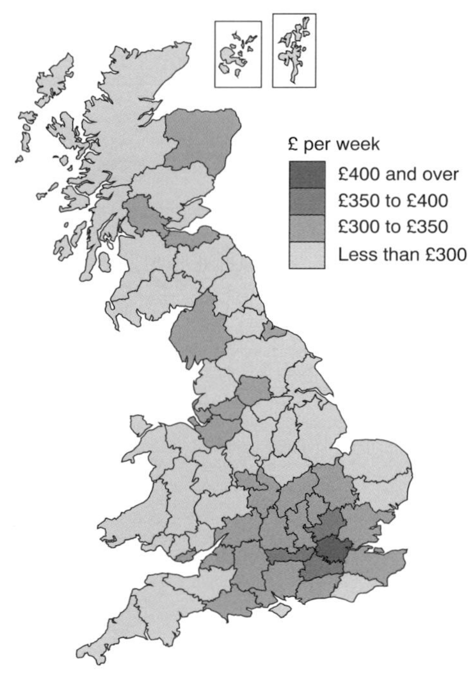

1 Full-time employees on adult rates whose pay was not affected for the survey period by absence.
Source: Employment Department

The New Earnings Survey, an annual survey of employers which collects information on full-time adult employees, is the main source of detailed earnings data. Chart 5.5 shows the distribution of gross earnings by area in Great Britain in April 1994. The highest earnings were concentrated in the South East of England, in particular Greater London where average weekly earnings were £415. Cornwall had the lowest average weekly earnings at £265. Earnings in Wales and Scotland were also low with seven out of the eight Welsh counties and six out of nine Scottish regions having average earnings below £300 a week.

It is worth noting that average earnings are affected by the occupational and industrial structure of the labour market in each county and that it does not necessarily follow that employees in areas with low average earnings are being paid at a lower rate than employees in similar occupations elsewhere.

The New Earnings Survey also allows us to look at how the distribution of earnings has changed over time. Chart 5.6 shows, for men and women separately, the growth in real weekly earnings since 1971. While the rise in earnings for those at the bottom decile point and the median of the earnings distribution has been fairly constant, the earnings of those at the highest decile point increased markedly in the 1980s. The earnings gap between the highest and lowest earners has therefore increased over time: for men the gap between those at the bottom and top decile points was £203 in 1971, rising to almost £402 in 1994; for women, the increase was not as large, £118 in 1971 compared with £279 in 1994.

The gap between average male and average female earnings for all three of the decile points shown has stayed fairly constant since 1971. When considering these data it should be remembered that it is not necessarily the same people who are in the top and bottom decile groups each year.

5.6

Real[1] gross weekly earnings[2]: by gender

Great Britain

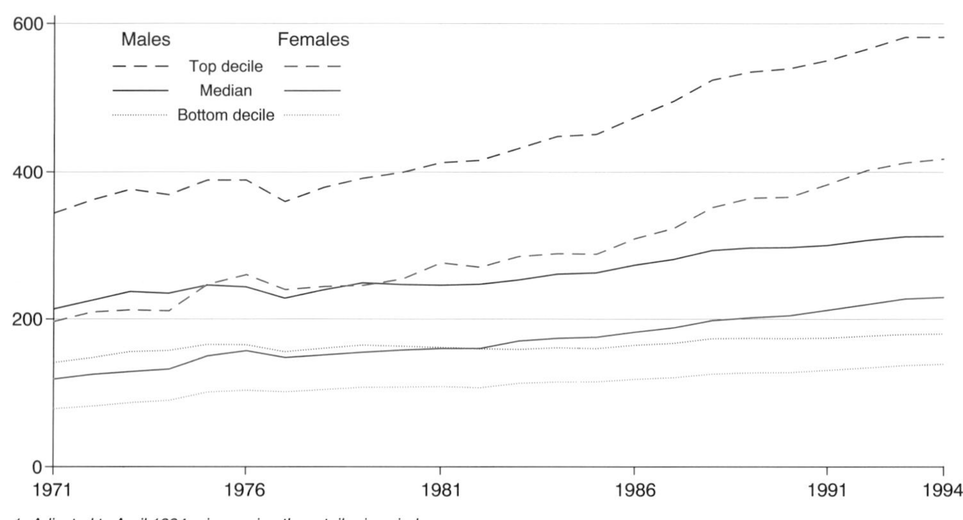

1 Adjusted to April 1994 prices using the retail prices index.
2 At April each year. Full-time employees on adult rates whose pay was not affected for the survey period by absence.
Source: Employment Department

Chart 5.7 shows the distribution of gross weekly earnings by gender in April 1994. The chart shows that there is a larger proportion of women then men at the lower end of the pay range. This is partly because women still form a large proportion of employees in those occupations that are traditionally lower paid. A third of women earned £190 per week or less compared with only 13 per cent of men. Conversely, nearly three quarters of men earned over £230 compared with only half of women.

Table 5.8 shows how real gross weekly earnings have changed for selected occupations since 1971. Of all the occupations shown, nurses have enjoyed the largest percentage increase in earnings since 1971, at over 120 per cent in real terms. The smallest increase was for bricklayers and carpenters, who had about a 28 per cent increase in real terms. In 1994 the lowest paid workers of all the occupations shown were waiters and waitresses while the highest paid were medical practitioners. The difference between the earnings of waiters/waitresses and medical practitioners in 1994 was about 375 per cent; the same difference as in 1971. Most professions have more or less kept their ranking in the table since 1971; nurses are the only group who have increased their rank by more than two places.

Whilst earnings from employment are the main source of income for many households, this is obviously not true for pensioners. The relative importance of different sources of income for pensioners changes depending on how long a

5.7

Average gross weekly earnings[1]: by gender, April 1994

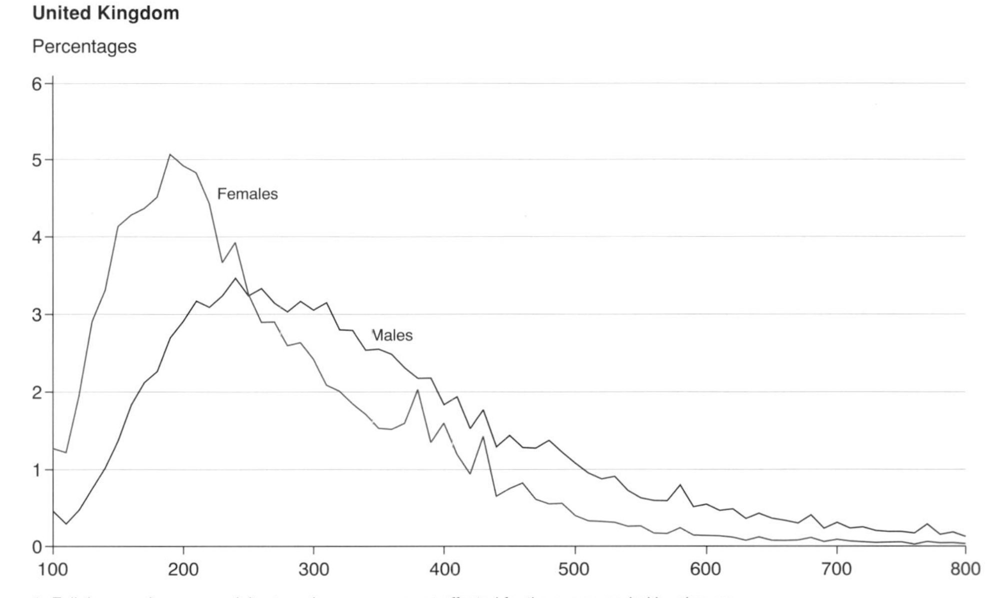

1 Full-time employees on adult rates whose pay was not affected for the survey period by absence.

Source: Employment Department

5.8

Real[1] gross weekly earnings[2]: by selected occupation

Great Britain — £ per week at April 1994 prices[1]

	1971	1976	1981	1986	1991	1994
Waiter/waitress	105	150	138	151	161	157
Bar staff	116	143	143	160	153	165
Cleaner	110	174	169	179	181	180
Receptionist	113	128	135	153	173	182
Caretaker	159	191	179	196	213	220
Bricklayer/mason	198	244	225	235	248	252
Carpenter/joiner	203	236	223	236	260	261
Nurse	142	187	188	216	298	316
Social worker	202	228	246	264	303	332
Primary tecaher	235	285	292	302	358	394
Secondary teacher	235	317	314	322	390	427
Mechanical engineer	322	365	375	423	493	511
Solicitor	347	379	367	418	590	569
Medical practitioner	499	488	550	592	669	746

1 Adjusted to April 1994 prices using the retail prices index.
2 At April each year. Full-time employees on adult rates whose pay was not affected or the survey period by abesence.

Source: Employment Department

5.9

Real income of pensioners[1]: by source[2], 1992

United Kingdom

Percentages

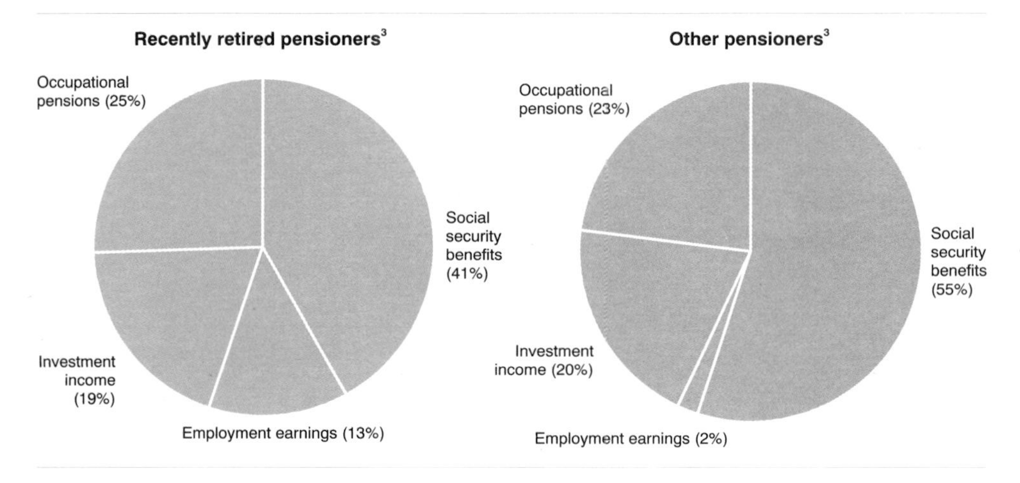

1 Pensioner units.
2 Other income forms less than 1 per cent of pensioner income and is excluded.
3 Recently retired pensioners are single women aged 60-64, single men aged 65-69 and couples where the husband is aged 65-69.
Source: Department of Social Security

5.10

Income tax payable: by income[1] range, 1994-95[2]

United Kingdom

	Number of taxpayers (millions)	Total tax payable (£ million)	Average rate of tax payable (percentages)	Average amount of tax payable (£)
Annual income				
£3,445-£4,999	2.2	290	*3*	130
£5,000-£7,499	4.1	1,790	*7*	440
£7,500-£9,999	3.8	3,470	*10*	900
£10,000-£14,999	6.0	10,100	*14*	1,670
£15,000-£19,999	3.9	10,800	*16*	2,750
£20,000-£29,999	3.6	15,200	*18*	4,250
£30,000-£39,999	1.1	7,890	*22*	7,370
£40,000 and over	0.9	19,400	*30*	20,890
All ranges	25.7	69,000	*17*	2,680

1 Total income of the individual for income tax purposes including earned and investment income. All figures in the table relate to taxpayers only.
2 Based on a projection from the 1992-93 Survey of Personal Incomes.
Source: Inland Revenue

pensioner has been retired. Chart 5.9 shows the income of pensioners who have recently retired to be £225 per week, whereas for other pensioners the average is £150 per week.

More recently retired pensioners receive a far higher income than other pensioners from all sources, in particular occupational pensions, investment income and employment earnings. Recently retired pensioners received occupational pensions of over £57 per week compared with only £34 per week for other pensioners, although these form almost equivalent percentages of their total income. Other pensioners rely more on social security benefits than recently retired ones: 55 per cent of their income came from this source.

The income of recently retired pensioners has increased by just over a half in real terms since 1981, whilst that of other pensioners has increased by about 47 per cent. This is partly attributable to the large increase in the amount of income from investments that recently retired pensioners have received compared to other pensioners.

Taxes

Inland Revenue have estimated that there will be nearly 26 million tax payers in 1994-95, with a total income tax bill of almost £70 billion (Table 5.10). The average rate of tax payable ranges from just 3 per cent for those with incomes less than £5,000 per year to 30 per cent for those with incomes more than £40,000 per year. Most people pay less than 18 per cent tax on average on their total income; only those with incomes of £30,000 or more (2 million people) pay a higher average rate of tax.

Income tax rates have been reduced markedly since 1978-79, particularly for those with higher incomes. The basic rate fell progressively from 33 per cent in April 1978 to 25 per cent in April 1988, and in 1992-93 a new lower rate of 20 per cent was introduced. The higher tax rates, which rose to a maximum of 83 per cent on earned income, have been replaced by one 40 per cent rate.

A single man on half average earnings will pay nearly 12 per cent of his income as income tax in 1994-95, whereas a married man (with a non-earning wife) on half average earnings will pay only 7 per cent (Table 5.11). This difference is less for men on average earnings and is very small for those on twice average earnings. The percentage of income paid as income tax is expected to rise in 1994-95 for married men, and for single men on twice average earnings, reversing the trend of recent years. The percentage of income paid in NI contributions has risen for those on average earnings from 5.8 per cent in 1971-72 to 8.4 per cent in 1994-95, and for those on twice average earnings from 3.3 per cent to 6.7 per cent over the same period. However, for men on half average earnings this percentage had been falling, though it is expected to rise slightly in 1994-95.

So far this chapter has looked at how earnings, income tax and NI contributions individually have changed over time. Table 5.12 overleaf shows the combined effect of these changes, after allowing for inflation. Of the family types shown, single women with two children have experienced the greatest real increase in income between 1971 and 1993, at over 145 per cent for someone on the lowest decile point of earnings who claims family credit. Over the same period real income for a single man on median earnings increased by 51 per cent. Although there have been real terms increases in income at all levels, these increases have generally been much less at the lower end of the distribution. Real income increased by nearly 38 per cent between 1971 and 1993 for a single man with no children at the lowest

5.11

Percentage of income paid in income tax and national insurance contributions[1]: by marital status and level of earnings[2]

Great Britain — Percentages

	1971-72	1981-82	1991-92	1994-95[3]
Single man				
Half average earnings				
Tax	*14.3*	*17.5*	*12.8*	*11.5*
NIC	*7.7*	*7.7*	*6.2*	*6.8*
Average earnings				
Tax	*22.2*	*23.7*	*18.9*	*18.3*
NIC	*5.8*	*7.7*	*7.6*	*8.4*
Twice average earnings				
Tax	*26.2*	*27.3*	*22.0*	*23.0*
NIC	*3.3*	*6.1*	*6.0*	*6.7*
Married man[4]				
Half average earnings				
Tax	*7.5*	*10.5*	*6.5*	*6.9*
NIC	*7.7*	*7.7*	*6.2*	*6.8*
Average earnings				
Tax	*18.8*	*20.2*	*15.7*	*16.0*
NIC	*5.8*	*7.7*	*7.6*	*8.4*
Twice average earnings				
Tax	*26.8*	*25.1*	*20.4*	*21.9*
NIC	*3.3*	*6.1*	*6.0*	*6.7*

1 Employees' contributions. Assumes contributions at Class 1, contracted in, standard rate.
2 Average earnings for full-time adult male manual employees working a full week on adult rates.
3 1993-94 based projections.
4 Assuming wife not in paid employment.

Source: Inland Revenue

decile point of earnings, but at the top decile point this increase was over 72 per cent. For a single woman with no children, these increases were 76 per cent and 106 per cent respectively. However, changes in the distribution of earnings do not necessarily indicate the movements in earnings of individuals or groups of individuals. They are caused by several factors including the change in the structure of employment. Over time, individuals move within the distribution.

Chart 5.13 shows net income after tax, NI contributions, rent and council tax payments have been deducted and receipts of benefits added for three different family types earning between £50 and £250 per week in October 1994. These data are not estimated from surveys of real families but are modelled. In order to model net income, it is assumed that there is no income other than the earnings of the head of the household and social security benefits, for which full entitlement is claimed; that they have only their personal tax allowances; that they live in local authority rented accommodation; and that they are not contracted out of the state pension scheme. Average local authority rent and council tax payments are taken off net income to arrive at net weekly spending power.

Entitlement to certain benefits changes as earnings change. At one time, it was possible for an increase in earnings to cause a fall in net income because of the withdrawal of benefits; this was known as the poverty trap. This poverty trap has been removed by social security reforms and, in general, net income increases with gross income. Despite this, the chart is fairly flat in places, showing that in some ranges of income spending power increases only very slowly. A lone parent with a child aged three only sees a large increase in net weekly spending power if their gross weekly earnings are greater than about £185. An increase in gross weekly earnings of £40, from £145 to £185, gives a rise of just under £8 in

5.12

Real[1] weekly earnings[2] after income tax, national insurance contributions, child benefit and family credit: by selected family type

Great Britain — £ per week at April 1993 prices[1]

	1971	1981	1991	1993
Single man, no children				
Lowest decile point	100	109	133	138
Median	148	162	214	224
Highest decile point	234	264	386	404
Single woman, no children				
Lowest decile point	64	82	105	113
Median	90	113	157	169
Highest decile point	140	183	267	288
Single woman, 2 children[3]				
Lowest decile point[4]				
Family credit claimed	70	115	164	172
Family credit not claimed[5]	70	115	137	143
Median	107	144	189	202
Highest decile point	157	211	299	321
Married man,[6] no children				
Lowest decile point	108	118	141	147
Median	156	171	223	232
Highest decile point	242	273	395	417
Married man,[6] 2 children[3]				
Lowest decile point[4]				
Family credit claimed	126	137	166	174
Family credit not claimed[5]	126	137	158	165
Median	174	190	240	250
Highest decile point	260	292	412	435

1 Adjusted to April 1993 prices using the retail prices index.
2 At April each year. Full-time employees on adult rates whose pay for the survey period was not affected by absence.
3 Aged under 11.
4 In years up to 1987, there was no entitlement to Family Income Supplement for this category.
5 Families with capital of more than £3,000 would only be eligible to receive reduced amounts of family credit, or may not be eligible at all.
6 Assuming no wife's earnings.

Source: Inland Revenue; Department of Social Security

net weekly spending power, while the same £40 increase in earnings, but from £185 to £225, gives a £26 rise in spending power.

Chart 5.14 shows direct taxes and social security benefits as a percentage of total personal income for the Group of Seven (G7) countries. These are major industrialised countries and together account for around two thirds of the world's GDP. In 1991 the percentage varied from 14 per cent in Japan to 21 per cent in Germany, with the United Kingdom at 16 per cent. Contributions as a percentage of personal income in Canada increased by 4 percentage points between 1981 and 1991, while those in the United Kingdom and United States of America fell by 1 percentage point. Of the other four countries, proportions in France, Japan and Italy all increased by 3 percentage points, while those in Germany remained the same.

When making international comparisons, it is necessary to make adjustments to definition and coverage. This means that the United Kingdom figures used here will not be strictly comparable with figures used elsewhere in this chapter. For example, the community charge is included here whereas in Table 5.11 it is not. A number of other factors must also be taken into account when making these comparisons, particularly the differing balance between direct and indirect taxation used by different countries. There is also considerable difference in government involvement in the provision of services and financial support (for example, medical care, pensions, etc) which are free at the point of use.

5.13

Net weekly spending power[1]: by gross weekly earnings[2] and type of family, October 1994

Great Britian

£ per week

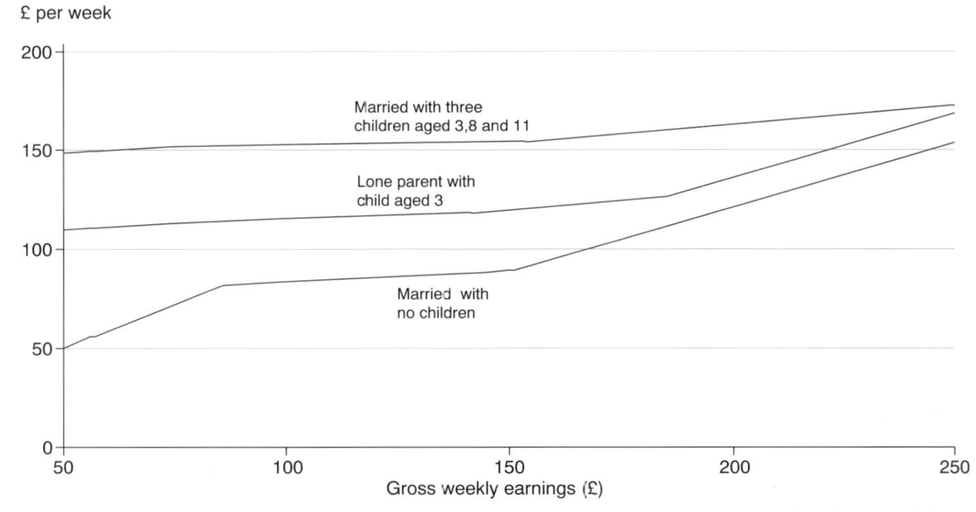

1 *Gross earnings less deductions for tax, national insurance, rent and council tax, plus receipts of all benefits which are applicable.*
2 *Gross earnings from full-time work where head of household only is in employment.*
Source: Department of Social Security

5.14

Direct taxes and social security contributions[1] as a percentage of personal income: G7 comparison, 1991

Percentages

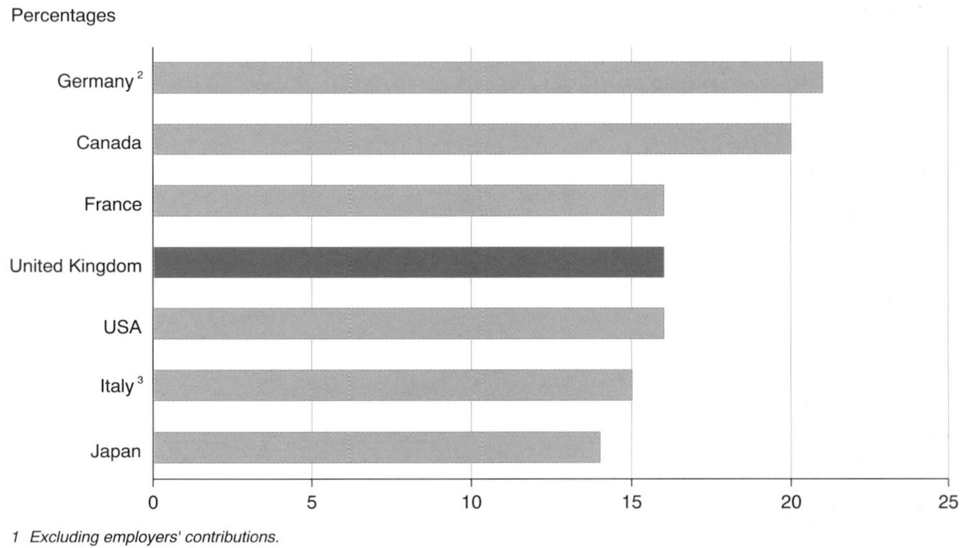

1 *Excluding employers' contributions.*
2 *As constitited since 3 October 1990.*
3 *1988 data.*
Source: OECD

5.15

Indirect taxes as a percentage of disposable income: by income grouping[1] of household, 1993

United Kingdom

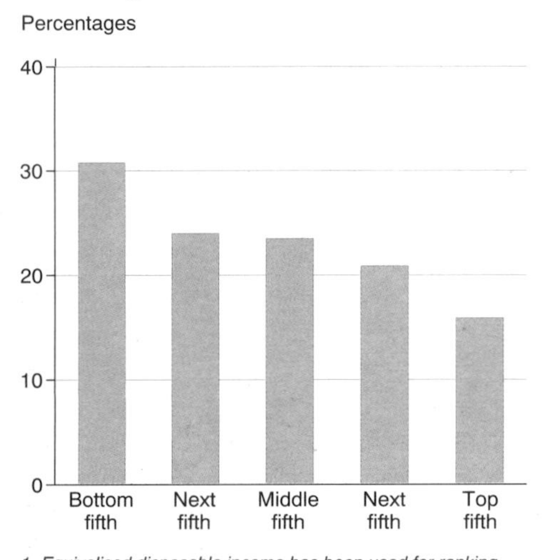

1 Equivalised disposable income has been used for ranking the households. See Appendix, Part 5: Equivalisation scales.
Source: Central Statistical Office

Another factor in the tax burden facing people is indirect taxation, such as VAT, customs duties and Vehicle Excise Duty. Chart 5.15 shows the percentage of household disposable income taken by indirect taxes. It can be seen that the lower the disposable income, the higher the proportion of income taken by indirect taxation. For all households, over 20 per cent of their disposable income was accounted for by indirect taxes; for households in the top fifth of the income distribution, the proportion was 16 per cent compared with 31 per cent for the bottom fifth. However, in absolute terms, the payment by the top fifth of households was much greater: on average, £4,900 per year compared with £1,710 per year (see Table 5.17).

Income distribution

Most government income is raised from households through direct and indirect taxes and social security contributions; its spending then benefits households. Some households will be taxed more than they benefit, and others will benefit more than they are taxed - this is the principle of redistribution of income. As we have seen in the first section, households initially receive income from various non-government sources: from their employment; from occupational pensions; from investments; and from other households - this is called original income. Cash benefits from the state (eg retirement pensions and income support) are added to original income to give gross income. This income is then reduced by income tax payments, NI contributions and local tax payments (such as council tax) to leave disposable income. The deduction of payments of indirect taxes, such as VAT, then leaves post-tax income. On the other hand, households benefit from government expenditure on services such as education and health and adding in the value of these gives a household's final income.

The redistribution statistics in the tables and charts in this section are generally presented by quintile group of household income. However, before considering these analyses it is important to look at which types of households are in which quintile groups. In 1993, 39 per cent of households in the bottom quintile group of disposable income were retired households, compared with only 7 per cent of households in the top quintile group. In addition lone parent households comprised 15 per cent of the households in the bottom quintile group, but only 1 per cent in the top quintile group (Table 5.16). It is households in the lower quintile groups on whom the bulk of the state benefits are targeted. Benefits are looked at in more detail in Chapter 8: Social Protection.

5.16

Quintile groups of household disposable income: by household type, 1993

United Kingdom Percentages

	Quintile groups of households[1]					
	Bottom fifth	Next fifth	Middle fifth	Next fifth	Top fifth	All households
Retired households	*39*	*47*	*24*	*15*	*7*	*26*
Non-retired households						
1 adult	*10*	*9*	*10*	*13*	*21*	*12*
2 adults	*9*	*9*	*20*	*26*	*36*	*20*
1 adult with children	*15*	*9*	*4*	*2*	*1*	*6*
2 adults with children	*21*	*17*	*27*	*27*	*23*	*23*
3 or more adults[2]	*6*	*9*	*16*	*16*	*12*	*12*
All households	*100*	*100*	*100*	*100*	*100*	*100*

1 Equivalised disposable income has been used for ranking the households into quintile groups. See Appendix, Part 5: Equivalisation scales.
2 With or without children.
Source: Central Statistical Office

5.17

Redistribution of income through taxes and benefits[1], 1993

United Kingdom — £ per year

	Quintile groups of households[2]					
	Bottom fifth	Next fifth	Middle fifth	Next fifth	Top fifth	All households
Average per household						
Wages and salaries	950	3,210	9,640	16,210	29,140	11,830
Imputed income from benefits in kind	10	10	80	300	920	270
Self-employment income	400	580	1,140	1,630	4,160	1,580
Occupational pensions, annuities	240	680	1,220	1,570	1,980	1,140
Investment income	190	360	570	880	2,620	930
Other income	140	180	210	260	550	270
Total original income	1,920	5,020	12,860	20,850	39,370	16,000
plus Benefits in cash						
Contributory	1,780	2,300	1,640	1,100	670	1,500
Non-contributory	2,670	2,050	1,430	830	390	1,470
Gross income	6,380	9,370	15,930	22,780	40,420	18,980
less Income tax[3] and NIC[4]	230	650	2,080	3,870	8,590	3,080
less Local taxes[5] (gross)	560	550	620	660	730	620
Disposable income	5,590	8,170	13,240	18,250	31,100	15,270
less Indirect taxes	1,710	1,950	3,100	3,790	4,900	3,090
Post-tax income	3,870	6,220	10,140	14,460	26,200	12,180
plus Benefits in kind						
Education	1,630	1,080	1,370	1,030	780	1,180
National Health Service	1,750	1,750	1,570	1,360	1,190	1,520
Housing subsidy	80	90	40	20	10	50
Travel subsidies	50	50	50	60	90	60
School meals and welfare milk	100	30	10	10	10	30
Final income	7,480	9,220	13,190	16,940	28,270	15,020

1 See Appendix, Part 5: Redistribution of income.
2 Equivalised disposable income has been used for ranking the households into quintile groups. See Appendix, Part 5: Equivalisation scales.
3 After tax relief at source on mortgage interest and life assurance premiums.
4 Employees' national insurance contributions.
5 Gross council tax, community charge, rates and water charges. Rates in Northern Ireland.

Source: Central Statistical Office

In 1993, original income ranged from an average of £1,920 per household for the bottom fifth of households to £39,370 for the top fifth (Table 5.17). After adding in cash benefits, deducting taxes and NI contributions, and adding in benefits in kind, final income ranged from £7,480 to £28,270 - narrowing the gap between the two groups.

Those households at the top of the income distribution pay the most taxes, both directly and indirectly, and receive least cash benefits. The bottom three fifths of the income distribution have gained from the income redistribution, while the other two fifths of households have lost.

5.18

Sources of gross household income[1]: by income grouping[2], 1993

United Kingdom

£ thousand per year

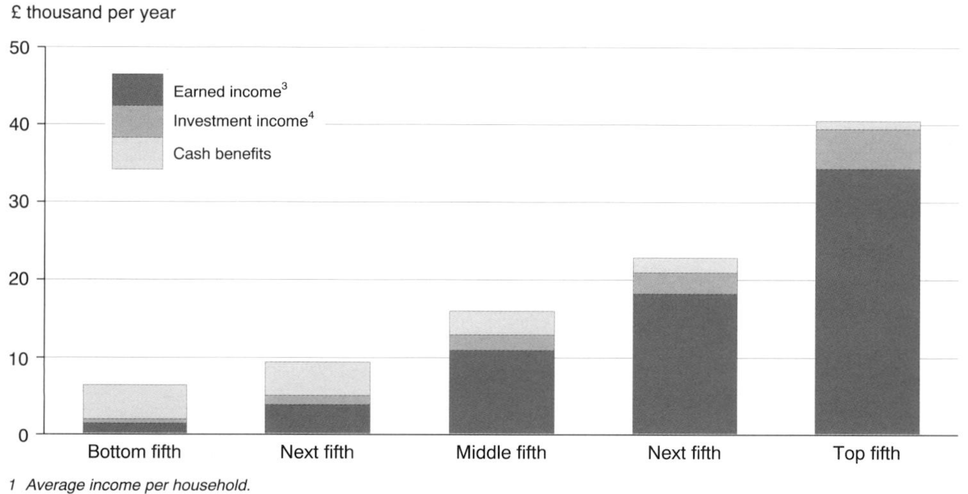

1 Average income per household.
2 Equivalised disposable income has been used for ranking the households into quintile groups. See Appendix, Part 5: Equivalisation scales.
3 Includes wages and salaries, self-employment income and income from 'fringe benefits'.
4 Includes occupational pensions and annuities.
Source: Central Statistical Office

Chart 5.18 shows the importance of different sources of gross income for each quintile group. Earned income accounted for the majority of income. For those households in the top quintile group in 1993: an average of £34,210 or nearly 85 per cent of income; investment income accounted for 13 per cent and cash benefits only 3 per cent. However, the lower the quintile group, the lower the income from earnings, both in real terms and as a percentage of total income; in the bottom quintile group earned income amounted to just £1,360 or 21 per cent of income. Income from cash benefits move in the opposite direction; they make up 70 per cent of the income of households in the bottom quintile group.

The Department of Social Security analyses the Family Expenditure Survey data, focusing on households below average income. The methodology used is different in several respects from that used earlier in this section; in particular it is based on quintile groups of individuals rather than households. On this basis the share of disposable household income taken by the bottom quintile group fell from 10 per cent in 1979 to 7 per cent in 1991-1992 (Table 5.19) Only the top quintile group had a larger share of total income in 1991-1992 than in 1979. When housing costs are taken into consideration, the trends are the same but the gap between the top and bottom groups widens: the share of the bottom quintile group fell by 4 percentage points while the top group increased its share by 8 percentage points. The table also shows that the deduction of housing costs has little effect on the share of income in the middle three quintile groups.

Some care should be exercised when interpreting these figures. The table does not monitor how the real income of individual households has changed over time, but compares the income share in 1991-1992

5.19

Shares of disposable household income[1]

United Kingdom — Percentages

	Quintile groups of individuals					
	Bottom fifth	Next fifth	Middle fifth	Next fifth	Top fifth	All individuals
Net income before housing costs						
1979	*10*	*14*	*18*	*23*	*35*	*100*
1981	*10*	*14*	*18*	*23*	*36*	*100*
1987	*9*	*13*	*17*	*23*	*39*	*100*
1988-1989	*8*	*12*	*17*	*23*	*40*	*100*
1991-1992	*7*	*12*	*17*	*23*	*41*	*100*
Net income after housing costs						
1979	*10*	*14*	*18*	*23*	*35*	*100*
1981	*9*	*14*	*18*	*23*	*36*	*100*
1987	*8*	*12*	*17*	*23*	*40*	*100*
1988-1989	*7*	*12*	*17*	*23*	*41*	*100*
1991-1992	*6*	*11*	*17*	*23*	*43*	*100*

1 The unit of analysis is the individual and the income measure is net equivalised household income. See Appendix, Part 5: Households Below Average Income and Equivalisation scales.
Source: Department of Social Security

of certain groups of households with the position of corresponding groups in earlier years. In addition, the composition of any quintile group is different from year to year as some households and individuals move from one group to another.

The British Household Panel Survey re-interviews the same sample of households over a period of time and so can show how the income of the same households changes from one year to the next. Table 5.20 shows changes in household equivalent income between 1991 and 1992. The income of each household in 1991 is ranked and decile groups are formed. In 1992 the household's income is again recorded and the 1991 decile group into which it would have fallen is recorded. It is then possible to identify households where income has moved from one decile group to another between the two years.

Overall almost three quarters of the households experienced relatively little income mobility (ie their household income did not move by more than one decile group). The proportion of households which experienced a marked drop was balanced by those which experienced a rise (13 per cent). However, the opportunities for substantial change depend somewhat on the initial starting point. Those in the lowest two decile groups cannot fall further (though they may of course experience a drop in living standards). Therefore the least mobility would be expected at the two ends of the distribution and the most in the middle. This is clearly true at the top end of the distribution, but relatively high (upward) mobility is experienced in the lowest decile group.

The Institute for Fiscal Studies has also analysed the Family Expenditure Survey to examine longer term trends in the income distribution using a similar methodology to the Department of Social Security (Chart 5.21) The percentage of people below average income increased by 3 percentage points between 1971 and 1992, to almost 63 per cent. However, the percentage of people below

5.20

Households moving between different income[1] groupings, 1991 to 1992

Great Britain — Percentages

	Income fell 4 or more deciles	Income fell 2-3 deciles	Income stable[2]	Income rose 2-3 deciles	Income rose 4 or more deciles
1991 income grouping					
Lowest decile	0.0	0.0	71.1	21.2	7.7
2nd decile	0.0	0.0	82.2	13.5	4.3
3rd decile	0.0	11.5	69.0	13.9	5.6
4th decile	0.0	14.9	68.3	13.3	3.6
5th decile	6.0	10.6	65.9	16.2	1.3
6th decile	8.1	10.6	68.0	10.9	2.3
7th decile	8.8	11.8	69.3	10.0	0.0
8th decile	7.1	11.2	75.4	6.3	0.0
9th decile	10.0	9.6	80.3	0.0	0.0
Highest decile	7.3	6.3	86.4	0.0	0.0
All households	4.7	8.6	73.6	10.6	2.5

1 Equivalised disposable income has been used for ranking the households. See Appendix, Part 5: Equivalisation scales.
2 Income did not change, or it fell by one decile or increased by one decile.
Source: The Research Centre for Micro-social Change

5.21

Percentage of people whose income is below various fractions of average income[1]

United Kingdom

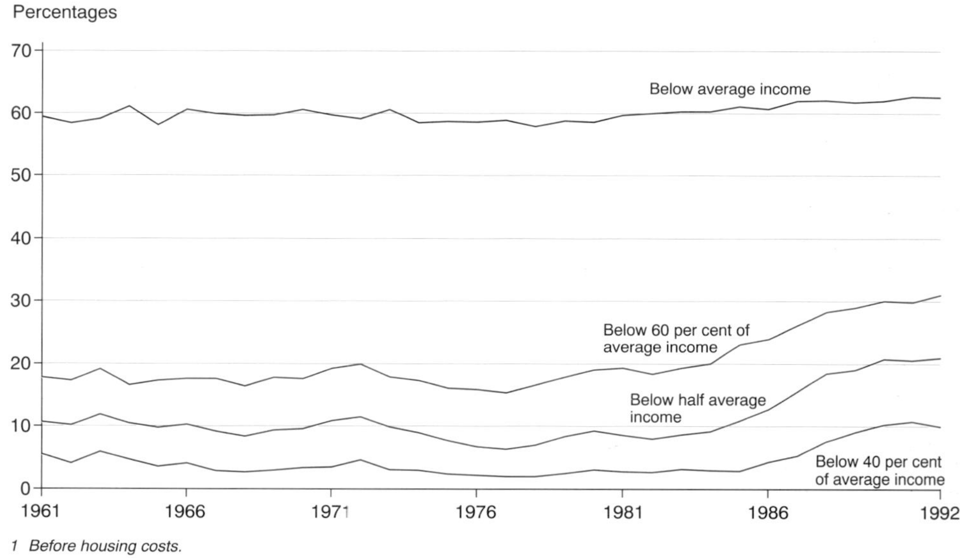

1 Before housing costs.
Source: Institute for Fiscal Studies

5.22

Composition of the net wealth[1] of the personal sector

United Kingdom — Percentages

	1971	1981	1991	1993
Dwellings (net of mortgage debt)	*26*	*36*	*37*	*30*
Other fixed assets	*10*	*10*	*5*	*5*
Non-marketable tenancy rights	*12*	*12*	*8*	*7*
Shares and deposits with building societies	*7*	*8*	*8*	*8*
National Savings, notes and coin and bank deposits	*13*	*10*	*9*	*9*
Stocks, shares and unit trusts	*23*	*8*	*8*	*11*
Life assurance and pension funds	*15*	*16*	*27*	*33*
Other financial assets net of liabilities	*-6*	*0*	*-2*	*-3*
Total (= 100%) (£ billion)	172	740	2,271	2,582

1 See Appendix, Part 5: Net wealth of the personal sector.

Source: Central Statistical Office

5.23

Distribution of wealth[1]

United Kingdom — Percentages

	1976	1981	1986	1991	1992
Marketable wealth					
Percentage of wealth owned by[2]					
Most wealthy 1%	*21*	*18*	*18*	*17*	*18*
Most wealthy 5%	*38*	*36*	*36*	*34*	*37*
Most wealthy 10%	*50*	*50*	*50*	*46*	*49*
Most wealthy 25%	*71*	*73*	*73*	*70*	*72*
Most wealthy 50%	*92*	*92*	*90*	*92*	*92*
Total marketable wealth (£ billion)	280	565	955	1,801	1,811
Marketable wealth less value of dwellings					
Percentage of wealth owned by[2]					
Most wealthy 1%	*29*	*26*	*25*	*29*	*29*
Most wealthy 5%	*47*	*45*	*46*	*51*	*53*
Most wealthy 10%	*57*	*56*	*58*	*64*	*65*
Most wealthy 25%	*73*	*74*	*75*	*80*	*82*
Most wealthy 50%	*88*	*87*	*89*	*93*	*94*

1 Estimates for 1976, 1981 and 1986 are based on the estates of persons dying in those years. Estimates for 1991 and 1992 are based on estates notified for probate in 1991-92 and 1992-93 respectively. Estimates are not strictly comparable between 1991 onwards and earlier years.

2 Applies to adult population aged 18 and over.

Source: Inland Revenue

the various fractions of average income shown have followed broadly the same pattern but risen at a faster rate. For example, the percentage of people below 60 per cent of average income increased by nearly 12 percentage points between 1971 and 1992, while the increase for those below half of average income was 10 percentage points. The largest year on year increases occurred between 1986 and 1988: generally earnings for those at the top decile point increased at a faster rate than for those at the bottom decile point (see Chart 5.6).

Wealth

The value of net wealth held by the personal sector was £2,582 billion in 1993 (Table 5.22), an increase of almost 5 per cent over 1991 in real terms. The percentage of net wealth in dwellings increased from 26 per cent in 1971 to peak at 43 per cent in 1988 and has since declined to 30 per cent in 1993 as house values fell. The largest increase between 1971 and 1993 has been for life assurance and pension funds which rose by 18 percentage points, to 33 per cent of net wealth in 1993; it now represents the largest share of wealth. Conversely, the percentage of net wealth held in stocks and shares fell by 15 percentage points between 1971 and 1981 (mainly attributable to a substantial fall in share prices during the early 1970s); in 1993 it stood at 11 per cent.

Table 5.23 shows the distribution of marketable wealth among the top half of the wealth distribution. Overall, there has been little change in the distribution of all marketable wealth since 1976: the percentage of marketable wealth held by the richest 50 per cent has remained steady at about 92 per cent. However, the share of the richest 1 per cent fell slightly at the beginning of the period, then remained steady from 1981 onwards at about 18 per cent.

The table also shows the distribution of marketable wealth after the value of dwellings (net of mortgage debt) has been removed. Wealth in this table differs from net wealth of the personal sector shown in Table 5.22 for several reasons - see Appendix, Part 5: Distribution of personal wealth. Wealth defined in this way is even more concentrated in the upper part of the distribution. For example, on this definition, the richest 10 per cent own 65 per cent of marketable wealth, compared with only 49 per cent of all marketable wealth. The proportion of wealth excluding dwellings held by the richest 50 per cent has increased from 88 per cent in 1976 to 94 per cent in 1992, an increase of 6 percentage points.

Table 5.24 shows that the way in which people hold their savings varies with income. Interest bearing bank and building society accounts are the most popular method of saving across all income groups, while National Savings are the next most popular. The proportion of people with savings in either of these two forms does not vary much with income, although the average amount of savings does. For example, people with an average income of over £25,000 have, on average, £3,187 invested in interest bearing accounts, whereas those with an income of £2,500 or less have only £965 invested in this type of account. Conversely, for National Savings, the amount invested tends to decrease as income increases. The proportion of people holding shares increases with income from only 5 per cent for those in the lowest income band to 29 per cent for those in the highest; the proportions with holdings in TESSAs and PEPs also increase with income.

5.24

People with financial investments: by type of investment and income, 1991-92

United Kingdom Percentages

	Interest accounts	National Savings	Shares	TESSAs[1]	PEPs[2]	Other[3]
£1-£2,500	*76*	*30*	*5*	*1*	*1*	*1*
£2,501-£4,500	*68*	*42*	*8*	*2*	*0*	*1*
£4,501-£6,500	*71*	*37*	*11*	*3*	*1*	*2*
£6,501-£7,500	*71*	*34*	*13*	*3*	*1*	*3*
£7,501-£9,500	*76*	*33*	*15*	*3*	*2*	*6*
£9,501-£11,500	*76*	*30*	*16*	*3*	*1*	*2*
£11,501-£13,500	*77*	*29*	*16*	*5*	*1*	*5*
£13,501-£15,500	*75*	*32*	*18*	*5*	*3*	*5*
£15,501-£17,500	*79*	*30*	*17*	*5*	*2*	*4*
£17,501-£25,000	*80*	*33*	*21*	*4*	*2*	*5*
£25,001 and over	*79*	*38*	*29*	*7*	*5*	*8*

1 Tax Exempt Special Savings Accounts.
2 Personal Equity Plans.
3 Primarily unit trusts, investment trusts and government securities.
Source: Institute for Fiscal Studies

An analysis of the share registers of UK listed companies found that the proportion of total equity held by individuals at end-1993 was 18 per cent; this compares with 54 per cent in 1963 (Chart 5.25). This fall has been offset to some extent by an increase in the proportion of shares held by unit trusts, which are

5.25

Individuals as a percentage of all shareholders[1]

United Kingdom

Percentages

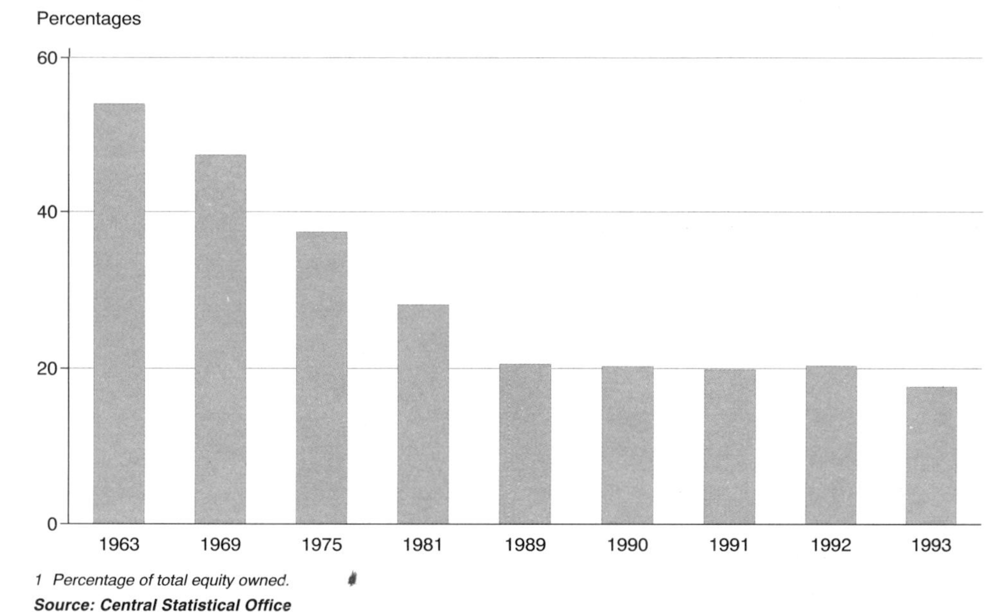

1 Percentage of total equity owned.
Source: Central Statistical Office

5.26

Membership of current employers' pension scheme: by socio-economic group, 1991-1993

Great Britain

Percentages

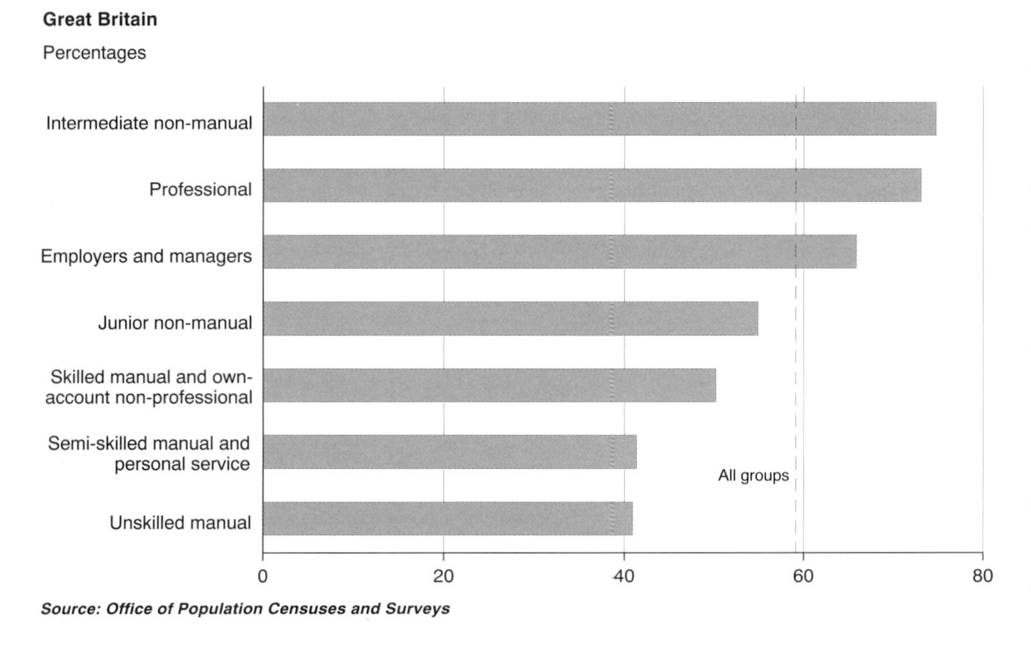

Source: Office of Population Censuses and Surveys

5.27

Gross domestic product[1]

United Kingdom

Volume index (1990 = 100)

1 At factor cost.

Source: Central Statistical Office

predominantly funded by individuals, to over 6 per cent. However, the largest increase over this period was in investments by pension fund and insurance companies who together accounted for half the total equity owned in 1993. Annual surveys to determine the number of individuals holding shares showed that in 1983 there were approximately 4 million individuals in Great Britain who held shares directly; this had risen to 10 million by 1993. It is thought that the number of shareholders peaked in 1990 following the privatisation of the electricity companies.

The proportion of people who are members of their employer's pension schemes has decreased since 1983. The percentage of full-time employees who were members of their employer's pension scheme was 58 per cent in 1993, compared with 61 per cent in 1983. After falling slightly between 1983 and 1987, the proportion of employees whose employer had no scheme then stayed fairly constant, at around a fifth. Membership of employer's pension schemes varies with socio-economic group (Chart 5.26). Around three quarters of both professional and intermediate non-manual workers were members of their employer's pension scheme in 1993, compared with only two fifths of semi-skilled or unskilled manual workers and personal service workers. This difference is partly explained by availability of pension schemes to employees in certain occupations.

National income

Gross Domestic Product (GDP) is one measure of the income of the nation. Chart 5.27 shows the real changes in GDP since 1951, by expressing GDP as an index based on 1990 prices. GDP at factor cost fell in the mid-1970s (the oil price shock), the early 1980s (the worldwide recession) and in the early 1990s (again due to recession). However, the general trend has seen growth in GDP at an annual average rate of about 2.5 per cent between 1951 and 1990; GDP has also been growing again in volume terms since 1992.

A regional breakdown of GDP is shown in Table 5.28. This uses indices based on GDP per head with the United Kingdom average equal to 100. This means that, in any year, a region with a value greater than 100 has a GDP per head higher than the United Kingdom average. The pattern, not surprisingly, is similar to that for gross weekly earnings (see Chart 5.5): the highest GDP per head in 1993 was in Greater London, the lowest in Northern Ireland. The North has seen the largest fall in GDP per head since 1981 while East Anglia has enjoyed the greatest rise.

The final item in this chapter, Chart 5.29, compares GDP per head for all the countries in the European Community (EC). These data, although presented in sterling, have been calculated using purchasing power parities. This makes the data more comparable by taking into account the different price levels in each country. For example, if a particular commodity, such as bread, is more expensive in one country than another then incomes would need to be higher in that country to reach the same standard of living. The chart shows that at over £13 thousand, Luxembourg has the highest GDP per head of countries in the EC. The United Kingdom has the 8th highest GDP per head at nearly £10 thousand, although this is still nearly twice that of Greece, the lowest, at just under £5 thousand per head.

5.28

Gross domestic product at factor cost and current prices: by region

Index per head (UK=100)

	1981	1986	1991	1993
United Kingdom[1]	100	100	100	100
North	94	90	90	89
Yorkshire & Humberside	92	94	92	91
East Midlands	97	97	97	96
East Anglia	97	101	100	102
South East	117	117	117	116
Greater London	128	126	126	125
Rest of South East	109	111	112	110
South West	93	95	94	97
West Midlands	91	92	92	93
North West	95	93	90	91
England	102	102	102	102
Wales	84	84	85	85
Scotland	97	95	97	98
Northern Ireland	79	79	81	82

1 United Kingdom less continental shelf.

Source: Central Statistical Office

5.29

Gross domestic product per head: EC comparison, 1991

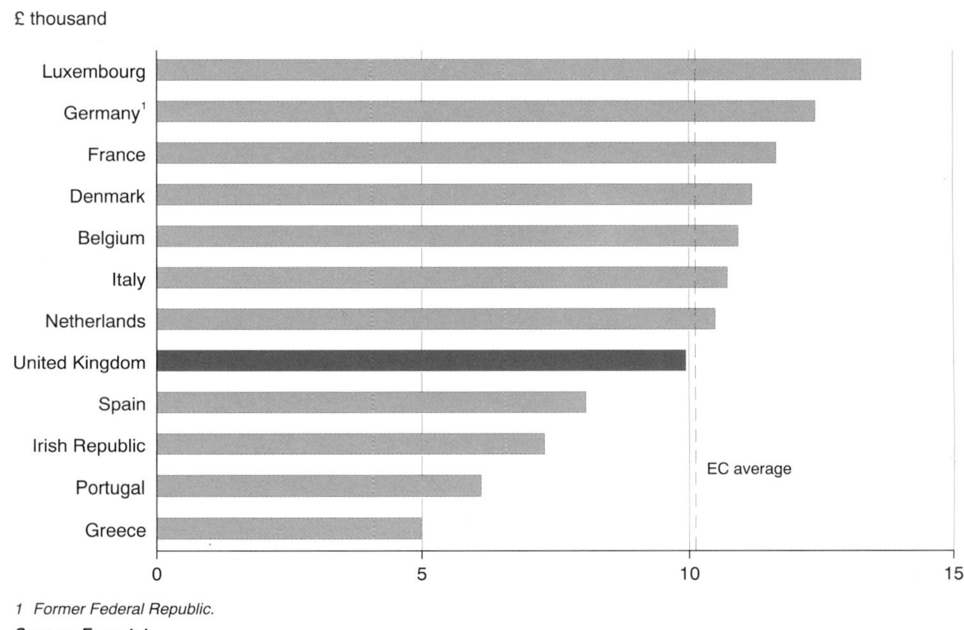

1 Former Federal Republic.

Source: Eurostat

References and further reading

The following list contains selected publications relevant to **Chapter 5: Income and Wealth**. Those published by HMSO are available from the addresses shown on the inside back cover of *Social Trends*.

Changing Households: The British Household Panel Survey 1990-1992, ESRC Research Centre on Micro-Social Change

Economic Trends, HMSO

Employment Gazette, Harrington Kilbride

Family Spending, HMSO

Fiscal Studies, Institute for Fiscal Studies

For Richer, For Poorer, Institute for Fiscal Studies

General Household Survey, HMSO

Households Below Average Income, A Statistical Analysis, HMSO

Inland Revenue Statistics, HMSO

New Earnings Survey, HMSO

Regional Trends, HMSO

Share Ownership - The Share Register Survey Report, HMSO

Social Security, Departmental Report, HMSO

Social Security Statistics, HMSO

Tax/Benefit Model Tables, Department of Social Security

The Distribution of Wealth in the UK, Institute for Fiscal Studies

The Personal Income Tax Base: A Comparative Study, OECD

United Kingdom National Accounts (The CSO Blue Book), HMSO

Contacts

Telephone contact points for further information relating to **Chapter 5: Income and Wealth.**

Central Statistical Office	
Effects of taxes and benefits	0171 217 4217
National accounts	0171 270 5944
Personal sector accounts	0171 217 4203
Retail prices	0171 217 4310
Regional accounts	0171 217 4197
Share register survey	0171 217 4187
Employment Department	
Average Earnings Index	01928 794847
New Earnings Survey	01928 794903/4
Department of Finance and Personnel, Northern Ireland	01232 521154
Office of Population Censuses and Surveys	0171 396 2327
Eurostat	00 352 4301 34447
Institute for Fiscal Studies	0171 636 3784

Chapter 6 Expenditure

Personal and household expenditure

Expenditure on clothing and footwear more than doubled in real terms between 1971 and 1993. (Table 6.2)

In 1993, 90 per cent of households had a telephone compared with 42 per cent in 1972. (Table 6.7)

Prices

In 1994, a single mother with a child would have had to have worked just over 10 hours to buy a standard class return rail ticket from London to Edinburgh, compared with nearly 31 hours in 1971. (Table 6.12)

A 1971 pound was worth just 14 pence in 1993 - a seventh of its original value. (Chart 6.13)

Consumer credit and household saving

Net lending to consumers in the United Kingdom reached £1.5 billion in the third quarter of 1994, the highest quarterly figure since 1989. (Chart 6.16)

Over three quarters of adults held at least one type of plastic payment or cheque guarantee card in 1993. (Table 6.17)

Public expenditure

Social security accounted for more than a third of general government expenditure in 1993. (Table 6.20)

The United Kingdom, Germany, France, Italy and the Netherlands were all net contributors to the European Community budget in 1993. (Table 6.21)

6.1

Retail prices index

Source: Central Statistical Office

6.2

Household expenditure[1]

United Kingdom

	1971	1981	1986	1990	1991	1992	1993 Indices/ percentages	1993 £ million (current prices)
Indices at constant 1990 prices								
Food	87	91	95	100	100	102	103	46,327
Alcoholic drink	74	95	100	100	97	94	94	24,395
Tobacco	136	121	101	100	98	94	91	10,829
Clothing and footwear	52	67	92	100	100	103	108	23,322
Housing	68	81	93	100	100	101	103	62,316
Fuel and power	86	94	103	100	108	106	109	14,618
Household goods and services								
Household durables	53	69	86	100	97	98	107	12,678
Other	66	68	84	100	99	102	106	13,482
Transport and communication								
Purchase of vehicles	51	59	82	100	81	77	86	18,046
Running of vehicles	47	65	84	100	99	98	101	30,460
Other travel	56	70	84	100	97	101	101	13,526
Post and telecommunications	33	63	80	100	100	101	107	7,592
Recreation, entertainment and education								
TV, video, etc	19	47	77	100	100	105	111	8,800
Books, newspapers, etc	101	97	92	100	95	96	99	5,462
Other	36	62	76	100	99	100	104	26,275
Other goods and services								
Catering (meals, etc)	55	58	72	100	93	91	93	34,746
Other goods	44	60	75	100	100	98	100	14,890
Other services	30	43	68	100	97	94	96	28,885
Less expenditure by foreign tourists, etc	48	72	94	100	86	89	97	-10,121
Household expenditure abroad	34	66	78	100	97	106	104	11,262
All household expenditure	59	72	85	100	98	98	101	397,790
Percentage of total household expenditure at current prices								
Food	*20.1*	*16.4*	*13.8*	*12.3*	*12.3*	*12.1*	*11.6*	46,327
Alcoholic drink	*7.3*	*7.3*	*6.9*	*6.4*	*6.6*	*6.3*	*6.1*	24,395
Tobacco	*4.8*	*3.6*	*3.1*	*2.5*	*2.7*	*2.7*	*2.7*	10,829
Clothing and footwear	*8.5*	*6.7*	*7.0*	*6.1*	*5.9*	*5.9*	*5.9*	23,322
Housing	*12.4*	*14.9*	*15.3*	*14.2*	*14.6*	*15.4*	*15.7*	62,316
Fuel and power	*4.5*	*5.1*	*4.6*	*3.6*	*4.0*	*3.8*	*3.7*	14,618
Household goods and services	*7.8*	*6.9*	*6.7*	*6.5*	*6.5*	*6.6*	*6.6*	26,160
Transport and communication	*14.3*	*17.2*	*17.5*	*18.3*	*17.3*	*17.3*	*17.5*	69,624
Recreation, entertainment and education	*8.8*	*9.4*	*9.4*	*10.0*	*10.0*	*10.1*	*10.2*	40,537
Other goods, services and adjustments	*11.4*	*12.5*	*15.6*	*20.0*	*20.0*	*19.9*	*20.0*	79,662
All household expenditure	*100*	*100*	*100*	*100*	*100*	*100*	*100*	397,790

1 See Appendix, Part 6: Household expenditure.

Source: Central Statistical Office

While the previous chapter looked at the sources of our income, this chapter shows what we spend our money on, and how its value is affected, as well as covering consumer credit, savings and government expenditure.

Personal and household expenditure

A breakdown of household expenditure at 1990 constant prices is given in Table 6.2. Overall, total household expenditure increased by 71 per cent in real terms between 1971 and 1993. However, expenditure on tobacco continues to fall; allowing for inflation, a third less was spent on it in 1993 than in 1971. Conversely, over the same period, spending on post and telecommunications more than tripled (further information on price changes for telephone calls and postage is given in Chart 6.14). The most notable increase in spending has been on TVs and videos. While TV ownership has risen only six percentage points since the early 1970s (see Table 6.7), the arrival of affordable video recorders has meant that spending on these items and their related products has seen nearly a sixfold increase in real terms.

Chart 6.3 illustrates how the pattern of household expenditure has been changing. Even though there has been a constant price increase of just over 18 per cent on food spending since 1971, its actual proportion of household expenditure has fallen by nearly 9 percentage points. Similarly, spending on clothing and footwear more than doubled between 1971 and 1993 in constant prices but as a proportion of expenditure it fell by almost 3 percentage points over the same period. Housing, however, now accounts for a higher proportion of household expenditure than 20 years ago. The drop in the housing figure between 1989 and 1990 is because domestic rates were included in the figure up to and including 1989, but both the community charge and its replacement, the council tax, are excluded because they are regarded as taxes rather than part of expenditure.

Whereas the previous two items give a general picture of spending, Table 6.4 (overleaf) compares the spending patterns of people in different income groups in 1991-1992. The table uses the measure before deducting housing costs. People in the bottom quintile group spent a high proportion of their household income on necessities such as food,

6.3

Household expenditure on selected items

United Kingdom

Percentages

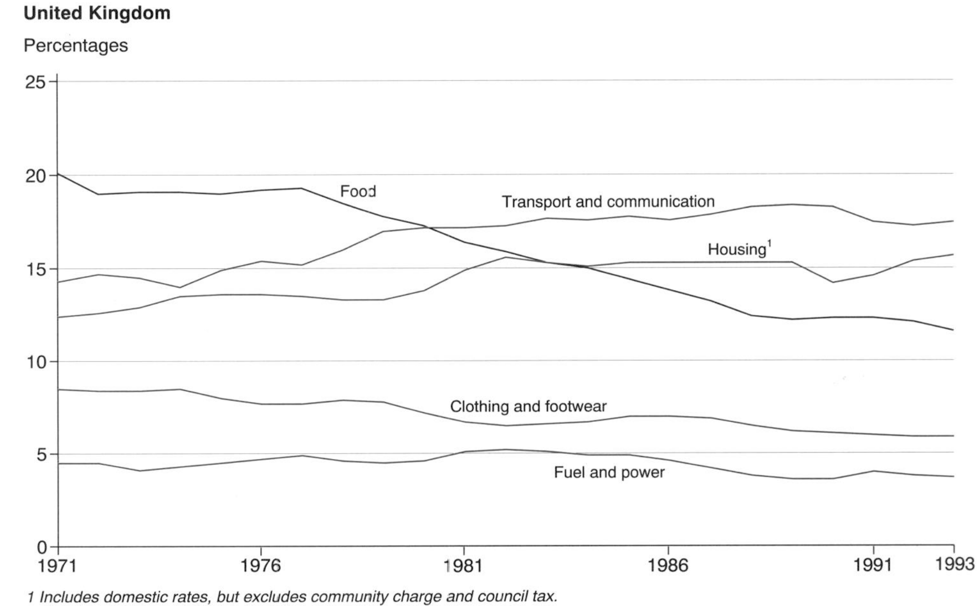

1 Includes domestic rates, but excludes community charge and council tax.

Source: Central Statistical Office

6.4

Household expenditure: by quintile group[1], 1991-1992

United Kingdom Percentages

	Bottom fifth	Next fifth	Middle fifth	Next fifth	Top fifth
Food	23	22	20	17	14
Housing	17	16	13	13	15
Travel	10	12	16	18	18
Leisure	10	11	13	14	18
Fuel	8	6	5	4	3
Tobacco and alcohol	8	7	7	7	5
Clothes	6	6	7	7	6
Personal services	3	4	4	4	4
Other	15	15	16	17	18
All household expenditure	100	100	100	100	100

1 The unit of analysis is the individual and the income measure is net equivalised household income. See Appendix, Part 5: Households Below Average Income and Equivalisation scales.

Source: Department of Social Security

fuel and housing which accounted for almost half of their spending. In contrast, the top quintile group spent just under a third of their income on these items. Over a third of their spending went on leisure and travel compared with only a fifth of that of the bottom quintile group.

Table 6.5 shows how average weekly expenditure of households, varies with the socio-economic group of the household head. In general, the higher social groups spent a smaller proportion of their expenditure on food and fuel than those in the lower social groups but a larger proportion on housing. Households headed by a retired or unoccupied person spent more than twice the proportion of their total household expenditure on fuel, light and power than those headed by a professional; although their average total expenditure is only two fifths of that in households headed by a professional. The contrast continues in an area where choice can be exercised more, namely alcohol and tobacco expenditure. On average, households headed by someone from the unskilled manual group spent nearly three times the proportion on these items than those headed by a professional, and twice the proportion than those headed by someone from the employers, managers or intermediate non-manual groups. There are, in fact, three times the proportion of smokers in the unskilled manual group than in the professional group (see Chapter 7).

Household spending differences can also be seen between the different parts of the United Kingdom (Table 6.6). In 1993, as in previous years, the South-East had the highest average household expenditure per week at £321 while the West Midlands had the lowest at £238. Both the North and Yorkshire

6.5

Household expenditure: by socio-economic group of head of household, 1993

United Kingdom Percentages

	Housing	Fuel, light and power	Food	Alcohol and tobacco	Clothing and footwear	Household goods and services	Motoring and fares	Leisure goods and services	Other goods and services	Average expenditure (=100%) (£ per week)
Professional	17.6	3.3	15.4	4.1	6.2	14.3	17.7	16.9	4.6	457.38
Employers and managers	18.5	3.6	15.8	5.4	6.6	13.7	14.8	16.5	5.1	445.54
Intermediate non-manual	17.7	3.6	15.3	5.2	6.4	13.9	17.1	14.6	6.3	366.33
Junior non-manual	17.6	4.3	16.7	5.6	6.7	13.9	18.4	12.4	4.5	291.34
Skilled manual	16.1	4.5	19.0	7.8	6.3	13.9	15.7	11.9	4.8	297.94
Semi-skilled manual	15.8	5.1	19.5	8.5	6.7	12.0	17.3	10.6	4.4	245.88
Unskilled manual	14.5	6.1	21.4	10.8	6.2	12.7	12.3	11.5	4.5	210.14
Retired and unoccupied	13.4	6.9	20.8	6.4	5.7	14.9	13.1	14.3	4.6	175.64
All households	17.2	4.1	17.1	6.3	6.5	13.6	16.3	14.0	5.0	335.73

Source: Central Statistical Office

6.6

Household expenditure: by region, 1993

United Kingdom — Percentages

	Housing	Fuel, light and power	Food	Alcohol and tobacco	Clothing and footwear	Household goods and services	Motoring and fares	Leisure goods and services	Other goods and services	Average expenditure (= 100%) (£ per week)
United Kingdom	*16.2*	*4.8*	*18.1*	*6.3*	*6.3*	*13.9*	*15.6*	*14.0*	*4.8*	276.68
North	*15.0*	*5.3*	*19.1*	*8.0*	*6.5*	*14.7*	*14.2*	*12.5*	*4.6*	245.94
Yorkshire & Humberside	*14.7*	*5.0*	*18.2*	*8.0*	*6.7*	*12.6*	*16.6*	*13.4*	*4.9*	263.06
East Midlands	*16.1*	*5.2*	*18.8*	*6.6*	*5.8*	*13.9*	*15.2*	*13.8*	*4.8*	262.15
East Anglia	*16.9*	*4.8*	*18.5*	*4.6*	*6.1*	*13.8*	*17.7*	*13.0*	*4.5*	260.46
South East	*18.2*	*4.1*	*16.8*	*5.2*	*5.9*	*14.8*	*15.2*	*15.0*	*4.8*	321.10
South West	*16.1*	*4.8*	*18.3*	*5.8*	*5.5*	*13.7*	*17.4*	*13.3*	*5.1*	268.14
West Midlands	*15.3*	*5.3*	*18.8*	*6.2*	*5.9*	*13.5*	*16.4*	*13.9*	*4.7*	238.19
North West	*15.7*	*5.0*	*18.0*	*7.4*	*7.0*	*13.6*	*14.7*	*14.3*	*4.3*	261.81
England	*16.7*	*4.7*	*17.8*	*6.2*	*6.1*	*14.0*	*15.7*	*14.2*	*4.7*	280.09
Wales	*15.7*	*5.6*	*19.5*	*7.2*	*7.1*	*13.6*	*15.1*	*12.3*	*3.9*	249.45
Scotland	*13.4*	*5.1*	*18.8*	*7.5*	*7.2*	*12.8*	*15.6*	*14.4*	*5.3*	264.84
Northern Ireland	*9.4*	*6.6*	*22.9*	*6.4*	*7.6*	*14.0*	*16.5*	*12.1*	*4.3*	255.32

Source: Central Statistical Office

and Humberside spent a higher proportion of their expenditure on alcohol and tobacco than any other region or country, at 8 per cent. Households in East Anglia spent under 5 per cent of their expenditure on alcohol and tobacco, but spent the highest proportion on motoring and fares. The South East was the only area to have spent more on housing than on food.

Table 6.7 illustrates the proportion of households with various types of consumer durables. The proportion of households with a television in 1993 was virtually at saturation point and had increased by only 2 percentage points since 1981. However, there has been a switch from black and white to colour; back in 1981 nearly a quarter of households had a black and white television only, compared with only 3 per cent in 1993. Since 1972, the proportion with a telephone more than doubled to become the second most widespread consumer durable after televisions: 9 in 10 households had a telephone in 1993. Between 1991 and 1993 there was a large increase in CD player ownership with the proportion of households with one increasing by two fifths. In 1993 four in ten households had a CD player while six in ten had a microwave and fewer than two in ten had a dishwasher.

6.7

Households with consumer durables

Great Britain — Percentages

	1972	1981	1991	1993
Colour television	} *93*	*74*	*95*	*96*
Black and white television only	}	*23*	*4*	*3*
Telephone	*42*	*75*	*88*	*90*
Washing machine	*66*	*78*	*87*	*88*
Deep-freezer/fridge freezer	..	*49*	*83*	*87*
Video recorder	..	..	*68*	*73*
Microwave	..	..	*55*	*62*
Tumble drier	..	*23*	*48*	*49*
Compact disc player	..	..	*27*	*39*
Dishwasher	..	*4*	*14*	*16*

Source: Office of Population Censuses and Surveys.

6.8

Consumer complaints, 1993

United Kingdom

Thousands

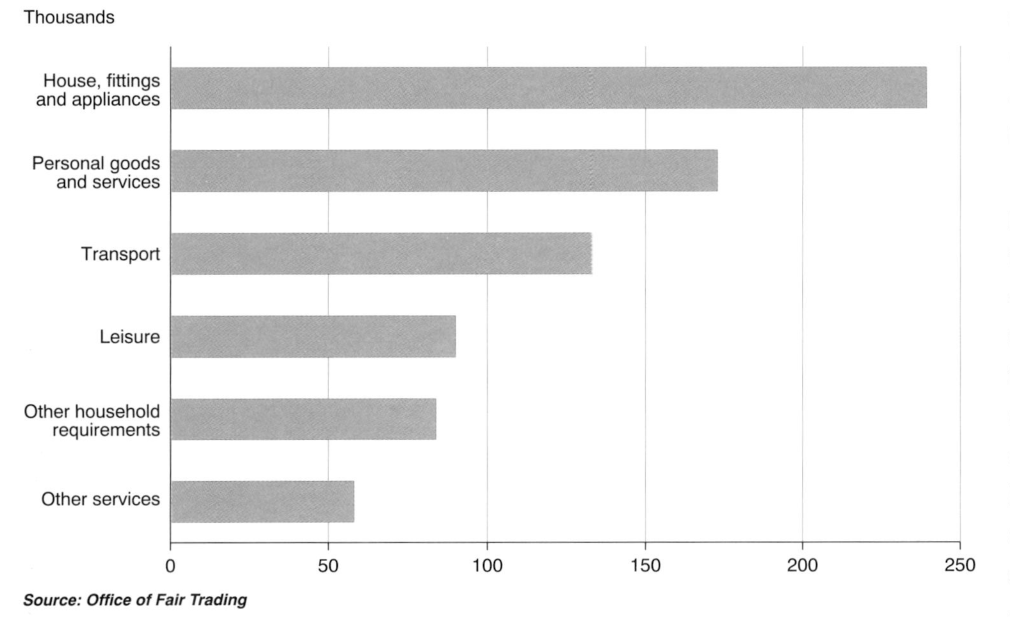

Source: Office of Fair Trading

Inevitably, when we make purchases, some goods and services do not meet our own or more general satisfaction standards. Chart 6.8 shows the number of consumer complaints notified by Trading Standards Departments to the Office of Fair Trading in 1993. Overall, complaints rose by just over 9 per cent on the previous year from 710 thousand to 776 thousand. By far the largest category was 'house, fittings and appliances' at nearly 240 thousand. Within this category, the largest number of complaints were about radio, TV and other electrical recreation goods (including their hire) at just over 60 thousand, the greatest cause being defective goods or substandard services. Between 1992 and 1993, air travel accounted for the biggest percentage increase in complaints, nearly doubling. Conversely, the greatest percentage falls were in time-sharing and footwear repair both of which fell by 30 per cent and complaints about jewellery, silverware, clocks and watches, down by nearly 40 per cent.

6.9

Volume of retail sales: weekly averages[1]

Great Britain

Indices (1990=100)

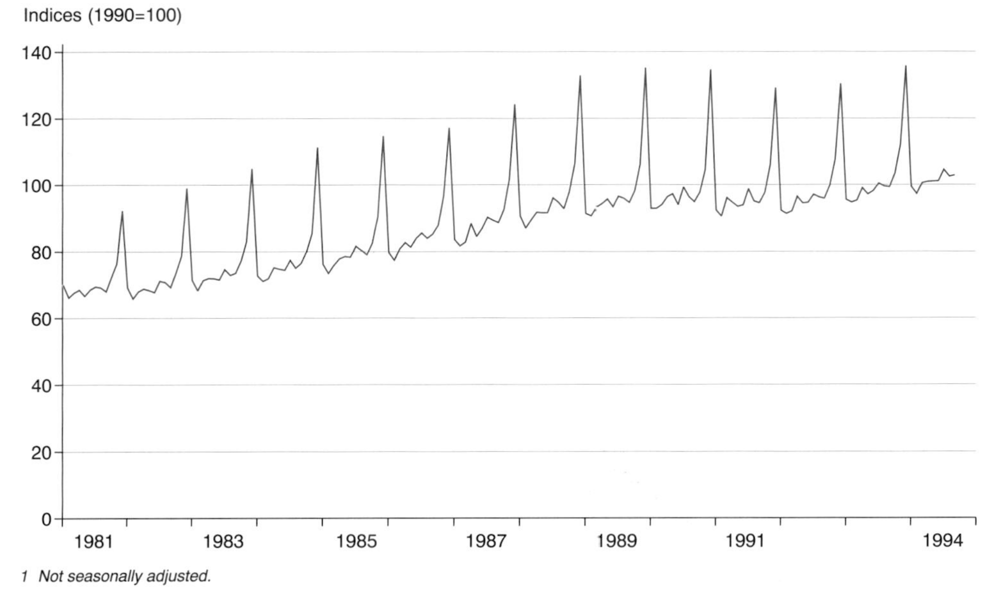

1 Not seasonally adjusted.

Source: Central Statistical Office

Retail sales reflect trends in overall consumers' expenditure; they account for around 35 per cent of total consumer expenditure. The retail sales index for all retailers rose by more than two fifths in volume terms between January 1981 and January 1994 (Chart 6.9). As can be seen from the chart, retail sales are highly seasonal, peaking in December each year. For example, the weekly average in December 1993 was nearly a third higher than the weekly average for the year as a whole. Conversely, in virtually all the years shown, February was the month with the lowest volume of weekly sales; the average for February 1993 was about 8 per cent lower than the average for the year as a whole.

6.10

Index of retail prices: rates of change

United Kingdom							Percentages
	Average annual percentage change						Weights
	1971	1976	1981	1986	1991	1993	1993
General index							
All items	*9.4*	*16.5*	*11.9*	*3.4*	*5.9*	*1.6*	1,000
All items except housing	*9.5*	*16.9*	*10.9*	*3.0*	*7.6*	*3.1*	836
All items except mortgage interest payments	..	*16.7*	*12.2*	*3.6*	*6.7*	*3.0*	952
Food	*11.1*	*20.0*	*8.4*	*3.3*	*5.2*	*1.8*	144
Catering	*13.4*	*18.8*	*9.7*	*6.3*	*10.0*	*5.2*	45
Alcoholic drink	*6.0*	*17.8*	*16.9*	*4.5*	*12.4*	*4.5*	78
Tobacco	*1.6*	*16.1*	*23.5*	*9.9*	*14.3*	*8.5*	35
Housing	*9.2*	*14.1*	*18.1*	*5.7*	*-1.8*	*-5.4*	164
Fuel and light	*10.4*	*23.7*	*21.3*	*1.3*	*7.9*	*-1.3*	46
Clothing and footwear	*6.9*	*10.9*	*1.4*	*2.8*	*3.0*	*0.8*	58
Household goods	..	*9.9*	*4.8*	*1.1*	*6.2*	*1.2*	79
Household services	..	*23.2*	*17.0*	*4.8*	*8.3*	*3.6*	47
Personal goods and services	..	..	..	..	*8.7*	*4.0*	39
Leisure goods	..	..	..	..	*4.7*	*1.4*	46
Leisure services[1]	*7.2*	*10.2*	*12.3*	*4.8*	*11.5*	*4.5*	62
Motoring expenditure	*9.0*	*13.1*	*11.9*	*-1.5*	*7.4*	*4.3*	136
Fares and other travel costs	*23.1*	*27.2*	*10.6*	*6.6*	*9.8*	*5.2*	21
Pensioner indices[2]							
All items except housing							
One-person households	*10.2*	*19.2*	*11.4*	*3.2*	*7.1*	*2.1*	1,000
Two-person households	*9.8*	*18.8*	*11.6*	*3.2*	*7.2*	*2.7*	1,000

1 The leisure services component includes foreign holidays with effect from February 1993 and holidays in the United Kingdom with effect from February 1994.
2 Pensioner indices relate to households in which at least 75 per cent of total income is derived from state pensions and benefits.
Source: Central Statistical Office

Prices

The growth of retail prices within the United Kingdom, usually referred to as the rate of inflation, is measured by changes in the retail prices index (RPI) (Chart 6.1). This index monitors the month to month percentage change in a representative 'basket' of goods and services bought by a typical household and indicates the impact of inflation on household budgets. The index can affect tax allowances, wages, and state benefits and pensions, as these and other types of payments are often uprated using the index.

The 'basket' is composed of more than 600 goods and services for which price movements are regularly measured in about 180 towns around the country, giving rise to around150 thousand separate price quotations. The 'basket' is regularly reviewed to ensure that it reflects current spending patterns. Thus, in the first half of the 20th century, the 'basket' contained articles such as candles and rubber roller table mangles, both of which disappeared from the mid-1950s. These items have been replaced with such commodities as light bulbs and washing machines. The price of candles had been monitored in one form or another since the 1500s and the price of pork, has been monitored in some form since the 1200s.

The 12 monthly change in the RPI peaked at 26.9 per cent in August 1975; it then fell sharply but rose again to secondary peaks of 17.7 per cent in June 1977 and 21.9 per cent in May 1980. It then steadied at around the 5 per cent mark in the mid-1980s. It began to rise towards the end of the 1980s and then fell during the early part of the 1990s to reach a low of 1.2 per cent in June 1993, its lowest level since February 1964. It then rose slightly and remained at around two and a half per cent throughout most of 1994.

Table 6.10 shows the changing prices for certain important goods and services included in the 'basket' of goods. The average annual percentage change in the RPI fell from 5.9 per cent in 1991 to 1.6 per cent in 1993. Within the

6.11

Purchasing power of the pound[1]: EC comparison, 1993

Indices (UK=100)

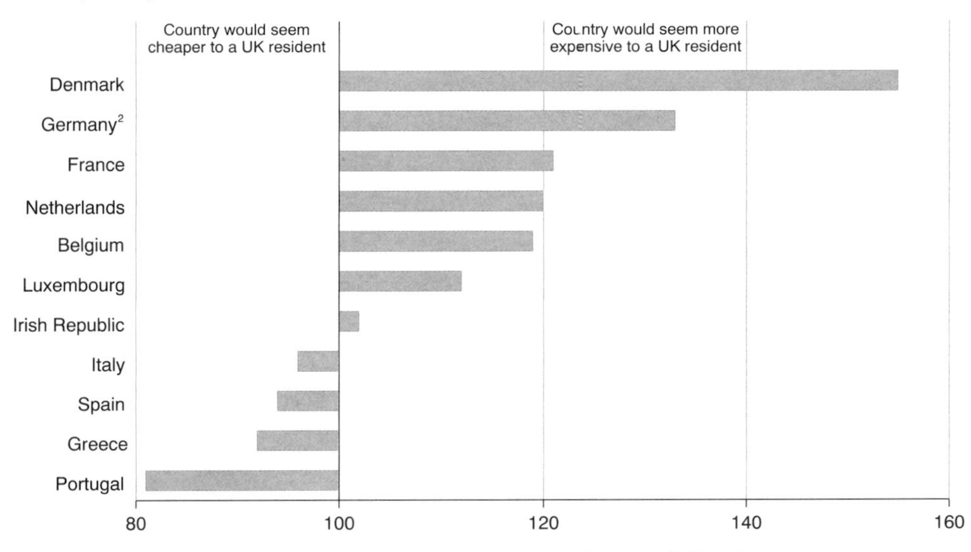

1 Price level indices for private consumption - the ratio of purchasing power parities to the official exchange rates.
2 As constituted since 3 October 1990.

Source: OECD

6.12

Length of time necessary to work to pay for selected commodities and services[1]

Great Britain								Hours and minutes
	Married couple with husband only working[2]				Single female parent with child			
	1971		1994		1971		1994	
	Hrs	Mins	Hrs	Mins	Hrs	Mins	Hrs	Mins
1lb back bacon (home produced)		32		19		47		22
1lb pork sausages		19		10		29		12
250g of butter (Danish)		14		7		20		8
1lb old potatoes, loose, white		2		2		3		3
Oranges, per lb		8		2		12		2
1lb of cod fillets		25		23		37		27
Chicken, per lb		20		8		30		10
1 pint of beer (draught bitter)		14		12		20		15
20 cigarettes (king size filter)		22		21		33		25
Ford Escort	2,193	43	1,787	56	3,258	31	2,118	44
Colour television licence	19	21	12	21	28	45	14	39
Return rail ticket from London to Edinburgh (2nd/Standard class)[3]	20	48	8	38	30	54	10	14
Copy of Social Trends	5	15	3	57	7	47	4	41

1 Length of time necessary for a person on average hourly adult earnings for all industries and services to work so that his/her net income pays for the various goods. The earnings figures are based on full-time employees on adult rates whose pay was not affected for the survey period by absence.
2 Married man with non-earning wife and two children under 11.
3 Standard return in 1971; Supersaver in1994.

Source: Central Statistical Office

overall index for 1993, prices rose for all the categories illustrated with the exception of housing costs which fell by 5.4 per cent and fuel and light, which fell by 1.3 per cent. Of those items which showed a rise, and in keeping with the pattern of recent years, the largest increase was in tobacco, which rose by 8.5 per cent.

The RPI is designed to be representative of typical household spending and for this reason, households with very high incomes (the top 4 per cent) and pensioner households (ie those households mainly dependent on state pensions and benefits) are excluded. Special indices for the latter category have been calculated, although for technical reasons they exclude housing costs. These are shown at the bottom of the table. In 1993 the price indices for both one and two person households increased at a slower rate than the general RPI excluding housing costs.

Chart 6.11 shows how the purchasing power of the pound fared in the European Community in 1993. The purchasing power parity between the United Kingdom and another country is the amount of that country's currency needed to buy the equivalent of goods and services costing one pound in the United Kingdom - in other words, to give the consumer the same purchasing power in that country as in the United Kingdom. If this is greater than the official exchange rate, that country would seem more expensive to a UK resident, while if it is smaller, it would seem cheaper. In 1981 only Germany and Denmark would have seemed more expensive to a UK resident. In 1992 only Greece and Portugal would have seemed cheaper but one year later, in 1993, these two countries were joined by Spain and Italy. Of those countries which seemed more expensive in 1992, all except the Irish Republic were even more so in 1993.

Over time, both prices and wages change and together they affect people's ability to buy certain goods and services. Table 6.12 compares how long it would have taken to earn the money to purchase certain goods and services in 1971 and 1994 for both a married man with a non-earning wife and two children under 11 and a single woman with a child. The table is based on net income for both groups. The gap between the two narrowed in the years between 1971 and 1994. The length of time it took to earn enough to pay for all the items shown in the table fell between 1971 and 1994 for both the married man and the single woman.

There is also a greater income parity between the groups. For example, in 1971 a single woman would have had to have worked a quarter of an hour longer than a married man to buy a pound of bacon. In 1994, this was only three minutes longer. If they wished to purchase a copy of Social Trends, although the price has risen by around nine times, neither would have had to work as long to buy a copy. A married man now has to work just under four hours (five and a quarter in 1971) and a single woman just over four and a half hours (nearly eight in 1971).

An obvious consequence of rising prices is that the amount of goods and services that can be purchased with a given sum of money, the purchasing power, decreases. Chart 6.13 shows how the value of a 1971 pound has fallen. By 1976, its value had nearly halved; in 1980 it was worth less than a third of its value in 1971. Steady inflation levels in the mid-1980s (see Chart 6.1) saw a steadying of its value at around the 20 pence mark, but by 1993 it was a seventh of its 1971 value at 14 pence.

The cost of various forms of communications is illustrated in Chart 6.14. However, care should be taken when making comparisons between post and telephone as there are certain other factors which need to be taken into account, such as telephone line rentals, special offers, discounts or options. Since 1971, the price of a first class stamp has risen by more than eight times from three pence to 25 pence. Over the same period, a second class stamp has risen over 7 times from two and a half pence to 19 pence. To give this some perspective, the average wage of a married man has risen by around ten and a half times. The biggest increase in stamp charges was in April 1975 for both classes; compared with April 1974, the price of a first class stamp doubled to 7 pence while a second class stamp increased by slightly less to 5.5 pence. In 1971, local daytime calls averaging 3 minutes would have cost just over a penny. By 1994 this had risen nearly ten times to stand at just under 12 pence. However, an average three minute 'b' rate cheap time call rose only four times over the same period from five and a half pence to just over 21 pence.

6.13

Purchasing power of a 1971 pound

United Kingdom

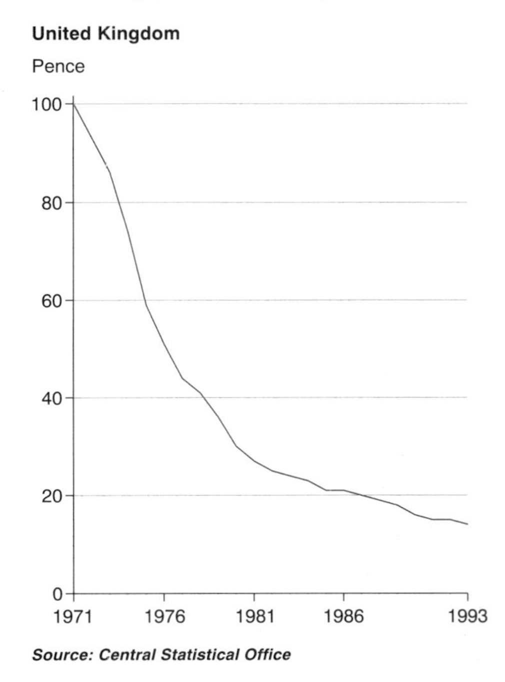

Source: Central Statistical Office

6.14

Cost of communicating by telephone[1] and post[2]

United Kingdom

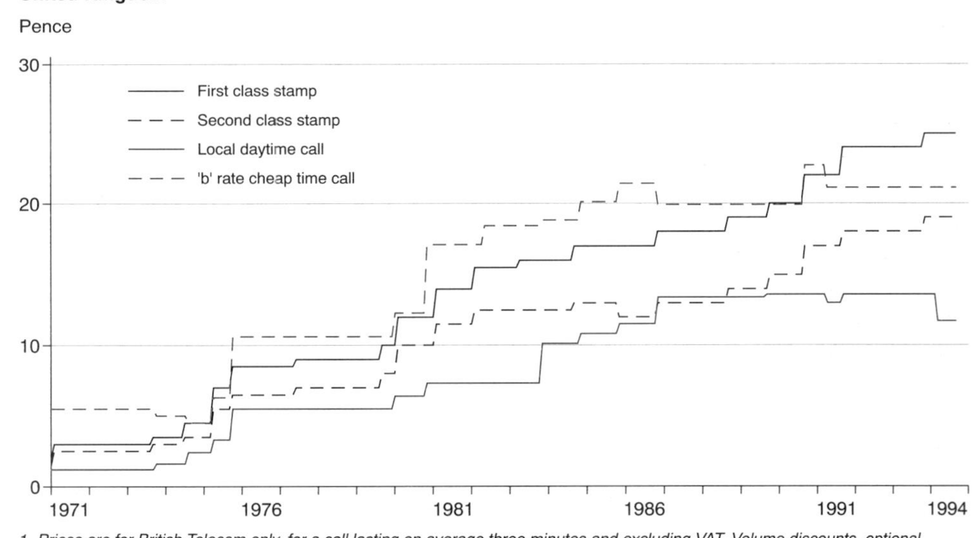

1 Prices are for British Telecom only, for a call lasting on average three minutes and excluding VAT. Volume discounts, optional packages and fixed costs (eg exchange line rentals) are excluded.

2 Four ounce letters in 1971 and two ounce (60 gram) letters in subsequent years.

Source: OFTEL; Post Office

6.15

Composition of consumer credit

United Kingdom					Percentages
	1981	1986	1991	1992	1993
Bank credit card lending	*12*	*17*	*18*	*19*	*20*
Bank loans[1]	*65*	*62*	*63*	*63*	*59*
Finance houses[2]	*9*	*12*	*10*	*10*	*12*
Insurance companies	*2*	*3*	*2*	*3*	*3*
Retailers	*12*	*6*	*5*	*5*	*5*
Building Society loans[3]	..	..	*1*	*1*	*2*
Credit outstanding at end of year (= 100%)(£ billion)	15.5	30.2	53.6	52.6	52.3

1 Banks and all other institutions authorised to take deposits under the Banking Act 1987.
2 Finance houses and other credit companies (excluding institutions authorised to take deposits under the Banking Act 1987)
3 Building Society unsecured loans to individuals or companies (i.e. Class 3 loans as defined in the Building Societies Act 1986).
Source: Central Statistical Office

6.16

Net lending to consumers[1]

United Kingdom

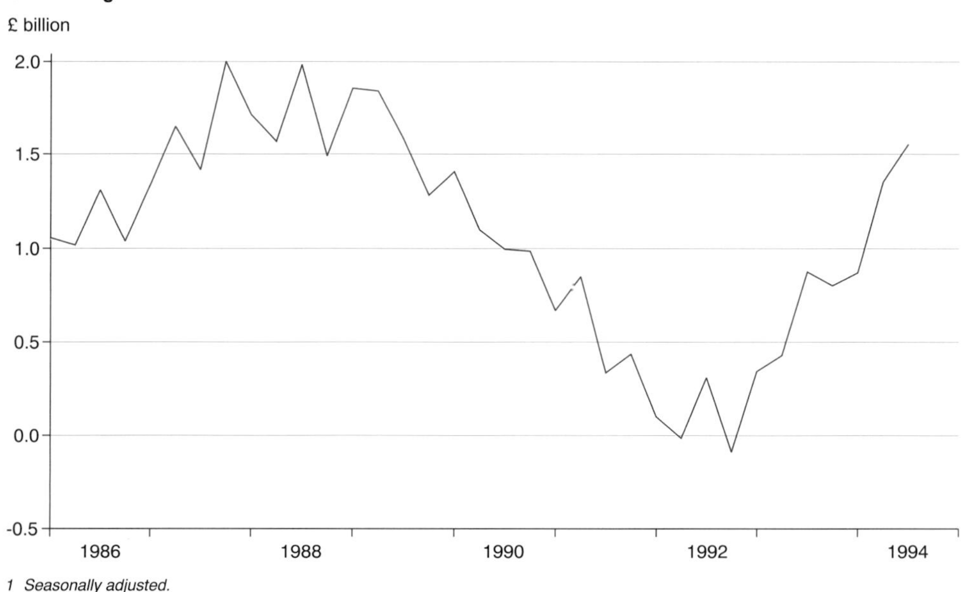

1 Seasonally adjusted.
Source: Central Statistical Office

Consumer credit and household saving

Bank loans, although still the largest source of consumer credit, continued to decline in importance to form 59 per cent of total consumer credit in 1993 (Table 6.15). Apart from bank loans, all other sources shown in the table increased their shares, with bank credit card lending continuing to rise from nearly 12 per cent of consumer credit in 1981 to 20 per cent in 1993. The amount of total credit outstanding at the end of 1993 was slightly lower than at the end of the previous year, continuing the recent downward trend from the peak of nearly 54 billion in 1991.

The amount of net lending to consumers illustrates the recent path of consumer credit. This peaked in the third quarter of 1988 at nearly £2 billion, and then fell sharply to a small net repayment in the second quarter of 1992 (Chart 6.16). Since then, net lending has been increasing to just over £1.5 billion in the third quarter of 1994 - back to nearly 80 per cent of its peak figure.

Figures from the payment industry suggest that sixteen pence in every pound spent by customers is by plastic payment card. Plastic card holding continues to grow; over three quarters of adults in Great Britain held at least one card in 1993 (Table 6.17). The largest increase has been in the possesion of debit cards: over half of adults held a debit card in 1993 compared with only 30 per cent in 1989. Cashpoint debit card holding also saw a similar rise to reach 62 per cent in 1993, the largest category of all the card types.

Chart 6.18 shows that from 1986 to 1990, household saving as a percentage of household disposable income was negative, that is, expenditure exceeded disposable income (sometimes called dissaving). From 1991, the figure became positive reaching nearly 5 per cent in 1992 but falling to just under four and a half per cent in 1993. Since household savings are measured as the difference between two much larger figures (disposable income and current expenditure), the estimates are subject to a wide margin of error. No independent estimates exist for total household saving.

Public expenditure

So far, this chapter has concentrated on individual or household spending. This final section looks at government spending. Like individuals, government spends money on goods, services and interest payments but it also makes transfer payments, such as social security benefits, grants and loans. The measure which includes all these payments is known as general government expenditure (GGE) and is used for analysing overall trends in public spending. Growth in GGE can be compared to growth in the economy as a whole by expressing it as a percentage of gross domestic product (GDP) - this is known as the GGE ratio.

6.17

Plastic cards[1]

Great Britain — Percentages

	1986	1989	1990	1991	1992	1993
ATM debit card	..	43	43	56	60	62
Debit card	..	30	40	45	51	52
Credit/charge card	33	37	39	39	38	38
Visa credit card	..	..	26	28	28	28
Mastercard	..	..	19	19	17	18
Retailer card	9	13	15	17	16	17
Any plastic card[2]	..	67	68	73	75	76

1 Percentage of persons aged 16 and over holding plastic cards.
2 Includes cheque guarantee cards.
Source: Association for Payment Clearing Services

6.18

Household saving[1] as a percentage of household disposable income

United Kingdom

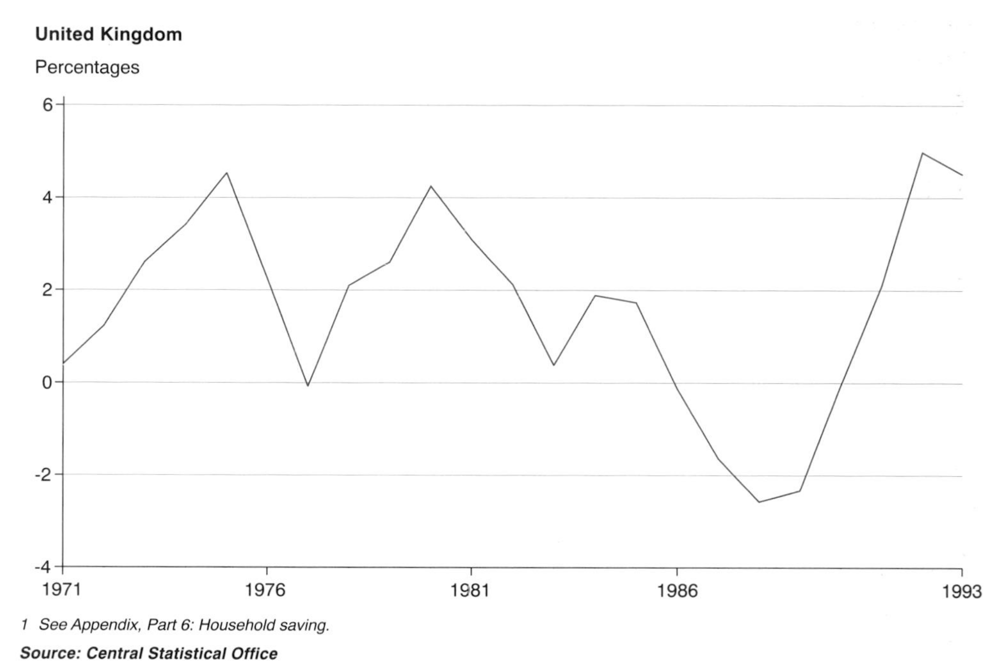

1 See Appendix, Part 6: Household saving.
Source: Central Statistical Office

6.19

General government expenditure as a percentage of GDP[1]

United Kingdom

Percentages

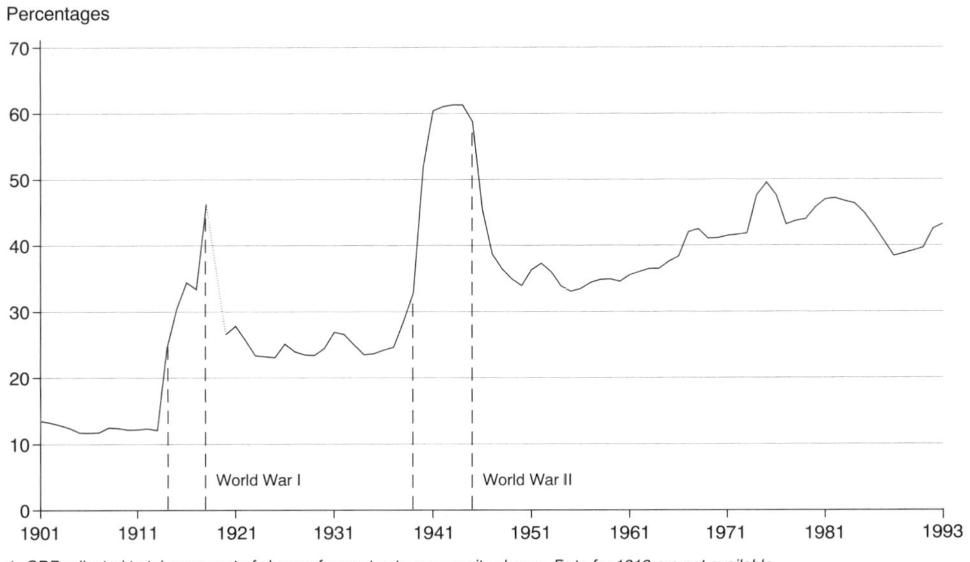

1 GDP adjusted to take account of change from rates to community charge. Data for 1919 are not available.

Source: Central Statistical Office

Two of the peaks in this ratio coincided with the two world wars (Chart 6.19); in 1918 GGE reached just over 46 per cent of GDP and in 1943 it reached just over 61 per cent - the highest percentage ever recorded. The GGE ratio fell back after each war but never to its pre-war levels. More recently, during the recession of the early 1980s, the ratio increased to 47 per cent in 1982 (largely due to social security and employment measures), while the boom of the late 1980s saw a fall to just over 38 per cent in 1988. As the recession of the early 1990s took hold, the ratio began to creep back up, reaching around 43 per cent in 1993.

Government expenditure is broken down by function in Table 6.20. In 1993, total government expenditure was £272.8 billion, a 7 per cent rise (£18.6 billion) on the previous year.

By far the biggest category of government expenditure remained social security, accounting for more than a third of total government expenditure. Health remained second although its proportion fell slightly on the previous year. Defence expenditure continued to fall to stand at around 9 per cent in 1993. Fuel and energy expenditure became a positive figure for the first time since 1986 at 0.3 per cent. It had been a negative figure since 1986 because the National Accounts treats privatisation proceeds as an offset to the relevant function and in the case of fuel and energy this gave rise to negative figures.

6.20

General government expenditure[1]: by function

United Kingdom — Percentages

	1981	1986	1991	1992	1993
Defence[1]	10.8	11.7	10.2	9.6	8.9
Public order and safety	3.7	4.2	5.7	5.4	5.5
Education	12.2	11.9	12.9	12.6	12.4
Health	11.4	11.8	13.6	13.7	13.5
Social security	26.6	30.8	32.3	33.3	34.2
Housing and community amenities	6.1	5.0	3.8	4.0	4.0
Recreational and cultural affairs	1.3	1.5	1.7	1.5	1.4
Fuel and energy	0.3	-0.7	-1.3	-0.2	0.3
Agriculture, forestry and fishing	1.4	1.3	1.2	1.2	1.4
Mining, mineral resources, manufacturing and construction	3.0	1.2	0.7	0.5	0.6
Transport and communication	3.6	2.3	2.9	2.5	2.5
General public services	3.9	3.9	5.0	5.0	4.6
Other economic affairs and services	2.5	2.5	1.9	1.8	1.8
Other expenditure	13.1	12.7	9.4	9.1	8.8
Total expenditure (=100%)(£ billion)	117.1	162.3	228.4	254.2	272.8

1 Includes contributions by other countries towards the United Kingdom's cost of the Gulf conflict - £2.1 billion in 1991.

Source: Central Statistical Office

Table 6.21 shows the amount the member states contributed to, and received from, the European Community budget in 1993. The United Kingdom, together with Germany and in recent years, France, has been a consistent net contributor to the EC budget (Italy and the Netherlands are also now becoming regular net contributors).

The United Kingdom is a net contributor because its share of agricultural support expenditure is low due to the relative size of its agricultural sector. Also, because we are a relatively prosperous member state, we do not receive a high share of structural funds receipts, which are primarily aimed at the poorer regions of the Community. The main beneficiaries of budget expenditure are the poorest member states, namely, Greece, Spain, Ireland and Portugal.

The United Kingdom's gross contribution is, though, significantly reduced by the abatement of its gross contributions, given in recognition of the lower level of United Kingdom receipts in the agricultural sector. The underlying level of the abatement is currently around £2 billion a year. The total of abatement made since the Fontainebleau agreement in 1984 will be about £16 billion by the end of 1994.

The changing priorities of the Community have led to support for agriculture falling from over three fifths of the total budget in 1983 to just over half in 1993. At the same time, structural actions expenditure has increased from under 15 per cent of the budget to about 25 per cent.

6.21

Contributions to, and receipts from, the European Community budget[1], 1993

£ billion

	Contributions	Receipts[2]
Germany[3]	14.9	5.6
France	9.0	8.2
Italy	8.0	6.8
United Kingdom	5.9	3.5
Spain	4.0	6.5
Netherlands	3.1	2.1
Belgium	1.9	1.9
Denmark	0.9	1.2
Greece	0.8	4.0
Portugal	0.7	2.6
Ireland	0.5	2.3
Luxembourg	0.2	0.3

1 From the Court of Auditors Report, 1993.
2 Excludes £4.9 billion which is mainly development aid and administrative expenditure for the other institutions. Community payments are to both the public and private sectors in member states.
3 As constituted since 3 October 1990.

Source: HM Treasury

References and further reading

The following list contains selected publications relevant to **Chapter 6: Expenditure**. Those published by HMSO are available form the addresses shown on the inside back cover of *Social Trends*.

British Tourism Survey, Monthly, British Tourist Authority

Business Monitor MM23 (Retail Prices Index), HMSO

Business Monitor SDM28 (Retail Sales), HMSO

Credit Business First Release, CSO

Economic Trends, HMSO

Employment Gazette, HMSO

Family Spending - A Report on the 1993 Family Expenditure Survey, HMSO

Financial Statistics, HMSO

Financial Statement and Budget Report, HMSO

General Household Survey, HMSO

Households Below Average Income: A Statistical Analysis 1979-1991/92, HMSO

International Passenger Survey, HMSO

Local Government Financial Statistics England, HMSO

Regional Trends, HMSO

Retail Prices 1914-1990, HMSO

Scottish Economic Bulletin, HMSO

The Government's Expenditure Plans, HMSO

United Kingdom National Accounts (The CSO Blue Book), HMSO

Welsh Economic Trends, HMSO

Contacts

Telephone contact points for further information relating to **Chapter 6: Expenditure.**

Central Statistical Office	
Consumer credit	0171 217 4814
Consumers' expenditure	0171 270 6207
General government expenditure	0171 270 6168
Household expenditure	0171 217 4206
Household saving	0171 217 4203
Retail prices	0171 217 4310
Retail sales	01633 812987
Department of Finance and Personnel, Northern Ireland	01232 521154
Employment Department	01928 794903/4
Her Majesty's Treasury	0171 270 4425
Inland Revenue	0171 438 7370
Office of Population Censuses and Surveys	0171 396 2327
Office of Telecommunications	0171 634 8937
Post Office Archives	0171 239 2572
Association for Payment Clearing Services	0171 711 6323

Chapter 7 Health

The nation's health

The average life span is increasing by an average of two years every decade. According to projected mortality rates for 1996 a boy born in that year can expect to live until he is 74, while a girl can expect to live until she is nearly 80. (Table 7.2)

Just over half of men and just over two fifths of women were overweight or obese in 1991-1992. (Chart 7.6)

Prevention

More than 1.6 million women in the United Kingdom were invited for breast screening in 1992-93: seven in ten of these attended. (Page 125)

Diet

We ate 4.5 ounces of breakfast cereal per person per week in 1993; three quarters more than we did in 1971. (Chart 7.18)

Social habits and health

In 1992, men in the unskilled manual group were three times more likely to smoke than those in the professional group. (Table 7.21)

In 1992, nearly two in five men aged 18 to 24 drank more than the recommended maximum sensible amount (21 units per week) of alcohol, compared with only one in six aged 65 and over. (Chart 7.24)

Causes of death

The death rates from lung cancer among males fell by almost a half between 1971 and 1992, while the rate for females increased by a sixth. (Chart 7.27)

Suicide is three times more common amongst men than women. (Chart 7.30)

7.1

Infant mortality

United Kingdom

Rate per 1,000 live births

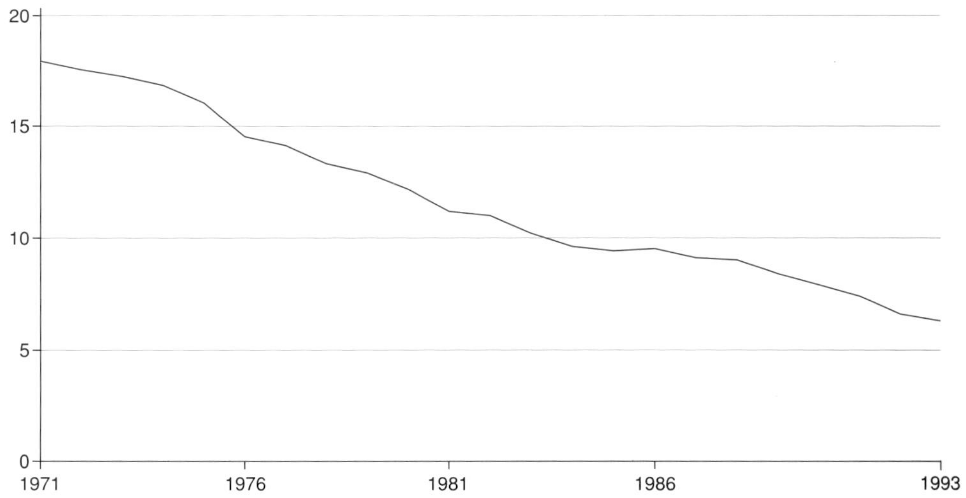

Source: Office of Population Censuses and Surveys; General Register Office (Scotland); General Register Office (Northern Ireland)

This chapter looks at various indicators of the nation's health, including some of the risk factors associated with premature death such as raised blood pressure levels and smoking. It also covers immunisation and screening measures designed to prevent disease or enable its early detection, as well as including information on diet and nutrition. The final section in the chapter looks at selected causes of death. Information on provision of health services is given in Chapter 8: Social protection.

The nation's health

All four countries in the United Kingdom have produced health strategies designed to address the major causes of premature death and preventable illness. The specific priorities and targets vary between the different countries, although they all include circulatory diseases, accidents, and certain cancers with their associated risk factors, such as smoking. While progress is being made towards meeting most of the targets, three continue to cause concern: cigarette smoking in young people; suicide in young men; and obesity. All these topics, together with others where improvements have been evident, are covered in this chapter.

The number of years which we can expect to live is a good overall indicator of the health of the nation. Death rates are continuing to fall at nearly all ages, at a rate which means that the average life span is increasing by about two years every decade. This rapid rate of increase in longevity is projected by the Government Actuary to decline gradually after 1996, but by the year 2021 the expectation of life is projected to be nearly four years greater than at present. According to the projected mortality rates for 1996 the expectation of life will be over 74 for males and nearly 80 for females compared with less than 58 and 62 respectively based on the mortality experience of 1931 (Table 7.2).

In order to be able to monitor trends in the nation's health the Department of Health commissioned the Health Survey for England. The first survey was carried out in 1991 and since then has been repeated every year. Similar surveys have been carried out in Wales, Scotland and Northern Ireland. In 1992 Northern Ireland carried out its Health and Activity Survey which set out to study the determinants of physical activity in relation to health and, like the England survey, gave particular emphasis to coronary heart disease and associated risk factors - one of the five key areas in the health of the nation strategies. In Wales a number of surveys have been carried out by Health

7.2

Expectation of life[1]: by gender and age

United Kingdom Years

	1901	1931	1961	1991	1992	1996	2001	2021
Males								
At birth	45.5	57.7	67.8	73.2	73.6	74.4	75.4	77.6
At age								
1 year	54.6	62.4	69.5	73.8	74.1	74.8	75.7	77.9
10 years	60.4	65.2	69.9	73.9	74.3	75.0	75.9	78.0
20 years	61.7	66.3	70.3	74.2	74.5	75.3	76.1	78.2
40 years	66.1	69.3	71.4	75.1	75.4	76.3	77.2	79.3
60 years	73.3	74.3	74.9	77.7	77.9	78.6	79.5	81.4
80 years	84.9	84.7	85.2	86.4	86.5	86.8	87.2	88.2
Females								
At birth	49.0	61.6	73.6	78.7	79.0	79.7	80.6	82.6
At age								
1 year	56.8	65.3	75.1	79.2	79.5	80.1	80.9	82.8
10 years	62.7	67.9	75.4	79.4	79.6	80.3	81.1	83.0
20 years	64.1	69.0	75.6	79.5	79.8	80.4	81.2	83.1
40 years	68.3	71.9	76.3	80.0	80.2	80.9	81.7	83.5
60 years	74.6	76.1	78.8	81.9	82.1	82.6	83.3	84.9
80 years	85.3	85.4	86.3	88.3	88.5	88.8	89.1	90.0

1 Total number of years which a person might expect to live. See Appendix, Part 7: Expectation of life.

Source: Government Actuary's Department

Promotion Wales in recent years. In 1995 the planned Welsh Health Survey will provide comprehensive prevalence, functioning and risk factor data for samples of the population with a range of medical conditions. However as it is not possible to aggregate the results from the various surveys the following four items contain combined data for 1991 and 1992 for England only.

Around a quarter of both men and women interviewed in the survey reported having at least one cardiovascular disease (CVD) disorder in their life. It is generally recognised that the main risk factors for CVD are raised blood pressure, raised cholesterol, smoking and lack of physical activity. Table 7.3 shows that the proportion of people who were either hypertensive (had high blood pressure) or were being treated for high blood pressure increases with age. Among men the proportion rises from 2 per cent of those aged 16 to 24 to nearly 60 per cent of those aged 75 and over. For women the proportion is negligible among the 16 to 24 year olds, but nearly two thirds of those age 75 and over either had, or were being treated, for high blood pressure. From the age of 55 upwards over a fifth of both men and women were classified as 'hypertensive untreated', ie they had high blood pressure but were receiving no treatment.

Obesity, severely elevated cholesterol levels and use of drugs that could affect blood pressure were also associated with raised blood pressure levels among both men and women. For men only, raised blood pressure was also associated with drinking more than the recommended level of alcohol. For example, men drinking over 21 units of alcohol per week were one and a quarter times as likely to have high blood pressure as would be expected from their age alone. However, those with very low alcohol consumption were also slightly more likely to

7.3

Blood pressure level[1]: by age and gender, 1991-1992

England Percentages

	16-24	25-34	35-44	45-54	55-64	65-74	75 and over	All aged 16 and over
Males								
Normotensive (untreated)	*98*	*97*	*91*	*84*	*62*	*52*	*42*	*81*
Normotensive (treated)	-	-	*2*	*3*	*9*	*11*	*7*	*4*
Hypertensive (treated)	*0*	*0*	*1*	*1*	*8*	*11*	*12*	*3*
Hypertensive (untreated)	*2*	*3*	*7*	*12*	*21*	*27*	*38*	*12*
All males	*100*	*100*	*100*	*100*	*100*	*100*	*100*	*100*
Females								
Normotensive (untreated)	*100*	*98*	*95*	*88*	*63*	*48*	*35*	*81*
Normotensive (treated)	-	-	*1*	*3*	*9*	*12*	*11*	*4*
Hypertensive (treated)	*0*	-	-	*2*	*8*	*13*	*18*	*4*
Hypertensive (untreated)	-	*2*	*3*	*8*	*20*	*26*	*36*	*11*
All females	*100*	*100*	*100*	*100*	*100*	*100*	*100*	*100*

1 See Appendix, Part 7: Blood pressure level.

Source: Office of Population Censuses and Surveys

7.4

Mean cholesterol levels[1]: by gender and age, 1991-1992

England		mmol/l
	Males	Females
18-24	4.80	4.87
25-34	5.40	5.14
35-44	5.82	5.43
45-54	6.15	6.05
55-64	6.16	6.71
65-74	6.17	7.13
75 and over	5.84	6.65
All aged 18 and over	5.78	5.93

1 Mean serum total cholesterol, for informants not currently taking lipid lowering drugs. See Appendix, Part 7: Serum total cholesterol.

Source: Office of Population Censuses and Surveys

have high blood pressure than would be expected from their age alone. Men had, on average, higher blood pressure levels than women. Men who were married or cohabiting were less likely to have high blood pressure than other men, after allowing for age differences.

Cholesterol level is used to monitor health partly because it can be modified by changes in lifestyle. The survey found that over two thirds of adults had cholesterol values above the desired level (over 5.2 mmol/l). The mean serum total cholesterol level in 1991-1992 was 5.78 mmol/l for men and 5.93 mmol/l for women (Table 7.4).

Cholesterol levels generally increase with age, up to the age of 74. Women between the ages of 25 and 54 had lower levels than men, whereas among those aged 55 and over, women had higher levels than men.

It has been recognised for some time that physical activity and exercise have an important and strong connection with health. In particular it is now widely accepted that moderate levels of physical activity can help to prevent CVD. There is also evidence that low levels of physical activity are associated with other risk factors for heart disease such as high blood pressure and obesity. Guidelines accepted in the United Kingdom suggest that moderate or vigorous exercise should be taken on at least three occasions a week and each occasion should last at least 20 minutes. Physical activity does not just relate to sport and exercise; the Health Survey also asked people about occupational activity, walking and home activities such as housework and gardening.

Around a fifth of all adults in England had taken no moderate or vigorous exercise for as long as 20 minutes (level 0) in the four weeks prior to interview (Table 7.5). Information from the Northern Ireland Health and Activity Survey suggests that people in Northern Ireland are more active: less than one in ten only attained level 0. In England (as in Northern Ireland) a slightly higher proportion of men than women (48 per cent compared with 42 per cent) had undertaken frequent activity of at least moderate intensity in the previous four weeks (ie were of level 3 or above). As might be expected, activity was strongly associated with age. Among men, for example, the proportion who had done frequent physical activity of which some was of vigorous intensity (level 4 or above), decreased from nearly one in

7.5

Physical activity level[1]: by gender and age, 1991-1992

England								Percentages
	16-24	25-34	35-44	45-54	55-64	65-74	75 and over	All aged 16 and over
Males								
Level 0	*7*	*10*	*12*	*16*	*24*	*33*	*51*	*19*
Level 1	*12*	*14*	*18*	*17*	*20*	*19*	*21*	*17*
Level 2	*14*	*15*	*19*	*18*	*13*	*20*	*12*	*16*
Level 3	*20*	*27*	*28*	*36*	*37*	*26*	*16*	*28*
Level 4	*22*	*17*	*13*	*8*	*5*	*1*	*0*	*11*
Level 5	*24*	*16*	*10*	*4*	*1*	*1*	*0*	*9*
All males	*100*	*100*	*100*	*100*	*100*	*100*	*100*	*100*
Females								
Level 0	*10*	*10*	*8*	*15*	*20*	*41*	*60*	*20*
Level 1	*18*	*16*	*18*	*15*	*18*	*18*	*19*	*17*
Level 2	*22*	*24*	*23*	*18*	*21*	*18*	*11*	*21*
Level 3	*24*	*28*	*34*	*41*	*35*	*21*	*10*	*29*
Level 4	*18*	*14*	*12*	*8*	*5*	*1*	*0*	*9*
Level 5	*8*	*7*	*4*	*2*	*1*	*1*	*0*	*3*
All females	*100*	*100*	*100*	*100*	*100*	*100*	*100*	*100*

1 See Appendix, Part 7: Physical activity level.

Source: Office of Population Censuses and Surveys

two of those aged 16 to 24, to one in four of those aged 35 to 44 and to one in twenty of those aged 55 to 64.

At the lower end of the activity scale, the proportion of men and women who had done no activity, even of moderate intensity, in the last four weeks (level 0) increased with age, particularly above the age of 55. Among both men and women aged 16 to 24 less than one in ten had had no physical activity compared with over half of those aged 75 and over. Information on participation in various sporting and physical activities is shown in Table 13.19 in the Leisure chapter.

There is a considerable amount of epidemiological evidence that obesity is related to ill health and results in increased risks of a number of diseases including hypertension and CVD. The most widely used measure of obesity is body mass index (BMI) which is calculated as weight (kg)/ height(m)^2. However it should be noted that the index tends to give an inflated measure of fatness for individuals with muscular physiques who are relatively heavy although lean.

Just over a half of men and just under a half of women aged 16 to 64 in England had a BMI of more than 25 and so would be classed as overweight or obese (Chart 7.6). Although a greater proportion of men than women are in these categories, women are more likely than men to be classed as obese: 15 per cent of women compared with 13 per cent of men had a BMI of more than 30. BMI also tends to increase with age. Among both men and women the proportions who were obese rose consistently between the ages of 16 to 64, peaking in the 55 to 64 age group for men and for women. The 1991 survey found that the average height was 1.75m among men and 1.62m among women aged 16 to 64, while average weight was 78kg and 66kg respectively; this resulted in average BMIs of 25.5 for men and 25.2 for women in 1991.

7.6

Body mass[1]: by gender, 1991-1992

England

Percentages

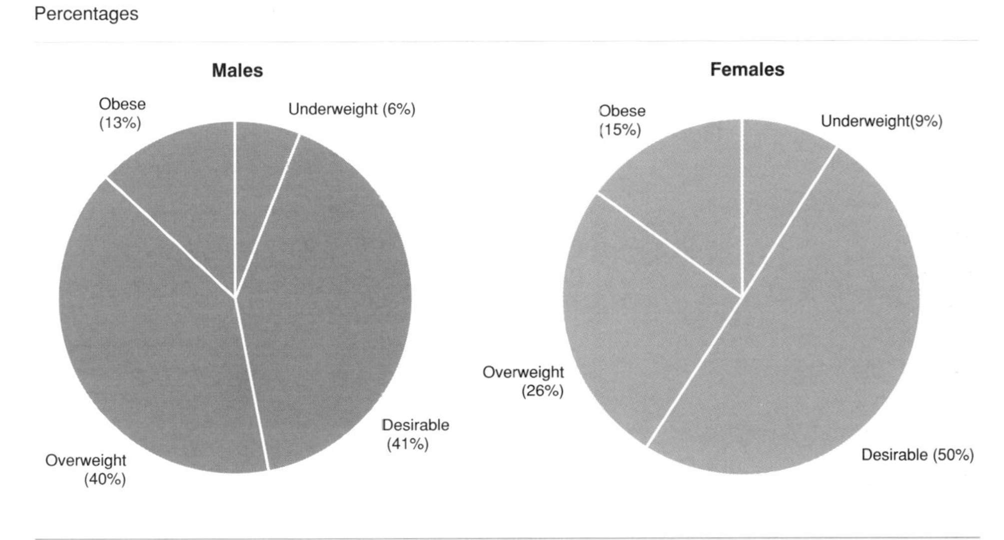

1 Body mass index of persons aged 16 to 64. See Appendix, Part 7: Body mass index.

Source: Office of Population Censuses and Surveys

There are links between BMI and several social factors. For example women who lived in households headed by a manual worker were more likely to be obese than women who lived in households headed by a non-manual worker; men and women who were ex-regular cigarette smokers had the highest BMI (information on smoking habits is given later in the chapter); men who were heavy drinkers had a higher average BMI than men who were non-drinkers while, conversely, women who were heavy drinkers had a lower average BMI than women who were non-drinkers and those with low alcohol consumption levels; married or cohabiting men had a higher BMI than other men.

7.7

Notifications of selected infectious diseases

United Kingdom

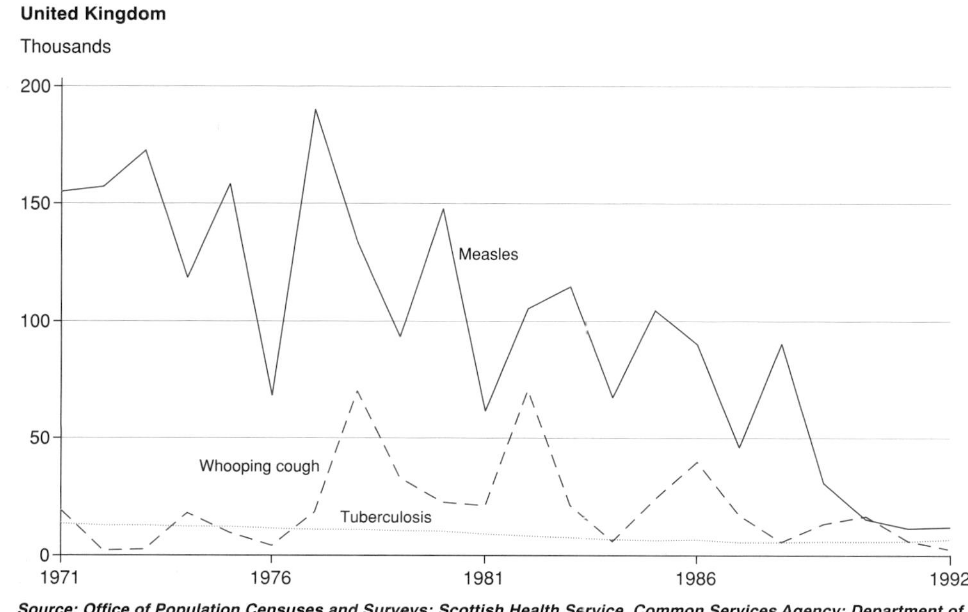

Source: Office of Population Censuses and Surveys; Scottish Health Service, Common Services Agency; Department of Health and Social Services, Northern Ireland

The number of reports of meningitis due to haemophilus influenzae type b fell dramatically in 1993: by 63 per cent among all age groups and by 85 per cent among the under 1s who are particularly susceptible. This was due to the introduction of the vaccine into the childhood immunisation programme in October 1992.

The Human Immunodeficiency Virus (HIV) is the virus which causes AIDS (Acquired Immune Deficiency Syndrome). However there can be a long period between infection with the virus and the onset of AIDS. It is estimated that ten years after infection about 50 per cent of people will have developed AIDS. In 1993 it is estimated that 2.1 thousand new AIDS cases will have been diagnosed in England and Wales (Chart 7.8). Sex between men still predominates as the main exposure category. However, sex between men and women accounted for nearly one in five of these cases in 1993 compared with only around one in nine in 1990.

The long incubation period of HIV means that these AIDS figures reflect patterns of transmission several years ago. A more accurate picture of current transmission is given by the annonymised HIV surveys. Data to the end of June 1993 indicate that in the ante-natal clinics being surveyed in London, prevalence among attenders has risen from 1 in 500 in 1990 to 1 in 380 in the first six months of 1993, while prevalence outside London has remained at over 1 in 9 thousand over the same period. Comparison of these results with the number of births to HIV infected women reported indicates that the majority of infections in pregnant women

7.8

AIDS - new cases per year[1]: by exposure category

England & Wales

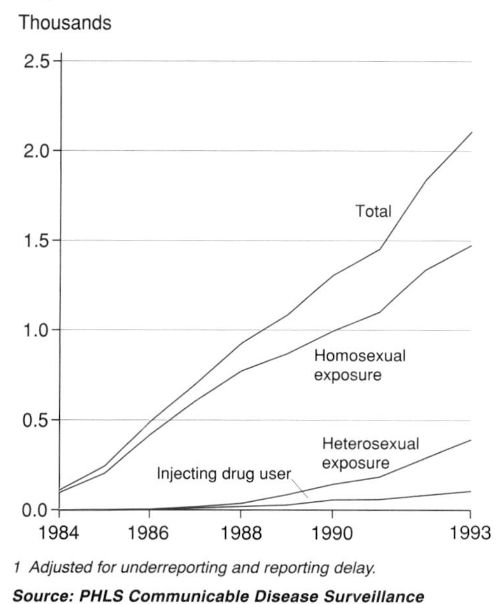

1 Adjusted for underreporting and reporting delay.

Source: PHLS Communicable Disease Surveillance Centre

Despite improvements in immunisation, antibiotics and hygiene, infectious diseases still occur and spread. Some diseases occur in epidemics which is reflected in the large year to year fluctuations seen in Chart 7.7. Before 1970, measles epidemics occurred about every two years. However with the introduction of immunisation against measles in 1968, the pattern became less regular and there was a general decrease in the total number of cases. Large scale immunisation during the measles epidemic of 1988, and the introduction of the combined measles, mumps and rubella vaccine from October 1988, reduced the number of cases in the United Kingdom still further to around 12 thousand in both 1991 and 1992. Further information on vaccination and immunisation is given in Table 7.15.

had not been diagnosed. In 1992 the Department of Health issued guidance to health authorities encouraging ante-natal clinics in higher risk areas to offer HIV testing to pregnant women. This was reissued with minor revisions in June 1994. By September 1994 a cumulative total of 9.9 thousand AIDS cases had been reported and 6.7 thousand deaths from AIDS were known to have occurred in the United Kingdom; females accounted for only 8 per cent of cases and 7 per cent of deaths.

In 1993 there were 1.6 thousand AIDS cases reported in the United Kingdom, a rate of 2.8 per 100 thousand population. Chart 7.9 compares the number of AIDS cases reported in 1993 in the various countries of the European Community (EC), expressed as a rate per 100 thousand population. Spain had the highest rate at 14.1 with France the second highest, at 9.9. The United Kingdom had one of the lowest rates in the EC; only Greece, the Irish Republic and Belgium had lower rates.

The General Household Survey collects information on people's own assessment of their health. Chart 7.10 compares the percentage of people who reported chronic sickness (ie a long standing illness, disability or infirmity) in 1974 and 1993. Since this measure of sickness is based on people's subjective assessments of their health, changes over time may reflect changes in people's expectations of their health as well as in the prevalence or duration of sickness. Nevertheless it can be argued that perceptions can have a direct relationship with the demand for health services.

7.9

New AIDS cases-total reported : EC comparison, 1993

Rate per 100,000 population

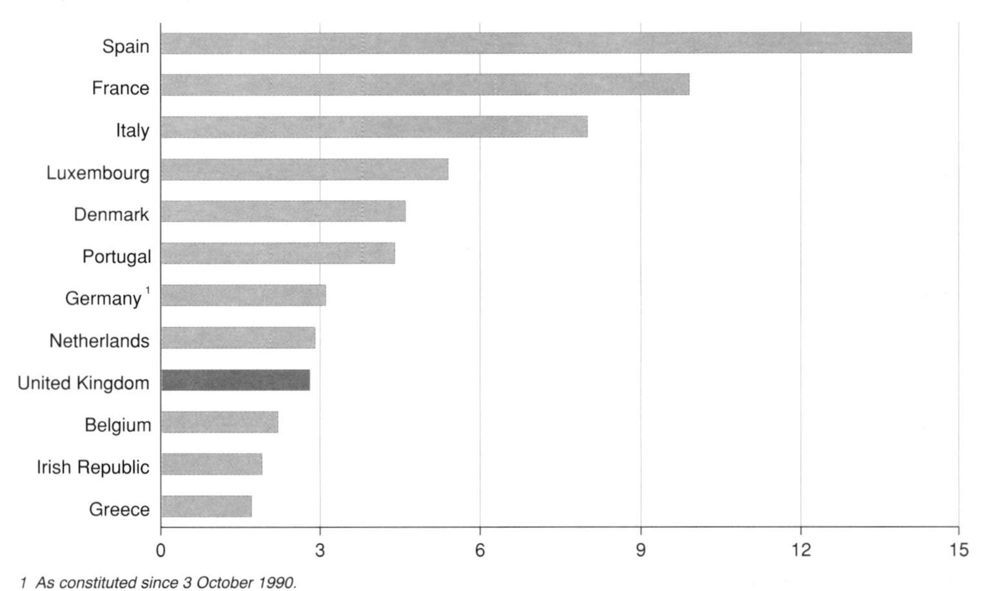

1 As constituted since 3 October 1990.

Source: Department of Health

7.10

Chronic sickness[1]: by age, 1974 and 1993

Great Britain

Percentages

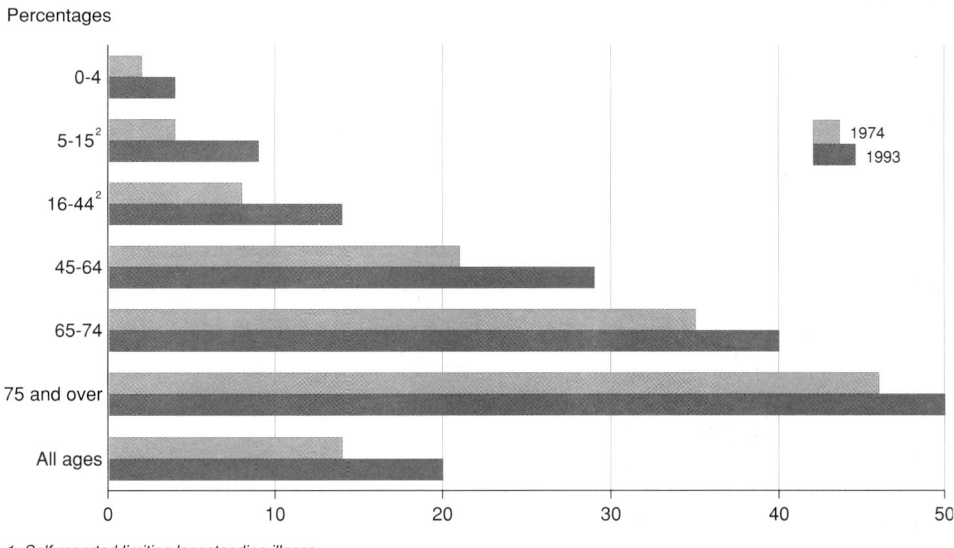

1 Self-reported limiting longstanding illness.
2 Aged 5 to 14 and 15 to 44 in 1974.

Source: Office of Population Censuses and Surveys

7.11

Difficulty with hearing: by gender and age, 1992

Great Britain			Percentages
	Wears an aid	Hearing difficulty, no aid	No hearing difficulty
Males			
16-44	-	*6*	*94*
45-64	*3*	*17*	*80*
65-74	*11*	*25*	*64*
75 and over	*20*	*25*	*55*
All aged 16 and over	*4*	*13*	*83*
Females			
16-44	-	*4*	*96*
45-64	*2*	*9*	*90*
65-74	*6*	*15*	*79*
75 and over	*17*	*24*	*59*
All aged 16 and over	*3*	*9*	*88*

Source: Office of Population Censuses and Surveys

In 1993 a higher proportion of both men and women, in all age groups, reported chronic sickness than did in 1974. The general trend has seen an increase in reporting of chronic sickness throughout the 1980s. However, towards the end of the decade the increase slowed and then a slight fall occurred between 1990 and 1991, before increasing again.

Not surprisingly, having a hearing difficulty is a condition which is strongly associated with age: around two in five of those aged 75 and over in Great Britain had difficulty with their hearing in 1992, compared with only 1 in 20 of those aged 16 to 44 (Table 7.11). Between 1979 and 1992 there was a small, but significant, rise in the proportion of people wearing hearing aids, from 2 per cent to 3 per cent. This can be largely attributed to a sharp rise among those aged 75 and over: 20 per cent of men in this age group were wearing a hearing aid in 1992 compared with only 12 per cent in 1979; for women there was a corresponding rise from 12 per cent to 17 per cent. Around four in five people who wore a hearing aid in 1992 had obtained their hearing aid from the National Health Service (NHS).

Between 1 September 1991 and 31 August 1992, 60 general practices in England and Wales took part in the fourth of a series of studies of GPs and their patients (MSGP4). Details of face-to-face contact with patients were recorded including the reason for the consultation. Table 7.12 shows some of the results from this study expressed as the number who consulted at least once during the year per 10,000 population. Both males and females were more likely to go to the doctor for respiratory problems than any other reason. Among those diseases confined to females, rates of 30 per 10,000 were reported for breast cancer and 3 per 10,000 for cervical cancer while for diseases confined to males a rate of 11 per 10,000 was reported for prostate cancer. Over the past decade there has been a striking increase in hospital admissions and GP consultations for asthma. This now affects over 2 million people in England, including some half a million below the age of 16, and causes over 1.6 thousand deaths annually. Further information on use of the health services is given in Chapter 8: Social protection.

Another way of finding out what sort of illnesses people suffer from is to look at the reasons why people stay in NHS hospitals. In 1992-93, of the 4.2 million main diagnoses of male in-patient cases in the United Kingdom, 13 per cent had digestive system complaints and a similar proportion had

7.12

Patients consulting GPs: by gender and selected disease or condition[1], 1991-92

England & Wales			Rates per 10,000 people at risk
	Males	Females	All persons
Dermatitis and eczema	636	879	760
Asthma	429	422	425
Hypertension	357	479	419
Neurotic disorders	202	481	344
Ischaemic heart disease	204	137	170
Normal pregnancy	.	287	147
Migraine	58	169	115
Diabetes	119	102	111
Obesity	38	125	82
Cerebrovascular disease	64	68	66
Acute reaction to stress	18	35	26
Drug dependence	19	19	19
Breast cancer	.	30	15
Alcohol dependence	20	6	13
Lung cancer	9	5	7
Malignant melanoma of the skin	2	3	2
All diseases and conditions	6,999	8,575	7,803

1 See Appendix, Part 7: Diseases and conditions - ICD codes.

Source: Office of Population Censuses and Surveys

circulatory system problems (Table 7.13). There were 4.5 million female diagnoses (excluding those associated with pregnancy); of these, diseases of the genito-urinary system accounted for 13 per cent of cases.

Marked changes in the incidence of, and mortality from, cancer have occurred since the beginning of this century. Currently about one person in three in England and Wales develops a cancer sometime in their life, and cancer now causes about one in four deaths. The latest figures for cancer registrations relate to 1989. Although trends must be interpreted with caution, registrations of all malignant neoplasms (with the exception of non-melanoma skin cancer where under-recording is suspected) showed increases of over 20 per cent between 1979 and 1988.

Malignant melanoma of the skin is a comparatively rare, but serious, form of skin cancer. There are three major reasons for the current concern over what may be largely a preventable cancer: the incidence, and mortality, rates have increased significantly over recent years; it has an impact on young adults as well as older people; and survival rates could be markedly improved if all patients were treated at an early stage. The disease, although generally rare, is more common in fair skinned populations of European origin living in sunny parts of the world such as Australia. The risk factors for the disease include having fair hair and skin, blue eyes and a tendency to burn but not tan after exposure to the sun; a person may also be at higher risk if their skin has a tendency to freckle. It is almost certain that intermittent (recreational) exposure to the sun is also an important risk factor.

7.13

Hospital in-patient cases: by gender and main diagnosis, 1992-93

United Kingdom — Percentages

	Males	Females
Infectious and parasitic diseases	*2*	*1*
Neoplasms	*11*	*11*
Endocrine, nutritional, metabolic and immunity	*2*	*2*
Blood	*1*	*2*
Mental disorders	*4*	*4*
Nervous system and sense organs	*6*	*7*
Circulatory system	*13*	*11*
Respiratory system	*9*	*7*
Digestive system	*13*	*12*
Genito-urinary system	*7*	*13*
Skin	*2*	*2*
Musculo-skeletal and connective tissue	*6*	*7*
Congenital anomalies	*2*	*1*
Perinatal conditions	*3*	*2*
Signs and symptoms	*9*	*10*
Injury and poisoning	*10*	*8*
All diagnoses (excluding pregnancy)(thousands)(=100%)	4,207	4,502
Complications of pregnancy (thousands)	.	1,145
Other reasons for contact with health services (thousands)	455	556
All in-patient cases (thousands)	4,662	6,203

Source: Department of Health; Welsh Office; Scottish Health Service, Common Services Agency; Department of Health and Social Services, Northern Ireland

7.14

For many years there has been a strong and consistent upward trend in the incidence of malignant melanoma of the skin in England and Wales (Chart 7.14). Over the period 1979 to 1986 the rate of increase was about 6 per cent per year but since then it has accelerated. This is one of the few cancers which is more prevalent in females than males. It is very rare in childhood but around 20 per cent of cases in 1988 occurred in young adults (aged 20 to 39) whereas under 4 per cent of all malignant neoplasms occurred in this age group.

Malignant melanoma of the skin: by gender

England & Wales

1 See Appendix, Part 7: Standardised registration ratios.

Source: Office of Population Censuses and Surveys

7.15

Immunisation of children[1]

United Kingdom Percentages

	1971[2]	1976	1981	1986	1991-92[3]	1992-93[3]
Diphtheria	*80*	*73*	*82*	*85*	*94*	*95*
Whooping cough	*78*	*39*	*46*	*66*	*88*	*91*
Poliomyelitis	*80*	*73*	*82*	*85*	*94*	*95*
Tetanus	*80*	*73*	*82*	*85*	*94*	*95*
Measles, mumps, rubella[4]	*46*	*45*	*54*	*71*	*91*	*92*

1 Children born two years earlier and immunised by the end of the specified year.
2 England & Wales only.
3 Scotland figures are for 1992 and 1993.
4 Includes measles only vaccine. Combined vaccine was not available prior to 1988.

Source: Department of Health; Welsh Office; Scottish Health Service, Common Services Agency; Department of Health and Social Services, Northern Ireland

7.16

Percentage of target population[1] screened for cervical cancer in the previous 5½ years[2]: by region

Percentages

	1989-90	1990-91	1991-92	1992-93
Northern	*64*	*79*	*83*	*86*
Yorkshire	*65*	*81*	*85*	*87*
Trent	*73*	*83*	*87*	*89*
East Anglia	*68*	*83*	*86*	*87*
North West Thames	*42*	*58*	*65*	*70*
North East Thames	*34*	*50*	*64*	*72*
South East Thames	..	*61*	*70*	*79*
South West Thames	*46*	*66*	*78*	*80*
Wessex	*75*	*86*	*88*	*89*
Oxford	*79*	*82*	*85*	*86*
South Western	*78*	*84*	*86*	*87*
West Midlands	*71*	*81*	*84*	*86*
Mersey	*72*	*79*	*82*	*84*
North Western	*61*	*79*	*84*	*86*
England	*62*	*74*	*80*	*83*
Wales	*62*	*73*	*85*	*86*
Northern Ireland[2]	*25*	*47*	*62*	*73*

1 Women aged 20 to 64.
2 Northern Ireland data refer to percentage screened in previous 5 years.

Source: Department of Health; Welsh Office; Department of Health and Social Services, Northern Ireland

Prevention

Around nine in ten children in the United Kingdom are now immunised by their second birthday against the major diseases shown in Table 7.15. The percentage of children immunised against whooping cough in 1992-93 was more than double the proportion in 1976, although this was low because of concerns about vaccine safety. In July 1994 plans were announced to offer protection against measles and rubella to all 5 to 15 year old children through an intensive immunisation programme beginning in November 1994; this is designed to prevent a predicted epidemic of measles in the next few years.

In addition, immunisation against Haemophilus influenzae type b was introduced into the childhood immunisation programme in October 1992. The launch of this immunisation programme was supported by an extensive publicity campaign aimed particularly at the parents of young children. The studies commissioned by the Health Education Authority to monitor the impact of the campaign found that, six months after the launch of the campaign, the existence of the vaccine was known by nearly three quarters of mothers of children under 36 months of age.

Cervical cancer is commonly preceded by a long pre-cancerous stage which can be treated. For women screened every five years the incidence of cancer can be reduced by over 80 per cent. In 1992-93, 83 per cent of women in the target population (ie those aged 20 to 64 less those with recall ceased) in England had undergone a test in the previous five and a half years (Table 7.16) This percentage had increased from just over 60 per cent three years previously.

In 1992-93 the highest screening rates, of nearly nine in ten of the target population, occurred in the Trent and Wessex Regional Health Authorities (RHAs); only the three Thames RHAs had rates below 80 per cent. Figures for Northern Ireland contained in the table are compiled on a slightly different basis: in 1992-93, 73 per cent of the target population had been screened in the previous 5 years, nearly three times the 1989-90 proportion.

Breast cancer remains one of the most significant diseases affecting women and is the cause of death of nearly 16 thousand women in the United Kingdom each year. In response to this the NHS has set up a breast screening programme which sends out invitations to women aged 50 to 64 for mammographic screening every three years; in addition mammography is available to women aged 65 and over three yearly on request. In 1992-93 more than 1.6 million women were invited for screening, a third of all women aged 50 to 64 in the United Kingdom. The uptake rate was 71 per cent, but varied around the country from 60 per cent in the North East Thames RHA to 79 per cent in the East Anglia RHA (Chart 7.17), reflecting the lower response to health promotion activities in urban areas than in rural areas.

Of the women screened in 1992-93, 54 in every thousand were recalled for further investigation and 7.8 per thousand had a biopsy; the cancer detection rate was 5.7 per thousand women screened. All three rates were lower than in the previous year. This is partly due to the maturity of the screening programme and partly to the fact that there is less breast cancer in the population being screened. Breast cancer rates increase with age. Women aged 53 to 64 have often been screened once by the programme and so the cancers which are present in this age group are only those which have become detectable since they were last screened.

Diet

There have been marked changes since the early 1970s in the type of food which we eat. We are slowly changing to a healthier diet. The consumption of breakfast cereals has increased dramatically: at 4.5 ounces per person per week we now eat nearly three quarters more than we did in 1971 (Chart 7.18). Conversely, on average, we now buy less than two eggs per person per week which is less than half the number in 1971. Packet sugar is another food of which our purchases have fallen almost continually throughout the period: in 1993 we purchased just over 5 ounces per person per week which is only a third of the amount purchased in 1971.

7.17

Breast cancer screening uptake rates: by region, 1992-93

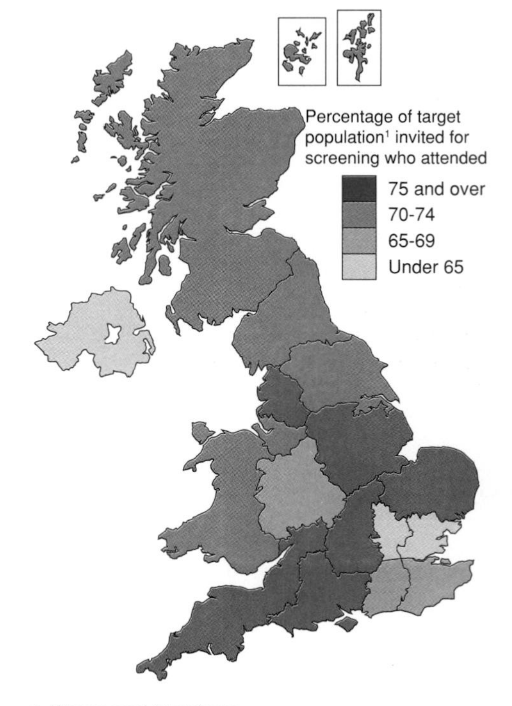

1 Women aged 50 and over.

Source: Department of Health

7.18

Changing patterns in the consumption of foods at home

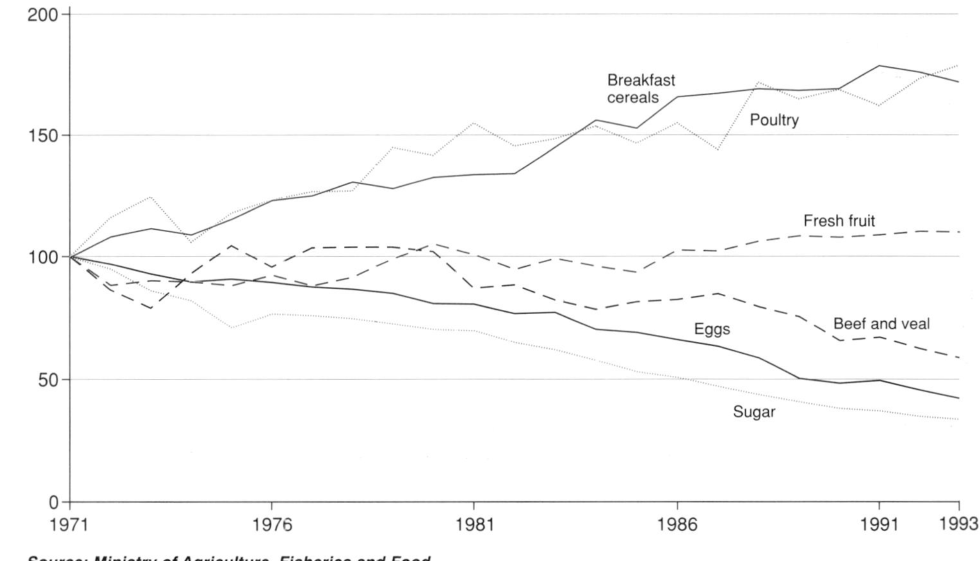

Source: Ministry of Agriculture, Fisheries and Food

7.19

Consumption of convenience foods at home

Great Britain

Ounces per person per week

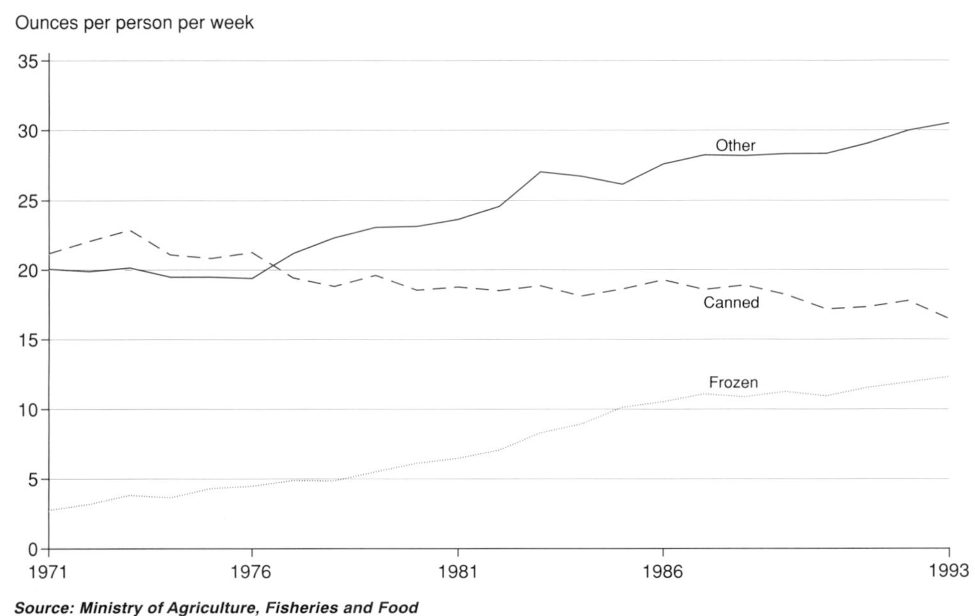

Source: Ministry of Agriculture, Fisheries and Food

7.20

Nutritional value of household food as a percentage of Reference Nutrient Intake[1], 1993

Great Britain

Percentages

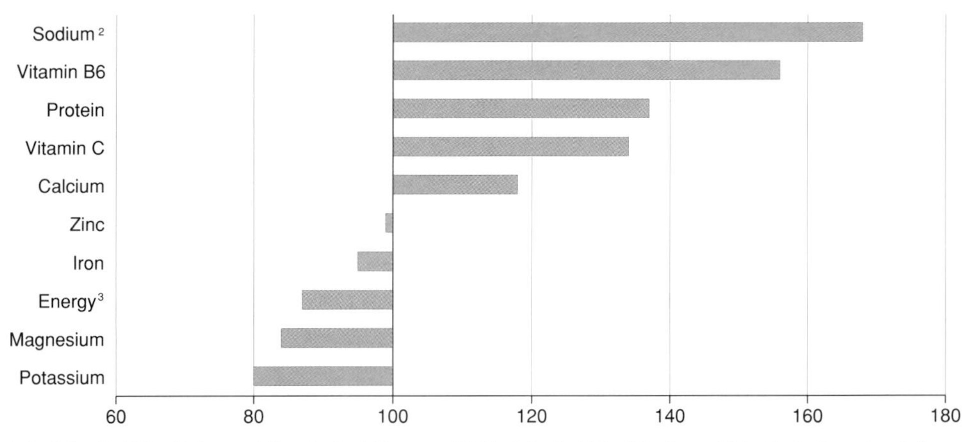

1 As defined in Dietary Reference Values for Food Energy and Nutrients for the United Kingdom published by the Department of Health in 1991. An allowance has been made for wastage and for meals not taken from the domestic food supply.
2 Excludes sodium from table salt.
3 As a percentage of Estimated Average Requirement.

Source: Ministry of Agriculture, Fisheries and Food

Although the amount of meat which we purchase for household consumption has fallen only slightly in the last twenty or so years there has been a marked switch from red to white meats. For example, in 1993 each person ate, on average, under 5 ounces of beef and veal per week, only about 60 per cent of the amount consumed in 1971. Conversely the consumption of poultry (including cooked poultry) has increased to over 8 ounces per week, nearly 80 per cent more than in 1971. We now eat slightly more fresh fruit than in 1971, at just under 22 ounces each a week. However, within this total, purchases of bananas continued to rise in 1993 while consumption of apples declined.

Convenience foods are an established part of the British diet with people increasingly buying more pre-cooked dishes instead of shopping for fresh ingredients. Total household consumption of convenience foods, including take away meals, rose by 10 per cent in the decade to 1993 and this growth does not yet seem to be slowing down. Purchases of canned foods are declining but this is more than offset by an increase in purchases of frozen and other convenience food (Chart 7.19). In the early 1970s canned convenience foods accounted for almost half of convenience food consumption, but this dropped to under a third in 1993.

Not surprisingly single adult households had the highest average expenditure on all types of convenience foods in 1993 at £5.32 per person per week, highlighting the benefits of convenience foods to those catering for one. However, many convenience foods are also popular with children and, the higher the number of children in the household, the higher the proportion of total expenditure spent on convenience foods.

The energy content of food brought into the home declined steadily from 1970 to 1990, but has stabilised since then; the average household diet (excluding soft and alcoholic drinks and confectionery) provided 1,830 kcals per person per day in 1993 compared with 2,600 in 1970. This fall is partly because less food is needed by an increasingly sedentary population and partly because food eaten outside the home, and confectionery and soft and alcoholic drinks are making an increasing contribution to total energy needs.

Chart 7.20 compares the nutritional value of food brought into the home with the Department of Health Dietary Reference Values, published in 1991. In this case an adjustment has been made for meals out, but additional energy and nutrients are obtained from confectionery, soft and alcoholic drinks and snacks. The inclusion of these items which are brought home raises the average daily intake in 1993 to 1,930 kcal, which is 92 per cent of the Estimated Average Requirement.

Social habits and health

Smoking is the greatest cause of preventable death in this country and can lead to diseases such as lung cancer, respiratory disease or heart disease. The Health Education Authority estimated that 110 thousand deaths in the United Kingdom in 1988 were attributable to smoking, representing about one in six deaths.

The prevalence of cigarette smoking among adults in Great Britain continued its downward trend in 1992 when 29 per cent of men and 28 per cent of women were smokers (Table 7.21) One of the Government's *Health of the Nation* targets is to reduce the prevalence of smoking among men and women to 20 per cent in England by the year 2000. If this is to be achieved the rate of decline among men and women needs to be slightly greater than it has been recently. Although the target is the same for men and women, 20 years ago men were much more likely than women to be smokers: in 1972, 52 per cent of men, compared with 41 per cent of women smoked cigarettes; this difference has now virtually disappeared.

7.21

Cigarette smoking[1]: by gender and socio-economic group

Great Britain — Percentages

	1972	1982	1992
Males			
Professional	*33*	*20*	*14*
Employers and managers	*44*	*29*	*23*
Intermediate and junior non-manual	*45*	*30*	*25*
Skilled manual	*57*	*42*	*34*
Semi-skilled manual	*57*	*47*	*39*
Unskilled manual	*64*	*49*	*42*
All aged 16 and over	*52*	*38*	*29*
Females			
Professional	*33*	*21*	*13*
Employers and managers	*38*	*29*	*21*
Intermediate and junior non-manual	*38*	*30*	*27*
Skilled manual	*47*	*39*	*31*
Semi-skilled manual	*42*	*36*	*35*
Unskilled manual	*42*	*41*	*35*
All aged 16 and over	*41*	*33*	*28*

1 Adults aged 16 and over except for 1972 which relates to those aged 15 and over.

Source: Office of Population Censuses and Surveys

7.22

Estimated cumulative proportion of pupils who will have tried smoking: by age and gender, 1992

England

Percentages

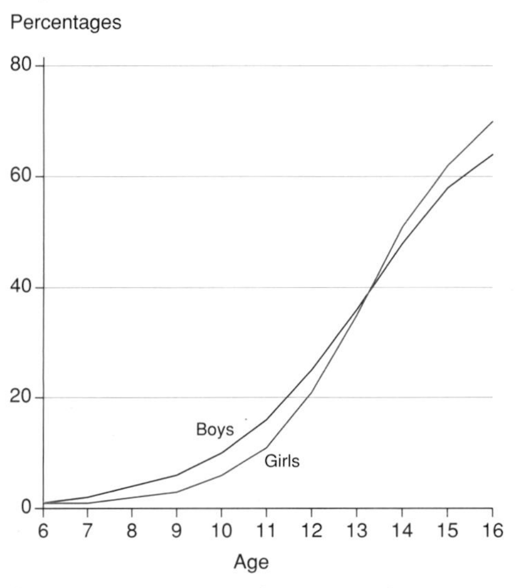

Source: Office of Population Censuses and Surveys

Although the proportion who smoke cigarettes has continued to decline in all social groups, the decline has been more marked in the non-manual than in the manual social groups, so differences between the groups have become even greater. In 1992, men in the unskilled manual group were three times more likely to smoke than those in the professional group. The difference for women showed a similar, although less marked, pattern. Women, however, smoked fewer cigarettes than men - 97 per week compared with 112 for men.

Health of the Nation targets have also been set to reduce smoking among children: the target for England is to reduce prevalence among 11 to 15 year olds by at least a third by 1994 (from about 8 per cent in 1988 to less than 6 per cent). Different targets exist in Wales and Scotland. In 1992 a survey on smoking and drinking among secondary schoolchildren was carried out by the Office of Population Censuses and Surveys on behalf of the health departments.

Chart 7.22 uses information obtained from this survey to show the cumulative proportion of children who have tried smoking by a given age in England. Boys tend to start experimenting with smoking earlier than girls, but by the age of 14 girls are more likely to have tried smoking than boys. By the age of 16, 70 per cent of girls have tried smoking compared with 64 per cent of boys.

The prevalence of cigarette smoking among secondary schoolchildren increases dramatically with age. Nearly a quarter of 15 year olds in England in 1992 were regular smokers, smoking at least once a week, while only 7 per cent of 13 year olds and 1 per cent of 11 year olds were regular smokers.

There is a clear link between children's smoking and that of their parents. In 1992 children in England whose parents both smoked were two and a half times more likely to be regular smokers than if neither parent smoked. There is also a link between children's smoking and drinking habits. Those who smoked regularly were almost ten times as likely as those who had never smoked to have drunk at least once a week.

7.23

When children last had an alcoholic drink: by gender and age, 1992

England — Percentages

	11	12	13	14	15	All aged 11 to 15
Boys						
During the last week	*8*	*13*	*15*	*32*	*49*	*24*
One to four weeks ago	*5*	*7*	*14*	*15*	*17*	*12*
One to six months ago	*4*	*10*	*17*	*18*	*14*	*13*
More than six months ago	*16*	*16*	*16*	*13*	*9*	*14*
Never	*68*	*54*	*39*	*21*	*12*	*37*
All boys	*100*	*100*	*100*	*100*	*100*	*100*
Girls						
During the last week	*5*	*7*	*11*	*25*	*40*	*17*
One to four weeks ago	*2*	*7*	*12*	*19*	*23*	*12*
One to six months ago	*6*	*10*	*16*	*23*	*17*	*14*
More than six months ago	*9*	*14*	*14*	*14*	*9*	*12*
Never	*78*	*62*	*48*	*18*	*12*	*44*
All girls	*100*	*100*	*100*	*100*	*100*	*100*

Source: Office of Population Censuses and Surveys

Just over a fifth of children aged between 11 and 15 years in England said that their last alcoholic drink had been during the week before they were interviewed: boys were more likely than girls to have had a drink in the last week - 24 per cent of boys had done so compared with only 17 per cent of girls (Table 7.23). Older pupils tended to have drunk more recently than younger pupils: only 6 per cent of 11 year olds, compared with 45 per cent of fifteen year olds, said that they had had a drink during the previous week.

Three quarters of children who had drunk alcohol in the week before interview had drunk beer, lager or cider - around 16 per cent of all pupils under 16. The other popular drink was wine - around one in ten of both boys and girls had drunk this in the previous week. The average amount drunk by all drinkers was six units - equivalent to three pints of beer or six glasses of wine.

Alcohol consumption above sensible levels is thought to be associated with increased likelihood of social problems and ill health. The recommended maximum sensible amounts for adults are 21 units per week for men and 14 units per week for women. The *Health of the Nation* targets include reducing the proportion of men aged 18 and over in England drinking more than 21 units a week from 28 per cent in 1990 to 18 per cent by 2005, and the proportion for women drinking more than 14 units a week from 11 per cent to 7 per cent over the same period. Similar targets apply in Wales and Scotland. In 1992, 27 per cent of men and 11 per cent of women aged 18 or over in Great Britain drank more than the sensible maximum amounts.

7.24

Consumption of alcohol above sensible[1] levels: by gender and age, 1992

Great Britain

Percentages

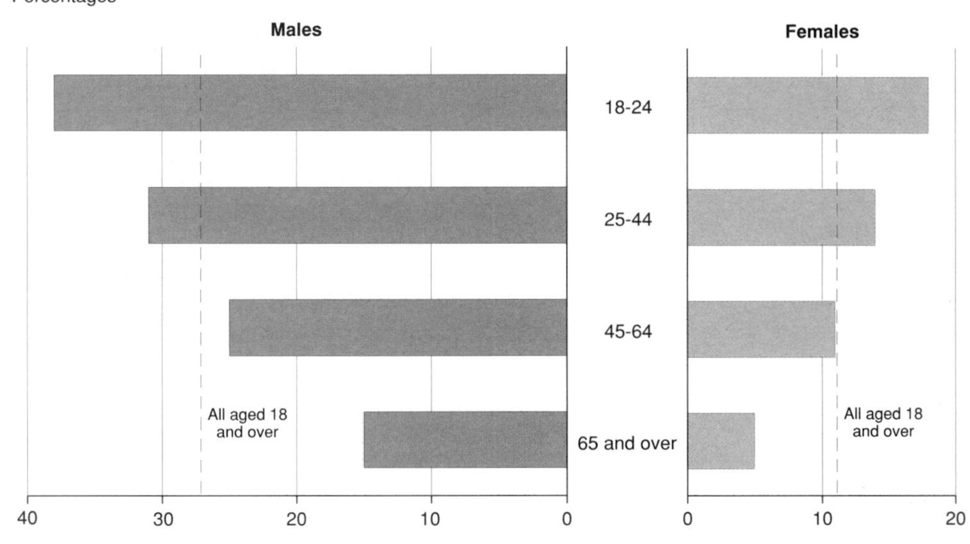

1 Maximum sensible levels are 21 units per week for men and 14 units per week for women

Source: Office of Population Censuses and Surveys

Younger people are more likely to be heavy drinkers than older people (Chart 7.24). In 1992, for example, nearly two in five men aged 18 to 24 drank more than the sensible maximum amount, compared with only one in six aged 65 and over. Among both men and women, the divorced or separated and those who had never married were the most likely to drink above the sensible maximum. However, it is thought that life cycle effects could exist here. Young single people drink more than others, possibly because they have fewer responsibilities and other calls on their time than married people, particularly those with young children. Consumption then tends to fall with marriage and the presence of young children in the household, but rises slightly when the children grow up. However there is a tendency for alcohol consumption to decline as people continue to get older, whatever their marital status.

7.25

New drug users[1]: by gender and age, 1992-93[2]

Great Britain

Thousands

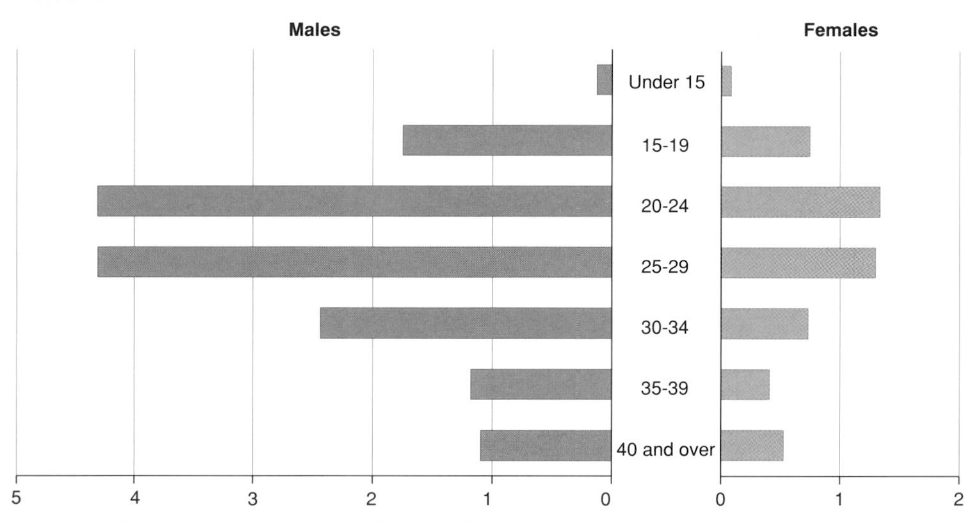

1 People with drug problems presenting to the services for the first time, or after an absence of six months or more.
2 1 October 1992 to 31 March 1993.

Source: Department of Health

7.26

People ever attending a sexually transmitted diseases clinic: by gender and number of lifetime partners, 1990-1991

Great Britain		Percentages
	Males	Females
Heterosexual partners		
0	*9*	*1*
1	*2*	*1*
2	*3*	*2*
3 to 4	*4*	*6*
5 to 9	*8*	*12*
10 or more	*20*	*27*
Homosexual partners		
0	*7*	*5*
1	*20*	*28*
2	*15*	*17*
3 to 9	*36*	*30*
10 or more	*67*	..
All persons	*8*	*6*

Source: Social & Community Planning Research

Chart 7.25 shows that during the six month period ending 31 March 1993, over 20 thousand people with drug problems went to drug services in Great Britain for the first time, or after an absence of six months or more. Three quarters of them were male and over half of both males and females were in their twenties. The main drug misused by each of them was also recorded: heroin was the most common, misused by 45 per cent, followed by methadone (15 per cent) and amphetamines (11 per cent). About two in five of users reported that they were injecting their main drug. The chart probably reflects only a small proportion of those people using drugs since not many will have gone to the drug services and so will not be recorded in the figures.

Between May 1990 and November 1991 Social and Community Planning Research carried out The National Survey of Sexual Attitudes and Lifestyles. The survey found that the likelihood of attending a sexually transmitted diseases (STD) clinic increases markedly with the number of heterosexual partners (Table 7.26). Over one in five of those who reported ten or more partners in their lifetime had ever attended an STD clinic. Among men reporting ten or more homosexual partners, around two thirds had attended at least once.

Care should be taken when interpreting the figures in this table as STD clinic attendance may be under-reported in the survey, although they are much in line with the figures reported by clinics. In addition, the proportion of men who reported STD clinic attendance but had never had a heterosexual partner is largely accounted for by those with homosexual partners.

There is substantial regional variation in the frequency of STD clinic attendance: around 7 per cent of both men and women in Greater London reported attending in the last five years compared with around 1 per cent in the North of England. The proportion attending also varied markedly by marital status. Only around 1 per cent of married women and men reported attending in the last five years; there was substantially higher attendance in all other marital status categories, with the exception of widowed women. This is probably due to a greater number of sexual partners among those who are not married.

Causes of death

There have been dramatic reductions in the levels of infant mortality since the beginning of this century. Chart 7.1, at the beginning of this chapter, shows that more recently, as very low levels of infant mortality have been reached, absolute improvements have been less pronounced although the rate is still falling in percentage terms. In 1993 there were 6.3 deaths per thousand live births, which is nearly a third less than the rate five years ago.

Some infant deaths occur without warning where the child appears otherwise perfectly healthy. The death rate for these so-called cot deaths, or more correctly Sudden Infant Death Syndrome, halved between 1991 and 1992, to 0.6 per thousand live births; this is about a third of the rate five years previously.

Age standardised death rates from breast cancer in England and Wales peaked in 1981 at 28.0 per 100,000 women under the age of 65 and fell to 25.2 per 100,000 in 1992 (Chart 7.27). The *Health of the Nation* target is to reduce deaths from breast cancer among all women by a quarter by the year 2000, from 95.1 per 100,000 women in 1990 to no more than 71.3 per 100,000. Information on the breast screening programme which is designed to help to bring about this drop in the mortality rate is shown in Chart 7.17.

Lung cancer is one of the most preventable carcinomas; at least 80 per cent of cases are due to tobacco smoke, inhaled either passively or actively. In 1992 the age standardised rates for lung cancer deaths in women under 65 were around half those for men under 65. However, these male death rates from lung cancer nearly halved between 1971 and 1992, while female rates actually increased by 16 per cent over the same period. Death rates, among both males and females, from stroke also halved over the same period.

Despite the fall in the death rate from heart disease it accounted for about a quarter of deaths in the United Kingdom in 1992. The highest death rates for heart disease occur in the northern parts of England, Scotland and Northern Ireland, while the lowest rates can be found in the East Anglia (Chart 7.28). Heart disease is both the largest single cause of death and the single main cause of premature death. The main risk factors for heart disease are cigarette smoking, raised cholesterol levels, raised blood pressure and lack of physical activity; these topics are covered earlier in this chapter. All the main risk factors can be influenced by changes in behaviour. For those who smoke, stopping smoking is the single most effective means of reducing risk of heart disease.

7.27

Death rates[1] for people aged under 65: by gender and selected cause of death

England & Wales

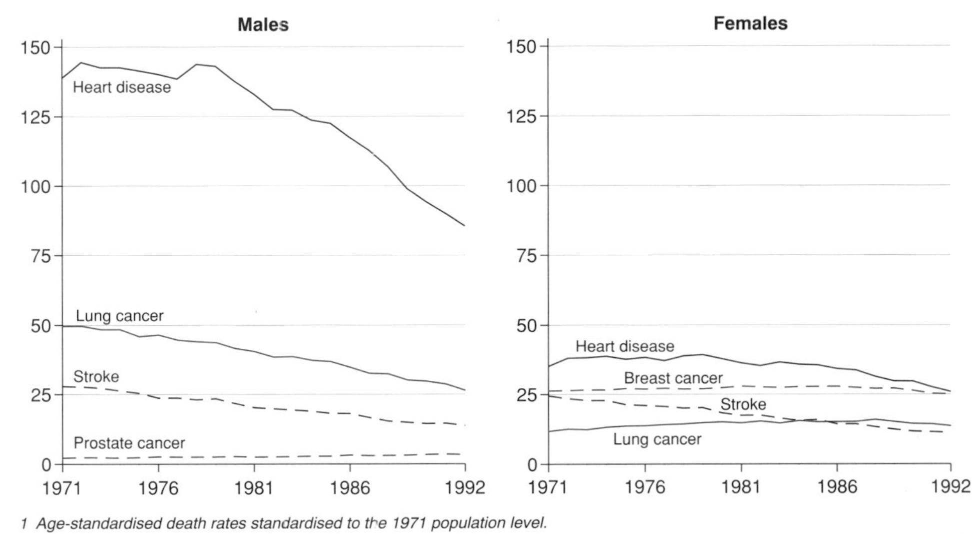

1 Age-standardised death rates standardised to the 1971 population level.

Source: Office of Population Censuses and Surveys

7.28

Death rates[1] from heart disease for people aged under 65: by area, 1992

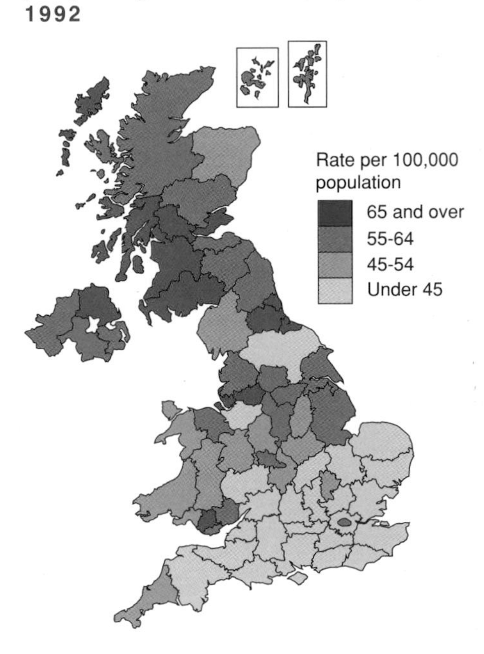

1 Adjusted for the age structure of the population. See Appendix, Part 7: Standardised death rates.

Source: Office of Population Censuses and Surveys; General Register Office (Scotland); General Register Office (Northern Ireland)

7.29

Death rates[1] from breast cancer; EC comparison, 1991

Rate per 100,000 females

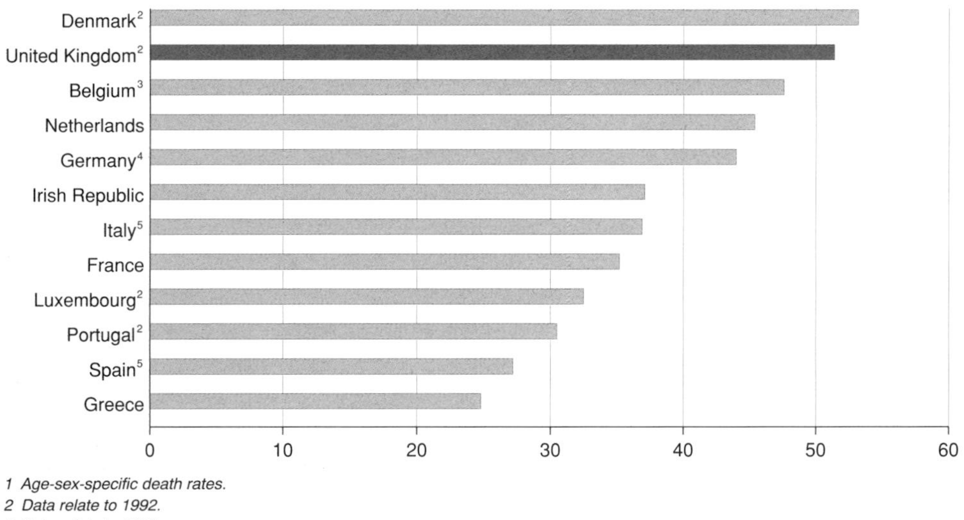

1 Age-sex-specific death rates.
2 Data relate to 1992.
3 Data relate to 1989.
4 As constituted since 3 October 1990.
5 Data relate to 1990.

Source: World Health Organisation

Although the death rate from breast cancer in the United Kingdom has dropped in recent years we have the second highest rate in the EC, after Denmark (Chart 7.29). The death rate in the United Kingdom is around twice that in the southern European countries of Spain and Greece.

The suicide rate among men is much higher than that for women in all age groups: suicide is three times as common in men as in women. Since the early 1970s suicide rates among men have generally been rising, while rates for women have continued to fall (Chart 7.30). However, among men aged 65 and over the suicide rate has been falling, while the rates for men aged between 25 and 44 have risen to such an extent that they now exceed the rates for those aged 45 to 64.

Changes in suicide rates are related to a complex set of social, economic and other changes. The Office of Population Censuses and Surveys has carried out research which suggests that, particularly for young men, the increasing numbers of men remaining single or becoming divorced may explain up to half of the increase in suicides observed since the 1970s. Of course this age group of men have also been affected by other factors which may increase the risk of suicide: such as high unemployment rates, exposure to armed combat, increasing risk of imprisonment, an increase in misuse of alcohol and other drugs, and the HIV virus.

7.30

Death rates from suicide: by gender and age

England & Wales

Rates per 100,000 population

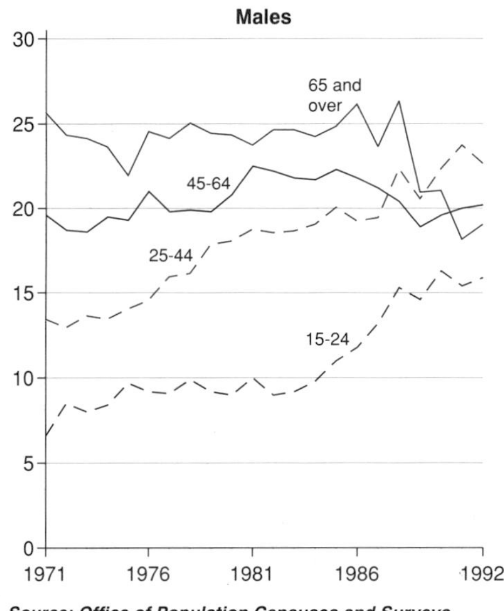

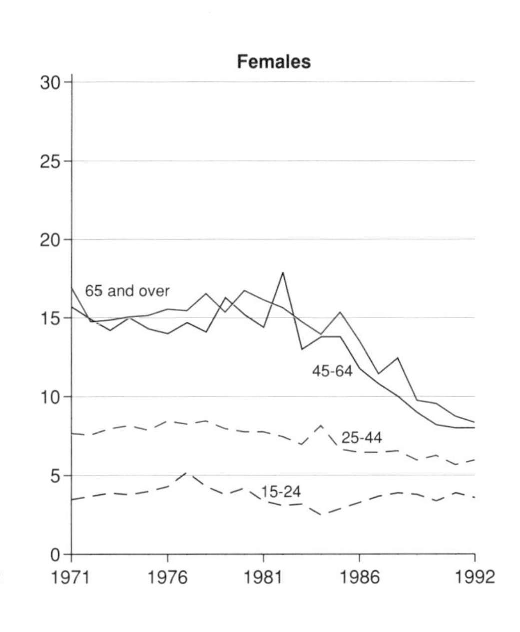

Source: Office of Population Censuses and Surveys

7.31

Accidents are the most common cause of death in people under the age of 30 in this country. The total number of deaths from accidents fell by around 37 per cent in Great Britain between 1971 and 1992 (Table 7.31). Accidents still accounted for 12.1 thousand deaths in 1992, of which 38 per cent were road accidents and 37 per cent were accidents in the home or communal establishments. Road accidents are discussed in more detail in Chapter 12: Transport.

Accidental deaths: by cause

Great Britain Numbers

	1971	1981	1991[1]	1992[1]
Railway accident	212	95	90	70
Road accident[2]	8,009	4,902	5,078	4,628
Other transport accident	222	144	111	122
Other accident				
At home or in communal establishments	7,045	..	4,717	4,521
Elsewhere	3,807	..	2,427	2,307
All other accidents[3]	10,905	10,039	7,203	7,277
All accidental deaths[3]	19,348	15,180	12,482	12,097

1 Excludes deaths under 28 days.
2 These figures are not comparable with those issued by the Department of Transport. See Appendix, Part 7: Accidental deaths.
3 Late effects of accidental injury are not available by place of occurrence for England and Wales but are included in the totals for other accidents and total accidental deaths.

Source: Office of Population Censuses and Surveys; General Register Office (Scotland)

References and further reading

The following list contains selected publications relevant to **Chapter 7: Health**. Those published by HMSO are available from the addresses shown on the inside back cover of *Social Trends*.

Annual Report of the Registrar General for Northern Ireland, HMSO
Annual Report of the Registrar General for Scotland, General Register Office (Scotland)
Cancer Registration in Wales, Welsh Office
Cancer Registration Statistics Scotland, Common Services Agency, National Health Service in Scotland
Cancer Statistics Registrations (Series MB1), HMSO
Communicable Disease Statistics (Series MB2), HMSO
Fifty Years of the National Food Survey 1940-1990, HMSO
General Household Survey, HMSO
Health and Personal Social Services Statistics for England, HMSO
Health and Personal Social Services Statistics for Northern Ireland, DHSS Northern Ireland
Health and Personal Social Services Statistics for Wales, Welsh Office

References and further reading (continued)

Health and Safety Statistics, HMSO
Health briefings on aspects of health and NHS activity in Scotland (various), Common Services Agency, National Health Service in Scotland
Health Related Behaviours in Wales, 1985-1993 Health Promotion Wales
Health Survey for England 1992, HMSO
Hospital Episode Statistics, Department of Health
Morbidity Statistics from General Practice: fourth national study, 1991-92 (Series MB5), HMSO
Mortality Statistics for England and Wales (Series DH1, 2, 3, 4), HMSO
National Food Survey, HMSO
NHS Hospital Activity Statistics for England, Department of Health
On the State of the Public Health, HMSO
Population Trends, HMSO
Regional Trends, HMSO
Scotland's Health, A challenge to us all, HMSO
Scottish Health Statistics, Common Services Agency, National Health Service in Scotland
Sexual Attitudes and Lifestyles, Johnson, Wadsworth, Wellings, Field, Blackwell Scientific Publications, Oxford
Smoking among Secondary School Children, HMSO
Social Focus on Children, HMSO

Contacts

Telephone contact points for further information relating to **Chapter 7:Health.**

Department of Health	
Demographic statistics	0171 972 5562
Drug misuse/legal status	0171 972 5547
Health service indicators	01532 545555
Ministry of Agriculture, Fisheries and Food	0171 270 8563
Office of Population Censuses and Surveys	
General Household Survey	0171 396 2327
Other inquiries	0171 396 2828
The Scottish Office	0131 244 5431
General Register Office (Scotland)	0131 314 4243
Scottish Health Service	0131 551 8899
Welsh Office	01222 825080
Department of Health and Social Services, Northern Ireland	01232 522519
Department of Finance and Personnel, Northern Ireland	01232 521481
Public Health Laboratory Service	0181 200 6868

Chapter 8 Social Protection

General

In 1992, two fifths of those in the professional socio-economic group undertook some voluntary work, compared with around a tenth of those in the unskilled manual group. (Table 8.4)

Health care

There were almost 26 million new outpatient attendances at NHS hospitals in 1993-94 - over a fifth more than in 1981. (Table 8.7)

On 31 March 1994, one in sixteen hospital patients had waited over a year for admission; on 31 March 1991 it was one in six. (Table 8.9)

Government expenditure on the NHS in 1993-94 was over three fifths more in real terms than in 1976-77. (Chart 8.14)

Social services

In 1993 there were 36 thousand children on child protection registers in England, Wales and Northern Ireland; over a third were considered at risk of physical injury. (Table 8.17)

Around 53 million meals were provided for the elderly and physically disabled in Great Britain in 1992-93 - 6 million more than in 1981-82. (Table 8.20)

Financial support

Nearly half of all social security payments in 1993-94 were made to the elderly. (Table 8.28)

Only 62 per cent of those eligible for family credit in Great Britain in 1990-1991 claimed it. (Table 8.31)

8.1

Real growth in social security benefit expenditure

United Kingdom

£ billion at 1993-94 prices[1]

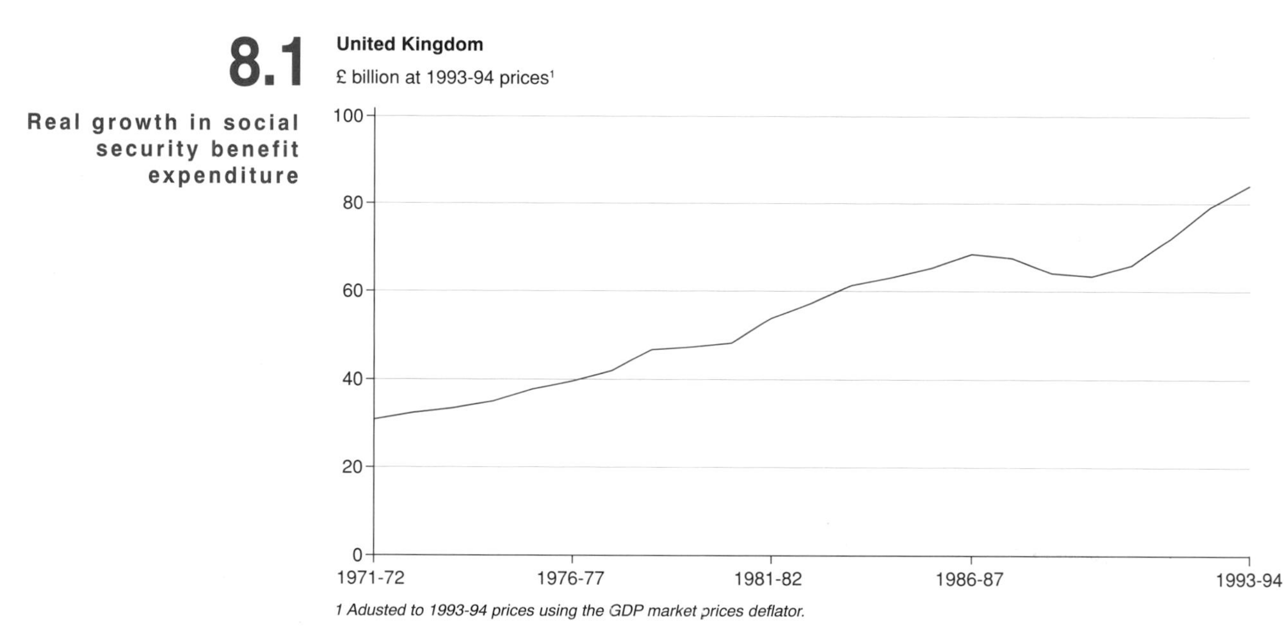

1 Adusted to 1993-94 prices using the GDP market prices deflator.

Source: Department of Social Security

8.2

Social protection expenditure: by function, 1992-93

United Kingdom				£ million
	Government programmes			
	Cash	In kind	Other (cash)	All benefits
Old age and survivors	44,839	3,757	16,505	65,101
Sickness	12,777	14,595	4,992	32,364
Invalidity, occupational accidents and diseases	12,689	4,684	550	17,923
Family and maternity	12,127	3,073	0	15,200
Unemployment and employment promotion	9,213	363	2,165	11,741
Housing	173	9,154	0	9,327
Other	1,835	533	0	2,369
Total expenditure	93,654	36,160	24,212	154,025

Source: Central Statistical Office

This new chapter of Social Trends describes the various ways in which central government, local authorities and the private and voluntary sectors act to help people in various kinds of need. Neediness may arise through ill health, infirmity, inadequate income or through other sorts of misfortune. Some of the topics dealt with here were included previously in the chapters on Health, Participation and Income and Wealth; others are new to Social Trends.

General

Some government expenditure programmes are designed specifically to protect people against common sources of hardship such as old age, sickness, unemployment, disability and so on. These programmes can be collectively described as expenditure on social protection, and are those from which households can most readily perceive a direct benefit, whether in cash or in kind. The Statistical Office of the European Communities has designed a framework for the presentation of information on such current expenditure and this has been adopted by Member Countries as the European System of Integrated Social Protection Statistics (ESSPROS). The sources of hardship or need to which the measures are directed are called 'functions' and the data for the United Kingdom, classified by social protection function, are given in Table 8.2.

Although the coverage of Table 8.2 is not complete for all non-government benefits, it can be seen that the majority of social protection expenditure comes from government programmes. Government expenditure on social protection constituted 21 per cent of GDP in 1992-93. In 1992-93 nearly £49 billion - almost two fifths of total government expenditure on social protection - was spent on the elderly and survivors (eg widowhood) functions. Of this, £45 billion was in the form of cash payments; the remainder was in the form of provision of services such day care facilities and home helps. Private sector contributions are also aimed principally at the elderly and

8.3

Social protection expenditure per head[1]: EC comparison, 1992

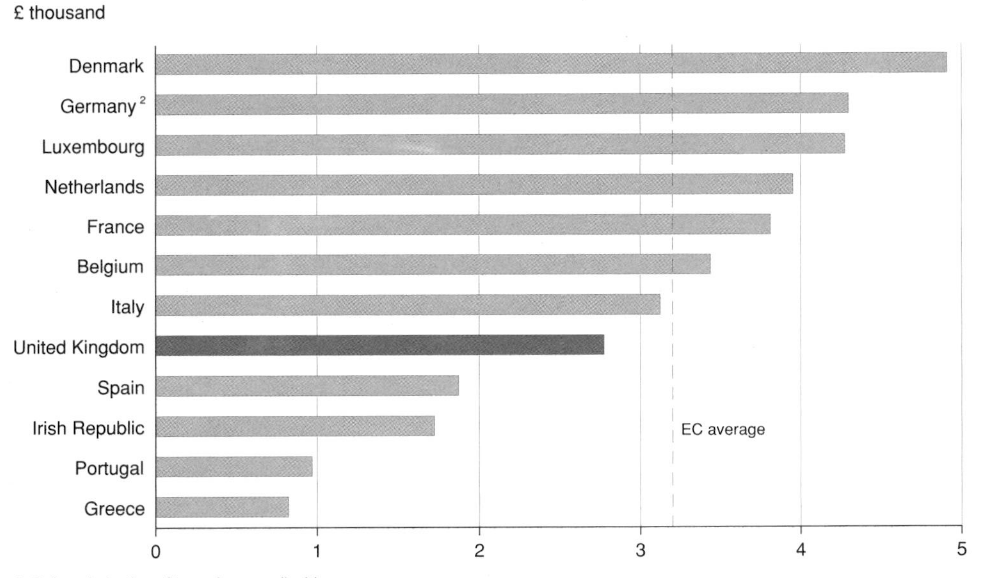

1 Before deduction of tax, where applicable.
2 Former Federal Republic.

Source: Eurostat

survivors, mainly in the form of occupational pension schemes and payments from Friendly Societies.

Chart 8.3 compares how much each member state of the European Community (EC) spent per head of population on social protection in 1992. Denmark spent more than any other country in the EC at around one and a half times the EC average. Conversely, Greece spent the least at just over a quarter of the EC average. The United Kingdom spent just below the EC average. However, it would be wrong to make assumptions about the well being of individuals in each country based solely on these data. For example, some benefits in some countries are subject to tax.

Many people give either their time or their money for the benefit of others. In 1992 the General Household Survey included questions about voluntary work. Voluntary work was defined as unpaid work done through a group or on behalf of an organisation; this included such activities as collecting or raising money, visiting people in institutions, providing information, organising events or serving on a committee. Table 8.4 shows that just over a fifth of men and just over a quarter of women interviewed in 1992 had undertaken some voluntary work within the previous 12 months. The table also shows that the likelihood of time being spent on voluntary work is greater in the non-manual socio-economic groups; two in five men from the professional group had undertaken some voluntary work during the previous year compared with under one in ten of those in the unskilled manual category. Just over a quarter of those who had undertaken some voluntary work had spent a maximum of 5 days on it during the year; a half had spent 20 days or more. Raising money was the most common type of voluntary work reported.

In 1993 the British Social Attitudes survey included a number of questions on people's attitudes towards giving to charities. As can be seen from Table 8.5, almost half of those included in the survey agreed that they could not refuse a collector at the door. On the other hand three fifths felt that it was not everyone's responsibility to give what they could afford to charity. Almost two thirds thought that we should support more charities which benefit people in Britain. There was strong support for the government supporting the needy rather than encouraging charities to do more.

8.4

Participation in voluntary work[1]: by socio-economic group, 1992[2]

Great Britain Percentages

	Males	Females
Professional	*40*	*41*
Employers and managers	*31*	*38*
Intermediate non-manual	*32*	*37*
Junior non-manual	*18*	*27*
Skilled manual	*14*	*24*
Semi-skilled manual	*13*	*19*
Unskilled manual	*8*	*14*
All socio-economic groups	*21*	*27*

1 Persons aged 16 and over.
2 In the year before interview.
Source: Office of Population Censuses and Surveys

8.5

Public opinion on giving to charities, 1993

Great Britain Percentages

	Agree	Disagree	Don't know[1]
There are so many charities - it is difficult to decide which to give to	*77*	*10*	*13*
We should support more charities which benefit people in Britain rather than overseas	*64*	*18*	*18*
It is not everyone's responsibility to give what they can to charities	*60*	*18*	*22*
I Can't refuse when someone comes to the door with a collecting tin	*46*	*36*	*18*
Most charities are wasteful of their funds	*40*	*25*	*35*
People should look after themselves and not rely on charities	*26*	*45*	*29*
The government should do less for the needy and encourage charities to do more instead	*8*	*76*	*16*

1 Includes those who neither agreed nor disagreed and those who did not answer the question.
Source: Social & Community Planning Research

8.6

Family practitioner and dental services

United Kingdom

	General medical and pharmaceutical services						General dental services	
	Number of doctors[1] in practice (thousands)	Average number of patients per doctor (thousands)	Prescriptions dispensed[2] (millions)	Average total cost[3] per prescription (£)	Average number of prescriptions per person	Average prescription cost[3] per person[4] (£)	Number of dentists[5] in practice (thousands)	Average number of persons per dentist (thousands)
1961	23.6	2.3	233.2	0.4	4.7	1.9	11.9	4.4
1971	24.0	2.4	304.5	0.8	5.6	4.3	12.5	4.5
1981	27.5	2.2	370.0	3.5	6.6	23.0	15.2	3.7
1986	30.2	2.0	397.5	5.1	7.0	36.0	17.3	3.3
1991	31.7	1.9	467.8	7.1	8.2	58.5	18.6	3.1
1992	32.0	1.9	488.2	7.6	8.6	65.5	18.6	3.1
1993	32.4	1.9	511.9	8.0	9.0	71.7	19.1	3.0

1 Unrestricted principals only. See Appendix Part 8: Unrestricted principals.
2 Includes items dispensed by community pharmacists and appliance contractors only.
3 Net ingredient cost (basic cost) less discount, and includes dispensing fees, container allowances, etc.
4 Based on the number of people on the NHS prescribing list.
5 Principals, assistants and vocational trainees.

Source: Department of Health

Health care

This section looks at the availability and use of a range of medical services including general practitioners (GPs), dentists and hospitals.

Table 8.6 shows that the number of doctors in general practice in the United Kingdom has been gradually increasing and in 1993 had reached a record 32.4 thousand. At the same time, the average number of patients per doctor fell between 1971 and 1988 since when it has remained constant. Between 1980 and 1993 the number of female GPs in England almost doubled and in 1993 they accounted for just over a quarter of all GPs. Between 1961 and 1993 the number of dentists rose by three fifths from 11.9 thousand to 19.1

8.7

National Health Service hospital activity: day cases and out-patients, all specialties

United Kingdom

	1971[1]	1976[2]	1981	1986	1991-92	1993-94
Day case attendances (thousands)	..	558	859	1,840	1,953	2,674
New out-patient attendances (thousands)						
Accidents and emergency	9,500	10,463	11,321	12,663	13,397	13,740
Other out-patients	9,319	9,178	9,810	10,713	11,059	11,939
Average attendances per new out-patient (numbers)						
Accidents and emergency	1.6	1.5	1.4	1.3	1.2	1.3
Other out-patients	4.1	4.2	4.4	4.3	4.1	4.0

1 Great Britain only.
2 Day case attendances data are for Great Britain only.

Source: Department of Health; Welsh Office; Scottish Health Service, Common Services Agency; Department of Health and Social Services, Northern Ireland

thousand. The average number of patients per dentist has remained constant in recent years. The table also shows that between 1961 and 1993 the number of prescriptions dispensed more than doubled.

In 1993-94 hospitals in the United Kingdom dealt with 2.7 million day-case attendances - over three times the number dealt with in 1981 (Table 8.7). New out-patient attendances increased by over a fifth between 1981 and 1993-94 to 25.7 million; over a half of these were accident and emergency cases. Figures for England show that in 1992-93 there were 7.8 thousand in-patient cases - an increase of nearly two fifths since 1982. This was despite a reduction of over a third in the average daily availability of beds over the same period. The increase in the numbers of patients treated was possible because of a reduction in the average length of time each patient spent in hospital and the more efficient use of beds.

The average stay as a hospital in-patient in 1993 was 9 days for a male and 7 days for a female (Table 8.8). Not surprisingly, however, this varies with age; the older we get the longer the stay. For example, the average stay for a 5 to 15 year old was just 4 days compared with 14 days for someone aged 75 and over.

Between 1991 and 1993, there were significant reductions in England and Northern Ireland in the proportion waiting over 12 months for hospital treatment either as an ordinary admission or as a day case; on 31 March 1991, 18.3 per cent had been waiting over 12 months but just 2 years later it was only 6.1 per cent. There was a slight deterioration in 1994 when the proportion rose to 6.3 per cent.

The length of time spent waiting for hospital treatment generally depends on the type of treatment sought and the urgency of the treatment. Table 8.9 shows that on 31 March 1994, only 4 per cent of those waiting for gynaecological treatment had been waiting for 12 months or longer compared with 13 per cent of those waiting for plastic surgery.

The length of time spent on a waiting list also varied according to location. Just over 12 per cent of patients in the North East Thames Regional Health Authority had been waiting a year or longer compared with none in the Mersey Regional Health Authority. In Scotland the proportion waiting for in-patient treatment fell from 10 per cent in 1993 to 5 per cent in 1994. From April 1995, under the Patient's Charter, no one will wait over 18 months for admission. The present guaranteed maximum wait is 24 months.

8.8

Nights[1] spent in hospital as an in-patient: by age and gender, 1993

Great Britain — Number

	Males	Females	All persons
Age			
0-4	7	4	6
5-15	3	4	4
16-44	5	5	5
45-64	9	9	9
65-74	14	13	13
75 and over	16	12	14
All persons	9	7	8

1 Average number during the last 12 months.

Source: Office of Population Censuses and Surveys

8.9

Patients[1] waiting over 12 months: by specialty

England & Northern Ireland — Percentages[2]

	1991	1992	1993	1994
Plastic surgery	46.6	24.0	10.9	13.1
Trauma and orthopaedics	20.5	10.4	8.1	7.4
Oral surgery	20.9	9.4	6.2	6.6
Urology	20.3	9.7	5.5	6.5
General surgery	18.5	8.6	5.9	6.2
Ophthalmology	14.1	9.0	6.2	6.0
Ear, nose and throat	14.4	7.7	4.6	5.0
Obstetrics and gynaecology	10.5	5.8	3.7	4.3
Other	11.2	7.0	5.4	4.8
All specialties	18.3	9.2	6.1	6.3

1 Ordinary (in-patient) and day cases combined.
2 At March each year.

Source: Department of Health; Department of Health and Social Services, Northern Ireland

8.10

Residents with a stay of over 5 years for mental handicap and mental illness in NHS hospitals and units

England and Scotland

Thousands

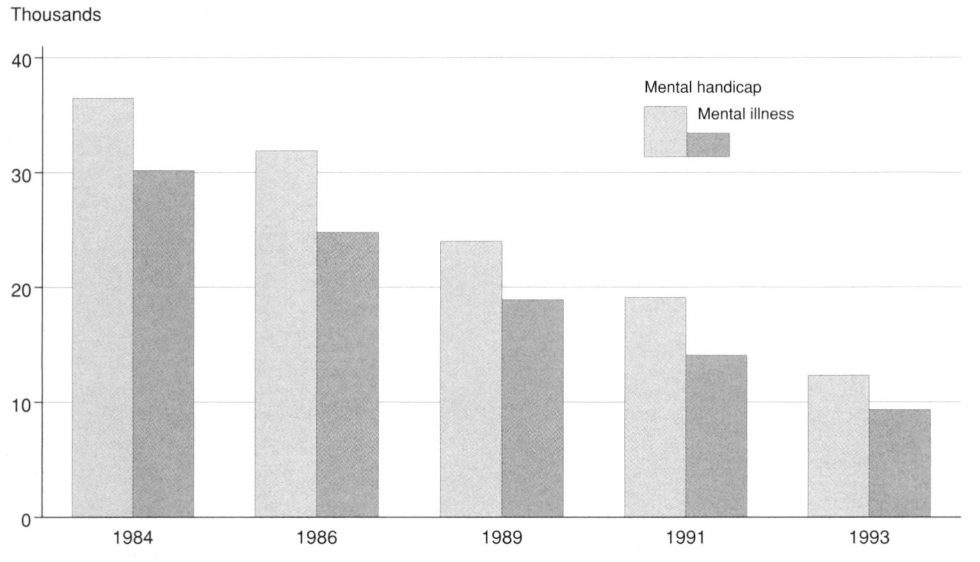

Source: Department of Health; The Scottish Office, Common Services Agency

Chart 8.10 shows that the number of mentally handicapped and mentally ill people resident in hospitals in England and Scotland for over five years fell from 67 thousand in 1984 to just 22 thousand in 1993. In Wales the number fell from 3.2 thousand in 1983 to just 1.2 thousand in 1993. In Northern Ireland there was a fall from 3 thousand in 1983 to 1.3 thousand in 1994.

These reductions were as a result of improved treatments and the Government's policy to provide care for as many people as possible in the community. In 1991 the Government introduced the Care Programme Approach requiring effective pre-discharge planning, the appointment of a key worker and regular reviews of the patient's need for care. Legislation is proposed to allow for more closely supervised aftercare of patients who might otherwise present a serious risk to themselves or others.

A ten point plan to improve care in the community for mentally ill people has been announced; it includes guidance on discharges, better training for those responsible for looking after the mentally ill in the community, and a review of standards of care for people with schizophrenia. The number of psychiatric nurses has increased fourfold in the last decade.

In 1993, 30 per cent of men and 36 per cent of women had had a sight test within the previous 12 months (Table 8.11). This shows an increase compared with 1991 when 26 per cent of men and 33 per cent of women had taken tests. Those in the non-manual socio-economic groups were the most likely to have had a sight test; almost two fifths of those in the

8.11

Percentage[1] who had a sight test in the year before interview: by socio-economic group and gender, 1991 and 1993

Great Britain Percentages

	1991			1993		
	Males	Females	All persons	Males	Females	All persons
Professional	*34*	*45*	*36*	*39*	*40*	*39*
Employers and managers	*30*	*36*	*32*	*34*	*39*	*36*
Intermediate non-managers	*32*	*37*	*35*	*37*	*40*	*39*
Junior non-managers	*31*	*33*	*33*	*29*	*38*	*36*
Skilled manual and own account non-professional	*21*	*31*	*23*	*26*	*33*	*28*
Semi-skilled manual and personal service	*22*	*30*	*27*	*26*	*34*	*31*
Unskilled manual	*23*	*28*	*26*	*22*	*29*	*27*
All socio-economic groups	*26*	*33*	*29*	*30*	*36*	*33*

1 Aged 16 and over.

Source: Office of Population Censuses and Surveys

professional group had taken a test in the previous year compared with only just over a quarter of those in the unskilled manual category. This follows the pattern seen from the 1992 General Household Survey which showed that over two thirds of the professional group wore glasses or contact lenses compared with just under a half of the semi-skilled manual group.

Chart 8.12 shows that the number of people who had private medical insurance increased sharply between 1971 and 1990 since when it has fallen back slightly, to 6.8 million. Figures prior to 1985 are taken from different sources and are not directly comparable with those for later years.

While the National Health Service and the private sector can provide essential health care services, more localised and specialised services are often provided by the voluntary sector. The United Kingdom has numerous organisations which provide help relating to specific medical problems. The organisations listed in Table 8.13 are just a small selection of such organisations. Their functions obviously vary but generally speaking they can advise on the availability of treatment, care, and welfare facilities, as well as sometimes providing such facilities themselves; provide support to relatives and friends of sufferers; raise funds; give grants; and undertake or support medical research. Both volunteers and professional staff may be employed.

The table shows the numbers of people that these organisations have helped. The counts are based on different criteria for different organisations but generally cover telephone inquiries, letters and personal callers. Clients may include patients, relatives of patients, employers and the organisation's own members. Although the numbers given for each organisation are not directly comparable, of the organisations shown, the Cancer Relief MacMillan Fund appears to have dealt with the largest number of clients -around 200 thousand in 1993. This is perhaps not surprising since (as mentioned in the previous chapter), one in three people contract cancer at sometime during their life and around a quarter of deaths are attributable to this disease. Some of the organisations, such as the Hyperactive Children's Support Group, and the Terrence Higgins Trust (which supports people with the Aids virus) deal with problems which have only been recognised in recent years.

8.12

People insured by private medical insurance[1]

United Kingdom

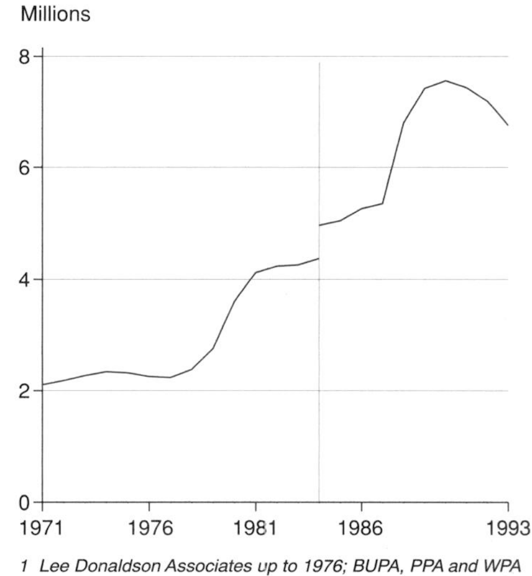

1 Lee Donaldson Associates up to 1976; BUPA, PPA and WPA 1977 to 1984; Department of Health 1984 onwards.

Source: Lee Donaldson Associates; BUPA; PPA; WPA; Department of Health

8.13

Clients of selected medical welfare organisations[1]

United Kingdom — Thousands

	1981	1991	1993
Cancer Relief Macmillan Fund	..	150	200
The Stroke Association	..	22	30
National Back Pain Association	8	19	26
Alzheimers Disease Society	2	15	20
Parkinson's Disease Society	..	14	18
Association for Spina Bifida and Hydrocephalus	..	..	15
Hyperactive Childrens Support Group	..	12	14
National Society for Epilepsy	1	11	14
Muscular Dystrophy Group of Great Britain	5	9	12
Leukaemia Care Society	2	6	8
Haemophilia Society	..	4	5
Terrence Higgins Trust	..	..	5
Hodgkin's Disease & Lymphoma Association	..	1	2
Schizophrenia Association of Great Britain	..	..	2

1 For details of coverage of individual organisations see Appendix, Part 8: Clients of selected medical welfare organisations.

Source: Organisations concerned

8.14

Real[1] cost of the National Health Service

United Kingdom

£ billion at 1993-94 prices[1]

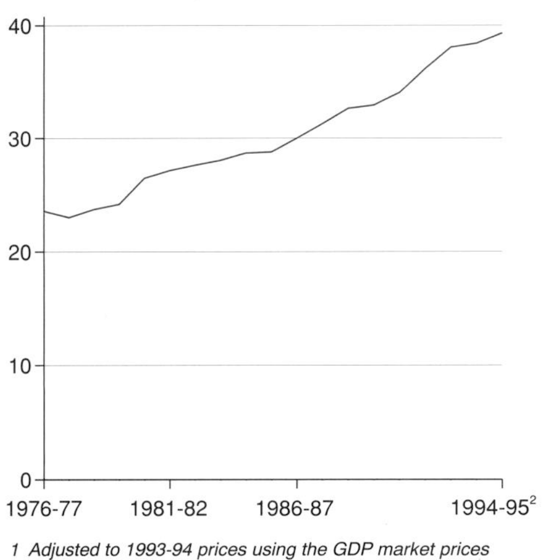

1 Adjusted to 1993-94 prices using the GDP market prices deflator.
2 Planned expenditure for 1994-95.
Source: Department of Health

8.15

Expenditure on health in real terms[1] of the top 400 charities[2]

United Kingdom

	Expenditure (£ million[1])	As a percentage of all expenditure[3]
1989-90	928	*36*
1990-91	871	*32*
1991-92	932	*34*
1992-93	942	*33*

1 At 1992-93 prices. Defalted by the GDP market prices deflator.
2 In each year based on voluntary income.
3 Of the top 400 charities.
Source: Charities Aid Foundation

Government expenditure, in real terms, on the NHS has increased steadily since 1977-78. Chart 8.14 shows that in 1976-77 gross expenditure on the NHS in the United Kingdom at 1993-94 prices was £23.5 billion pounds. By 1993-94 it had risen in real terms by over three fifths to £38.4 billion. It is planned to rise still further to £39.3 billion in 1994-95.

In 1993, three fifths of central government expenditure on the NHS in England went to the Health Authorities who are responsible for hospitals and local authority health services. The majority of the remainder was spent by the Family Health Service Authorities whose responsibilities include GPs, dentists and pharmaceutical services. In 1993-94 United Kingdom gross expenditure on the NHS represented 5.9 per cent of gross domestic product.

As well as NHS expenditure on health, numerous voluntary organisations also provide health related services. In 1993 over 170 thousand voluntary organisations were registered as charities in the United Kingdom. Organisations may qualify for charitable status if they are established for purposes such as relief of poverty, the advancement of education or religion, the protection of health or certain other purposes for public benefit. The Charities Aid Foundation, an independent body, is one of the main organisations that aids the flow of funds to charities from individuals, companies and grant-making trusts.

The Charities Aid Foundation is able to identify expenditure by charities according to broad sectors. Table 8.15 shows that in 1992-93 the top 400 charities (in terms of voluntary income) spent £942 million on health - £14 million pounds more in real terms than in 1989-90. Expenditure on health in 1992-93 represented a third of the total expenditure of the top 400 charities. It included expenditure by charities concerned with cancer, physical handicap, chest and heart problems, blindness, mental health, aids, terminal care, and hospitals.

Social services

Personal social services assist the elderly, the disabled, children and their families. They also help those who have responsibility for looking after others. Services provided include residential and day care, help for people confined to their homes and various forms of social work. The services are provided directly by local authorities, voluntary organisations or the private sector under contract to local authorities or independently by voluntary organisations and the private sector.

Demand for these services is rising because of the increasing number of elderly people (see Table 1.4) - especially those aged 85 and over - the heaviest users of services and because of the move towards care in the community.

Local authorities must provide accommodation for children who need it. This may be due to a child having no parent or guardian, because they have been abandoned or because their parents are unable to provide for them. They also have the power to accommodate children if they consider that to do so would safeguard or promote their welfare.

Table 8.16 shows that the total number of children looked after by local authorities in England, Wales and Northern Ireland fell from 99 thousand in 1981 to 60 thousand in 1992. At the same time there was a shift away from the provision of accommodation in local authority homes (including those controlled or assisted by local authorities); 28 per cent of children were accommodated in this way in 1981 but only 14 per cent in 1992. Over the same period there was a corresponding increase in placements with foster parents which increased from 38 per cent to 58 per cent of the total. In 1992 just five in every thousand children aged under 18 were looked after by local authorities - a fall from 7.6 per thousand in 1981. In England just over three fifths of children in care were in the 5 to 15 age group. A quarter of children had been looked after for less than a year while a further quarter had been looked after for 5 years or more.

All social services Departments hold a central Register which lists all of the children in the area who are considered to be at risk of abuse. Registration takes place following a case conference which sets out a protection plan. The registers are not records of child abuse: some children on the register will not have been the victim of abuse; other children who have been victims of abuse will not have been placed on the register if there was no need for a protection plan. A child may be on the register of more than one authority at a time.

Some children are considered to be at risk from a specific category of abuse. Table 8.17 shows that in England, Wales and Northern Ireland in 1993, over a third of boys and just over a quarter of girls were on a Child Protection Register because they were at risk of physical injury. Risk of sexual abuse, on the other hand, was a more common reason for registration of girls than boys; just over a quarter of girls on the register were there for this reason compared with a seventh of boys. However, 6 per cent of boys and 7 per cent of girls were considered to be at risk from more than one form of abuse. Hence the percentages at risk from each of the categories shown is understated.

The total number of children on child protection registers in England fell from 41 thousand in 1989 to 32 thousand in 1993. This was attributable more to an increase in the rate of deregistrations rather than a decrease in the rate of registrations. Almost two fifths of children on the register in 1993 were aged under 5. Due to changes in the categories of abuse, it is not possible to make direct comparisons with earlier years.

8.16

Children looked after by local authorities[1]: by type of accommodation

England & Wales and Northern Ireland — Percentages

	1981	1991	1992
With foster parents	*38*	*58*	*58*
In local authority homes	*28*	*16*	*14*
Placement with parent regulations	*19*	*13*	*12*
Schools for children with special educational needs	*3*	*2*	*2*
Voluntary homes and hostels	*4*	*2*	*2*
Other accommodation	*7*	*10*	*12*
All children in care (=100%) (thousands)	99	66	60
All children in care per 1,000 population aged under 18	7.6	5.5	5.0

1 At 31 March.

Source: Department of Health; Welsh Office; Department of Health and Social Services, Northern Ireland

8.17

Children on child protection registers: by category and gender, 1993[1]

England & Wales and Northern Ireland — Percentages

	Boys	Girls
Physical injury only	*34*	*27*
Neglect only	*23*	*20*
Sexual abuse only	*15*	*27*
Emotional abuse[2]	*11*	*10*
Grave concern	*10*	*9*
Multiple categories[3]	*6*	*7*
Number of children (=100%)(thousands)	17.6	17.9

1 At end March.
2 Where it is the main or sole form of abuse.
3 Children registered under some combination of neglect, physical injury and/or sexual abuse.

Source: Department of Health; Welsh Office; Department of Social Services, Northern Ireland

8.18

Attendance[1] at local authority day centres: by client group, 1993

England				Thousands
		Under contract using		
	Directly admin-istered	Voluntary sector	Private sector	All sectors
Aged 16-64				
Physical and/or sensory disability	33.4	3.2	0.1	36.7
Learning disabilities	208.4	3.8	0.3	212.5
Mental illness	26.6	8.5	-	35.1
Others	2.5	2.0	-	3.5
Client group unknown	7.3	0.4	-	7.6
All aged 16-64	278.2	17.8	0.5	296.4
Aged 65 and over	92.1	30.5	0.4	123.1
All clients	370.3	48.3	0.9	419.5

1 Attendance counted separately on each day of survey week (week commencing 27 September).

Source: Department of Health

A wide range of social services is provided for those that need them; they include day centres, home care services, the provision of meals and facilities to help those whose mobility is impaired. Table 8.18 shows attendances at day care facilities provided or purchased by local authorities in England. The table shows that in September 1993 over two thirds of all attendances were by people aged 16 to 64, of which just over 70 per cent had learning disabilities. Under a third of day centre attendances were accounted for by those over 65. At the same time there were 2.8 thousand day centres providing services for local authority clients, of which just under a half were primarily intended for people aged 16-64 and just over two fifths for elderly people. Of all centres providing services for local authority clients, nearly three in four were directly provided by local authorities; the majority of the remainder were operated by the voluntary sector under contract. Around 1 per cent were operated under contract using the private sector. In Wales in 1993, almost 16 thousand people attended day centres directly controlled by local authorities; here, however, a smaller proportion - less than half of all users - were in the 16-64 age group. Day care for children generally caters for a different kind of need and is covered in Tables 3.3, 3.5 and 3.6.

8.19

Households receiving local authority home help or home care services: by sector and age[1], 1993[2]

England				Thousands
		Under contract using		
	Direct	Voluntary sector	Private sector	All sectors
Under 18	3.3	0.1	-	3.5
18-64	44.9	0.7	1.3	47.0
65-74	81.6	0.5	1.7	83.8
75-84	203.0	0.8	4.1	207.9
85 and over	139.8	0.6	3.2	143.6
All ages[3]	495.0	5.0	12.6	512.6

1 Of oldest client.
2 Week commencing 27 September 1993.
3 Includes age unknown.

Source: Department of Health

The same survey in England found that over 1.7 million hours of home help and home care were provided or purchased by local authorities in England during the survey week; just over half a million households received such services. Over two thirds of homecare services (which include the home helps to assist with cleaning and washing and the provision of night sitters) were provided for households where the oldest resident was aged 75 or over (Table 8.19). In two fifths of these households the oldest resident was aged 85 or over. The majority of home help and home care services were provided directly by local authorities; services provided under contract using the voluntary and private sectors accounted for only 3 per cent of the total. Around two fifths of all clients received only one visit during the survey week, while 8 per cent received 10 or more visits. In Scotland, 88 thousand people were receiving home care services as at 31 March 1993 of which again just over two thirds were aged over 74. In Northern Ireland 31 thousand people used home care services at 31 March 1993 although this also included the provision meals at home.

Table 8.20 shows that between 1971-72 and 1992-93 the number of meals provided for the elderly and physically disabled in Great Britain more than doubled to 53 million. Almost three quarters of the meals provided in 1992-93 were served at home. In England, local authorities provided around two thirds of the meals themselves with the remainder mostly being provided by the voluntary sector.

In Great Britain in 1993 there were 264 thousand residents living in homes for the elderly and 8 thousand people living in homes for physically disabled people (Table 8.21). Together, the number of people in these types of homes rose by over two fifths between 1981 and 1991; since then it has fallen slightly. In 1993 there were also 37 thousand residents living in homes for people with learning disabilities and 12 thousand in homes for mentally ill people. In Northern Ireland in 1993 there were 2.7 thousand residents in statutory homes covering all of the categories mentioned above. This was a fifth less then the number for 1991. Data for voluntary sector homes in Northern Ireland are not available. As with other social services, homes and hostels are operated either by local authorities, the voluntary sector or the private sector. In respect of homes for the elderly and younger physically disabled people, there has been a move away from local authority homes and towards the private sector. In part this reflects the transfer by local authorities of their own homes to the independent sector. In 1983 less than a quarter of all elderly and physically disabled residents in England were in private sector homes but by 1993 that proportion had risen to nearly three fifths. Over the period the percentage of residents financed by local authorities decreased while the percentage of residents financed by central government through Income Support increased. From April 1993 the funding arrangements changed and local authorities are now responsible for funding placements for people who cannot afford the fees for themselves.

8.20

Meals provided for elderly and physically disabled people

Great Britain — Millions

	1971-72[1]	1981-82	1991-92	1992-93
Served at home	16	31	37	38
Served elsewhere	9	16	16	15
All meals served	25	47	54	53
Meals served per person aged 65 and over (numbers)	4.1	5.7	6.1	5.9

1 England only.

Source: Department of Health; Welsh Office; The Scottish Office, Social Work Services Group

8.21

Residents in homes and hostels

Great Britain — Thousands

	1981	1991	1993
For elderly people	198 (elderly and physically disabled combined)	272	264
For physically disabled people		8	8
For people with learning difficulties	..	33	37
For mentally ill people	..	10	12
All residents in specified homes and hostels	..	323	321

Source: Department of Health, Welsh Office; The Scottish Office, Social Work Services Group

8.22

Carers: by relationship with dependant, 1990

Great Britain			Percentages
	In the same household	In another private household	All
Dependant			
Parent	*23*	*39*	*35*
Friend/neighbour	*2*	*25*	*19*
Other relative	*10*	*20*	*18*
Parent-in-law	*6*	*15*	*13*
Spouse	*41*	*0*	*10*
Child over 16	*10*	*10*	*3*
Child under 16	*8*	*0*	*2*
All carers (=100%) (millions)	1.6	5.2	6.8

Source: Office of Population Censuses and Surveys

In 1990 the General Household Survey asked people in Great Britain if they were carers, ie looked after anyone who was sick, disabled or elderly. This included helping with personal care (such as washing), giving medicine, physical help, paperwork, providing company and keeping an eye on a dependant. Overall 15 per cent of people aged 16 and over were carers - 17 per cent of women and 13 per cent of men. Table 8.22 shows that over a third of those who were carers were looking after a parent while almost a fifth were looking after a friend or neighbour. Two fifths of the parents being cared for lived at a different address to their son or daughter. The peak age for caring s 45 to 64, presumably because at this age a person's parents may become in need of care. Among this age group a fifth of men and over a quarter of women were carers. The time spent caring appears to be related to whether or not the dependant is in the same household. Two thirds of carers looking after someone at the same address spent 20 hours or more a week caring. Where the dependant was at a different address, less than one in ten spent this amount of time. Overall, almost a quarter of carers spent 20 hours or more a week looking after someone; while one in ten devoted at least 50 hours a week.

For many people getting about can be difficult. They may be physically disabled, have limited or no sight or simply be elderly and infirm. There are many ways in which these people can lead independent lives.

For those that have the use of a car, there is the Orange Badge Scheme. This enables holders to park in otherwise restricted areas and parking areas designated for disabled people. Over 1.3 million badges were on issue at March 1994. Many local authorities now operate special bus services for people with mobility impairments. On these services assistance with boarding and alighting is provided, wheelchair users can be carried and routes are flexible in order to reduce walking distance. Many service buses now also have special features such as brightly coloured grab rails, high visibility destination blinds and low steps and low floor levels. Some local authorities also provide subsidised taxi journeys. To assist with shopping, Shopmobility provides (usually free of charge) use of manual and motorised wheelchairs and scooters. The first scheme was set up in 1981 and by the end of 1994

8.23

Clients of selected advisory and counselling services[1]

United Kingdom				Thousands
	1971	1981	1991	1993
Citizens Advice Bureaux	1,500	4,515	8,278	8,253
Samaritans	..	1,700	2,500	2,400
Law Centres Federation	1	155	452	525
Youth Access	..	30	113	250
Disablement Information and Advice Lines	.	40	75	184
ChildLine	.	.	69	81
Relate	22	38	70	76
Alcoholics Anonymous	6	30	45	47
Cruse Bereavement Care	5	9	23	29
Turning Point	..	..	..	22
Catholic Marriage Advisory Council	3	3	17	20
Al-Anon Family Groups	1	7	13	12

1 For details of coverage of individual organisations see Appendix, Part 8: Selected advisory and counselling services.

Source: Organisations concerned

120 schemes were in operation covering most major towns and cities in Great Britain. Other features which have been developed to help those with mobility problems are ramps into buildings, dropped kerbs at road junctions and road crossings and visual and audible signals at pedestrian crossing points.

In addition to the medical welfare organisations shown in Table 8.13, the United Kingdom also has many other counselling and advisory services which between them deal with a wide range of issues. All of the organisations shown in Table 8.23 saw large increases in the numbers of clients during the 1970s and 1980s - a trend which has continued into the 1990s for most of them. Because these organisations record the number of clients or enquiries in different ways, it is difficult to make direct comparisons between them. However, it appears that, of the organisations show in the table, the Citizens Advice Bureaux dealt with the most enquiries - 8.3 million in 1993. This was more than a fivefold increase on the number dealt with in 1971.

Table 8.24 looks in more detail at the work of the Citizens Advice Bureaux. In 1993-94, of the 8.3 million enquiries dealt with, almost a quarter were concerned with social security matters; consumer, trade and business problems (including consumer debt) accounted for almost the same proportion. Between 1980-81 and 1993-94 the number of queries relating to travel and leisure fell by almost a third while those relating to social security increased more than fourfold.

8.24

Citizens Advice Bureaux: by type of enquiry

United Kingdom — Percentages

	1980-81	1991-92	1993-94
Social security	*9.8*	*23.1*	*24.0*
Consumer, trade and business[1]	*18.6*	*23.4*	*23.3*
Employment	*10.0*	*11.3*	*11.2*
Housing, property and land	*15.8*	*10.6*	*10.5*
Family and personal	*14.7*	*8.9*	*9.9*
Administration of justice	*8.4*	*6.2*	*5.8*
Taxes and duties[2]	*2.7*	*4.6*	*4.2*
Holidays, travel and leisure	*4.5*	*1.9*	*1.6*
Health[2]	*3.6*	*1.9*	*1.6*
Other	*11.8*	*7.3*	*7.8*
All enquiries (=100%) (thousands)	4,345	8,277	8,253

1 Includes consumer debt.
2 Not included as a separate category in Scotland in 1991-92 and 1993-94.
Source: National Association of Citizens Advice Bureaux; Citizens Advice Scotland

Twenty years ago Victim Support was set up in Bristol to help people who had been victims of crime. Since then over 5 million people in England, Wales and Northern Ireland have been offered emotional and practical help such as helping to sort out matters of compensation and liaising with the police and courts. Most people are referred to the organisation by the police although some people (including those who have not reported a crime) approach the organisation directly. Witnesses of crime who have to give evidence in court are offered support by Victim Support's witness service. Table 8.25 shows that in 1993-94 just over a million people were referred to Victim Support. Over a half of these had suffered a burglary while 180 thousand had experienced some form of violent crime.

8.25

People referred[1] to Victim Support

England & Wales and Northern Ireland — Thousands

	1991-92	1992-93	1993-94
Burglary	468	570	582
Theft	135	176	207
Criminal damage	37	47	58
Sexual crime (other than rape)	8	10	11
Arson	2	3	3
Rape	2	3	3
Road deaths	1	1	1
Homicides	1	1	1
Other violence	109	136	161
Other crime	17	26	25
Non-crime	4	6	6
All users	785	978	1,058

1 Includes self-referrals.
Source: Victim Support

8.26

Local authority net current expenditure in real terms[1] on personal social services

England and Scotland £ million[1]

	1989-90	1990-91	1991-92	1992-93
Elderly	2,225	2,292	2,234	2,248
Children	1,624	1,719	1,718	1,784
People with learning difficulties	600	658	721	776
Young physically disabled	259	267	316	363
Mentally ill	107	114	177	218
Other	216	223	257	248
Total expenditure	5,030	5,270	5,424	5,638

1 At 1992-93 prices.Deflated by the GDP market prices deflator.

Source: Department of Health; The Scottish Office, Social Work Services Group

8.27

Expenditure on welfare in real terms[1] of the top 400 charities[2]

United Kingdom

	Expenditure (£ million[1])	As a percentage of all expenditure[3]
1989-90	649	*25*
1990-91	624	*23*
1991-92	675	*25*
1992-93	705	*25*

1 At 1992-93 prices. Deflated by the GDP market prices deflator.
2 In each year based on voluntary income.
3 Of the top 400 charities.

Source: Charities Aid Foundation

As with health, spending on social services is split between the public, private and voluntary sectors. Details of local authority expenditure on personal social services in England and Scotland are given in Table 8.26. This shows that in 1992-93, £5.6 billion was spent by local authorities on personal social services. Two fifths of this was spent on looking after the elderly and a further third on children. In real terms, the total spent on personal social services increased by 12 per cent between 1989-90 and 1992-93. Spending on mentally ill people doubled over the same period to £218 million in 1992-93. Local authority spending in Wales on personal social services, totalled £306 million in 1992-93 - a 17 per cent increase in real terms compared with 1990-91. Total gross expenditure on personal social services (excluding central administration costs) in Northern Ireland in 1992-93 was £183 million.

Table 8.27 shows that in 1992-93 the top 400 charities (in terms of voluntary income) spent £705 million on welfare - almost a tenth more in real terms than in 1989-90. Since 1989-90 this expenditure has represented around a quarter of all expenditure by the top 400 charities. This includes expenditure on elderly people, children, service and ex-service people, benevolent funds and religious groups

Financial support

Around a third of government expenditure is currently devoted to the social security programme. Chart 8.1 (at the beginning of the chapter) shows that in real terms social security expenditure in the United Kingdom has been increasing steadily since 1971-72. In 1993-94, £84.3 billion was spent - almost three times more in real terms than in 1971-72. A longer times series shows that since 1951-52, there has been an almost eight fold increase in real terms in expenditure on social security benefits.

Table 8.28 shows benefit expenditure broken down by recipient group. Nearly half of total expenditure in Great Britain in 1993-94 was accounted for by the elderly. Just over a further fifth went to the long-term sick and disabled. In real terms, total expenditure on benefits increased more than two and a half times between 1971-72 and 1993-94. However, expenditure on the long-term sick and disabled and on families increased more than fivefold over the same period. Between 1993-94 and 1996-97 expenditure on benefits is planned to rise by a further 7 per cent in real terms.

Some benefits are termed contributory. Eligibility for these is governed by the individual's record of contributions to the National Insurance Fund; either by their employer on their behalf or by themselves as employees or self employed. Table 8.29 shows the number of people receiving the principal types of contributory benefits in Great Britain in 1993-94. The state retirement pension, including lump sum payments accounted for the majority of contributory benefits. These were received by 19 million people and accounted for £28.2 billion of expenditure. The number of people receiving these benefits is, of course, increasing as the average age of the population increases.

Some social security payments are non-contributory which means that they are financed from general taxation; some of these are income related. The numbers receiving non-contributory benefits in Great Britain are given in Table 8.30 (overleaf). In 1993-94 child benefit was the most significant non-income-related benefit in terms of both numbers of recipients and expenditure. The majority of income related benefits fall into three main categories - income support, (received by 5.8 million

8.28

Benefit expenditure in real terms[1]: by beneficiary group[2]

Great Britain — £ billion at 1993-94 prices[1]

	1971-72	1981-82	1986-87	1991-92	1993-94	1996-97[3]
Elderly	16.7	27.2	32.1	33.6	36.8	38.4
Long-term sick and disabled	2.9	5.7	8.9	12.8	17.2	19.2
Short-term sick	2.4	1.4	1.6	1.5	1.2	0.5
Family	2.8	9.3	11.5	12.2	14.4	16.4
Of which lone parents	..	2.0	3.9	6.0	8.0	9.8
Unemployed	2.8	7.1	10.6	8.1	9.7	9.9
Widows and others	2.5	1.8	1.8	1.8	1.7	1.8
All benefit expenditure	30.1	52.4	66.4	70.0	80.9	86.2

1 Adjusted to 1993-94 prices using the GDP market prices deflator.
2 See Appendix, Part 8: Groups of beneficiaries.
3 Planned.
Source: Department of Social Security

8.29

Recipients of contributory benefits[1]: by type of benefit

Great Britain — Thousands

	1981-82	1991-92	1993-94
Lump sum payments to contributory pensioners[2]	9,074	9,567	9,568
Retirement pensions	8,877	9,425	9,442
Invalidity benefit	683	1,439	1,536
Unemployment benefit	1,090	695	607
Statutory sick pay	.	345	342
Widows benefit	397	326	313
Sickness benefit	393	138	142
Statutory maternity pay	.	85	85
Maternity allowance	..	11	11
Industrial disablement/ death benefit	219	.	.

1 All estimates are at a point in time. See Appendix, Part 8: Social security benefits.
2 Graduated pension cases only.
Source: Department of Social Security

8.30

Recipients of selected non-contributory benefits[1]: by type of benefit

Great Britain — Thousands

	1981-82	1991-92	1993-94
Non-income-related benefits			
Child benefit[2]	13,079	12,401	12,662
One-parent benefit	508	821	914
Industrial disablement[3]/ death benefit	.	228	227
War pension	336	250	296
Attendance allowance	364	1,059	996
Invalid care allowance	7	167	240
Severe disablement allowance	143	302	311
Mobility allowance[4]	218	699	.
Disability living allowance	.	.	1,320
Income-related benefits			
Supplementary pension	1,705	.	.
Supplementary allowance	2,185	.	.
Income support	.	5,030	5,791
Family credit	.	352	513
Housing benefit - rent rebates and allowances	4,151	4,200	4,664
Rate rebates/ community charge benefit	6,555	6,506	5,526

1 All estimates are at a point in time. See Appendix, Part 8: Social security benefits.
2 The number of qualifying children.
3 The number of pension assessments. A person may be in receipt of more than one pension.
4 Mobility allowance was replaced by Disability living allowance from April 1992.

Source: Department of Social Security

8.31

Take-up of benefits: by expenditure and caseload, 1991

Great Britain — Percentages

	Expenditure	Caseload[1]
Housing benefit	*93-97*	*90-95*
Income support	*85-95*	*77-90*
Family credit[2]	*68*	*62*

1 Number of people claiming as a proportion of those eligible.
2 Relates to 1990-1991.

Source: Department of Social Security

people in 1993-94), council tax rebates (5.5 million) and housing benefit (4.7 million). In 1992 two new benefits were introduced - the disability living allowance (DLA) and disability working allowance. There were 1.3 million recipients of DLA in 1993-94; it has replaced attendance allowance for people disabled before the age of 65 and mobility allowance.

Not everyone who is entitled to receive social security benefits claims them. Take-up varies according to the type of benefit and the family structure of those claiming. In 1991 between 90 and 95 per cent of people eligible to claim received housing benefit. Between 93 and 97 per cent of the total amount that would have been spent if everyone who was eligible had claimed was actually taken up. (Table 8.31). Take-up was highest among lone parents and lowest among those in private rented accommodation. Income support take-up was in the range 77 to 90 per cent by caseload and between 85 and 95 per cent by expenditure. Take-up was again highest among lone parents but lowest among pensioners. For family credit, in 1990-1991 take-up was thought to be 62 per cent by caseload and 68 per cent by expenditure. Take-up is naturally higher among non-income related benefits; for example, take up of child benefit and the retirement pension is believed to be close to 100 per cent.

8.32

In 1993 the British Social Attitudes survey asked for people's views on aspects of the social security system. Over a half thought that people were made to feel inferior if they received social security benefits (Table 8.32). Around a quarter of respondents agreed with the statement that many of those receiving social security did not deserve it. Around a third thought that most people were probably concealing information in order to get benefits. However, just over half said that the government should spend more on welfare benefits (even if taxes would have to be raised as a result); only a fifth disagreed. Between a quarter and a third of people did not express a view one way or the other on these issues.

Public opinion on social security, 1993

Great Britain — Percentages

	Agree	Disagree	Don't know[1]
People receiving social security are made to feel like second class citizens	*55*	*22*	*23*
The government should spend more on welfare benefits for the poor even if it leads to higher taxes	*53*	*20*	*27*
Most people on the dole are fiddling in one way or another	*31*	*38*	*31*
Around here most unemployed people could find a job if they really wanted one	*27*	*52*	*21*
If welfare benefits weren't so generous, people would learn to stand on their own two feet	*25*	*52*	*23*
Many people who get social security don't really deserve any help	*24*	*50*	*26*

1 Includes those who neither agreed nor disagreed and those who did not answer the question.

Source: Social & Community Planning Research

References and further reading

The following list contains selected publications relevant to **Chapter 8: Social Protection**. Those published by HMSO are available from the addresses shown on the inside back cover of *Social Trends*.

Activities of Social Service Departments, Welsh Office

Annual Report of the Registrar General for Northern Ireland, HMSO

Annual Report of the Registrar General for Scotland, General Register Office (Scotland)

British Social Attitudes survey series, SCPR

Charity Commissioner's Report, HMSO

Charity Trends, Charities Aid Foundation

Children in Care in England and Wales, Department of Health

General Household Survey, HMSO

Health and Personal Social Services Statistics for England, HMSO

Health and Personal Social Services Statistics for Northern Ireland, DHSS Northern Ireland

Health and Personal Social Services Statistics for Wales, Welsh Office

Health and Safety Statistics, HMSO

Health Survey for England 1991, HMSO

Hospital and Health Service Yearbook, Health and Saftey Executive

Hospital Waiting List Statistics: England, Department of Health

Individual Giving and Volunteering in Britain (6th Edition), Charities Aid Foundation

NHS Hospital Activity Statistics for England 1974-1989/90, Department of Health

Personal Social Services Statistics, CIPFA

Population Trends, HMSO

Regional Trends, HMSO

Report on Voluntary Work, HMSO

Residential Accommodation for the Elderly and for Younger Physically Handicapped People, HMSO

Scotland's Health: A Challenge to us all, HMSO

Scottish Health Service Costs, The Scottish Office

References and further reading (continued)

Scottish Health Statistics, Common Services Agency, Scottish Health Service

Social Protection Expenditure and Receipts, Eurostat

Social Security Departmental Report, HMSO

Social Security Statistics, HMSO

Social Work Services group of The Scottish Office, Statistical Bulletins

Statistical Publications on aspects of Health and Personal Social Services activity in England (various), Department of Health

Statistics of Elective Admissions and Patients Waiting, Department of Health

Survey of Children and Young Persons on Child Protection Registers, Department of Health

Tax/Benefit Model Tables, Department of Social Security

The Tax/benefit Position of Production Workers, OECD

Contacts

Telephone contact points for further information relating to

Chapter 8: Social Protection.

Department of Health	
Adults' services	0171 972 5585
Children's services	0171 972 5575
Community and environmental health services	0171 972 5536
Financial data	0171 972 5595
General dental and community dental service	0171 972 5394
General medical services manpower	01532 545909
General ophthalmic services	0171 972 5507
General pharmacy services	0171 972 5504
Mental illness/handicap	0171 972 5546
NHS medical staff	01532 545881
NHS non-medical manpower	01532 545985
Non-psychiatric hospital activity	0171 972 5525
Personal social services budget data	0171 210 5699
Prescription analysis	0171 972 5519
Staffing	0171 972 5595
Waiting lists	01532 545549
Department of Health and Social Services, Northern Ireland	01232 522800
Office of Population Censuses and Surveys	0171 396 2327
The Scottish Office	
Social WorkServices Group	0131 244 5431
Eurostat	00 352 4301 34567
Charities Aid Foundation	01732 771333
Citizens Advice Scotland	0131 667 0156
National Association of Citizens Advice Bureaux	0171 833 2181
Social & Community Planning Research	0171 250 1866 extn 369

Chapter 9 Crime and Justice

Offences

There was one notifiable offence recorded by police for every ten people in England and Wales in 1993. (Chart 9.2)

The cost of crime to retailers in Great Britain in 1992-93 was estimated at £2 billion. (Page 156)

Offences cleared up

Less than one in five offences of vehicle crime in England and Wales was cleared up in 1993. (Table 9.12)

Offenders

More than half of all offenders commencing probation orders or community service or discharged from prison are reconvicted within two years. (Table 9.16)

Police and courts action and sentencing

Almost 210 thousand cautions were issued in England and Wales in 1993 - more than twice as many as in 1981, but less than in 1992. (Table 9.17)

Prisons and probation

Nearly one in ten of the sentenced prison population is serving a life sentence. (Chart 9.26)

Crime prevention

Over 5 million homes in England and Wales are covered by a neighbourhood watch scheme. (Page 168)

Resources and legal aid

The number of criminal legal aid applications granted fell by 15 per cent between 1991 and 1993, after quadrupling in the 20 years to 1991. (Chart 9.36)

9.1

Prison accommodation and population

Great Britain

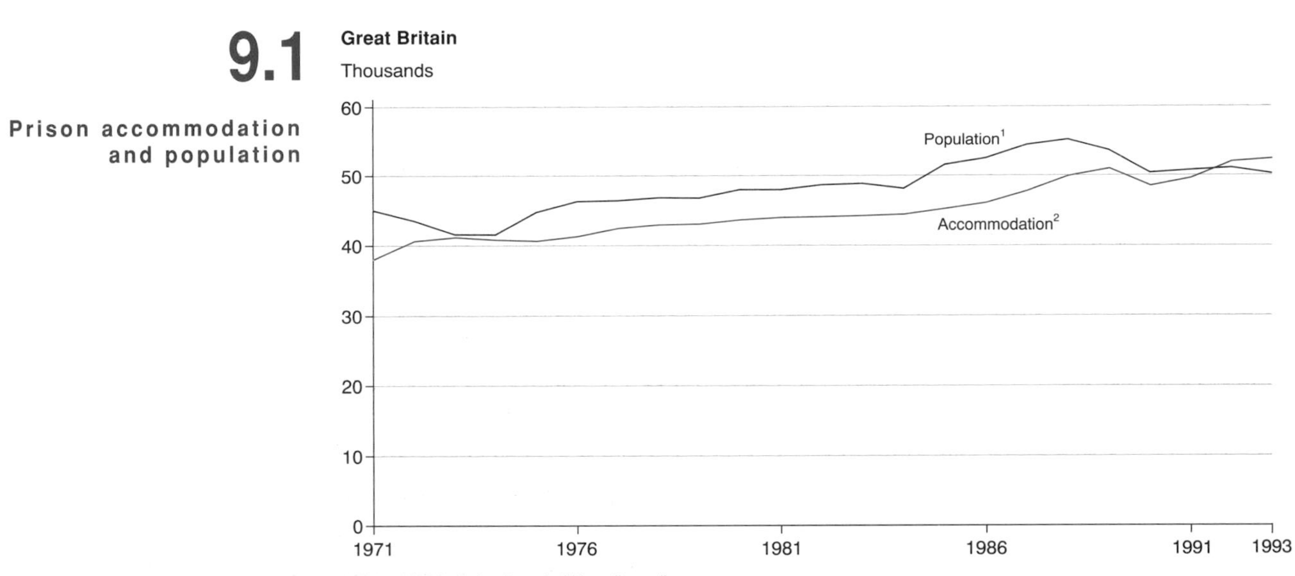

1 From 1980 includes those held in police cells.
2 Certified Normal Accommodation in England & Wales for 1993 excludes accommodation which is not yet operational.
Source: Home Office; The Scottish Office Home and Health Department

9.2

Notifiable offences[1] recorded by the police

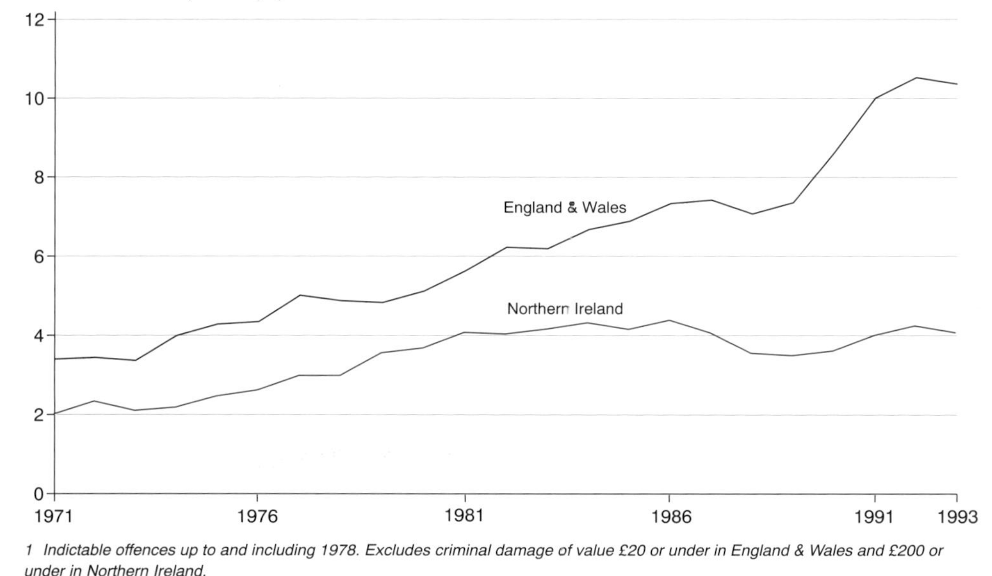

1 Indictable offences up to and including 1978. Excludes criminal damage of value £20 or under in England & Wales and £200 or under in Northern Ireland.

Source: Home Office; Royal Ulster Constabulary

This chapter looks at crime and justice in the United Kingdom, from the number of people who commit offences to the actions taken for dealing with them. It also looks at broader issues such as crime prevention and issues of civil justice.

In this chapter England and Wales, Scotland and Northern Ireland are often shown separately because of their different legal systems.

Offences

The first two items in this section cover notifiable offences recorded by the police. This is a measure of the amount of crime with which the police have to deal.

Notifiable offences are not a measure of the 'true' level of crime as many offences are either not reported to the police or not

9.3

Notifiable offences[1] recorded by the police: by type of offence

Thousands

	England & Wales			Scotland			Northern Ireland		
	1981	1991	1993	1981	1991	1993	1981	1991[2]	1993[2]
Violence against the person	100.2	190.3	205.1	8.0	15.5	13.8	2.9	4.0	4.6
Sexual offences,	19.4	29.4	31.3	2.1	3.1	3.7	0.3	0.9	1.2
of which: rape	1.1	4.0	4.6	0.3	0.5	0.5	-	0.1	0.2
Burglary	718.4	1,219.5	1,369.6	95.7	116.1	97.8	20.5	16.6	15.7
Robbery	20.3	45.3	57.8	4.2	6.2	5.6	2.7	1.8	1.7
Drug trafficking	..	11.4	14.8	1.6	3.3	5.2	-	-	-
Theft and handling stolen goods,	1,603.2	2,761.1	2,751.9	201.1	284.3	250.4	25.4	32.0	33.2
of which: theft of vehicle	332.6	581.9	597.5	32.5	44.3	42.8	5.1	8.4	9.0
theft from vehicles[3]	379.6	913.3	925.8	..	..	89.4	6.5	7.2	6.7
Fraud and forgery	106 7	174.7	162.8	21.4	26.4	23.7	2.6	4.8	5.5
Criminal damage[4]	386.7	821.1	906.7	61.7	89.7	84.2	5.2	2.4	2.9
Other notifiable offences	8.9	23.2	26.1	12.4	48.1	58.6	2.8	1.0	1.1
All notifiable offences	2,963.8	5,276.2	5,526.3	408.2	592.8	543.0	62.5	63.5	66.2

1 Includes attempted offences. Scottish figures of 'crime' have been grouped in an attempt to approximate to the classification of notifiable offences in England & Wales and Northern Ireland. However, differences in the legal systems, recording and counting practices and classification problems mean that Scottish figures should not be compared with those for England & Wales and Northern Ireland.
2 No longer includes assault on police and communicating false information regarding a bomb hoax. These offences have been removed from the categories 'Violence against the person' and 'Other notifiable offences'.
3 In Scotland data have only been collected from January 1992. The figures include theft by opening lockfast places, from motor vehicles and other theft from motor vehicles.
4 In Northern Ireland, the figures exclude criminal damage valued at £200 or less.

Source: Home Office; The Scottish Office Home and Health Department; Royal Ulster Constabulary

recorded by them because the complainant may decide not to proceed, or the police may decide that there is not enough evidence to warrant a criminal investigation. Unrecorded crime is covered in Chart 9.4.

Although the name of the series has changed over the years, the offences which are covered have remained more or less the same. The definition used in Northern Ireland is broadly comparable with that of notifiable offences in England and Wales. Due to the differences in the legal system, recording practices and classification, recorded crimes and offences in Scotland are not directly comparable with recorded notifiable offences in England and Wales. In Scotland the term 'crimes' is used for the more serious criminal acts (roughly equivalent to indictable offences); the less serious are termed 'offences'.

Because the number of offences recorded over time is affected by the size of the population, a better picture of trends is given by the crime rate. Chart 9.2 shows the number of notifiable offences recorded per 100 population. The rate tripled in England and Wales between 1971 and 1992 but then fell by nearly 2 per cent in 1993 when there was one offence recorded for every ten people. The rates for Northern Ireland and Scotland have also increased since 1971; they then also fell between 1992 and 1993, by 4 per cent and 8 per cent respectively.

Around half of all offences notified to the police in the United Kingdom in 1993 were for theft and handling of stolen goods (Table 9.3). Crimes against property (burglary, fraud, forgery and criminal damage together with theft and handling of stolen goods) constituted over 90 per cent of crimes in England and Wales, and only slightly smaller proportions in Scotland and Northern Ireland. In England and Wales the largest increase between 1991 and 1993 was for drug trafficking, which increased by 30 per cent. More detailed information on drug offences is shown in Table 12.6.

The British Crime Survey (BCS), which covers England and Wales, conducts interviews with the public about their experiences of crime to give a fuller count of the number of offences than the number recorded by the police. The most recent survey was carried out in 1994 and provides estimates of crime committed in 1993. A similar survey, the Scottish Crime Survey (SCS), was carried out in Scotland in 1993 which asked members of the public about their experiences of crime in 1992.

The BCS examines crimes against individuals and their property; it does not include crimes against organisations such as company fraud and shoplifting or crimes such as drug abuse where the victim is also the perpetrator. Results from the survey, in Chart 9.4, show that certain crimes are more likely to be recorded than others. In 1993 theft of motor vehicles was the crime most likely to be reported: 95 per cent were recorded by the police. This is probably because people have to report such a theft for insurance purposes. The least likely crimes to be reported were robbery or theft from the person (12 per cent) and vandalism (14 per cent).

9.4

Percentage of offences recorded by the police: by type of offence, 1993

England & Wales

Percentages

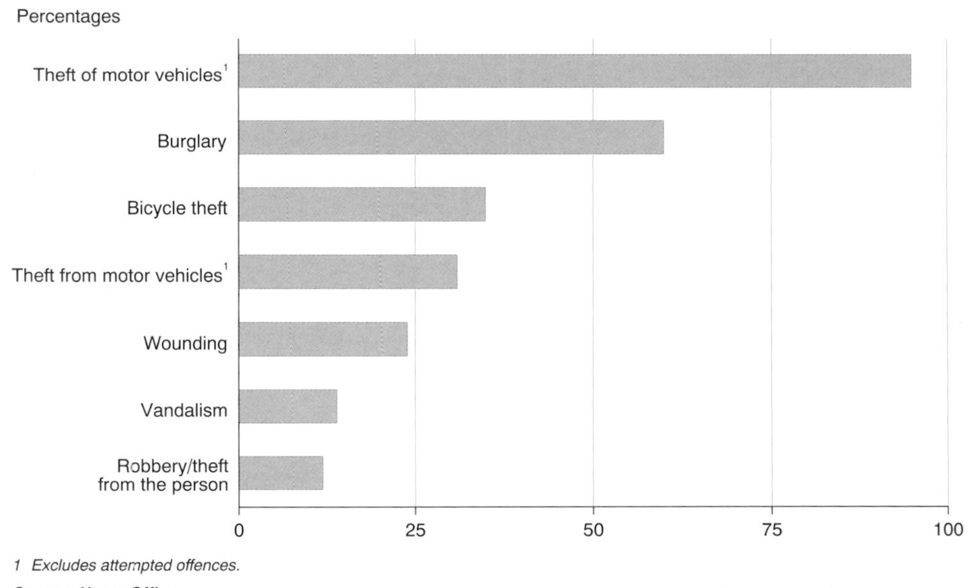

1 Excludes attempted offences.

Source: Home Office

9.5

Retail crime costs, 1992-93

Great Britain

Percentages

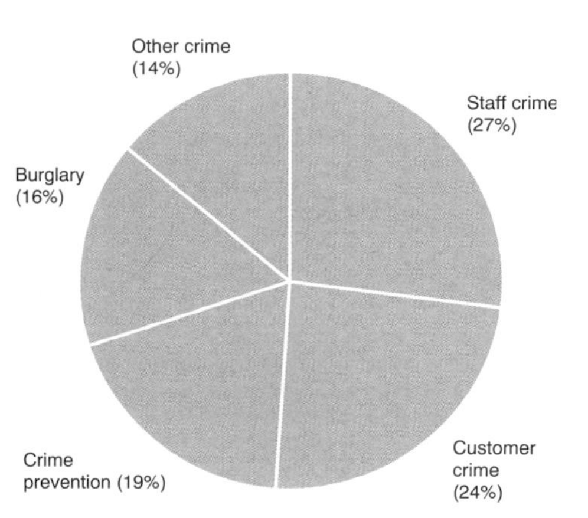

Source: British Retail Consortium

In 1993 a survey on retail crime was carried out by the British Retail Consortium. This drew responses from 54 thousand retail outlets in Great Britain and investigated crime affecting retail companies in 1992-93. The overall cost of retail crime in 1992-93 was estimated at £2 billion; a breakdown of this cost is shown in Chart 9.5. External crime (comprising customer theft, burglary and other crimes such as arson and robbery) accounted for just over half the total cost compared with just over a quarter for staff crime; crime prevention measures accounted for the remainder.

Retail premises were the target of almost 180 thousand burglaries. Certain types of business are more likely to be burgled: risks are highest for grocery and electrical shops, gas showrooms and music shops. It is estimated that there were also nearly 28 thousand cases of staff being involved in theft. The average value recovered from suspects of such incidents was £159: only just over half were reported to the police. The cost of fraud to the retailer was estimated as being relatively minor, only costing an estimated £22 million. However, the cost of fraudulent payment card transactions are usually borne by the financial institutions.

One or two major drug seizures can have a significant effect on the quantity of drugs seized in any one year. Table 9.6 shows that the quantities of cocaine seized doubled between 1991 and 1992 but then fell to a third of its 1992 level by 1993, despite there being more seizures in total. Since 1981 there have been dramatic increases in quantities seized for many drugs, especially 'ecstasy' which was very rare in the United Kingdom in 1981. Quantities of 'ecstasy' and LSD are measured in doses. In 1992 there were over half a million doses of both LSD and 'ecstasy' seized although these amounts fell to 450 thousand doses of LSD and 300 thousand doses of 'ecstasy' in 1993. Still by far the most common illegal drug is cannabis - in 1993 over 60 thousand kilograms were seized, by either Customs or police, almost a fifth up on the previous year.

9.6

Quantity[1] and number of seizures[2] of class A drugs: by type of drug

United Kingdom

	Quantity seized (kilogrammes)				Number of seizures			
	1981	1991	1992	1993	1981	1991	1992	1993
Cocaine	21.1	1,077.8	2,248.2	708.6	503	1,984	2,365	2,983
Heroin	93.4	493.2	546.6	655.7	819	2,640	2,968	3,679
Opium	16.5	8.0	3.8	8.2	137	49	57	64
Morphine	6.5	0.4	1.5	1.7	243	119	106	141
Pethidine	0.3	-	16.9	-	135	33	24	18
Methadone	1.0	0.8	0.5	28.9	402	427	441	620
LSD	..	..	..	..	384	1,636	2,474	2,513
MDMA (Ecstasy)	..	..	..	..	..	1,735	2,399	2,341
Other class A	0.6	14.4	18.4	33.6	119	541	748	717

1 See Appendix, Part 9: Drugs seizures.
2 A seizure can include more than one type of drug.

Source: Home Office

In 1993, The British Social Attitudes Survey, carried out by Social and Community Planning Research included questions about people's attitudes to cannabis. Around one in five people in Great Britain agreed with the statement that 'Smoking cannabis should be legalised' while almost half disagreed strongly. This shows a change in attitudes since 1983 when only one in eight agreed and more than six in ten disagreed strongly. Cannabis was thought of as a cause of crime and violence by over half of those interviewed in 1993, while almost one in three felt that it is not 'nearly as damaging to users as some people think'.

Table 9.7 shows the proportion of various types of offences where firearms have been used. Although the percentage of all offences in which they have been used has increased, less than one in three hundred offences involved the use of a firearm in 1993. Firearms are most likely to be used in homicides and robberies: they were used in around one in ten of these offences. Just under 16 thousand offences in the United Kingdom in 1993 involved a firearm; over 40 per cent of these were robberies and a further third were cases of criminal damage. In Northern Ireland, the security situation has led to much higher levels of crime involving firearms - around one in eight of all offences and about two thirds of all homicides.

9.7

Percentages of selected offences in which firearms were reported to have been used

England & Wales — Percentages

	1971	1981	1991	1993
Homicide	*8.3*	*6.1*	*7.6*	*11.0*
Robbery	*7.7*	*9.3*	*11.7*	*10.2*
Attempted murder/acts endangering life	*5.7*	*5.0*	*5.9*	*6.1*
Other violence against the person	*2.0*	*2.9*	*1.0*	*0.9*
Criminal damage[1]	*0.3*	*1.4*	*0.6*	*0.7*
All offences	*0.1*	*0.3*	*0.2*	*0.3*

1 Includes damage valued at £100 or more in 1971, £20 or more in subsequent years.

Source: Home Office

Victims

Risks of crime vary across different types of areas; the BCS collected information as to which kinds of area were most susceptible to burglary and car crime. The classifications are taken from the 1991 Population Census and describe the broad characteristics of each area. Roughly speaking, thriving areas are the wealthiest while striving are the poorest - mostly inner city council estates. Table 9.8 shows that risks are lowest in the most prosperous areas and highest in the poorest areas with the notable exception of rising areas which tend to be wealthy but in cities. The risk of car crime in striving, less prosperous areas is approaching twice the national average while the risk in the most wealthy areas is only half of the national average.

9.8

Victims of burglary and car crime: by type of area[1], 1993

England & Wales — Indices

	Burglary	Car crime[2]
Thriving	58	52
Expanding	60	63
Rising	177	148
Settling	82	82
Aspiring	90	106
Striving	162	190
All areas	100	100

1 See Appendix, Part 9: Type of area.
2 Thefts and attempted thefts of/from cars taking place in private and semi-private parking areas by the home or in nearby streets. Risks are based on car owners.

Source: Home Office

9.9

Offences currently recorded as homicide: by age of victim, 1993

United Kingdom

Rate per million population

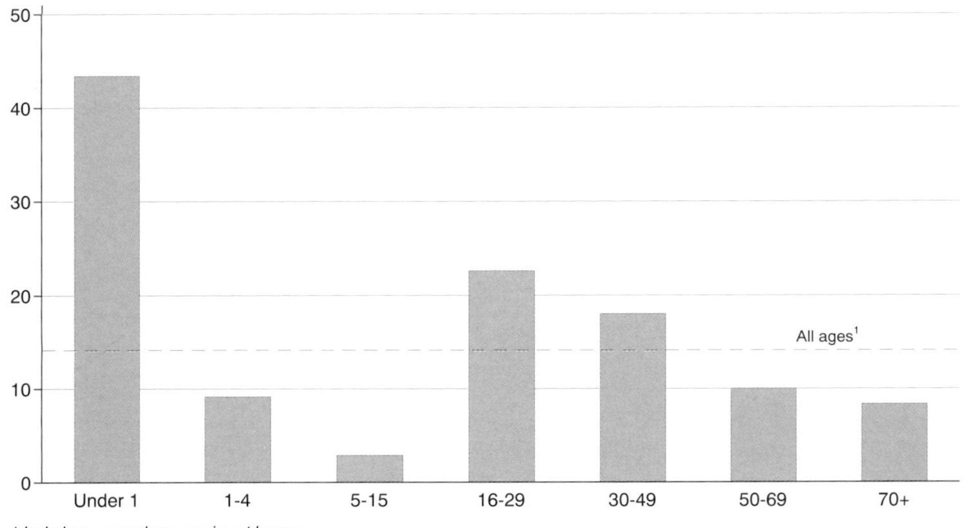

1 Includes cases where age is not known.

Source: Home Office; The Scottish Office Home and Health Department; Royal Ulster Constabulary

9.10

Northern Ireland: deaths and injuries due to the security situation

Thousands

Source: Royal Ulster Constabulary

Homicides are still rare - there were only 829 in the United Kingdom in 1993, 5 per cent less than in the previous year. Chart 9.9 shows the homicide rate per million population. Infants, aged under 1, are more at risk than any other age group while children aged between 5 and 15 are the age group least likely to be murdered. Generally males are more likely than females to be a victim of homicide; in 1993 they accounted for around two thirds of homicide victims in the United Kingdom.

Between 1969 and 1993 the security situation in Northern Ireland led to over 3 thousand deaths and nearly 36 thousand injurie (Chart 9.10). In 1993 there were 84 deaths, 70 of whom were civilians. In 1994 there were 58 deaths up until September.

Despite the IRA 'cease-fire' from 1st September, and similar actions by the Loyalist para-militaries from 14th October, two further deaths had occurred by mid December.

Many people could be considered to be victims of crime albeit indirectly because their quality of life is affected by the fear of crime. For example, they may be afraid to go out at night. Table 9.11 gives results from the British Crime Survey and shows that men worry most about theft of their cars while more women report being worried about burglary. In almost all instances older people were less likely to report being 'very worried' than younger people, with mugging being the only crime which older people found more worrying.

Similar results came from the Scottish Crime Survey in 1992 although in general more women than men reported being 'very worried'. Also with the exception of housebreaking, younger respondents were more likely to be 'worried'.

Offences cleared up

Offences can be cleared up by the police in a number of ways: a person can be charged, summonsed or cautioned for an offence. Alternatively an offence may be admitted and taken into consideration by the court (although the system is different in Scotland), or the police may not proceed with a case even if there is sufficient evidence to make a charge.

One in four of all notifiable offences was cleared up in England and Wales in 1993 (Table 9.12). However the rate is much higher for certain offences, with three quarters of violent and sexual crimes being cleared up. For vehicle crime, both theft of and from vehicles, less than one in five offences is cleared up. Drug trafficking has a high clear up rate because the offence is only identified by detecting a suspect. In Scotland and Northern Ireland the overall clear up rates are higher at 34 per cent and 36 per cent respectively.

9.11

Fear[1] of crime: by gender, age and type of crime, 1993

England & Wales — Percentages

	Males				Females			
	16-29	30-59	Over 60	All over 16	16-29	30-59	Over 60	All over 16
Theft of car	*34*	*27*	*22*	*27*	*34*	*28*	*26*	*29*
Theft from car	*28*	*23*	*18*	*23*	*23*	*21*	*18*	*21*
Burglary	*22*	*22*	*20*	*22*	*33*	*29*	*29*	*30*
Mugging	*13*	*12*	*14*	*13*	*33*	*26*	*29*	*29*
Rape	..	..	..	..	*38*	*22*	*21*	*25*

1 Percentage feeling 'very worried'.

Source: Home Office

9.12

Clear-up rates for notifiable offences[1]: by type of offence

Percentages

	England & Wales			Scotland			Northern Ireland		
	1981	1991	1993	1981	1991	1993	1981	1991[2]	1993[2]
Violence against the person	*75*	*77*	*76*	*83*	*81*	*77*	*47*	*62*	*62*
Sexual offences,	*73*	*76*	*75*	*65*	*77*	*77*	*71*	*87*	*74*
of which: rape	*68*	*76*	*74*	*74*	*79*	*76*	*45*	*80*	*76*
Burglary	*30*	*23*	*19*	*20*	*15*	*16*	*22*	*22*	*20*
Robbery	*25*	*23*	*22*	*26*	*27*	*27*	*15*	*17*	*15*
Drug trafficking	..	*97*	*96*	*99*	*100*	*100*	*100*	*82*	*93*
Theft and handling stolen goods,	*38*	*28*	*23*	*28*	*23*	*24*	*27*	*34*	*34*
of which: theft of vehicles	*28*	*24*	*18*	*26*	*21*	*21*	*14*	*29*	*30*
theft from vehicles[3]	*23*	*19*	*13*	..	..	*12*	*12*	*12*	*10*
Fraud and forgery	*70*	*55*	*51*	*78*	*70*	*77*	*66*	*67*	*62*
Criminal damage[4]	*27*	*19*	*16*	*22*	*19*	*19*	*17*	*32*	*35*
Other notifiable offences	*91*	*96*	*95*	*90*	*98*	*98*	*33*	*79*	*82*
All notifiable offences	*38*	*29*	*25*	*31*	*31*	*34*	*27*	*36*	*36*

1 Includes attempted offences. Scottish figures of 'crime' have been grouped in an attempt to approximate to the classification of notifiable offences in England & Wales and Northern Ireland. However, differences in the legal systems, recording and counting practices and classification problems mean that Scottish figures should not be compared with those for England & Wales and Northern Ireland.
2 No longer includes assault on police and communicating false information regarding a bomb hoax. These offences have been removed from the categories ' Violence against the person' and 'Other notifiable offences'.
3 In Scotland data have only been collected from January 1992. The figures include theft by opening lockfast places, from motor vehicles and other theft from motor vehicles.
4 In Northern Ireland, the figures exclude criminal damage valued at £200 or less.

Source: Home Office; The Scottish Office Home and Health Department; Royal Ulster Constabulary

9.13

Primary clear up rates for recorded notifiable offences: by police force area, 1993

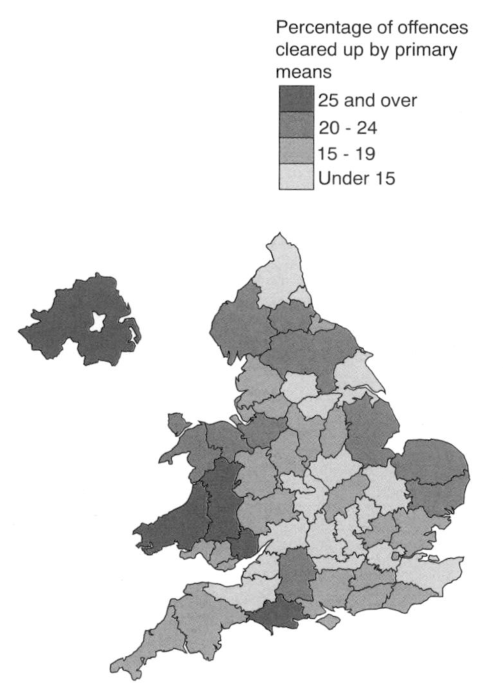

Source: Home Office; Royal Ulster Constabulary

Offences may be cleared up by primary or secondary methods. Primary clear up occurs when someone is summonsed, charged or cautioned for the offence, whereas secondary clear up includes offences taken into consideration in court or additional offences admitted when a convicted prisoner who admits to further offences. Primary methods accounted for around six in ten of all offences cleared up in 1993. Chart 9.13 contains primary clear up rates by police force area. Generally, more rural areas have higher clear up rates. The highest primary clear up rate in 1993 in England and Wales was in Gwent, at 35 per cent, while the Metropolitan Police Force Area had the lowest rate at 10 per cent. In Scotland where rates are not comparable, no distinction is made between primary and secondary clear up; the percentage of crimes cleared up ranges from around three in ten in Strathclyde to nearly six in ten in the Northern area.

Offenders

Theft and handling of stolen goods accounted for about three in five offences committed by boys aged between 10 and 13, compared with only two in five for those over 18 (Table 9.14). Over four in five offences committed by girls aged 10 to 13 were theft and handling of stolen goods. Over two fifths of all offenders found guilty or cautioned were under 21.

9.14

Offenders found guilty of, or cautioned for, indictable offences: by gender, age and type of offence, 1993

England & Wales — Percentages

	Males					Females				
	10-13	14-17	18-20	21 and over	All aged 10 and over	10-13	14-17	18-20	21 and over	All aged 10 and over
Theft and handling stolen goods	*61*	*48*	*38*	*39*	*42*	*84*	*72*	*65*	*64*	*68*
Violence against the person	*10*	*13*	*11*	*14*	*13*	*8*	*14*	*9*	*9*	*10*
Burglary	*18*	*13*	*15*	*9*	*12*	*4*	*4*	*3*	*1*	*2*
Drug offences	*1*	*9*	*17*	*13*	*12*	-	*3*	*9*	*7*	*6*
Criminal damage	*5*	*3*	*3*	*3*	*3*	*1*	*2*	*1*	*1*	*1*
Sexual offences	*1*	*2*	*1*	*2*	*2*	-	-	-	-	-
Robbery	*2*	*2*	*1*	*1*	*1*	-	*1*	*1*	-	-
Other indictable offences	*2*	*6*	*15*	*20*	*16*	*1*	*4*	*13*	*17*	*12*
All indictable offences (=100%) (thousands)	22.2	78.0	77.5	244.1	421.8	7.7	21.6	13.0	51.3	93.7

Source: Home Office

Chart 9.15 shows likelihood of offending by age. The peak offending age for males in England and Wales and in Scotland is 18. In England and Wales the peak offending age for females is 15. A 15 year old girl is more likely to commit an offence than a man aged 31 or over. In Northern Ireland, the peak ages for offending are higher at 19 for males and 18 for females.

Table 9.16 shows that over half of offenders commencing probation or community service or discharged from prison are reconvicted within two years. The likelihood of reoffending generally increases with the number of previous convictions, but decreases with age. More than seven in ten of those under the age of 21 who have been to prison are reconvicted within two years of release compared with only four in ten of those aged 30 or over. Differences between reconviction rates for different types of sentences reflect not only the effectiveness of the sentences involved but also the different characteristics of offenders receiving sentences.

9.15

Known offenders[1] as a percentage of the population: by age and gender, 1993

England & Wales

Percentages

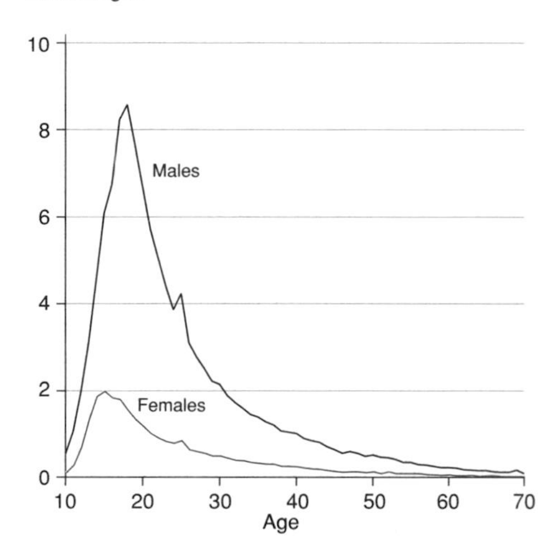

1 Persons found guilty or cautioned for indictable offences.

Source: Home Office

9.16

Percentage of persons reconvicted within 2 years[1]: by number of previous convictions[2], age and type of sentence last received

England & Wales Percentages

	Number of previous convictions					
	0	1-2	3-6	7-10	11 or more	All
Aged under 21						
Probation	*43*	*58*	*76*	*85*	*93*	*63*
Community service	*45*	*59*	*77*	*84*	*92*	*65*
Immediate custody	*43*	*64*	*78*	*84*	*90*	*71*
Aged 21-24						
Probation	*27*	*50*	*56*	*74*	*81*	*55*
Community service	*30*	*41*	*59*	*65*	*71*	*52*
Immediate custody	*19*	*36*	*59*	*71*	*80*	*58*
Aged 25-29						
Probation	*21*	*34*	*51*	*59*	*69*	*47*
Community service	*20*	*34*	*48*	*58*	*72*	*47*
Immediate custody	*16*	*33*	*40*	*54*	*74*	*50*
Aged 30 and over						
Probation	*17*	*32*	*36*	*48*	*60*	*39*
Community service	*19*	*16*	*31*	*52*	*62*	*37*
Immediate custody	*5*	*16*	*31*	*41*	*69*	*40*

1 Offenders commencing orders or discharged during 1987. Convictions are for standard list offences and reconvictions may include offences committed before the sentencing date.
2 Only one conviction is counted for each court appearance.

Source: Home Office

9.17

Offenders cautioned: by type of indictable offence[1]

England & Wales — Percentages

	1971[2]	1981	1991	1993
Violence against the person	3.0	5.4	10.8	11.5
Sexual offences	5.0	2.7	1.8	1.6
Burglary[3]	16.0	10.8	7.4	6.1
Robbery	0.3	0.1	0.3	0.3
Theft and handling stolen goods	69.2	76.2	60.3	55.9
Fraud and forgery	1.3	1.3	3.1	3.9
Criminal damage	4.7	2.0	2.1	2.0
Drug offences	0.4	0.3	11.8	16.7
Other[3]		1.3	2.3	2.0
All offenders cautioned[1] (=100%)(thousands)	77.3	103.9	179.9	209.6

1 Excludes motoring offences.
2 Adjusted to take account of the Criminal Damage Act 1971.
3 See Appendix, Part 9 : Offenders cautioned for burglary.

Source: Home Office

Police and courts action and sentencing

When the police in England and Wales detect an alleged offender they can either take no action; issue a formal caution; or start a prosecution. The Crown Prosecution Service (CPS) decide whether or not to continue the prosecution, which can be discontinued by the CPS if it is felt that there is insufficient evidence to give a realistic prospect of conviction or to proceed would not be in the public interest. The number of offenders cautioned in England and Wales doubled between 1981 and 1993 is shown in Table 9.17 overleaf. However, the number cautioned in 1993 was 6.6 thousand less than in 1992, with the fall occurring in the last quarter. This probably reflected the issue of draft Home Office guidance in October 1993 which discouraged the use of cautions for serious offences and for offenders who had been cautioned previously.

A third of all offenders sentenced for indictable offences in England, Wales and Northern Ireland in 1993 were fined (Table 9.18). Only one in seven offenders was sentenced to immediate custody. However for the more serious offences like robbery and sexual offences, a custodial sentence is by far the most likely outcome.

9.18

Offenders sentenced for indictable offences: by type of offence and type of sentence, 1993

England & Wales and Northern Ireland — Percentages

	Discharge	Fine	Community sentence	Fully suspended sentence	Immediate custody: Under 5 years	Immediate custody: 5 years and over	Other	Total sentenced (=100%) (thousands)
Violence against the person	24	20	29	2	18	1	5	40.6
Sexual offences	9	14	26	3	34	11	2	4.5
Burglary	12	11	46	1	29	-	1	41.4
Robbery	3	-	24	1	51	16	4	5.2
Theft and handling stolen goods	27	37	25	1	8	-	1	124.7
Fraud and forgery	24	26	30	3	14	-	2	18.1
Criminal damage	30	19	30	2	9	1	9	10.5
Drug offences	16	51	15	1	14	2	-	22.3
Motoring	6	68	14	1	10	0	-	10.9
Other	17	55	12	1	11	-	4	37.6
All indictable offences	21	33	26	1	14	1	3	315.8

Source: Home Office; Northern Ireland Office

9.19

Court proceedings for persons[1] with charge proved: by type of crime or offence and outcome, 1992

Scotland — Percentages

	Custody	Community service	Probation	Fine	Admonished	Compensation order	Other	All outcomes (=100%) (thousands)
Crime								
Non-sexual crimes of violence	*35.6*	*10.0*	*8.4*	*32.9*	*10.3*	*0.8*	*1.9*	4
Crimes of indecency	*12.6*	*1.9*	*11.5*	*62.4*	*10.5*	*0.3*	*0.9*	1
Crimes of dishonesty	*20.9*	*8.3*	*7.9*	*48.5*	*11.7*	*2.0*	*0.6*	34
Crimes against property	*6.2*	*3.2*	*4.0*	*65.8*	*10.1*	*9.9*	*0.9*	6
Other crimes	*15.0*	*4.9*	*4.9*	*60.0*	*14.4*	*0.1*	*0.6*	10
All crimes	*19.1*	*7.1*	*7.1*	*51.6*	*11.9*	*2.4*	*0.7*	54
Offences								
Miscellaneous offences	*6.0*	*2.1*	*2.3*	*73.7*	*14.4*	*0.7*	*0.8*	53
Motor vehicle offences	*1.3*	*0.8*	*0.3*	*93.4*	*4.0*	-	*0.2*	69
All offences	*3.4*	*1.4*	*1.1*	*84.8*	*8.5*	*0.3*	*0.5*	122
All crimes and offences	*8.2*	*3.2*	*3.0*	*74.6*	*9.6*	*0.9*	*0.6*	176

1 Includes companies.

Source: The Scottish Office Home and Health Department

9.20

The equivalent breakdown for Scotland is given in Table 9.19. Fines are a much more common outcome of court proceedings, accounting for three quarters of cases where the charge is proved. For all categories of crime or offence a fine is the most common outcome except for crimes of violence where custody is more likely than a fine. For offenders under 21, fines account for only around 60 per cent of outcomes with custody and admonishments each accounting for over 10 per cent. Over 20 per cent of young female offenders are admonished while overall for females, admonishments are more than nine times as likely as custody.

In 1993 in England and Wales nearly 7 million offences relating to motor vehicles were dealt with - almost 80 per cent more than in 1971

Action taken for offences relating to motor vehicles

England & Wales — Percentages

	1971	1981	1991	1993
Fixed penalty notice	*51*	*60*	*68*	*59*
Court proceedings	*43*	*35*	*27*	*35*
Vehicle defect rectification scheme	..	..	*2*	*3*
Written warning issued	*6*	*5*	*3*	*3*
Total offences dealt with (=100%) (thousands)	3,907	6,900	8,368	6,976

Source: Home Office

(Table 9.20). However it must be remembered that car ownership doubled over the same period. In 1993 nearly six in ten offences resulted in a fixed penalty notice (mostly for obstruction, waiting and parking offences). In addition there were a further half a million fixed penalty notices issued in Scotland in 1993.

9.21

Average sentence length[1] for defendants aged 21 or over sentenced to immediate custody at the Crown Court : by gender and type of offence

England and Wales Months

	Males				Females			
	1981	1986	1991	1993	1981	1986	1991	1993
Violence against the person	17	18	20	22	14	19	20	22
Sexual offences	29	32	38	39	20	23	29	28
Burglary	17	16	16	16	11	12	13	14
Robbery	39	47	48	48	21	32	34	32
Theft and handling stolen goods	11	11	10	11	7	8	8	9
Fraud and forgery	16	15	16	15	10	11	12	10
Criminal damage	19	22	22	27	14	24	25	31
Drug offences	26	30	32	31	19	24	37	31
Motoring offences	6	6	8	8	4	4	9	8
Other	11	13	12	12	11	7	14	12
All offences	17	18	21	22	11	14	18	18

1 Excludes life sentences.

Source: Home Office

When the sentence is for immediate custody, different courts have different limitations. Magistrates' courts in England and Wales are restricted to custodial sentences of 6 months or less while the Crown Courts have no limitations, apart from those placed on particular offences. Table 9.21 shows the average sentence lengths imposed by the Crown Courts in England and Wales for different offence types. This has increased since 1981 for both males and females, although robbery is still the most severely penalised. Criminal damage is the only offence for which, on average, females get longer sentences than males. Average sentence lengths in Scotland and Northern Ireland are longer, with the average for males in each country being over 50 months.

9.22

Appeals against conviction or sentence: by type of court and type of appeal[1]

England & Wales

	Number of appeals				Percentage successful			
	1971	1981	1991	1993	1971	1981	1991	1993
Crown Court								
Against conviction	7,950	6,202	8,537	11,226	..	*27*	*38*	*38*
Against sentence		10,735	10,113	13,823	..	*51*	*49*	*53*
Court of Appeal								
Against conviction	1,627	1,418	1,711	1,967	*11*	*10*	*13*	*16*
Against sentence	5,664	4,757	5,407	5,322	*8*	*20*	*26*	*33*

1 Appeals against both sentence and conviction are counted in both categories

Source: Home Office

After conviction and sentencing, the defendant can appeal against either the sentence, the conviction or both, although only a small percentage do so. In England and Wales appeals against decisions made at magistrates' courts are heard at the Crown Court while appeals against Crown Court decisions are made at the Court of Appeal. Appeals to the Crown Court have a higher success rate than those at the Court of Appeal; half the Crown Court appeals against sentence in 1993 were successful (Table 9.22). Appeals against sentence have a better chance of success than appeals against conviction.

Prisons and probation

Chart 9.1, at the beginning of this chapter, shows how the prison population of Great Britain has fluctuated since 1971, reaching a peak of 55 thousand in 1988 when it exceeded the certified accommodation by just over 10 per cent. Since then, accommodation has increased and in 1992 and 1993 exceeded the prison population. Although some overcrowding still exists in many prisons, the number of prisoners sharing two or three to a cell designed for one has fallen sharply. The practice of 'trebling' - holding prisoners three to a cell designed for one person - has been virtually eliminated. As recently as 1987-88, over 5 thousand prisoners were held three to a cell: by February 1994 this had been reduced to only 54. The number of prisoners held two to a cell intended for one person has more than halved from nearly 18 thousand in January 1987 to just over 8 thousand in February 1994.

Twenty four hour access to sanitation for prisoners has also increased in line with recommendations made in the Woolf report following the riot at Strangeways prison and other establishments in 1990. In January 1994 nearly nine in ten prisoners had 24 hour access to sanitation, compared with less than half in 1981.

Over a quarter of prisoners are remand prisoners, either untried or convicted but unsentenced. The average time in custody for an untried prisoner in Great Britain is around 49 days whilst for those held after conviction in custody whilst awaiting sentence the average is around 33 days (Chart 9.23). The average time in custody for convicted unsentenced prisoners has remained fairly constant over the last 15 years; the average time for untried prisoners has increased by 90 per cent since 1977. Average time in custody for remand prisoners is lower in Scotland than in England and Wales.

9.23

Average time spent in prison service establishments by remand prisoners

Great Britain

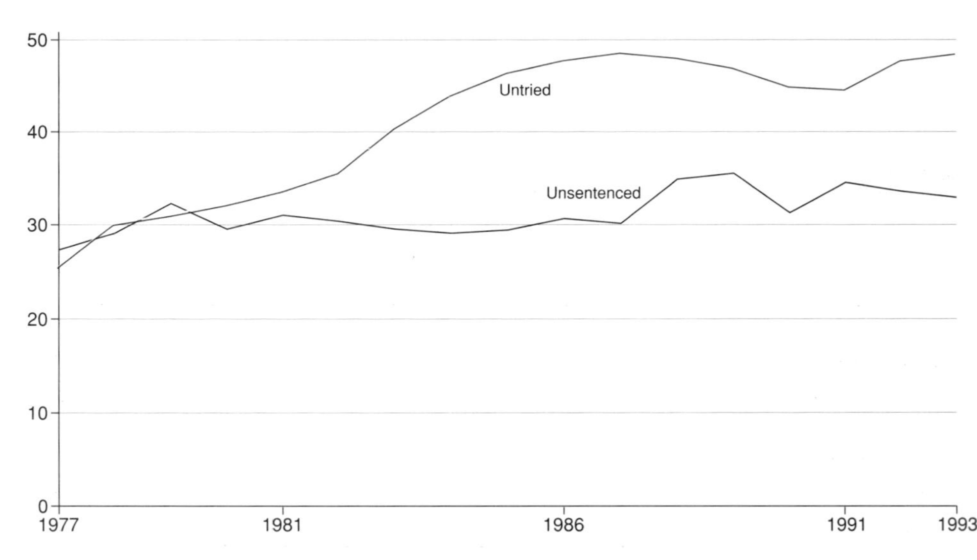

Source: Home Office; The Scottish Office Home and Health Department

9.24

Sentenced male adult prisoners: by ethnic origin and type of offence, 1993

England & Wales Percentages

	White	Black[1]	Indian Pakistani or Bangladesh	Other ethnic minoriy groups	All ethnic groups
Violence against the person	*22*	*20*	*25*	*20*	*22*
Rape	*4*	*7*	*6*	*5*	*5*
Other sexual offences	*6*	*1*	*3*	*3*	*5*
Burglary	*15*	*10*	*4*	*9*	*14*
Robbery	*13*	*18*	*10*	*17*	*14*
Theft and handling	*9*	*5*	*7*	*6*	*8*
Fraud and forgery	*3*	*2*	*7*	*3*	*3*
Drugs offences	*8*	*20*	*22*	*21*	*11*
Other offences	*11*	*6*	*11*	*8*	*11*
Offence not recorded	*6*	*8*	*4*	*6*	*6*
Fine defaulters	*2*	*1*	*1*	*1*	*2*
All sentenced adult male prisoners (=100%)(thousands)	22.1	3.8	0.7	1.1	27.7

1 Black Caribbean, Black African and Black Other.

Source: Home Office

Over a fifth of the male prison population in 1993 had been convicted of violence against the person (Table 9.24) with robbery and burglary being the next most common types of offence. This pattern varies according to ethnic origin with over a fifth of non-white sentenced offenders in prison having been convicted of drug offences. In some cases, sentenced prisoners may be foreign nationals who have a quite different distribution of offence types with almost one in three offenders convicted of drugs offences.

Males are more than 20 times as likely to go to prison under sentence than females (Table 9.25); amongst males the rate is highest for 17 to 20 year olds. Only 1 in every 10 thousand females went to prison in 1993. The composition of the prison population has been changing in recent years, in part as a result of changes in criminal justice policy and practice. A much higher proportion of sentenced offenders are serving longer sentences, or life sentences, for violent or drugs related offences. Among those serving an immediate custodial sentence, 60 per cent had been convicted of violent or drugs offences compared with around a third in 1981.

Life sentences are mandatory for convictions of murder and can also be passed as a result of other serious offences. The population of life sentence prisoners has risen over time; in 1993 nearly 10 per cent of the prison population were serving a life sentence (Chart 9.26). The time spent in prison by life sentence prisoners varies considerably but the average time served by life prisoners when they are first released on life licence has increased from just over 10 years in 1982 to over 14 years in 1993 when 120 life prisoners were released on licence.

9.25

Receptions into prison service establishments[1]: by gender and age, 1993

England & Wales and Northern Ireland Rate[2]

	Males	Females	All
15-16	26	1	14
17-20	85	3	45
21-24	73	3	39
25-29	45	3	24
30-39	24	1	13
40-49	10	1	6
50-59	4	-	2
60 and over	1	-	-
All aged 15 and over	24	1	12

1 Receptions under sentence excluding fine defaulters and prisoners held in police cells.
2 Per 10,000 population.

Source: Home Office; Northern Ireland Office

9.26

Percentage of the sentenced prison population serving a life sentence

United Kingdom

Percentages

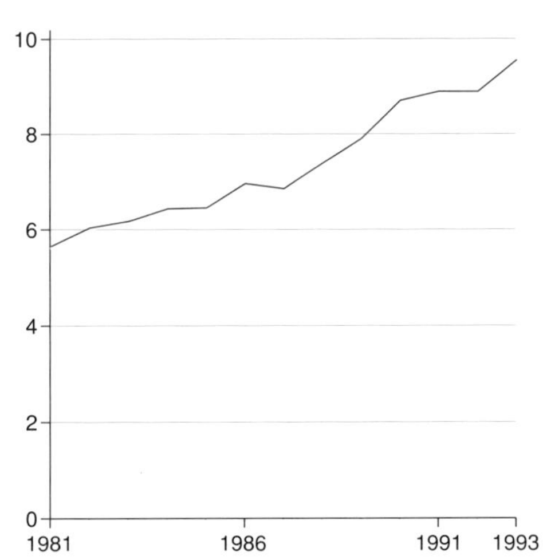

Source: Home Office; The Scottish Office Home and Health Department; Northern Ireland Office

The United Kingdom has the second highest number of prisoners per head of population in the European Community (Chart 9.27). However, this does not necessarily imply a higher crime rate or more punitive sentencing as national differences in sentencing and imprisonment policies make comparisons between countries difficult. A country with a high prison population may not have a high crime rate, but a tougher sentencing policy which might mean either that offenders are more likely to be imprisoned or that those offenders who are imprisoned receive longer sentences.

The Prison Service collects information on the time use of prisoners. The average amount of time spent on 'purposeful activities' (which includes education, training and work around the prison) has increased from under 22 hours per week at the beginning of 1990-91 to over 25 hours at the beginning of 1994. However this varies according to the type of prison service establishment; for example, male prisoners in local prisons and remand centres spend less than 19 hours a week on these activities which is only two fifths of the time spent by male prisoners in open prisons. Chart 9.28 shows a breakdown into the different types of purposeful activity. On average, domestic or farm/garden work accounts for over 9 hours a week, which is two fifths of the total time spent on purposeful activities, while over 4 hours a week is spent on education.

The National Prison Survey was conducted in England and Wales in 1991; among other things, it collected information on prisoners' attitudes towards the prison regime. Table 9.29 shows the percentage of prisoners who agreed with six statements (three positive and three

9.27

Prison population[1]: EC comparison, 1992

Rate per 100,000 population

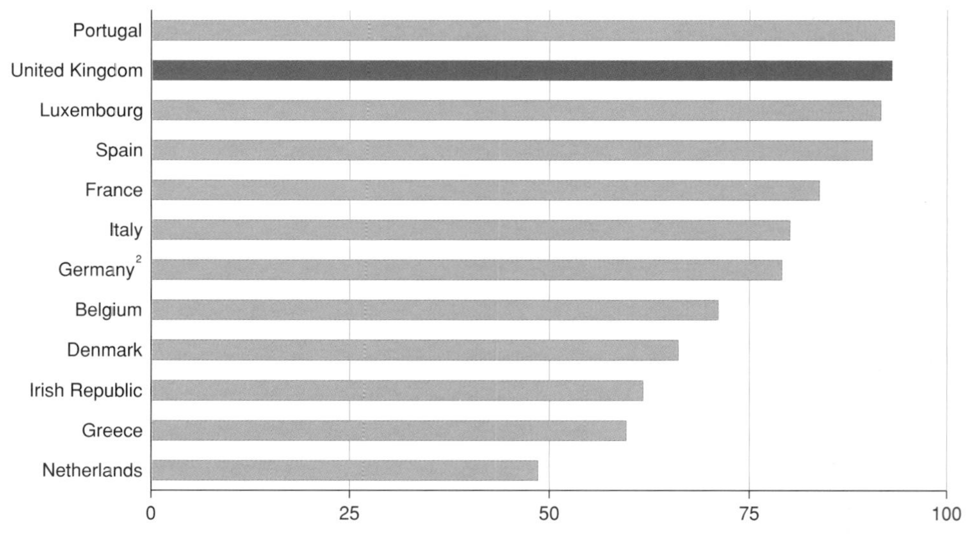

1 At 1 September.
2 As constituted since 3 October 1990. Data relate to 1 September 1991.
Source: Council of Europe; Home Office

9.28

Time spent by prisoners on purposeful activities, 1992-93

England & Wales

Percentages

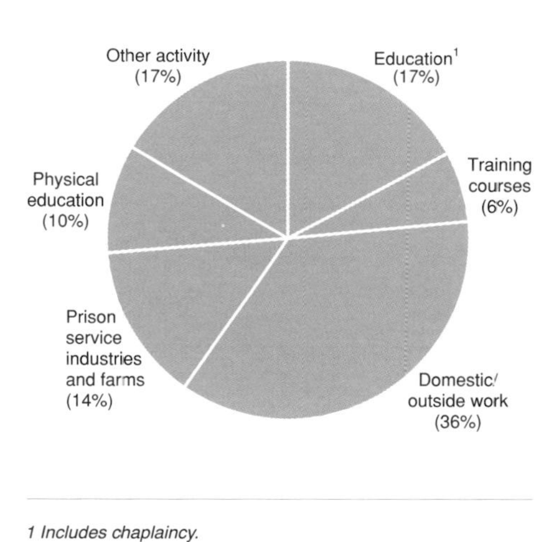

1 Includes chaplaincy.
Source: Home Office

9.29

Prisoners' attitudes to prison officers[1], 1991

England & Wales Percentages

	1991
Some prison officers have been helpful to me here	*78*
Most prison officers treat prisoners fairly here	*71*
It is easy to talk to prison officers here	*50*
The prison officers could be more helpful	*76*
Prison officers don't really care about prisoners here	*43*
Some prison officers assault prisoners here	*25*

1 Prisoners stated whether or not they agreed with the six statements read out.
Source: Home Office

9.30

Persons receiving criminal supervision[1]: by gender and age

England & Wales				Percentages
	1982	1986	1991	1993
Males				
Under 17	*9*	*5*	*1*	*1*
17-24	*55*	*54*	*49*	*42*
25-40	*26*	*31*	*38*	*44*
40 and over	*9*	*10*	*12*	*14*
All males (=100%) (thousands)	123.0	117.4	125.4	133.3
Females				
Under 17	*6*	*3*	*1*	*1*
17-24	*44*	*46*	*42*	*36*
25-40	*34*	*38*	*45*	*50*
40 and over	*15*	*14*	*12*	*13*
All females (=100%) (thousands)	23.5	20.0	16.4	14.7
Total				
Under 17	*9*	*5*	*1*	*1*
17-24	*54*	*53*	*48*	*41*
25-40	*27*	*32*	*39*	*44*
40 and over	*10*	*11*	*12*	*14*
All (=100%) (thousands)	146.5	137.4	141.8	148.0

1 Includes supervision under the Children and Young Persons Act 1969 following care proceedings.

Source: Home Office

9.31

Neighbourhood watch schemes[1]

England & Wales

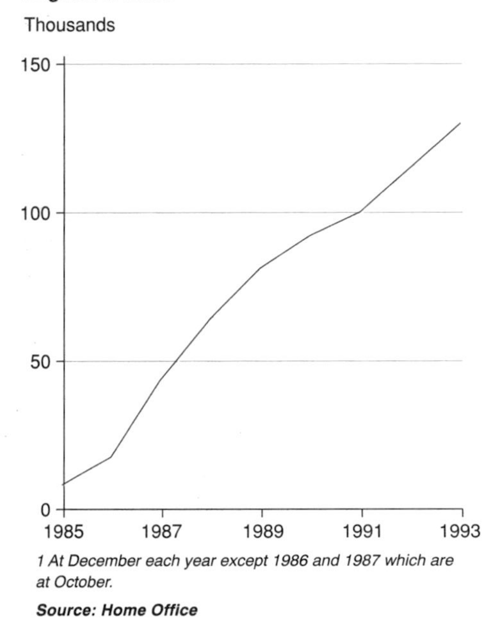

1 At December each year except 1986 and 1987 which are at October.

Source: Home Office

negative) about their prison officers. Nearly four in every five prisoners agreed that some prison officers had been helpful to them but one in four said that some officers assault inmates. Generally, inmates in local prisons and remand centres were more negative than those in open prisons or training prisons. The survey also asked prisoners about things that annoyed them - treatment by officers and bureaucracy were the most common replies; overcrowding was not seen as a big problem. A similar survey was carried out in Scotland - findings suggested that relationships were generally positive between prisoners and staff and among prisoners but nearly four in ten had been concerned about their safety at some time in prison.

The number of people receiving criminal supervision by the probation service in 1993 stood at almost 150 thousand, nine in ten of whom were male (Table 9.30). While the total number receiving supervision in 1993 was slightly higher than in 1982, the number who were under 17 had fallen - this is partly due to the increased use of the caution for young offenders.

Crime prevention

Neighbourhood Watch schemes are an increasingly popular method of crime prevention (Chart 9.31). The scheme started up in Cheshire in 1982; by December 1993, 130 thousand schemes had been set up in England and Wales covering over 5 million households. Information from the 1992 BCS suggested that members of Neighbourhood Watch schemes were more likely to take security precautions such as marking property and telling neighbours when their home will be empty. However these schemes are more likely to operate in areas with a lower risk of burglary. In Scotland Neighbourhood Watch started in 1989; in 1993 there were about three and a half thousand schemes.

Another way in which members of the public can help prevent crime is by becoming a Special Constable. Since the early eighties the number of special constables, who are recruited on a divisional basis to supplement the regular police force, has increased by more than a third to over 20 thousand.

The BCS also collects information on security devices which people use to protect their homes. Results show that in 1993 an increasing proportion of households were using devices such as burglar alarms, extra locks and sensors. The survey also found that households which have been a victim of residential burglary are more likely to have security devices than those which had not; also they were more likely to be protected when interviewed than when the burglary occurred (Table 9.32).

Civil justice

Table 9.33 shows complaints made to ombudsmen ie those officials responsible for dealing with complaints about the services provided by various bodies. Each organisation has its own system of recording complaints or cases and some are affected by certain legislation so the figures are not strictly comparable. When a complaint which is within the jurisdiction of an ombudsman is received, it will be investigated and if it is upheld, compensation or other legal redress may be provided.

Complaints on the grounds of race discrimination are dealt with by the Commission for Racial Equality (CRE); the

9.32

Percentage of households protected by selected security devices, 1993

England & Wales — Percentages

	Victims of burglary[1]		
	At time of incident	Currently	Non-victims
Burglar alarm	*12*	*26*	*18*
Double/dead locks on doors	*48*	*73*	*69*
Window locks	*44*	*66*	*62*
Light timers/sensors	*20*	*38*	*31*
Window bars/grilles	*3*	*9*	*7*

1 Excludes victims of a burglary at a previous address.

Source: Home Office

9.33

Number of complaints received by Ombudsmen[1]

United Kingdom — Numbers

	1981	1991	1993
Police Complaints Authority[2]	.	18,065	17,991
Commissioners for Local Administration	3,295	14,060	16,507
Banking Ombudsman	.	6,327	10,231
Building Societies Ombudsman	.	8,264	9,142
Insurance Ombudsman	1,517	4,334	8,133
Independent Commission for Police Complaints for Northern Ireland	.	2,530	2,419
Corporate Estate Agents Ombudsman	..	1,236	2,340
Pensions Ombudsman	..	2,186	2,179
Health Service Commissioners	686	990	1,384
Legal Services Ombudsman	.	1,248	1,235
Broadcasting Complaints Commission	114	1,048	1,049
Parliamentary Commissioner for Administration	917	801	986
Northern Ireland Parliamentary Commissioner and Commissioner for Complaints	654	547	605
Scottish Legal Services Ombudsman	41	303	295
Investment Ombudsman	.	67	103

1 See Appendix, Part 9: Ombudsmen.
2 England and Wales only.

Source: Ombudsmen concerned

9.34

Enquiries answered by the Equal Opportunities Commission and applications[1] to the Commission for Racial Equality

Great Britain				Numbers
	1981	1986	1991	1993
Equal Opportunities Commission				
Employment	1,352	2,087	9,060	14,136
Education and training	232	1,028	1,596	1,917
Goods, facilities and services	376	530	804	989
Other discrimination	357	453	763	799
Advertising	815	1,914	2,968	3,183
Family policy[2]	..	500	2,172	1,822
General[3]	..	..	..	2,074
Communications and external relations[3]	..	..	..	14,637
All enquiries	3,132	6,512	17,363	39,557
Commission for Racial Equality				
Employment	547	619	1,203	1,160
Services	317	380	375	425
Out of scope of Race Relations Act	..	17	77	45
All applications	864	1,016	1,655	1,630

1 Applications for assistance or advice with a formal complaint under the Race Relations Act.
2 Included under other headings prior to 1986.
3 Coverage of enquiries was expanded in 1992 with some enquiries reclassified.
Source: Equal Opportunities Commission; Commission for Racial Equality

Equal Opportunities Commission (EOC) deals with discrimination on the basis of gender or marriage. The EOC collects information on enquiries (although one enquiry may identify a situation affecting a large number of people), while the CRE collects details of applications for assistance or advice, but not on general enquiries.

The numbers of enquiries or cases dealt with by the two organisations are shown in Table 9.34. EOC enquiries relating to employment increased by more than half between 1991 and 1993, whilst CRE employment related applications fell slightly.

Resources and legal aid

Public expenditure on justice and law stood at £14.5 billion in 1993, over half of which was spent on the police (Table 9.35). For the third consecutive year total public expenditure on justice and law was over 5 per cent of general government expenditure; this compares with 3.5 per cent in 1982.

9.35

Public expenditure on justice and law[1]

United Kingdom				£ million
	1982	1986	1991	1993
Police	2,780	3,691	6,468	7,685
Law courts	505	726	2,091	2,537
Prisons	635	1,071	1,827	1,626
Legal aid	211	345	898	1,228
Parliament	324	530	806	1,084
Probation	109	148	262	355
All expenditure	4,564	6,511	12,352	14,515
As a percentage of general government expenditure	*3.5*	*4.0*	*5.4*	*5.3*

1 Costs are not included for social work staff employed in Scotland on aspects related to the criminal justice system which in England and Wales are undertaken by the probation service.
Source: Central Statistical Office

Expenditure on legal aid, a scheme which provides legal assistance and advice for those who cannot afford it, rose sixfold between 1982 and 1993. Chart 9.36 shows that 571 thousand applications were granted in England and Wales in 1993 for criminal legal aid - around three and a half times more than in 1971. A further 25 thousand applications were granted in Northern Ireland and 78 thousand in Scotland in 1992-93.

Nearly 66 thousand applications for criminal injuries compensation were made in Great Britain in 1992-93 (Chart 9.37). This was higher than ever before, although the number of awards made, at 37 thousand, was lower than in the previous year.

More people were employed in the criminal justice system in England and Wales in 1993 than ever before, at around 240 thousand (Table 9.38). Over three quarters of this total worked in the police force, either as police or civilian staff. However, Prison service employment has grown faster: it has more than doubled since 1971 while the number working in the police force has increased by only two fifths. In addition, 18 thousand staff were employed in the police or prison services in Northern Ireland and over 22 thousand in Scotland.

9.36

Criminal legal aid[1]: applications granted[2]

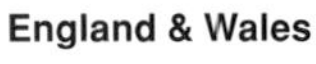

England & Wales

Thousands

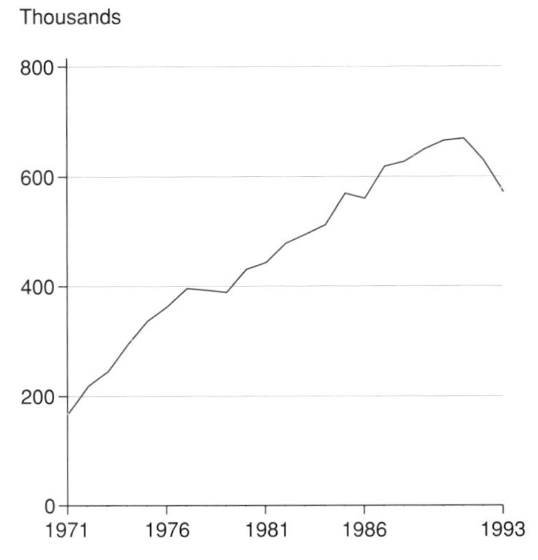

1 See Appendix, Part 9: Legal aid.
2 Total of all criminal proceedings and appeals. Includes care proceedings prior to 1992.

Source: Lord Chancellor's Department

9.37

Criminal injuries compensation

Great Britain

Thousands

80
60
40
20
0
1964-65
1971-72
1981-82
1992-93
Applications received
Awards made

Source: Criminal Injuries Compensation Authority

9.38

Employment in the criminal justice system[1]

England & Wales | Thousands

	1971	1981	1991	1993
Police service				
Police	96.8	119.6	127.1	127.7
Civilian staff[2]	33.9	42.2	52.0	55.2
All police service	130.7	161.8	179.1	182.8
Prison service[3]				
Prison officer class[4]	11.7	16.8	24.7	23.8
Governor class	0.5	0.5	0.8	1.0
Other non-industrial staff	3.1	4.1	5.1	10.3
Industrial staff	1.9	2.2	2.5	2.8
All prison service	17.3	23.7	33.1	38.0
Probation service[5]				
Probation officers	3.8	5.7	7.5	8.1
Probation services officers	..	1.0	2.0	2.1
Other staff[6]	..	5.9	8.3	8.6
All probation service	..	12.5	17.7	18.7

1 At December each year.
2 Includes traffic wardens, clerical and technical staff.
3 Prior to 1993 excludes headquarters staff.
4 Prior to 1993 excludes trainees.
5 Full-time plus part-time workers and includes some temporary officers and also some trainees from 1981 onwards.
6 Excluding non-probation officer grade hostel staff.

Source: Home Office

References and further reading

The following list contains selected publications relevant to **Chapter 9: Crime and Justice**. Those published by HMSO are available from the addresses shown on the inside back cover of *Social Trends*.

Annual Report of the Scottish Legal Aid Board, SLAB

Civil Judicial Statistics, Scotland, HMSO

Chief Constables's Annual Report, Royal Ulster Constabulary

A Commentary on Northern Ireland Crime Statistics, HMSO

Digest of Information on the Northern Ireland Criminal Justice System 1992, HMSO

Crime in Scotland, findings from the 1988 British Crime Survey, The Scottish Office

Crime and the quality of life The Scottish Office

Criminal Injuries Compensation Board Report and Accounts, HMSO

Criminal Statistics, England and Wales, HMSO

Criminal Statistics, Scotland, HMSO

Criminal Victimisation in the Industrialised World: 1989 and 1992 International Crime Survey, The Hague, Ministry of Justice

Crown Prosecution Service, Annual Report, HMSO

Digest 2: Information on the Criminal Justice System in England and Wales, Home Office

Equal Opportunities Commission Annual Report, EOC

Home Office Statistical Bulletins Series, Home Office

Judicial Statistics, England and Wales, HMSO

Legal Aid Annual Reports, (England and Wales), HMSO

Legal Aid Reports, (Northern Ireland), HMSO

Northern Ireland Judicial Statistics, Northern Ireland Court Service

Northern Ireland Prison Service Annual Report, HMSO

National Prison Survey, HMSO

Police Statistics, England and Wales, CIPFA

Prison Statistics, England and Wales, HMSO

Prison Service annual report and accounts, HMSO

Prisons in Scotland Report, HMSO

Probation Statistics, England and Wales, Home Office

Race and the Criminal Justice System 1994, Home Office

Report of the Parole Board for England and Wales, HMSO

Report of the Parole Board for Scotland, HMSO

The Scottish Office Statistical Bulletins Series, The Scottish Office

Statistics of Drugs Seizures and Offenders Dealt With, United Kingdom, Home Office

Ulster Year Book, HMSO

The Work of the Prison Service, HMSO

Contacts

Telephone contact points for further information relating to **Chapter 9: Crime.**

Home Office	0181 760 2850
Northern Ireland Office	01232 527537
The Scottish Office	0131 244 2224
Central Statistical Office	0171 270 6168
Criminal Injuries Compensation Authority	0141 331 5830
Northern Ireland Court Service	01232 328594 extn 216
The Royal Ulster Constabulary	01232 650222 extn 2413
British Retail Consortium	0171 371 5185

Chapter 10 Housing

Housing stock and supply

In 1993 the total number of dwellings in the United Kingdom exceeded 24 million for the first time. (Chart 10.1)

In 1993, 34 thousand new dwellings were built by housing associations in the United Kingdom, more than three times the number in 1971. (Chart 10.3)

Housing standards

In 1991, 10 per cent of dwellings in both Greater London and the North West were classified as unfit - a higher proportion than in any other English region. (Chart 10.9)

Despite official advice to householders to fit smoke detectors, by 1991 less than half had done so. (Page 178)

Housing costs and expenditure

Average house prices rose in every English region between the second quarter 1993 and second quarter 1994, whereas in the other countries of Great Britain they fell. (Chart 10.15)

There were 153 thousand mortgages in arrears by 6 to 12 months in the United Kingdom at the end of June 1994. (Table 10.17)

Characteristics of occupants

In 1993 households who owned their own dwelling outright had lived at the same address the longest - more than seven out of ten had lived at their present address for over 10 years. (Table 10.20)

Homelessness

Just over a third of homeless households who were found accommodation in 1993 originally became homeless because parents, relatives or friends with whom they had been living were no longer willing or able to accommodate them. (Chart 10.25)

10.1

Stock of dwellings: by tenure

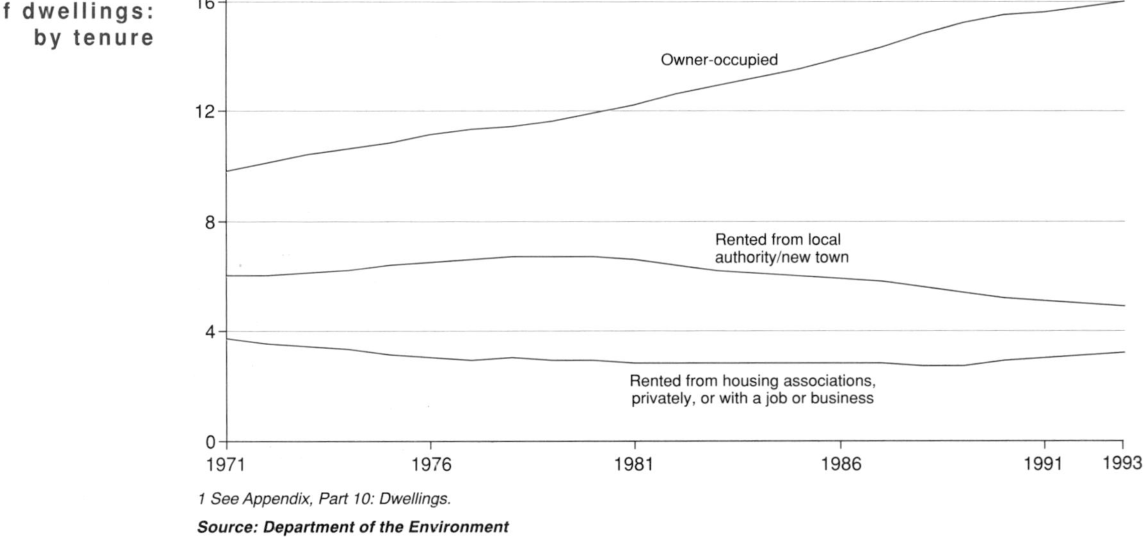

1 See Appendix, Part 10: Dwellings.

Source: Department of the Environment

10.2

Average annual change in dwelling stock

United Kingdom — Thousands

	1950 -1959	1960 -1969	1970 -1979	1980 -1989	1990 -1993
New construction					
Private enterprise	90	197	166	163	154
Housing associations	4	4	14	16	25
Local authorities	175	148	120	36	9
New towns	8	8	12	3	1
Government departments	7	5	2	0	0
Total new construction	284	362	314	218	188
Other changes					
Slum clearance[1]	-35	-78	-63	-16	-7
Other[2]	-19	-25	-21	4	11
Total other changes	-54	-103	-84	-12	4
Total net gain	230	259	230	206	192

1 Northern Ireland figures for 1985 are not available and are for demolitions only in other years.
2 Comprises net gains from conversions and other causes, and losses other than by slum clearance. Excludes figures for Wales and Northern Ireland. Figures for Scotland are not available between 1981 and 1985.

Source: Department of the Environment; Welsh Office; The Scottish Office; Department of the Environment, Northern Ireland

10.3

Housebuilding completions: by sector

United Kingdom

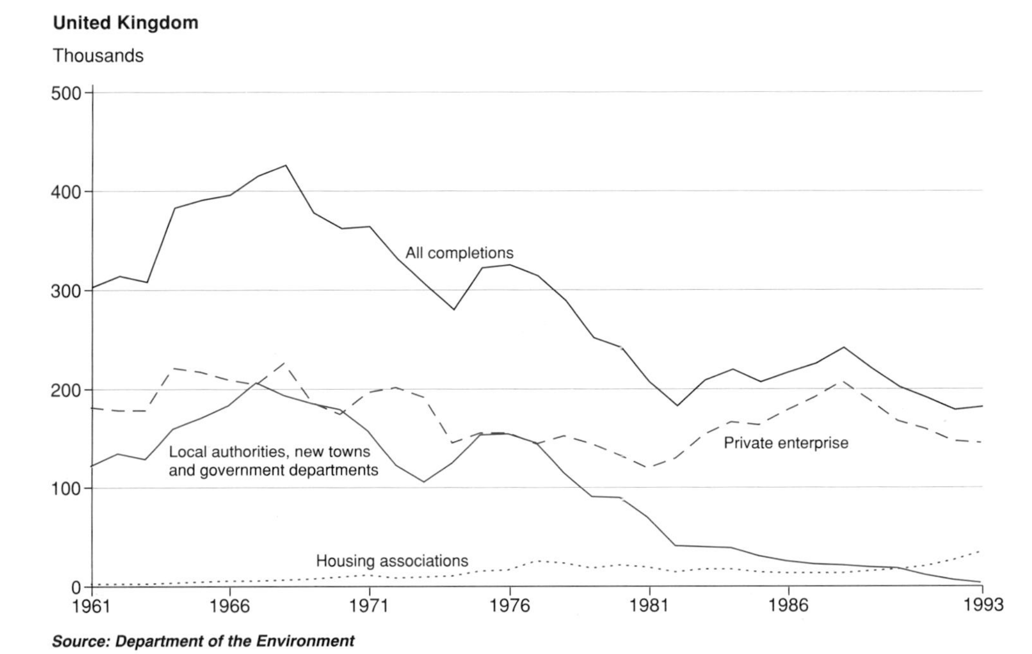

Source: Department of the Environment

This chapter initially analyses housing in terms of the stock and its present condition and goes on to consider the cost of housing and expenditure on housing. The characteristics of the occupants of the various types are then analysed and the chapter closes by presenting data on those people who apply as homeless to local authorities.

Housing stock and supply

In 1993 there were 16 million owner-occupied dwellings in the United Kingdom, an increase of nearly two thirds since 1971 and representing two thirds of the total number of dwellings, which exceeded 24 million for the first time (Chart 10.1). The number of dwellings rented from local authorities or new towns continued to decline, and reached the lowest level for almost 30 years in 1993. Conversely the decline in the number of other rented dwellings halted in 1989, since when it has risen slightly.

On average, 188 thousand new dwellings were built each year in the United Kingdom between 1990 and 1993, which was about half the rate of the 1960s (Table 10.2). More than eight out of ten new dwellings built between 1990 and 1993 were constructed by private enterprise. The number of dwellings built by local authorities, new towns and government departments has fallen steadily since 1976 (Chart 10.3), while private enterprise completions have fallen since 1988. This has been caused in part by the effects of the recession and the fall in new house prices which is shown in Table 10.15. The housing association sector was the only sector to construct more dwellings in recent years; two and a half times more dwellings were constructed in 1993 than in 1988.

While new dwellings are being constructed, others are lost as a result of demolitions and other causes. However, the number of dwellings demolished through slum clearance has been declining since the 1960s and now stands at less than a tenth of the average for that decade. Figures for England have been collected since before the Second World War. In the 1930s around 30 thousand dwellings were cleared annually. This had more than doubled to around 70 thousand dwellings in 1971, but has since declined sharply to just 2 thousand dwellings in 1991-92.

A further change in dwelling stock has occurred since 1988-89. Over 30 local authorities have transferred all or a large part of their housing stock to housing associations after their tenants have opted to change landlord. The first of these 'Large Scale Voluntary Transfers' in England took place in December 1988 when around 5 thousand tenants of Chiltern District Council voted to change. Up to May 1994 over 140 thousand dwellings had been transferred, the majority of which were in the South East. The largest transfer took place in 1992 when over 12 thousand dwellings formerly administered by the London Borough of Bromley were transferred.

Table 10.4 shows the age and type of dwellings occupied in Great Britain. In 1993 households occupying dwellings built before 1919 were more likely to be living in a terraced house than any other type of dwelling, whereas household occupying dwellings built between 1919 and 1964 were most likely to be living in semi-detached houses; those occupying dwellings built after 1964 were most likely to be living in a detached house. Results from the Continuous Household Survey for 1992-93 for Northern Ireland indicate that the majority of occupied dwellings built before 1919 are detached houses, while the majority of those built between 1919 and 1964 were terraced, as in Great Britain; those occupying dwellings built after 1964 were most likely to be living in a detached house.

A convenient indicator of the size of a dwelling is the number of bedrooms it contains. Since 1971 there has been a move away from building three bedroomed in favour of two bedroomed and larger dwellings. Of the dwellings constructed in England and Wales in 1971 about a quarter contained two bedrooms, compared with over a third in 1993 (Table 10.5). In 1971 three bedroomed homes comprised over half of dwellings constructed, but this had declined to a third by 1993.

10.4

Construction date: by type of dwelling, 1993

Great Britain — Percentages

	Before 1919	1919 -1944	1945 -1964	1965 or later
House or bungalow				
Detached	*15*	*16*	*15*	*28*
Semi-detached	*15*	*46*	*45*	*24*
Terraced	*48*	*26*	*22*	*23*
Purpose built flat or maisonette	*6*	*9*	*16*	*23*
Converted flat or maisonette	*15*	*3*	*2*	*2*
Other	*1*	*1*	-	-
All households	*100*	*100*	*100*	*100*

Source: Office of Population Censuses and Surveys

10.5

Housebuilding completions: by number of bedrooms

England & Wales — Percentages

	1971	1981	1986	1991	1993
1 bedroom	*15*	*22*	*19*	*19*	*15*
2 bedrooms	*23*	*25*	*28*	*31*	*34*
3 bedrooms	*55*	*39*	*36*	*30*	*33*
4 or more bedrooms	*7*	*14*	*17*	*20*	*18*
All houses and flats (= 100%)(thousands)	310	180	188	165	155

Source: Department of the Environment; Welsh Office

10.6

Local authority and housing association dwellings which are vacant

England & Wales

Percentages

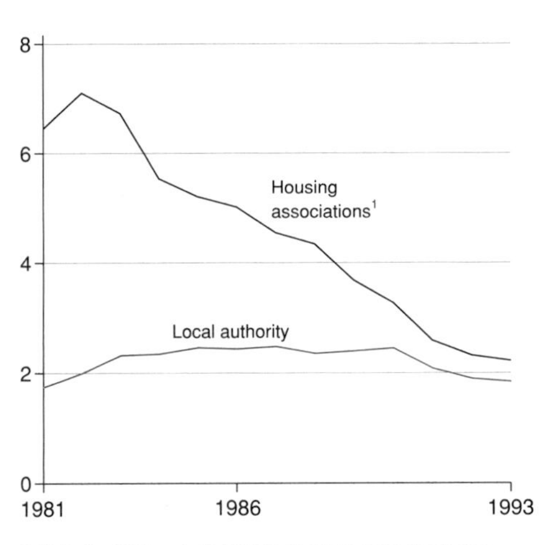

1 Data for 1993 exclude 10,500 dwellings in England. See Appendix, Part 10: Housing Market Package.

Source: Department of the Environment; Welsh Office

Conversely four or more bedroomed homes accounted for just 7 per cent of homes completed in 1971, but 18 per cent in 1993.

An alternative method of assessing dwelling size is 'usable floor area'; this comprises the internal floor area but excludes integral garages and storage space accessed from outside the dwelling. In 1991 the average usable floor area for a dwelling in England was 80 square metres. For terraced houses, the average was 75 square metres, compared with 77 square metres for a semi-detached house and 114 square metres for a detached house. Flats generally are smaller with 57 square metres for a purpose built flat and 66 square metres for converted flats. Most houses stand on plots between 100 and 500 square metres in size, with houses that were built before 1850 standing on the largest plots; those built between 1850 and 1900 have the smallest plots.
In 1993, there were over 23 million households in the United Kingdom, but 24 million dwellings. There are a number of reasons for this apparent surplus of dwellings. Some dwellings, for example, are vacant while undergoing repairs or awaiting sale, and some households own more than one dwelling. After making allowances for these factors the surplus of dwellings disappears.

Information from the English House Condition Survey estimates that there were 639 thousand vacant dwellings in England in 1991, around 3 per cent of the total housing stock. Dwellings are vacant for a variety or reasons, the most common reason being that they are awaiting sale. This reflects the fact that the bulk of vacant dwellings are in private ownership; in 1991 around 80 per cent of vacant dwellings were in private ownership. Public sector vacant dwellings are more likely to be of recent construction than those in the private sector, with a disproportionate number of flats built in the 1960s and 1970s; these tend to be difficult to let.

In 1993 there were around 88 thousand public sector vacant dwellings in England and Wales; over 80 per cent of these dwellings were owned by local authorities. In 1993 the percentage of local authority dwellings which were vacant in England and Wales was almost identical to the percentage recorded back in 1981 (Chart 10.6) although it had risen to a peak in the mid 1980s. The percentage of housing association dwellings which were vacant in England and Wales has been declining since 1982; in 1993 it constituted around two and a quarter per cent of total stock. However, this proportion excludes 10.5 thousand dwellings in England acquired under the Housing Market Package - see Appendix, Part 10: Housing Market Package.

10.7

Allocation of local authority housing

United Kingdom

	1986-87	1990-91	1992-93
New tenants (percentages)			
Homeless[1]	*22*	*29*	*33*
Ordinary waiting list	*65*	*57*	*52*
Others	*13*	*14*	*14*
New tenants (=100%)(thousands)	315.6	310.3	293.3
Tenants transferring or exchanging[2] (thousands)	229.2	205.5	210.3
All tenants (thousands)	544.9	515.7	503.6

1 See Appendix, Part 10: Homeless households.
2 Data for Wales include dwellings let to tenants through the 'tenants exchange scheme'.

Source: Department of the Environment; Welsh Office; The Scottish Office; Department of the Environment, Northern Ireland

Table 10.7 illustrates how local authority housing has been allocated in the United Kingdom; in 1986-87, 65 per cent of new tenants came from the ordinary waiting list compared with around a half in 1992-93. Conversely the group which has shown the largest increase in allocation of local authority housing are the homeless, which constituted a third of new local authority tenants in 1992-93, up from a fifth in 1986-87.

Since 1980 tenants of local authorities and other public bodies in Great Britain have had the right to buy their homes, as a result of the introduction of *The Housing Act 1980* and its Scottish equivalent. These acts gave tenants the right to buy their homes with a discount if they had been a tenant for more than three years. This was subsequently reduced to two years by the *Housing and Building Control Act 1984*, which also increased the maximum discount from 50 to 60 per cent. Subsequently in January 1987 the maximum discount for flats was increased again to 70 per cent. In Northern Ireland tenants have had the right to buy their homes since the adoption of *The Housing Order 1983*. However, the Northern Ireland Housing Executive had been selling homes to tenants since 1979.

Annual sales in the United Kingdom peaked at just over 200 thousand in 1982 with a slightly smaller peak in 1989. In 1993, 65 thousand were sold which was the lowest figure since 1980 when the first act was introduced (Chart 10.8).

The Department of Environment's Survey of English Housing conducted in 1993-94 asked council tenants about their expectations of buying. It found that couples with dependent children were the most likely to expect to buy their homes sometime. Furthermore half of those tenants not expecting to buy their homes said they would like to, with a quarter of these tenants saying that they would buy if the council gave them a cash incentive.

Housing standards

The 1989 Local Government and Housing Act defined through a new fitness standard whether a premises was fit for human habitation. This replaces, redefines and extends the provisions of the previous fitness standard contained in the *1985 Housing Act*. Under the new standard around 1.5 million dwellings in England or 7.6 per cent of the total, were found to be unfit in 1991. The most common reasons for unfitness were either the scale of repair required to the building or unsatisfactory facilities for the preparation of food.

Chart 10.9 illustrates the differences by region. In 1991, the English region with the highest percentage of dwellings which were unfit was Greater London, where more than one out of ten dwellings was unfit. The regions with the lowest proportion of unfit dwellings were the West Midlands and the South East outside Greater London, where the number of unfit dwellings was nearly half the percentage in Greater London. The Welsh Housing Condition Survey carried out in 1993 found that more than one in eight dwellings in Wales was unfit, which is greater than the 1991 figure for Greater London. In Scotland a different standard is employed, this has some similarities to the definition of unfitness but excludes the provision that the dwelling should be free from serious disrepair. In Scotland in 1991 4.6 per cent or 95 thousand dwellings fell below this standard.

10.8

Right to buy applications for, and sales of, dwellings owned by local authorities and new towns

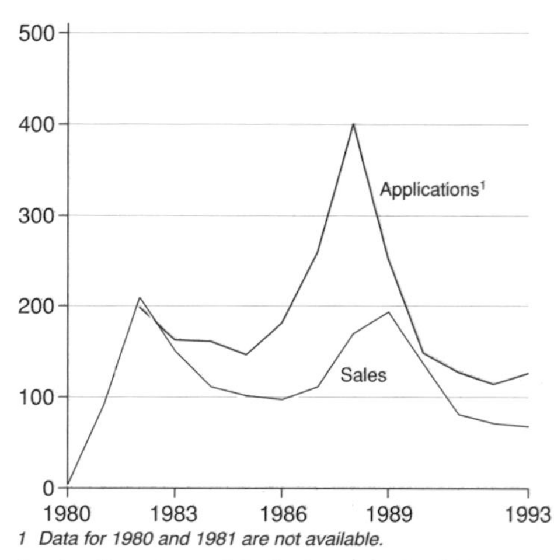

1 Data for 1980 and 1981 are not available.

Source: Department of the Environment; Department of the Environment, Northern Ireland

10.9

Unfit dwellings[1]: by region, 1991

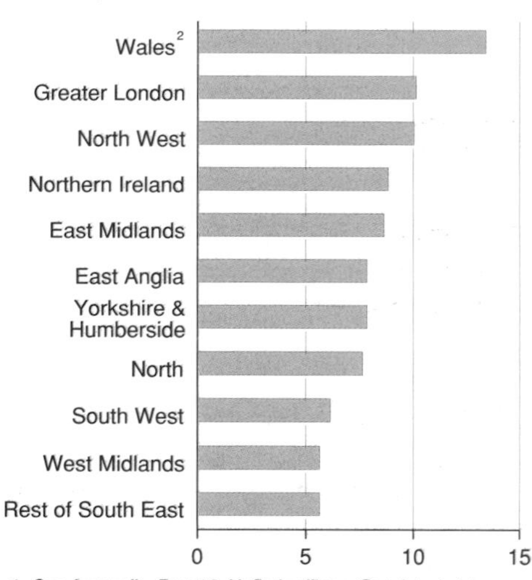

1 See Appendix, Part 10: Unfit dwellings. Consistent data are not available for Scotland.

2 Data are for 1993 and include occupied first homes only.

Source: Department of the Environment; Welsh Office; Department of the Environment, Northern Ireland

10.10

Overcrowding: by ethnic group of head of household, 1991-1993

Great Britain					Percentages
	Two or more above bedroom standard	One above bedroom standard	Equals bedroom standard	One or more below bedroom standard	All households
Ethnic minority group					
Indian	*24*	*32*	*33*	*11*	*100*
Pakistani/Bangladeshi	*13*	*21*	*35*	*31*	*100*
Black Caribbean	*19*	*26*	*45*	*10*	*100*
Other	*16*	*35*	*41*	*7*	*100*
All	*19*	*30*	*39*	*12*	*100*
White	*30*	*38*	*29*	*3*	*100*
All ethnic groups	*30*	*38*	*29*	*3*	*100*

Source: Office of Population Censuses and Surveys

Another important factor governing housing conditions is overcrowding. The extent to which a dwelling is overcrowded or under-occupied may be calculated from a number of indicators. One commonly used measure is the bedroom standard which compares the number of bedrooms available to a household with a calculation of its bedroom requirements - see Appendix, Part 10: Bedroom standard. Using this standard 1991 results for England suggest that 3 per cent of households had insufficient bedrooms, ie they were living in overcrowded conditions, whilst around 68 per cent of households had spare bedrooms.

The incidence of overcrowding varies according to many factors, such as tenure, housing type and location. Table 10.10 looks at overcrowding in Great Britain in the period 1991-93, using bedroom standard, by the ethnic group of the head of the household. Households headed by a Pakistani or a Bangladeshi were the most likely to be living in overcrowded conditions, with just under a third of households in this group having insufficient bedrooms. Conversely those households headed by a White or an Indian were most likely to have surplus bedrooms; 30 per cent and 24 per cent respectively had two or more bedrooms above the standard.

In addition to fundamental standards we expect a number of basic facilities to be present in our homes. Over the years our expectations have changed in line with technological developments. For many years the Census has included questions on the amenities available in each household, which are detailed in Table 10.11. Results from the 1951 Census, the first conducted after the Second World War, indicated that over a third of households in Great Britain lacked a fixed bath, whilst around 8 per cent possessed neither an internal or external flush toilet. At the last Census, conducted in 1991, less than half a per cent lacked either a bath or shower, and a similar proportion lacked an internal flush toilet.

The English House Condition Survey in 1991 collected information on the availability of 21 facilities, including more modern facilities such as burglar alarms, smoke detectors, double glazing and parking provision. It found that the sector with the best provision of facilities was the owner occupied sector. However, across all sectors it found that 86 per cent of households had a mains gas supply, 91 per cent had loft insulation, 52 per cent had double glazing, 11 per cent had burglar alarms and 40 per cent had smoke detectors.

10.11

Households lacking basic amenities

Great Britain					Percentages
	1951	1961	1971	1981	1991
Bath or shower[1]	*37.6*	*22.4*	*9.1*	*1.9*	*0.3*
Flush toilet					
Internal or external	*7.7*	*6.5*	*1.2*	..	..
Internal	..	..	*11.5*	*2.7*	*0.5*
Hot water tap	..	*21.8*	*6.4*	..	..
Central heating	..	..	..	..	*18.9*

1 Prior to 1991 data relate to fixed bath only.

Source: Office of Population Censuses and Surveys

Housing costs and expenditure

Rents in the private rented sector have risen rapidly since deregulation in 1989. Deregulation meant that market rents could be charged for new lettings, starting in 1989 or later, although regulation was retained for lettings already in existence. The increase in rents was largest in the furnished part of the sector, where net rents (after deduction of housing benefit) doubled between 1989 and 1993 (Chart 10.12). Most furnished lettings are of short duration, so the proportion let at market rents increased most rapidly in this sector. Between 1985 and 1988, rents paid by private tenants of unfurnished accommodation were lower on average, after housing benefit, than those paid by housing association tenants. By 1993 however median net rents were twice as high. The apparent drop in rent levels in the local authority and housing association sectors in 1993 can be explained by the increased proportion of tenants receiving housing benefit; the gross rents have not actually fallen. Net rents in the private sector continue to be higher than in the public sector; in 1993 the median net rent paid by tenants of unfurnished privately rented accommodation was more than three times the corresponding rent paid by local authority tenants. It should be noted that comparisons are affected by the higher proportion of local authority and housing association tenants than private tenants whose rents are reduced by housing benefit.

Mortgage payments have fallen since 1991 with the reduction in interest rates. In all years the median payment is reduced by the inclusion of some mortgagors who bought 20 or more years ago, when house prices were lower.

10.12

Median net rent[1] and mortgage payments[2]: by tenure

Great Britain

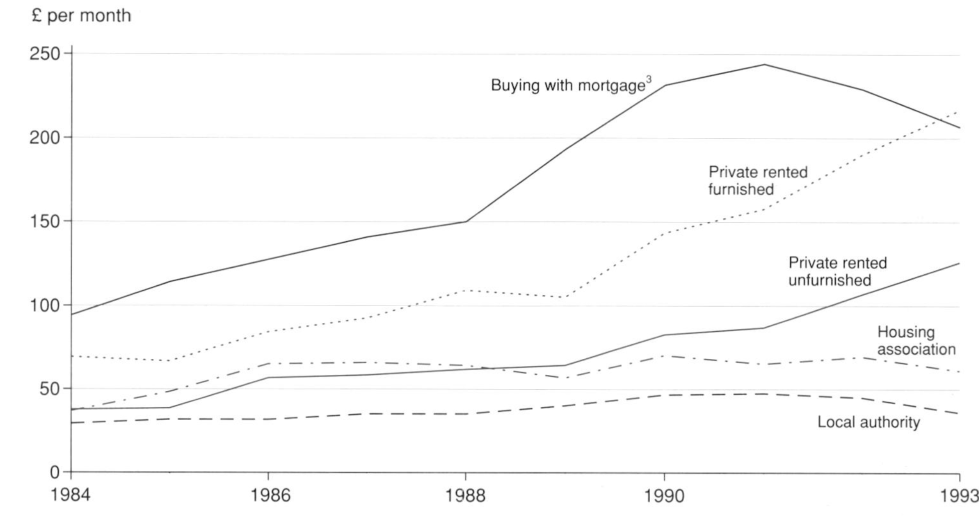

1 Gross rent less any rent rebate (housing benefit) received.
2 Mortgage payment after the deduction of tax relief.
3 Data prior to 1988 comprise only households in receipt of Mortgage Interest Relief at Source (MIRAS).

Source: Department of the Environment

Chart 10.13 shows the proportion of council tenants who were either in rent arrears in 1993, or had been in the last 12 months. Care should be taken when interpreting these data as they are based on self-reporting and are

10.13

Council tenants with rent arrears: by type of household, 1993

England

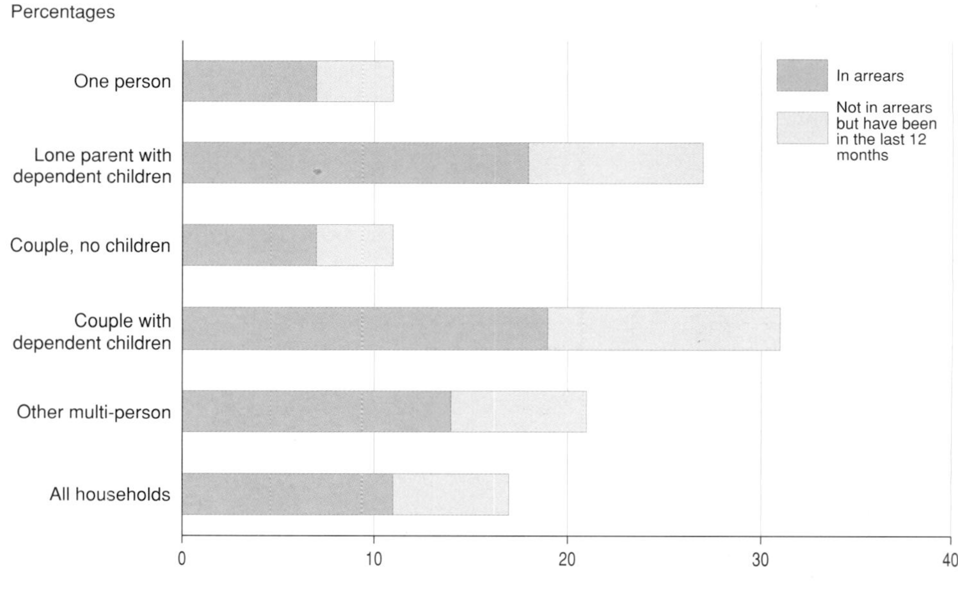

Source: Department of the Environment

10.14

Dwelling prices[1]

United Kingdom				£
	Average price			Mix-adjusted dwellings price index (1990=100)
	New dwellings	Other dwellings	All dwellings	
1971	5,609	5,640	5,632	7.9
1976	13,084	12,618	12,704	17.9
1981	28,119	23,642	24,188	36.8
1986	43,562	35,464	36,276	57.2
1987	49,692	39,336	40,391	66.7
1988	61,873	47,961	49,355	83.8
1989	73,544	52,568	54,846	101.3
1990	75,037	57,760	59,785	100.0
1991	73,507	60,986	62,455	98.6
1992	73,190	59,226	60,821	94.9
1993	73,234	59,753	61,223	92.5
1994[2]	73,259	63,241	64,391	94.7

1 See Appendix, Part 10: Mix-adjusted series.
2 Third quarter.
Source: Department of the Environment

10.15

Changes in average house prices[1]: by region, 1993-1994[2]

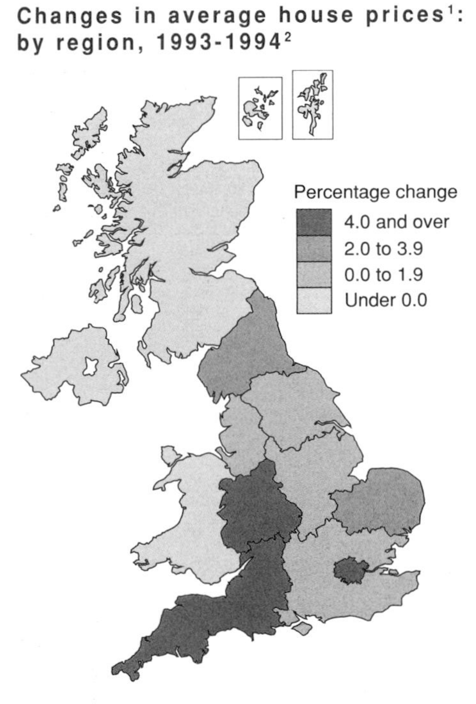

1 Mix-adjusted house price index. See Appendix, Part 10: Mix-adjusted series.
2 From second quarter 1993 (April to June) to second quarter 1994.
Source: Department of the Environment

thought to underestimate the true level of arrears. Couples with dependent children were the type of household most likely to have been in arrears; just over three in ten were either in arrears or had been in the last 12 months. The proportion for lone parents with dependent children was only slightly lower, at 27 per cent. One person households and childless couples were the least likely to be in arrears, now or in the recent past.

Those council tenants in employment were as likely as those who were unemployed to be in rent arrears. The most common reason given by tenants for their debt was a decrease in earnings, caused either by job loss or a reduction in working time. Other reasons for arrears included other debts and problems with housing benefit. The pattern of tenants in arrears is much the same for those in housing association accommodation. However, among private sector tenants, lone parents with dependent children are more likely than any other household to be in arrears, while couples with dependent children are among the least likely. Among householders with a mortgage, single parent households with dependent children are the most likely to be in arrears with their mortgage payments: 13 per cent in 1993.

Between 1985 and 1989 house prices, as measured by the mix adjusted dwelling price index, more than doubled. Then, with the recession in the housing market it fell by 9 per cent over the next four years, before rising again in 1994 (Table 10.14). Since the mix (ie type, size, location and age) of dwellings being bought and sold changes over time, this index provides a better measure of true house price movements than an index based on the simple average price. The average price for a new dwelling peaked in 1990 at over £75,000 and then declined to stabilize at between £73,000 and £73,500 from 1991. However, other dwellings have fared somewhat better, after dipping slightly they rose back to their highest ever level in the second quarter 1994.

Chart 10.15 shows that all the regions in England experienced a rise in average house prices between the second quarters of 1993 and 1994. Greater London had the largest percentage rise of 7 per cent, with the South West (6 per cent) and West Midlands (5 per cent) having the next largest increases. Conversely, prices fell in Wales and Scotland. These price movements are the exact opposite of what happened between 1992 and 1993, when only Wales and Scotland experienced a rise in house prices; prices fell in all the English regions, with the South West and West Midlands seeing the greatest percentage falls at that time.

Between 1992 and 1993, the average mortgage payment as a percentage of average income fell by 4 percentage points for first time buyers and 6 percentage points for moving owner occupiers, continuing the downward trend since the peak in 1990 (Chart 10.16). The percentage of income spent on mortgages by both first time buyers and moving owner occupiers has roughly halved over these three years. This is mainly due to lower mortgage interest rates, falling house prices and increases in real earnings. In 1993, the initial average annual mortgage repayment level for first time buyers was just under £2,500, its lowest level since 1988, and property was at its most affordable since 1983, initial mortgage payments accounting for less than 14 per cent of income.

Between 1971 and 1994, the number of mortgages in the United Kingdom has more than doubled. However, the proportion of mortgaged properties that were taken into possession in 1994 was nine times higher than in 1971, even though it has been falling since 1991 (Table 10.17). In June 1994, around 300 thousand mortgages were in arrears by six months or more, a fall of 16 per cent from the peak of over 350 thousand at the end of 1992.

The warning given with every mortgage is that 'your home is at risk if you do not keep up repayments on a mortgage or other loan secured on it'. The same is true of rented property. When people fall significantly behind with rent or mortgage payments and are unable to reach an alternative payment arrangement with their landlord or mortgage lender, a county court possession summons might be issued, with the view to obtaining a court order. Not all orders will result in

10.16

Average mortgage repayment as a percentage of average income

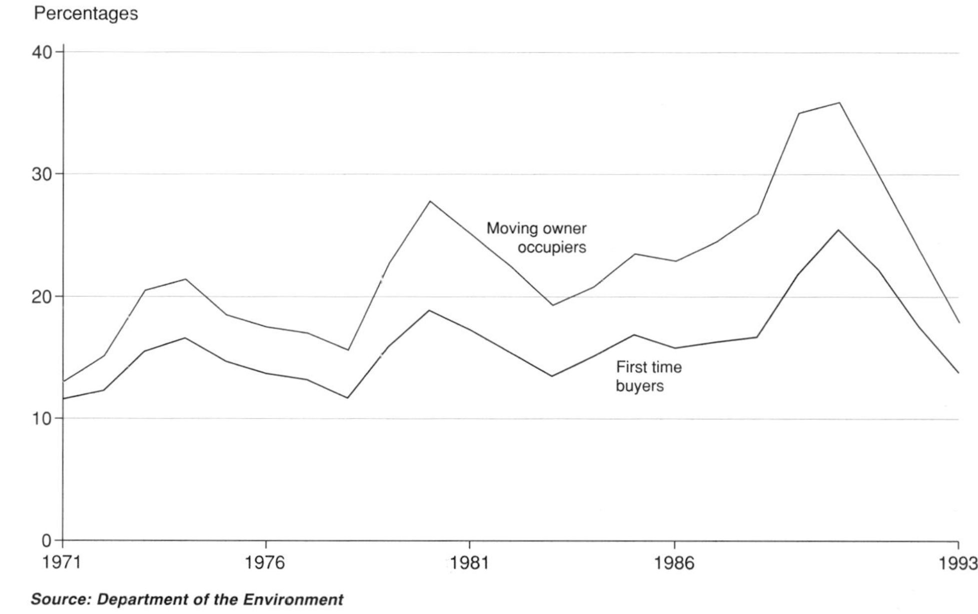

Source: Department of the Environment

10.17

Number of mortgages, arrears and possessions[1]

United Kingdom — Thousands

	Number of mortgages	Loans in arrears at end-period: By 6-12 months	Loans in arrears at end-period: By over 12 months	Properties taken into possession in period
1971	4,506	17.6	..	2.8
1976	5,322	16.0	..	5.0
1981	6,336	21.5	..	4.9
1986	8,138	52.1	13.0	24.1
1988	8,564	42.8	10.3	18.5
1989	9,125	66.8	13.8	15.8
1990	9,415	123.1	36.1	43.9
1991	9,815	183.6	91.7	75.5
1992	9,922	205.0	147.0	68.5
1993	10,137	164.6	151.8	58.5
1994	10,375	153.3	142.2	25.0

1 All data are as at 31 December in each year except 1994, which is 30 June. Estimates cover only members of the Council of Mortgage Lenders; these account for 95 per cent of all mortgages outstanding.

Source: Council of Mortgage Lenders

10.18

Repossession of properties[1]: warrants issued and executed

England & Wales

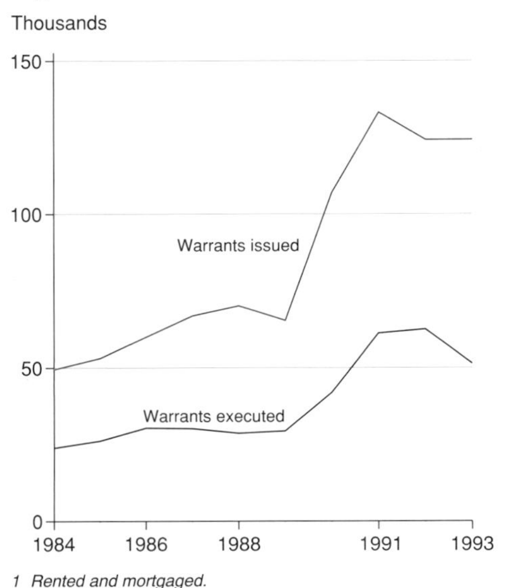

1 Rented and mortgaged.

Source: Lord Chancellor's Department

possession; it is not uncommon for courts to make suspended orders which provide for arrears to be paid off within a reasonable period. If the court decides not to adjourn the proceedings or suspend a possession order, the warrant will be executed and the home repossessed by the landlord or mortgage lender.

The number of warrants issued and executed for repossession of properties in England and Wales are shown in Chart 10.18. The number of warrants issued peaked at 133 thousand in 1991; it then fell slightly in 1992 and stayed at the same level in 1993. The number of possession warrants peaked at 62 thousand in 1992, but then fell by nearly a fifth in 1993.

Characteristics of occupants

Table 10.19 shows that in 1993 more than three quarters of households in Great Britain headed by professionals and employers and managers were buying their homes with a mortgage. However, the group most likely to own their own homes outright were the economically inactive, most of whom had retired. Those households headed by an unskilled manual worker were the group most likely to rent their home, with six out of ten households renting in 1993. Nevertheless, even amongst this group around a third were buying their own home.

The General Household Survey (GHS) looked at the amount of time households of different tenures had lived at the same address in Great Britain in 1993. Those households who owned their own homes were the least mobile with more than seven out of ten having lived at their present address for more than ten years (Table 10.20). The group which was the most mobile were those households living in rented furnished accommodation, where more than six out of ten households had lived at their current address less than a year.

Other results from the GHS indicate that local authority tenants are more likely to have been at their current address longer than housing association tenants; though possibly these results could, in part, reflect the contraction of the local authority sector and the expansion of the housing association sector. Results for 1992-93 for Northern Ireland follow the same trend for the rest of the United Kingdom, with more

10.19

Tenure: by socio-economic group of head of household, 1993

Great Britain Percentages

	Owned with mortgage	Owned outright	Rented[1]	All tenures
Professional	*79*	*11*	*10*	*100*
Employers and managers	*76*	*13*	*12*	*100*
Intermediate non-manual	*72*	*11*	*17*	*100*
Junior non-manual	*53*	*14*	*33*	*100*
Skilled manual	*57*	*15*	*28*	*100*
Semi-skilled manual	*44*	*11*	*45*	*100*
Unskilled manual	*31*	*11*	*58*	*100*
Economically inactive	*10*	*45*	*45*	*100*

1 Includes renting from a housing association and those renting with a job or business.

Source: Office of Population Censuses and Surveys

than three quarters of households who owned their own dwelling living at their present address for more than ten years.

The British Household Panel Survey conducted by the ESRC Research Centre for Micro-social Change enables analysis of adults who moved between Autumn 1991 and Autumn 1992, in terms of whether the whole household or only some adult members moved (Table 10.21). Only around 40 per cent of people moved as a result of the whole household moving which perhaps runs counter to some expectations of migration as a collective household activity.

Adults living in privately rented accommodation were, on average, much more mobile than those in other tenures, and one third of adults living in this sort of accommodation moved between Autumn 1991 and Autumn 1992 . Of these movers, two thirds experienced a change in household composition on moving.

In 1993 almost half of households in Great Britain consisting of one adult aged 60 or over were renting their accommodation; a higher proportion than for any other household type shown in Table 10.22. Households containing two adults, one or both of whom were aged over 60, were the households most likely to own their home outright, whereas households consisting of 2 adults aged 16 to 59 were most likely to be buying their home with a mortgage. Amongst all households in Great Britain in 1993 the most numerous type of home was the semi-detached house with around a third of all households occupying such a dwelling.

10.20

Length of time at current address: by tenure, 1993

Great Britain Percentages

	Under a year	1-4 years	5-10 years	Over 10 years	All households
Owner occupied					
Owned with mortgage	7	29	33	31	100
Owned outright	2	8	16	73	100
Rented unfurnished					
Local authority	8	27	23	42	100
Housing associations	19	37	26	18	100
Privately	24	26	13	37	100
Rented furnished	63	29	5	4	100
Rented with job or business	15	39	22	24	100

Source: Office of Population Censuses and Surveys.

10.21

Adults moving between Autumn 1991 and Autumn 1992: by tenure

Great Britain Percentages

	Whole household	Part of household	All movers
Local authority	4	5	9
Other rented	11	21	32
Owned with mortgage	3	5	8
Owned outright	2	3	4
All tenures	4	6	10

Source: ESRC Research Centre for Micro-social Change

10.22

Household type[1]: by tenure, 1993

Great Britain Percentages

	Owned with mortgage	Owned outright	Rented[2]	All tenures
One adult aged 16-59	44	11	45	100
Two adults aged 16-59	64	14	22	100
Small family	61	5	34	100
Large family	52	5	42	100
Large adult household	54	22	23	100
One adult aged 60 or over	4	48	48	100
Two adults, one or both aged 60 or over	14	60	26	100

1 See Appendix, Part 10: Household type.
2 Includes those renting from a housing association and those renting with a jcb or business.
Source: Office of Population Censuses and Surveys

10.23

Household type[1]: by type of dwelling, 1993

Great Britain						Percentages
	House or bungalow					
	Detached	Semi-detached	Terraced	Flat or maisonette	Other dwellings	All dwellings
One adult aged 16-59	*9*	*19*	*25*	*47*	*1*	*100*
Two adults aged 16-59	*22*	*31*	*28*	*18*	*1*	*100*
Small family	*17*	*34*	*34*	*14*	*1*	*100*
Large family	*18*	*35*	*38*	*9*	-	*100*
Large adult household	*27*	*38*	*28*	*6*	*1*	*100*
One adult aged 60 or over	*13*	*26*	*27*	*34*	-	*100*
Two adults, one or both aged 60 or over	*27*	*34*	*25*	*13*	-	*100*

1 See Appendix, Part 10: Household type.
Source: Office of Population Censuses and Surveys

Detached houses were occupied by around one in five of all households, while a further one in five of households lived in a flat or maisonette. Not surprisingly, people who live on their own are more likely than any other household to live in a flat or maisonette. Nearly half of households consisting of one adult aged 16 to 59, and a third of those containing on adult aged 60 or over, lived in a flat or maisonette (Table 10.23).

Homelessness

Part III of the *Housing Act 1985*, and its Scottish equivalent, requires local authorities to help homeless people in defined categories of 'priority need'. Essentially these are families with young children, women expecting babies and those vulnerable through old age, physical disability, mental handicap or illness. They may help others not in these categories, either by securing accommodation or by providing advice and assistance to enable them to find accommodation themselves.

A council's first responsibility is to satisfy itself that an applicant is homeless or threatened with homelessness. Once satisfied it must determine whether the applicant has a priority need. If this is the case then the council has responsibility to provide permanent accommodation. The legislation does not require councils to provide local authority accommodation in all cases, but allows them to make arrangements homeless people to be housed by a housing association or in private accommodation.

In 1993 nearly 340 thousand households in Great Britain applied to local authorities in Great Britain to be accepted as homeless (Table 10.24). Around half of them were found to be in priority need. Of those households in

10.24

Homeless households - applications and households found accommodation[1]

Great Britain				Percentages
	1986	1989	1991	1993
Households applying as homeless				
Total enquiries (thousands)	249.1	333.0	346.8	339.4
Homeless households in priority need found accommodation				
Household with dependent children	*65*	*68*	*65*	*60*
Household member pregnant	*14*	*13*	*13*	*12*
Household member vulnerable because of:				
Old age	*7*	*6*	*4*	*5*
Physical handicap	*3*	*3*	*3*	*4*
Mental illness	*2*	*2*	*3*	*5*
Other reasons[2]	*9*	*7*	*11*	*13*
All in priority need[3] (= 100%)(thousands)	107.7	128.7	160.7	154.1
Homeless households not in priority need found accommodation (thousands)	10.2	13.2	9.8	6.7
All households found accommodation (thousands)	117.9	142.0	170.5	160.8

1 See Appendix, Part 10: Households found accommodation.
2 Includes 'homeless in emergency'.
3 Includes actions where priority need category is not known.

priority need found accommodation in 1993, 60 per cent were households with children and a further 12 per cent had a pregnant household member. The proportion of households with a household member who was vulnerable because of mental illness has more than doubled since 1989, but still only accounted for 5 per cent of those households in priority need. In Northern Ireland in 1993 around 10 thousand households applied to the Northern Ireland Housing Executive in the province to be accepted as homeless.

The most common reason for households being homeless in 1993 was that they were no longer able to live in accommodation which was currently being provided by parents, relatives or friends (Chart 10.25). Those homeless households found accommodation because of a breakdown in relationship with their partner accounted for just over 20 per cent of all cases in 1993 compared with only 16 per cent in 1981.

A survey carried out by Social and Community Planning Research in 1991 on behalf of the Department of the Environment, indicated that statutorily homeless households are offered permanent accommodation immediately in just under a quarter of local authorities. However, virtually all London boroughs placed households in temporary accommodation first, compared with 70 per cent of the non-metropolitan districts. After steadily increasing up to 1992, the number of households in Great Britain who were living in temporary accommodation at the end of the year, awaiting permanent rehousing by local authorities, fell by 13 per cent in 1993, to 58 thousand (Table 10.26). Seventy per cent of these households were accommodated in property leased by local authorities on a short-term basis. This accommodation included dwellings such as mobile homes, privately leased dwellings and permanent accommodation used on a temporary basis. The use of bed and breakfast accommodation has declined dramatically over the last two years. It accounted for nearly one in ten households living in temporary accommodation in 1993, compared with one in five in 1991. The number of households in Great Britain living in this type of accommodation in 1993 was 5.5 thousand, the lowest figure since 1984. In 1993 around 2 thousand Northern Ireland homeless households were living in temporary accommodation; three quarters of these were living in dwellings rented from the private sector.

10.25

Homeless households[1] found accommodation by local authorities: by reason[2] for homelessness, 1993

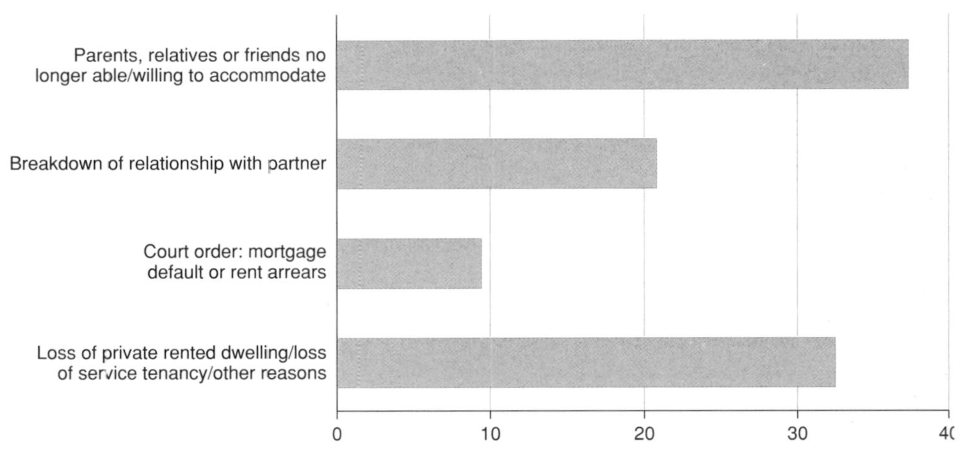

1 See Appendix, Part 10: Homeless households.
2 Categories in Wales and Northern Ireland differ slightly from those in England so cases have been allocated to the closest English category. Data for Wales include priority cases given advice and assistance but excludes those that fall into the non-priority category.
Source: Department of the Environment; Welsh Office; The Scottish Office; Department of the Environment, Northern Ireland

10.26

Homeless households living in temporary accommodation[1]

Great Britain Thousands

	Bed and breakfast	Hostels	Short life leasing	Total
1982	2.0	3.7	4.8	10.5
1983	3.0	3.6	4.5	11.1
1984	4.2	4.2	5.3	13.7
1985	5.7	5.0	6.7	17.3
1986	9.4	5.0	8.3	22.7
1987	10.6	5.7	10.5	26.8
1988	11.2	6.8	14.2	32.3
1989	12.0	8.6	19.9	40.5
1990	11.7	10.4	27.0	49.1
1991	12.9	11.7	39.7	64.3
1992	8.4	12.6	46.6	67.6
1993	5.5	12.0	41.0	58.4

1 Data are at end year and include households awaiting the outcome of homeless enquiries. Households made temporarily homeless through flooding in Wales in 1990 and 1993 are excluded.
Source: Department of the Environment; Welsh Office; Scottish Office

References and further reading

The following list contains selected publications relevant to **Chapter 10: Housing**. Those published by HMSO are available from the addresses shown on the inside back cover of *Social Trends*.

English House Condition Survey, 1991, HMSO
General Household Survey, HMSO
Housebuilding in England by Local Authority Areas, HMSO
Housing and Construction Statistics (Great Britain), annual and quarterly, HMSO
Housing Finance, Council of Mortgage Lenders
Inland Revenue Statistics, HMSO
Labour Force Survey Housing Trailer, HMSO
Local Housing Statistics: England and Wales, HMSO
Northern Ireland Housing Statistics, HMSO
Regional Trends, HMSO
Rent Officer Statistics, Department of the Environment
Scottish Development Department Statistical Bulletins on Housing, The Scottish Office
Social Focus on Children, HMSO
Social Security Statistics, HMSO
Welsh House Condition Survey, 1993, Welsh Office
Welsh Housing Statistics, Welsh Office
1988 Private Renters Survey, HMSO

Contacts

Telephone contact points for further information relating to **Chapter 10: Housing.**

Department of the Environment	0171 276 3496
Department of the Environment for Northern Ireland	01232 540808
Office of Population Censuses and Surveys	
General Household Survey	0171 396 2327
Other enquiries	0171 396 2828
The Scottish Office	0131 244 2687
Eurostat	00 352 4301 34567
Council of Mortgage Lenders	0171 437 0655

Chapter 11 Environment

Environmental concern and conservation Chemicals in rivers and seas and the disposal and import of toxic waste were the environmental issues of most concern to adults in England and Wales in 1993. (Table 11.2)

The global atmosphere Chlorofluorocarbons are the main man-made source of damage to the ozone layer - sales in the EC in 1993 amounted to two-fifths of the value of sales in 1976. (Chart 11.8)

Carbon dioxide accounts for almost three quarters of the global greenhouse effect. (Chart 11.9)

Air quality Road transport accounted for nine tenths of carbon monoxide emissions and just over half of nitrogen oxide emissions in 1992. (Table 11.10)

Water quality Average concentrations of lead in major rivers in Great Britain in 1992 amounted to a fifth of the amount in 1976; concentrations of zinc and copper halved over the period. (Chart 11.15)

Land cover and land use A tenth of the land area of the United Kingdom is covered by forest - double the proportion at the beginning of the century. (Page 197)

Natural resources Flushing the toilet uses a third of the domestic water supply. (Chart 11.23)

The average United Kingdom resident uses around half of the energy consumed by a Luxembourg resident but nearly three times more than that used by a resident of Spain. (Chart 11.24)

11.1

Carbon dioxide emissions: by source

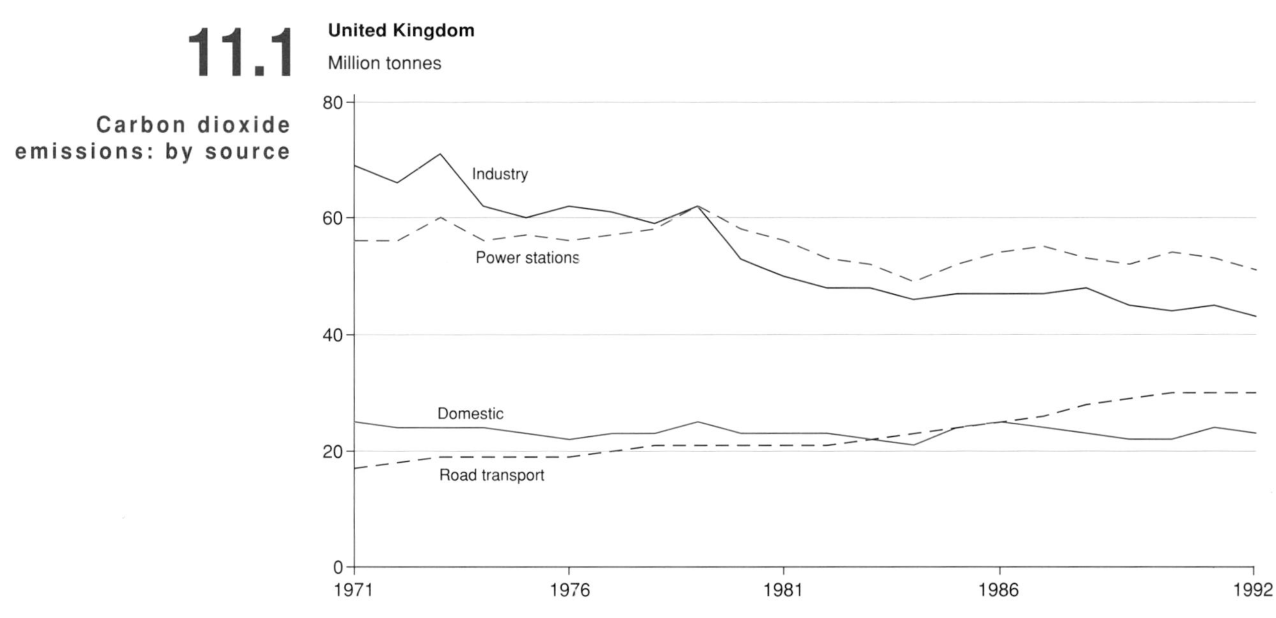

Source: National Environmental Technology Centre

11.2

People who were 'very worried' about various environmental issues

England & Wales Percentages

	1989	1993		1989	1993
Chemicals in rivers/seas	64	63	Fumes and smoke from factories	34	35
Toxic waste: disposal/import	..	63	Traffic congestion	..	35
Radioactive waste	58	60	Global warming	44	35
Sewage on beaches/bathing water	59	56	Acid rain	40	31
Oil spills at sea/on beaches	53	52	Litter/rubbish	33	29
Tropical forest destruction	44	45	Fouling by dogs	29	29
Loss of plants/animals in UK	..	43	Using up United Kingdom's natural resouces	..	27
Ozone layer depletion	56	41	Decay of inner cities	22	26
Traffic exhaust fumes/urban smog	33	40	Household waste disposal	..	22
Drinking water quality	41	38	Need for more energy conservation	..	21
Loss of plants/animals abroad	..	38	Vacant/derelict land/buildings	16	19
Use of insecticides/fertilizers	46	36	Not enough recycling	..	19
Loss of trees/hedgerows	34	36	Noise	13	16
Losing Green Belt land	27	35			

Source: Department of the Environment

11.3

Objections to noise[1], 1991

Great Britain
Percentages

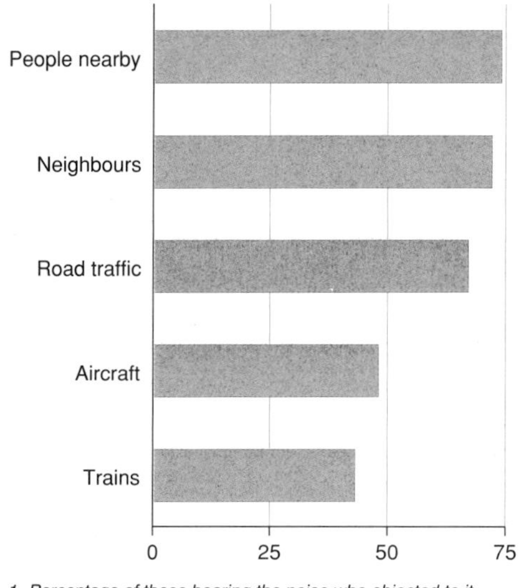

1 Percentage of those hearing the noise who objected to it.
Source: Building Research Establishment

The environment in which we live is affected by many issues: some of local concern, such as planning matters; some of national concern, such as the pollution rivers; and others of global concern, such as the 'greenhouse effect'. This chapter looks at a range of environmental issues which affect the air, water and land around us. It also looks at the extent and use of our natural resources.

Environmental concern and conservation

A Department of the Environment survey on public attitudes to the environment carried out in 1993 suggested that 85 per cent of adults in England and Wales were either 'quite concerned' or 'very concerned' about the environment. Table 11.2 shows that the two issues of greatest concern were chemicals being put in rivers and the sea and the disposal and import of toxic waste. Some issues, such as traffic exhaust fumes and urban smog, appear to be of increasing concern. In 1989 only 33 per cent of respondents said that they were very worried about this issue compared with 40 per cent in 1993; more people said that in 20 years time they would be concerned about traffic congestion, fumes or noise than any other environmental issue. Only 10 per cent, however, said that they had used public transport on a regular basis instead of a car for environmental reasons.

Over half of those surveyed in 1993 were also 'very concerned' about radioactive waste, sewage on beaches and in bathing water and oil spills at sea with the consequential damage to beaches.

The results of a similar survey in Northern Ireland in 1990 showed that of greatest concern was the disposal of sewage and the risks from nuclear power stations; 56 per cent of people interviewed were 'very concerned' about these issues. Over two fifths of people were 'very concerned' about the use of insecticides, pesticides and chemical sprays, the loss of plant and animal species and the quality of drinking water.

A survey conducted by MORI in 1993 showed that children are also aware of environmental problems. Litter was seen as the most important local issue for those aged 8 to 12 while 13 to 15 year olds felt that traffic fumes were more of a problem. On global issues, around nine in ten children felt that deforestation and polluted oceans were a problem.

A survey on public attitudes also showed that many people are concerned about noise. A study by the Building Research Establishment in 1991 set out to assess the problem of noise and how it affects people. It found that some noises such as birds, laughter and, in some instances, children are actually appreciated; some people even said that a degree of noise from neighbours was welcomed because it provided a sense of human contact. Noise from neighbours and children crying or screaming, however, and noise from traffic, aircraft and trains was considered unacceptable by many people. Overall, just under a third of people said that noise spoiled their home life to some extent.

Chart 11.3 shows that almost three quarters of those who experienced noise from neighbours and other people nearby objected to it. Respondents to the survey who objected to noise said that it caused emotional reactions such as annoyance, anger, anxiety and resentment. A measure of the increasing problem of noise may be taken from the number of complaints to Environmental Health Officers; in 1980 there were around 1.3 thousand complaints per million people in England and Wales but by 1991 this had more than tripled to almost 4.1 thousand complaints per million people.

Some people feel that they can help protect the environment by joining an organisation. Table 11.4 shows that membership of such organisations has increased dramatically in recent years. Greenpeace, for example, had only 30 thousand members in 1981; in 1993 it had over 400 thousand. The National Trust which is concerned with the preservation and protection of selected buildings and areas of land had well over 2 million members in 1993.

11.4

Membership of selected voluntary environmental organisations

United Kingdom — Thousands

	1971	1981	1991	1993
National Trust	278	1,046	2,152	2,189
Royal Society for the Protection of Birds	98	441	852	850
Greenpeace	..	30	408	410
Royal Society for Nature Conservation	64	143	250	248
National Trust for Scotland	37	110	234	235
Civic Trust[1]	214	..	222	222
World Wide Fund for Nature	12	60	227	207
Woodland Trust	..	20	150	150
Friends of the Earth[2]	1	18	111	120
Ramblers Association	22	37	87	94
Council for the Protection of Rural England	21	29	45	45
British Trust for Conservation Volunteers[3]	1	..	9	12
British Trust for Ornithology	5	7	9	10
Scottish Wildlife Trust	1	7	9	9
National Council for the Conservation of Plants and Gardens	..	..	7	7
Campaign for the Protection of Rural Wales	..	2	4	4

1 Members of local amenity societies registered with the Civic Trust.
2 England, Wales and Northern Ireland only.
3 Data for 1971 and 1991 relate to two years earlier.
Source: Organisations concerned

Recycling can benefit the environment by saving energy and resources. The Government's 1990 White Paper on the Environment set a target of recycling half of all recyclable household waste by the year 2000. Table 11.5 shows that there has been an increase in the level of recycling in a number of key industrial sectors in recent years. In 1992 the amount of paper and board recycled and waste paper used in news print was equivalent to around a third of consumption during the year; for glass it was around a quarter. The proportion of aluminium cans recycled nearly tripled between 1990 and 1992 to 16 per cent; it is targeted to rise to 50 per cent by the year 1997-98.

11.5

Recycling levels: by material

United Kingdom — Percentages

	1990	1991	1992	2000 (target)
Paper and board	*31*	*34*	*34*	..
Waste paper used in news	*27*	*28*	*31*	*40*
Glass	*21*	*21*	*26*	*50*
Aluminium cans[1]	*6*	*11*	*16*	*50*
Steel cans	*9*	*10*	*12*	..
Plastics	*2*	..	*5*	..

1 Target figure refers to 1997-98.
Source: BGMC; BS; SCRIB; BP&BIF; PPIC

11.6

Designated areas: by region, 1993

Percentages

	National Parks	Areas of Outstanding Natural Beauty[1]	Green Belt areas[2]	Defined Heritage Coasts (kilometres)[3]
North	23	15	3	114
Yorkshire & Humberside	20	2	15	82
East Midlands	6	3	5	.
East Anglia	0	7	1	121
South East	0	24	21	72
South West	7	29	5	638
West Midlands	2	10	19	.
North West	1	11	33	0
England	7	15	12	1,027
Wales	20	4	0	496
Scotland	0	13	2	7,546
Northern Ireland	0	20	17	-

1 National Scenic Areas in Scotland.
2 1992 data.
3 Preferred Coastal Conservation Zones in Scotland, including mainland and islands.

Source: Department of the Environment

11.7

Bat population

United Kingdom

Indices (1978=100)

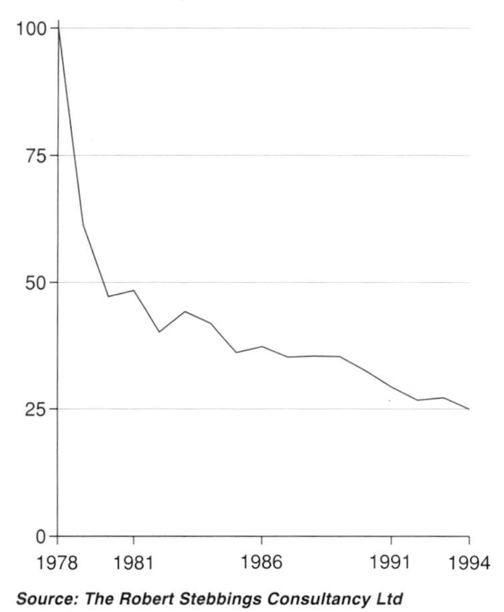

Source: The Robert Stebbings Consultancy Ltd

Many parts of the United Kingdom are protected in some way. For example, in England and Wales there are 12 National Parks, 40 Areas of Outstanding Natural Beauty and 45 stretches of Heritage Coast. Scotland has 40 National Scenic Areas and almost three quarters of the Scottish mainland and island coastline is classified as a Preferred Coastal Conservation Zone. Northern Ireland has 9 areas of Outstanding Natural Beauty. Table 11.6 shows that the North has the greatest proportion of its area designated as a National Park (almost a quarter) while the South West has the largest proportion of its area (over a quarter) designated as Areas of Outstanding Natural Beauty.

Green Belts were established to restrict urban development, protect the surrounding countryside from further encroachment, protect the special character of historic towns and assist in urban regeneration. The largest Green Belt is around London although a third of the North West is also designated as Green Belt. Overall, Green Belts cover 1.5 million hectares in England, around 155 thousand hectares in Scotland and about 200 thousand hectares in Northern Ireland. There are no Green Belts in Wales.

Other parts of the United Kingdom are protected in different ways. For example, at the end of 1993 there were almost 6 thousand Sites of Special Scientific interest in Great Britain covering, in total, almost 19 thousand square kilometres. Northern Ireland has 48 Areas of Special Scientific Interest. Other areas protected by statute include National and Local Nature reserves, Marine Nature reserves, 'Ramsar' Wetland Sites and Environmentally Sensitive Areas.

The United Kingdom has an estimated 30 thousand species of animals (excluding marine microscopic and less well known groups). A number of these species is considered to be endangered or rare and hence are protected under the *Wildlife and Countryside Act, 1981*. This includes all 15 species of bat which are or have been resident in Great Britain. One species, the mouse-eared bat, has recently become extinct and some others are now very rare. Under the *Wildlife and Countryside Act, 1981* it is illegal to injure, kill or disturb bats when they are roosting or to damage, destroy or obstruct bat roosts. Every year the Robert Stebbings Consultancy Ltd organises the National Bat Colony Survey. This is undertaken by volunteers counting the number of bats emerging from their roosts in the evenings in June. Trends in the bat population are calculated by comparing the results of counts made at the same site and same time each year. Chart 11.7 shows that in Summer 1994 it was estimated that the United Kingdom bat population was only a quarter of what it was in 1978.

The global atmosphere

Some environmental problems such as the depletion of the ozone layer are of global concern and can only be dealt with effectively by concerted global action. The ozone layer helps prevent short wavelength ultraviolet-C radiation and ultraviolet-B radiation reaching the earth's surface. Ultraviolet B can cause skin cancer and have harmful effects on plants and marine life. The increase in the concentrations of man-made gases since the 1950s has led to a significant depletion of the ozone layer. The principal man-made ozone depleters are chlorofluorocarbons (CFCs) and halons.

Chart 11.8 shows that sales of CFCs in the European Community (EC) in 1993 amounted to less than two fifths of that sold in 1976; this was mainly attributable to the replacement of CFCs in aerosols by other less harmful gases. In order to ensure that future damage to the ozone layer is limited, the 1987 Montreal Protocol introduced limits on the production and consumption of CFCs and halons. The provisions of the Protocol were strengthened in 1990 and further in 1992. CFCs and halons are now to be phased out by 1996 and a timetable for phasing out hydrofluorocarbons by 2030 has been agreed.

A change in climate can affect natural vegetation, wildlife and effect a rise or fall in sea levels. The First Assessment Report of the Intergovernmental Panel on Climate Change concluded that average global temperatures increased by between 0.3 degrees centigrade and 0.6 degrees centigrade during the last century and that without intervention an increase of around 0.3 degrees centigrade per decade is likely in the future.

These changes in temperature levels have been attributed to the so called 'enhanced greenhouse effect': sunlight penetrates the atmosphere and warms the earth, then some of this heat is reflected back from the earth but is trapped by the greenhouse gases which act as a blanket keeping the heat in and causing an increase in temperature.

Since the industrial revolution increasing amounts of greenhouse gases have been added to the atmosphere mainly by the release of carbon dioxide as a result of the use of fossil fuels for heating, transportation and the generation of electricity as well as by the increasing destruction of forests. Chart 11.9 shows that almost three quarters of the global greenhouse effect is attributable to carbon dioxide.

11.8

EC sales of CFCs[1]: by use

Thousand tonnes

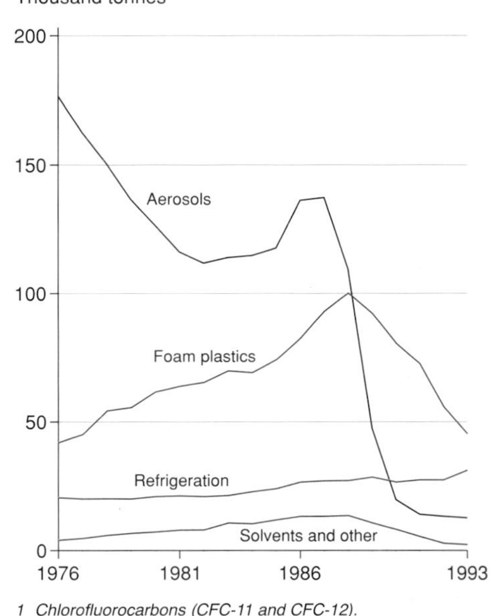

1 Chlorofluorocarbons (CFC-11 and CFC-12).

Source: European Commission

11.9

Relative direct contribution to the greenhouse effect of the emissions of various gases[1], 1992

Percentages

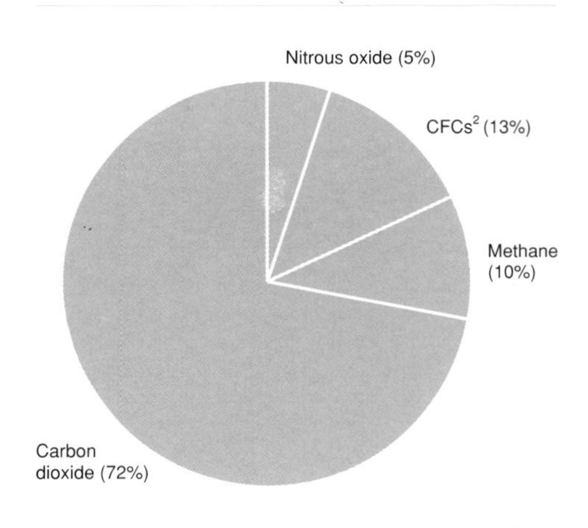

1 Man-made emissions.
2 Chlorofluorcarbons.

Source: Inter Governmental Panel on Climate Change

11.10

Air pollutants: by source, 1992

United Kingdom Percentages

	Carbon dioxide	Carbon monoxide	Sulphur dioxide	Nitrogen oxides	Volatile organic compounds	Black smoke
Road transport	*19*	*90*	*2*	*51*	*37*	*47*
Electricity supply	*33*	*1*	*69*	*25*	-	*5*
Domestic	*15*	*4*	*3*	*3*	*1*	*28*
Other	*33*	*5*	*26*	*21*	*62*	*20*
Total (=100%) (million tonnes)	155.0	6.7	3.5	2.8	2.6	0.5

Source: National Environmental Technology Centre

11.11

Lead concentrations at selected sites[1]

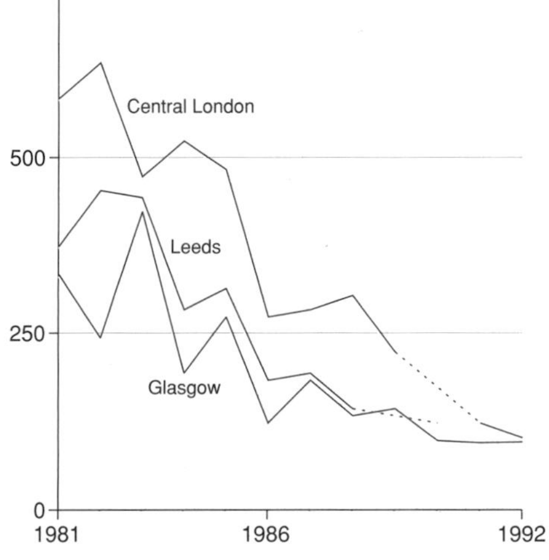

1 Annual mean. Leeds data for 1989 and 1991 onwards and Central London data for 1990 are not available.
Source: National Environmental Technology Centre

Air quality

Poor air quality has a detrimental effect on humans, wildlife, plant life and even on building materials. As can be seen from Table 11.10, in terms of weight carbon dioxide is the main pollutant; in 1992 a third of these emissions came from the production of electricity. The same source, however, accounted for over two thirds of emissions of sulphur dioxide and a quarter of those from nitrogen oxides.

The Clean Air Acts of 1956 and 1968 created smokeless zones which considerably reduced pollution from smoke and sulphur dioxide (produced by the combustion of coal). However, emissions of nitrogen oxides and carbon monoxide increased throughout the 1970s and 1980s mainly because emissions of both gases from road transport doubled over the period. In recent years emissions of these gases from road transport have stabilised and in 1992 they began to fall.

The increase in emissions of volatile organic compounds was also largely attributable to road transport. In 1992 road transport still accounted for nine tenths of all emissions of carbon monoxide, around a half of those from black smoke and nitrogen oxides and almost two fifths of those from volatile organic compounds. Projections of road traffic emissions of carbon monoxide, volatile organic compounds and nitrogen oxides suggest that levels will fall until around 2010 as a result of the use of catalytic converters, and then rise again as a result of increased traffic levels.

Around 7,500 million tonnes of carbon dioxide are produced annually from man-made sources around the world; just over 2 per cent of this comes from sources within the United Kingdom. Chart 11.1 shows that in 1992 power stations were the source of over 50 million tonnes of carbon dioxide - a reduction on the 56 million tonnes emitted in 1971. In both years this accounted for around a third of all carbon dioxide emissions by source. Carbon dioxide emissions from road transport (as already mentioned) almost doubled over the same period reaching 30 million tonnes in 1990 since when the figure has remained unchanged.

Emissions from industry (including refineries, iron and steel producers, and commercial and public service operations), on the other hand, declined by almost two fifths between 1971 and 1992. Domestic users accounted for only 15 per cent of carbon dioxide emissions by source in 1992 - almost the same proportion as in 1971. In 1992 almost two fifths of carbon dioxide emissions came from the burning of coal - a proportion which has declined steadily from just over a half since 1970.

Road traffic is also responsible for emissions of lead. The largest single source of lead in the air originates from the burning of leaded petrol although lead also gets into the atmosphere from coal burning and metal smelting. Accumulations of lead in the body can cause health problems especially in children. In order to ensure that lead emissions are kept within safe limits, the government has set up a number of monitoring sites - some at roadside locations and some at industrial locations. Lead concentrations are controlled by an EC directive which limits airborne concentrations to 2,000 nanograms/m^3.

Since monitoring began in 1985, only one site (in Walsall) has exceeded the limit. Chart 11.11 shows recorded emissions of lead at three sites all of which show generally downward trends. This is attributed to the increased use of unleaded petrol which in Autumn 1994 accounted for 59 per cent of all sales compared with just 1 per cent in Summer 1988. This increase in sales is in part, at least, due to the lower duty on unleaded petrol compared with leaded. By 2012 virtually all petrol-engined vehicles should be running on unleaded petrol.

Everyone is exposed to radiation, the majority of which comes from natural sources. Chart 11.12 shows that half of all exposure comes from radon. This is a gas produced by the decay of trace amounts of uranium that occur in virtually all rocks. In the open air radon disperses quickly. However, in enclosed spaces, especially in areas of porous rocks which contain above average levels of uranium, it can be a health hazard. It has been estimated that radon is the cause of around 5 to 6 per cent of all deaths from lung cancer. In Devon and Cornwall around 12 per cent of homes have radon concentrations above the recommended action level. The majority of radiation exposure from artificial sources comes from medical X-ray examinations. Fallout from the testing of nuclear weapons has been declining steadily since the early 1960s.

The Chernobyl nuclear power station accident in 1986 caused a sharp increase in fallout (albeit from a very low level). By 1993, however, this had fallen back to just a fifth of its 1986 level. In 1993 radiation from all non-medical artificial sources (such as fallout from nuclear weapons) accounted for just half of 1 per cent of total radiation exposure.

Soil is a vital limited resource upon which we depend for the growing of food crops and the supply of timber. Many plants and animal species are similarly dependent upon the soil. Loss of organic matter, erosion, contamination, subsidence and acidification can all reduce the effectiveness of the soil. Although acidification is a natural process, it can be intensified by the emission of acidifying gases such as nitrogen oxides, sulphur dioxide and ammonia. In wet weather these gases fall to ground in rain or snow - the so called 'acid rain'.

The extent of damage to the soil is dependent upon three things: the level of acidifying gases in the air, the level of rainfall and the extent to which the soil is susceptible to damage. At some point, an increase in the concentrations of these gases or an increase in rainfall may damage the soil. The point at which this long term damage occurs is called the critical load. Chart 11.13 shows that areas where the soils are most affected by acid rain are generally the areas of high rainfall including the hills close to the west coast of Scotland, the Pennines, the Lake District, parts of Cheshire and the Welsh mountains.

11.12

Radiation exposure of the population: by source, 1993

United Kingdom

Percentages

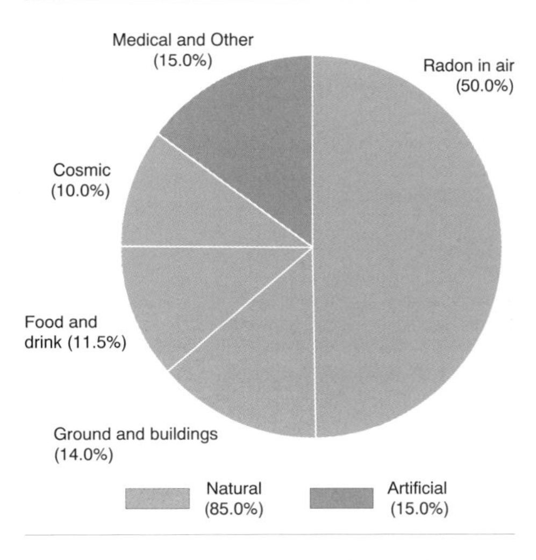

Source: National Radiological Protection Board

11.13

Exceedance of critical load for acidity of soils[1], 1989-1991

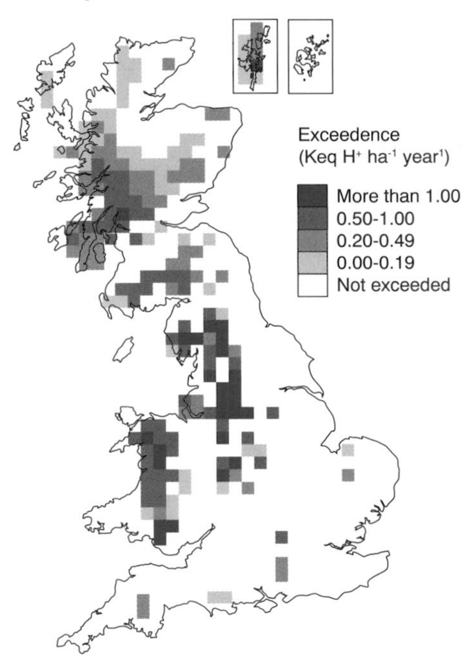

1 Areas where critical loads for acidity of soils are exceeded by annual mean total non-marine sulphur deposition.

Source: Warren Spring Laboratory; Institute of Terrestrial Ecology

11.14

River and canal quality: by region, 1992

Percentages

	Good	Fair	Poor	Bad
Northumbria/Yorkshire	*54*	*28*	*16*	*3*
Anglian	*22*	*56*	*19*	*3*
Thames	*39*	*51*	*9*	*1*
Southern	*51*	*40*	*8*	*1*
South Western	*69*	*26*	*4*	*1*
Severn-Trent	*38*	*45*	*14*	*3*
North West	*53*	*28*	*15*	*4*
Welsh[1]	*86*	*11*	*3*	*1*

1 Regional boundaries are based on river catchment areas.

Source: National Rivers Authority

11.15

Annual average concentrations of selected heavy metals in freshwater

Great Britain[1]

Micrograms/litre

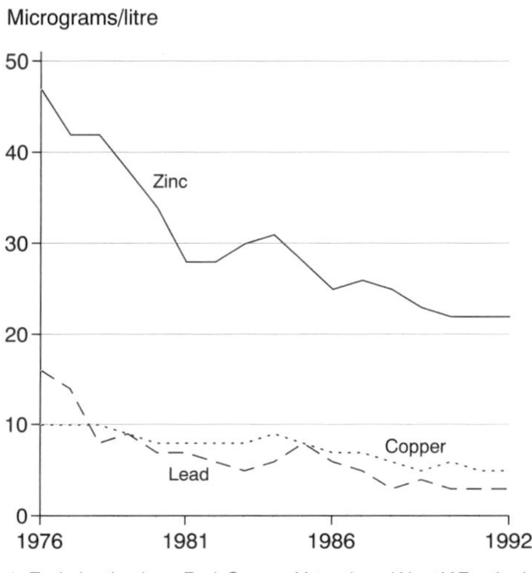

1 Excludes the rivers Red, Carnon, Ystwyth and Nant Y Fendrod.

Source: National Rivers Authority; Scottish River Purification Boards

Water quality

Like soil, water is also a limited resource which can be damaged by man's activities. In 1992 a new classification system for measuring river and canal quality was introduced in England and Wales. Figures in Table 11.14 are, therefore, not comparable with those given in earlier editions of *Social Trends*, or with current figures for Scotland and Northern Ireland. In 1992 there were considerable variations in the quality of river and canal water in England and Wales. In the Welsh region, for example, 97 per cent of water was of good or fair quality compared with only 78 per cent in the Anglian region.

The 1990 Countryside Survey found that water quality varied in different types of landscape; in arable landscapes, for example, a lower proportion of water courses were of good quality than in upland landscapes. As well as quality, the reliability of the water supply is also important. The prolonged drought from April 1988 to June 1992 mainly affected eastern and southern England where groundwater resources were depleted during a succession of four dry winters. Between 1989 and 1992, 194 drought orders were issued by the National Rivers Authority; there were none at all during the previous four years.

The quality of freshwater is affected by discharges from sewage works, factories and farms and also by spillages and the leaching of contaminants from soils and rocks. In England and Wales the quality of water is controlled through a system of consents. All discharges of certain substances considered dangerous to the aquatic environment must have prior consent from the National Rivers Authority (NRA). These conditions are designed to achieve Environmental Quality Standards (EQSs). The NRA enforces EQSs in inland and coastal waters as statutory Water Quality Objectives under the *Water Resources Act 1991*. Regulated substances include copper, lead and zinc. As can be seen from Chart 11.15, between 1976 and 1992 there were notable reductions in the concentrations of all three metals in freshwaters in Great Britain.

Spillages from ships and offshore installations are a source of pollution at sea. Table 11.16 shows that in 1992 there were 611 reported oil spills; less than in each of the previous three years but more than in each of the eight years before that. The steady increase in the number of reported incidents between 1986 and 1990 is likely, in part at least, to be due to improved surveillance techniques. In 1992, almost a third of reported incidents were in the North Sea. One of the largest spillages of oil in recent years was an estimated 84 thousand tonnes from the MV Braer off the coast of Shetland in January 1993. The high clean up costs in 1990 were attributable to the clearing of oil off the south west coast of England following the collision between an oil tanker and a fishing vessel. In addition to spillages, oil is also discharged from offshore installations; this accounted for around 11 thousand tonnes in 1992.

The quality of seawater bathing areas is monitored against mandatory standards set by an EC directive. This imposes a limit on the presence of coliforms - a group of bacteria - in the water. Chart 11.17 shows the percentage of seawater bathing areas in each EC country in 1993 which failed to meet the standards required by the directive. The best record was held by the Netherlands where all bathing waters met the standard; the United Kingdom had the worst rate. All countries except Ireland, France and Belgium had improved their rates of compliance since the 1990 survey.

The same EC directive is also used to monitor water quality on a regional basis within the United Kingdom. In 1993 less than 10 per cent of identified bathing waters in Yorkshire, Thames and Northern Ireland failed to comply while three fifths in the North West failed to meet the standard.

11.16

Oil spills reported

United Kingdom — Numbers

	1981	1986	1990	1991	1992
Number of incidents	552	436	791	705	611
Spills over 100 gallons[1]	93	103	174	143	100
Spills requiring clean-up	171	126	136	169	156
Costs incurred (£ thousands at 1992 prices)[2]	219	190	1,310	305	127

1 Not directly comparable with 'number of incidents'.
2 Deflated by the retail prices index.
Source: Advisory Committee on Protection of the Sea

11.17

Seawater bathing areas not complying with mandatory coliform standards[1]: EC comparison, 1993

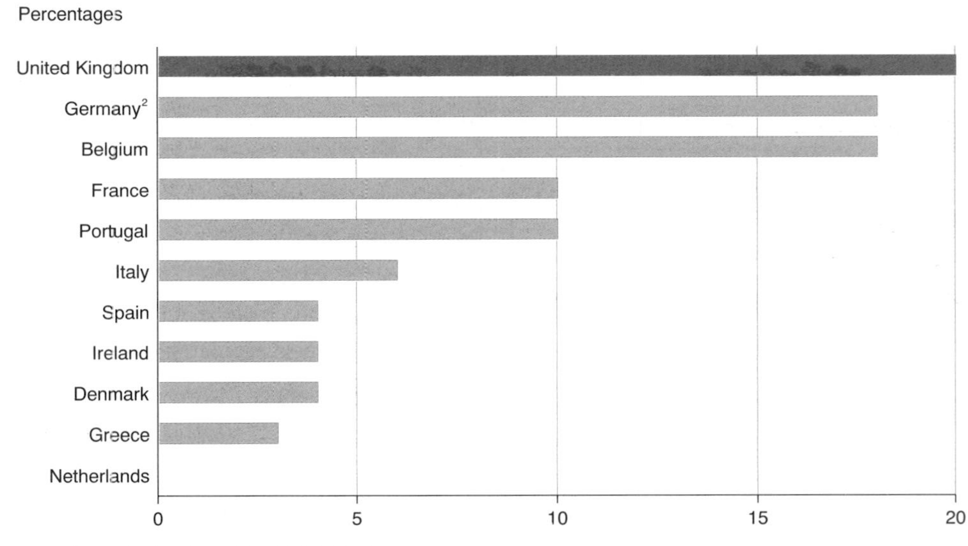

1 See Appendix, Part 11: Quality of bathing water.
2 As constituted since 3 October 1990.
Source: European Commission

11.18

Land cover, 1990

Percentages

	England	Wales	Scotland	Great Britain
Managed grassland	*33*	*38*	*15*	*27*
Heath/marsh/moor[1]	*11*	*27*	*51*	*26*
Tilled land	*32*	*5*	*8*	*21*
Urban/suburban	*10*	*3*	*2*	*7*
Broadleaved/mixed wood	*6*	*12*	*2*	*5*
Inland water/sea/estuary	*2*	*3*	*6*	*4*
Coniferous wood	*2*	*4*	*6*	*3*
Other	*4*	*7*	*10*	*6*
Total area (=100%) (thousand square kilometres)	134	22	85	240

1 Includes rough grassland and bracken.

Source: Department of the Environment; Institute of Terrestrial Ecology

11.19

Agricultural land use[1]

United Kingdom Thousand hectares

	1961	1971	1981	1991	1993
Crop areas, of which:	4,276	4,838	4,995	4,956	4,519
Wheat	739	1,097	1,491	1,980	1,759
Barley	1,549	2,288	2,327	1,393	1,164
Other cereals (excluding maize)	768	424	161	127	107
Rape grown for oil seed[2]	..	5	125	440	377
Sugar beet not for stockfeeding	173	190	210	196	197
Potatoes (early and maincrop)	285	256	191	176	170
Other crops	761	577	490	644	744
Bare fallow	123	74	76	64	47
Grasses	7,999	7 240	7,013	6,846	6,770
Sole right rough grazing[3]	7,359	5 550	5,021	4,685	4,611
Woodland	..	154	277	368	411
Set-aside[4]	.	.	.	97	677
All other land on agricultural holdings	..	131	211	248	267
Common rough grazing	..	1,128	1,214	1,233	1,229
Total agricultural land[5]	19,757	19 115	18,808	18,498	18,530

1 Includes estimates for minor holdings in England and Wales throughout and in Northern Ireland from 1991, but not for Scotland.
2 England and Wales only for 1971 and 1981.
3 The 1961 figure includes common rough grazing.
4 Applied only to England in 1991.
5 Excludes woodland and all other land on agricultural holdings in 1961.

Source: Ministry of Agriculture, Fisheries and Food; Welsh Office; The Scottish Office Agriculture and Fisheries Department; Department of Agriculture, Northern Ireland

Land cover and land use

The 1990 Countryside Survey involved a field survey of 508 one kilometre squares, 11,500 vegetation plots and 360 watercourses. It also used data collected by satellite. The survey looked at a number of aspects including land cover, plant diversity, lengths of hedgerows and walls and the quality of water courses. A summary of the results of the land cover study based on the satellite images is given in Table 11.18. It shows that in 1990 just over a fifth of Great Britain was tilled land; managed grassland accounted for just over a quarter and heath, marsh, moorland, rough grassland and bracken accounted for just over another quarter. As would be expected, there were considerable regional variations. Heath, marsh, moor, rough grassland and bracken accounted for just over a half of the land area in Scotland but only just over a tenth of the area of England. Between 1984 and 1990 there was a 4 per cent reduction in both tilled land and field boundaries.

Table 11.19 shows that the proportion of land used for agriculture was 6 per cent less in 1993 than in 1961. However, the area devoted to crops rose from 4.3 million hectares in 1961 to 5.0 million hectares in 1981; between 1991 and 1993 it fell back from 5.0 to 4.5 million hectares. Between 1961 and 1993 the area devoted to individual crops varied considerably. For example, in 1991 the area of land used for wheat production (2.0 million hectares) was over two and a half times greater than it was in 1961; between 1991 and 1993, however, there was an 11 per cent fall. Similarly, the area devoted to barley rose by a half between 1961 and 1981. The 1993 figure (1.2 million hectares) was just half of that for 1981. The reduction in land devoted to crops in recent years is at least in part a result of the EC's Common Agricultural Policy (CAP) to subsidise farmers for taking land out of production.

Trees serve a number of important functions; they provide timber, a habitat for wildlife and act as reservoirs to free carbon from carbon dioxide thereby reducing the effects of global warming. The United Kingdom was once heavily forested, with about 80 per cent tree cover according to some estimates, much of which was felled for agriculture, settlements and roads so that by the start of this century forest cover stood at an all time low of around 5 per cent. Today that proportion has doubled to around 10 per cent.

As well as planting and controlling the felling of trees, it is also prudent to monitor the health of trees. This is done under a joint EC-UNECE monitoring programme which involves measuring the density of foliage against a 'perfect' tree. For all species there were sharp increases in the numbers with more than 10 per cent loss of foliage between 1990 and 1992. Of the trees shown in Table 11.20, the Norway Spruce appeared to be in best health in 1993 although only 57 per cent of even this species had foliage within 25 per cent of the optimum density. Only a fifth of oak trees came within the same category. Changes in tree health can be attributed to droughts and possibly air pollution.

As a control over land use we have a planning system which is designed to help people plan the use of their land, help local authorities act in the public interest (by, for example, designating land for a particular use) and stop developers acting against the public interest. It also gives an opportunity for all those affected by proposals to air their views. Under the *Planning and Compensation Act 1991* all local planning authorities must have a current development plan of policies and proposals relating to the development of their area.

11.20

Forest health

United Kingdom — Percentages[1]

	1987	1989	1991	1992	1993
Norway spruce	*57*	*64*	*52*	*51*	*57*
Sitka spruce	*50*	*46*	*51*	*56*	*55*
Beech	*44*	*64*	*41*	*48*	*53*
Scots pine	*53*	*55*	*43*	*37*	*48*
Oak	*34*	*42*	*29*	*20*	*20*

1 Trees within 25 per cent of the 'perfect tree'.

Source: Forestry Commission

Table 11.21 shows that the number of planning decisions made fell from just under 600 thousand in 1989-90 to 483 thousand in 1991-92; after falling further in 1992-93 (to 441 thousand), it then rose again to 447 thousand in 1993-94. Almost all of these decisions resulted from applications to district councils; the remainder were county matter applications

11.21

Planning applications: by type

England — Thousands

	Decisions made			Applications granted (percentages)
	1989-90	1991-92	1993-94	1993-94
District councils				
Householder developments	226	185	169	*92*
Dwellings	115	76	60	*78*
Change of use	52	43	39	*79*
Advertisements	35	29	30	*81*
Listed building consents	31	29	27	*81*
Industrial	33	22	18	*91*
Retail distribution and servicing	28	21	18	*87*
Conservation area consents	.	.	6	*89*
Other new developments	59	57	61	*89*
Other	16	20	17	..
All district council decisions	596	482	445	..
County matter decisions[1]	2	2	2	*87*
All decisions	597	483	447	..

1 Predominately relate to minerals and waste disposal developments.

Source: Department of the Environment

11.22

Out of town shopping developments[1]

United Kingdom

Numbers

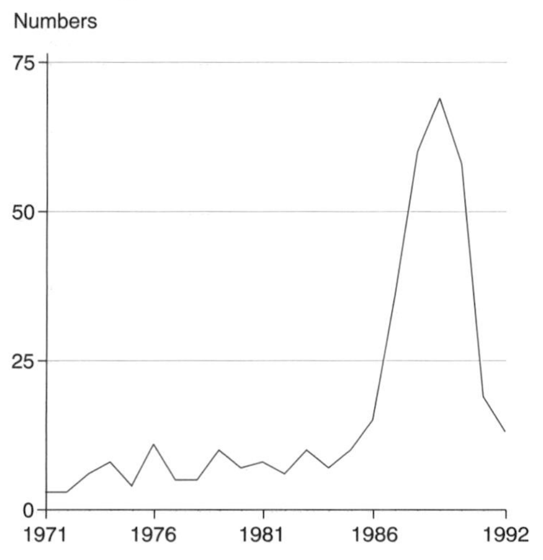

1 Number of developments completed each year over 5,000 square metres or 50,000 square feet.

Source: Oxford Institue of Retail Management; British Council of Shopping Centres

11.23

Domestic water use, 1992

England & Wales

Percentages

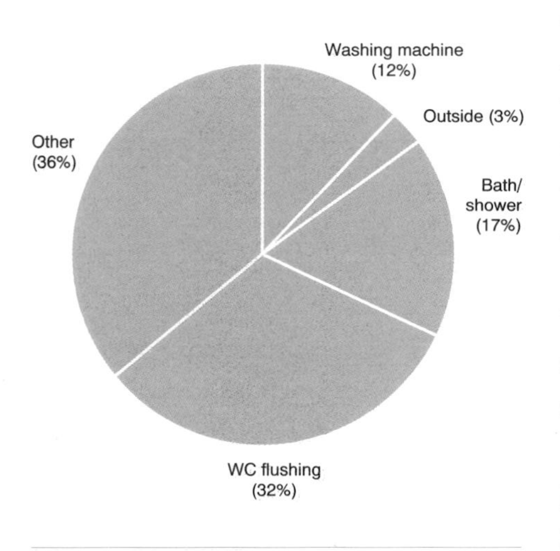

Source: Water Services Association

which relate mainly to minerals and waste disposal. Just under two fifths of the decisions made by district councils were in respect of householder development applications. The proportion of applications granted varied according to the type of application. For example, 92 per cent of householder decisions found in favour of the applicant while only 78 per cent of those relating to dwellings were granted. In Wales, in 1993, there were 32 thousand planning applications. Of the 29 thousand decisions made, 87 per cent were granted.

Up to the 1960s the majority of people relied on public transport to get them to work and for leisure and shopping journeys. The most convenient place to shop was therefore the town or village centre. As car ownership has increased town and village centres with their restricted parking facilities and traffic jams have become less attractive. This has encouraged developers to look for out-of-town sites where large car parks can be provided and where the traffic congestion of the town centre can be avoided. These developments also provide a controlled environment in terms of heating and lighting (warm in winter and air conditioned in summer) making them all year round attractions. The apparent attractiveness of these centres, encourages people to travel relatively long distances to visit them but they may be less convenient for those who do not have a car.

The number of developments over 5 thousand square metres or 50 thousand square feet completed each year rose to a peak of 69 in 1989 (Chart 11.22) since when it fell back to just 13 in 1992. Developments completed in recent years include the Gateshead Metro Centre, Meadowhall in Sheffield, Lakeside in Essex and Merryhill in the West Midlands. Despite the rise in the popularity of these types of centres, the number of new town centre developments over 5 thousand square metres or 50 thousand square feet has remained broadly constant since 1971 at around 15 to 30 per year except in 1990 when it rose to 38. However, this overestimates the extent of development in town centres as there is also a loss of floor space due to closures.

Natural resources

In 1992 an average of 68 thousand megalitres a day of water was extracted from surface and groundwater sources in England and Wales. Of this, nearly three fifths was used for the production of electricity while just over a quarter went into the public water supply. Of the 20 thousand megalitres per day put into the United Kingdom public water supply, 28 per cent was metered and used mainly by industry and the remainder was unmetered and used mainly by domestic and commercial users.

Of the 140 litres per person per day consumed in households in England and Wales, almost a third is used for flushing the toilet (Chart 11.23) Not all water put into the public water supply is used effectively; leakages in the pipes owned by the water companies and by consumers are thought to account for loses that in some cases can be as high as 25 per cent. The metering of water supplies has been shown to reduce demand by about 11 per cent.

Chart 11.24 shows that domestic energy consumption per head varies considerable between the EC member states. Luxembourg had by far the highest consumption rate in 1992 with the equivalent of 1,341 tonnes of oil consumed per million population. This is over five times as much as Spain where the equivalent of only 251 tonnes of oil per million population were consumed. The United Kingdom was just above the EC average at 725 tonnes per million population.

Climate is obviously one factor which has a major bearing on fuel consumption hence all of the southern EC countries (Italy, Greece, Portugal and Spain) are low users of energy. Other factors affecting energy use are type and age of housing. Looking at the Community as a whole, 72 per cent of energy consumed in households is for space heating, 13 per cent for water heating and 6 per cent for cooking. Some countries, however, use more energy for particular purposes. For example, France and Greece use the most energy for cooking and the United Kingdom uses the most for heating water.

The production of primary fuels in 1993 was almost double that in 1971. However, as can be seen from Chart 11.25 there has been a significant change in the importance of each type of fuel. Coal accounted for almost four fifths of fuel production in 1971 while oil accounted for less than one per cent. By 1993 coal production accounted for less than a fifth of the total while oil accounted for almost a half. The big dip in coal production in 1984 was due to industrial action by coal miners. Transport is the largest single energy user accounting for 33 per cent of the total in 1993 while domestic users and industry took 30 per cent and 24 per cent respectively.

11.24

Domestic energy consumption: EC comparison, 1992

Tonnes of oil equivalent per million population

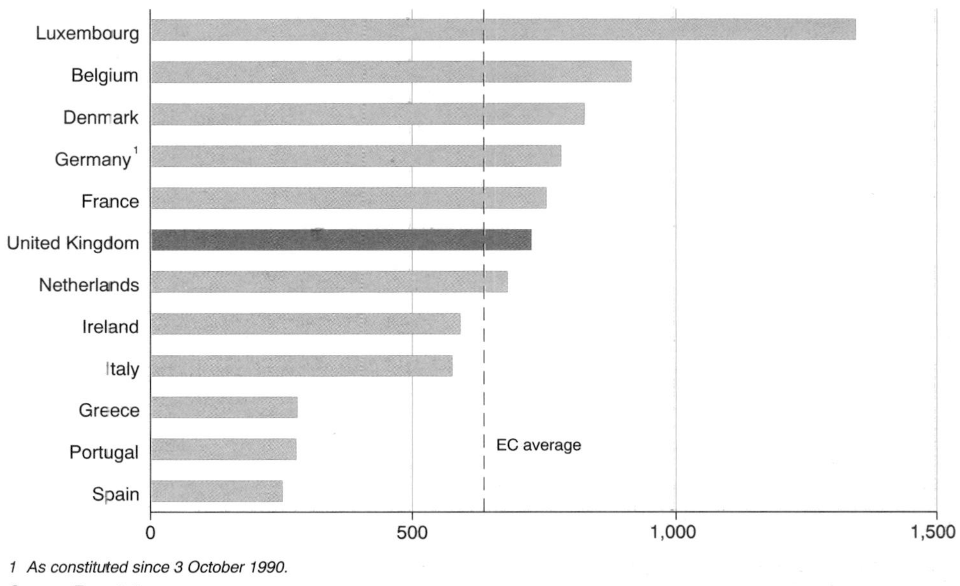

1 As constituted since 3 October 1990.

Source: Eurostat

11.25

Production of primary fuels

United Kingdom

Million tonnes of oil equivalent

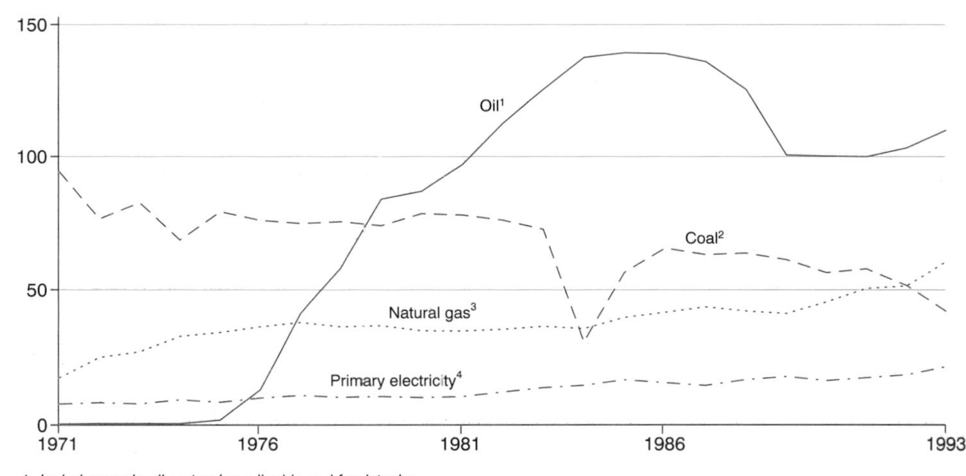

1 Includes crude oil, natural gas liquids and feedstocks.

2 From 1988 includes wood, waste, etc.

3 Includes colliery methane and from 1988 landfill gas, sewage gas, etc.

4 Nuclear, natural flow hydro-electricity and from 1988 other renewable primary electricity sources.

Source: Department of Trade and Industry

11.26

Oil and gas reserves, 1993

United Kingdom continental shelf

	Oil (million tonnes)	Gas (billion cubic metres)
Fields already discovered		
Proven reserves	2,265	1,550
Probable reserves	800	805
Possible reserves	690	480
Total initial reserves in present discoveries	2,265-3,755	1,550-2,835
of which already recovered	1,659	918
Estimates in potential future discoveries	560-3,360	300-1,295
Total recoverable reserves	2,825-7,115	1,850-4,130
Potential additional reserves	130-390	125-280

Source: Department of Trade and Industry

Over 70 per cent of proven reserves of oil and around 60 per cent of proven reserves of gas have already been recovered (Table 11.26). However, new discoveries mean that estimates of recoverable oil and gas reserves are continuing to increase. In 1993 development plans for six new oil or gas-condensate fields were agreed. These included two fields in Liverpool Bay - the first for the west coast of Britain. Five new offshore gas fields and one onshore field were authorised in 1993. In 1994, by end November ten new oil fields (all offshore and 12 new gas fields (three onshore and nine offshore) had been authorised.

References and further reading

The fo lowing list contains selected publications relevant to **Chapter 11: Environment**. Those published by HMSO are available from the addresses shown on the inside back cover of *Social Trends*.

Biodiversity: The UK Action Plan, HMSO
Development of the Oil and Gas Resources of the United Kingdom, DTI
Digest of Agricultural Census Statistics, HMSO
Digest of Environmental Protection and Water Statistics, HMSO
Environment Statistics, Eurostat
Environmental Digest for Wales, Welsh Office
OECD Environmental Data Compendium, Eurostat
Scottish Environmental Statistics, The Scottish Office
Survey of Public Attitudes, Department of the Environment
Sustainable Development, the UK Strategy, HMSO
The Energy Report, Volume 2: Oil and Gas Resources of the United Kingdom, HMSO
The UK Environment, HMSO
This Common Inheritance, HMSO

Contacts

Telephone contact points for further information relating to **Chapter 11: Environment.**

Department of the Environment	0171 276 8422
Department of the Environment, Northern Ireland	01232 540808
Department of Trade & Industry	0171 238 3590
Eurostat	00 352 4301 34567
Ministry of Agriculture, Fisheries and Food	01904 455329
National Radiological Protection Board	01235 831600
National Rivers Authority	01454 624353

Chapter 12 Transport

Passenger transport use

Shopping journeys accounted for a fifth of the distance travelled by those aged 60 and over in the period 1991 to 1993. (Table 12.2)

Three quarters of people used public transport to travel to work in Central London in 1991-1993 compared with 16 per cent of people in Great Britain as a whole. (Table 12.3)

Road

Two out of every three people aged 17 and over in Great Britain were licensed to drive a car in 1991-1993. (Page 205)

In 1993 around seven out of ten people in Great Britain stated that they were in favour of many more streets in cities and towns being reserved for pedestrians only. (Table 12.10)

Over a half of cars and over a third of motorcycles exceeded the speed limit at a sample of free-flow motorway sites in 1993. (Table 12.12)

Rail

The distance people travelled by train in 1993 was virtually the same as in 1971. (Chart 12.1)

To fulfil its obligations under the Citizens Charter, British Rail paid out nearly £5 million in season ticket discounts and compensation in 1993-94. (Page 210)

Water and air

The number of domestic air passengers using United Kingdom airports more than doubled between 1972 and 1993. (Table 12.20)

12.1

Road and rail passenger transport use

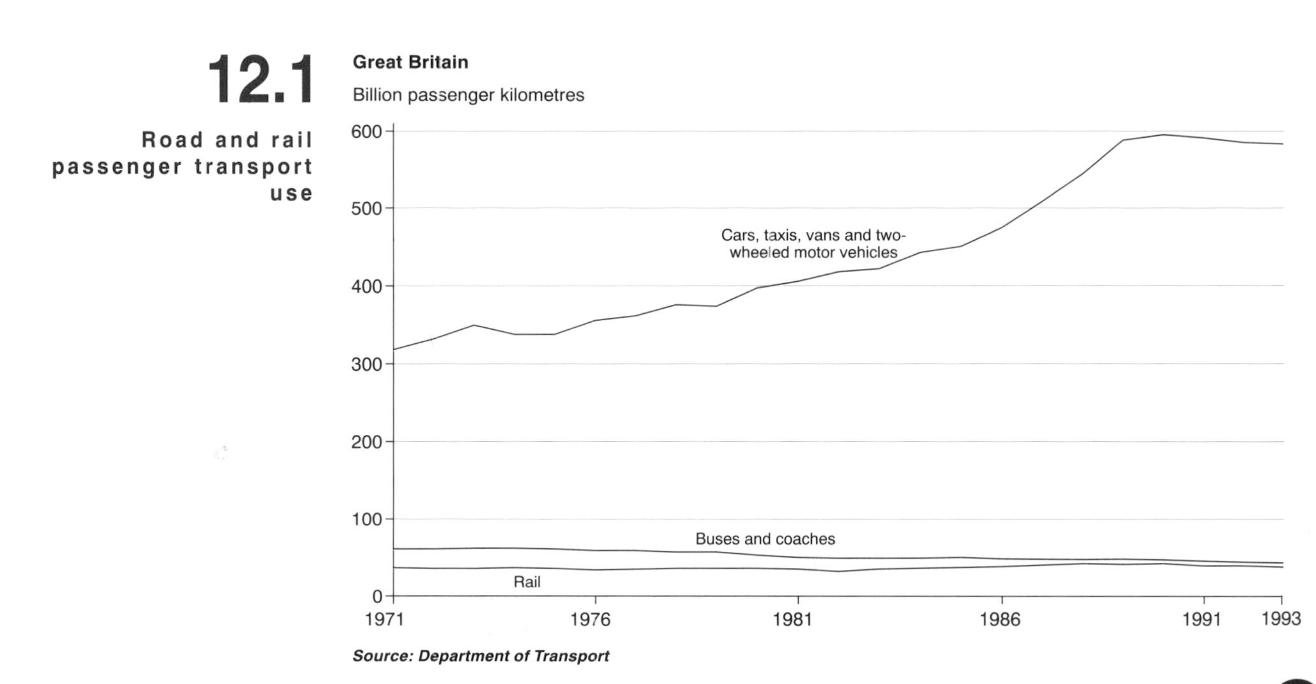

Source: Department of Transport

12.2

Distance travelled[1] per person per year: by age and purpose[2], 1991-1993

Great Britain — Miles

	Under 16	16-29 Males	16-29 Females	30-59 Males	30-59 Females	60 and over	All persons
Commuting	29	2,285	1,420	3,173	1,045	214	1,199
Business	6	1,165	337	2,253	367	176	676
Education	429	410	266	46	46	6	171
Escort education	49	22	40	85	144	13	64
Shopping	394	593	801	810	1,052	796	747
Other personal business[3]	656	813	654	1,160	929	549	797
Social/entertainment	1,472	2,578	2,295	2,115	1,901	1,238	1,803
Holiday/other	816	855	866	930	942	949	900
All purposes	3,851	3,722	6,679	10,573	6,427	3,942	6,357

1 Excludes all journeys under one mile.
2 See Appendix, Part 12: Journey purpose.
3 Includes other escort journeys.
Source: Department of Transport

Transport is a vital element in the economy of the country. This chapter focuses on the use of transport by people in their daily lives, in terms of travel to and from work and in other social and leisure activities.

Passenger transport use

In 1993 people in Great Britain travelled a total of over 660 billion kilometres by road and rail, a drop of 3 per cent since the peak in 1990 (Chart 12.1). Private motor vehicles and taxis were used for around 90 per cent of distance travelled. Travel by this form of transport has shown the greatest increase since 1971, rising by over 80 per cent. Conversely, travel by public transport has declined over the same period, with the distance travelled by bus and coach falling by nearly a third since 1971. However, the distance travelled by train was virtually the same in 1993 as it was in 1971.

The distance that we travel varies between men and women, and changes as we get older. Not surprisingly amongst the groups shown in Table 12.2 those who travel the most are men aged 30 to 59, who travelled over 10,500 miles a year in the period 1991 to 1993 (the equivalent of over 200 miles a week). Indeed this is the only group where the distance travelled commuting was greater than that for any other journey purpose. In all other groups the main purpose of travel was in connection with a social or entertainment event. Shopping trips accounted for around double the proportion of travel for women than men: around 12 per cent for women aged 16 to 29, and over 16 per cent for those aged 30 to

12.3

Usual mode of transport to work: by place of work, 1991-1993

Great Britain — Percentages

	Central London	Outer London	Urban	Rural	All areas
Rail[1]	*66*	*12*	*2*	*1*	*6*
Bus	*9*	*13*	*10*	*5*	*10*
Car	*18*	*60*	*69*	*68*	*66*
Motorcycle	*2*	*1*	*2*	*2*	*2*
Bicycle	*2*	*2*	*4*	*5*	*4*
Walk	*3*	*11*	*13*	*17*	*13*
Other	-	-	*1*	*2*	*1*
All modes of transport to work	*100*	*100*	*100*	*100*	*100*
Average distance travelled (miles)	13	8	8	8	8

1 Includes London Underground.
Source: Department of Transport

59. Both these percentages have increased since the period 1989 to 1991. Amongst the over 60s, 20 per cent of the distance they travel each year represents journeys to the shops.

Outside London nearly seven out of ten journeys to work in the period 1991 to 1993 were made by car (Table 12.3). The lowest use of public transport was by people working in rural areas, with just 6 per cent travelling in this way. Central London on the other hand shows a totally different picture: three out of four journeys were made by public transport, with rail and underground outnumbering bus journeys by more than seven to one. The average journey to work in Central London takes much longer than elsewhere in Britain, nearly twice as long as journeys into other conurbations and two and a half times as long as travel into other urban areas.

Table 12.4 looks at travel by public transport in terms of journey stages made. A journey may consist of one or more stages. A new stage is defined as commencing when there is a change in the form of transport or when there is a change of vehicle requiring a separate ticket. Nearly half of journeys by train in Great Britain in the period 1991 to 1993 were for commuting, with leisure being the next most common purpose. Conversely shopping was the main reason for people travelling by bus, while commuting was the second most common purpose. Journey stages by train were the longest, the average in 1991-1993 being about 26 miles, whereas journeys by taxi, at just under four miles are among the shortest. In 1991-1993 around half of all taxi journeys were made for leisure, with people from London recording the highest mileage per year by taxi, about 65 miles per person per year. Charts 12.5 and 12.14 and Table 12.6 illustrate some results from the London Area Transport Survey 1991, the fourth in a series of large scale surveys of travel and transport in London. The focus of the study was the area within the M25 orbital motorway. The main survey components were a large household survey in London and a major programme of roadside interviews of vehicles entering and travelling within the London area. In addition, data on rail travel were provided by British Rail (Network South East) and London Transport (London Underground Ltd) from passenger surveys. Further, smaller, surveys were undertaken to fill gaps in the main ones.

More than a million people travelled into Central London each weekday morning in 1991 for purposes such as work, shopping and sightseeing. The most common time for travelling into Central London was between 8am and 9am, when the transport system coped with almost half a million people (Chart 12.5). For travel out of Central London the peak was between 5pm and 6pm.

12.4

Public transport use: by purpose, 1991-1993

Great Britain			Percentages[1]
	Rail	Bus	Taxi
Commuting	*48*	*22*	*11*
Business	*7*	*1*	*5*
Education	*6*	*13*	*5*
Shopping	*9*	*32*	*13*
Other personal business	*7*	*11*	*15*
Leisure	*22*	*21*	*52*
All purposes	*100*	*100*	*100*

1 Of journey stages.

Source: Department of Transport

12.5

Weekday journeys to and from Central London: by hour[1] of day, 1991

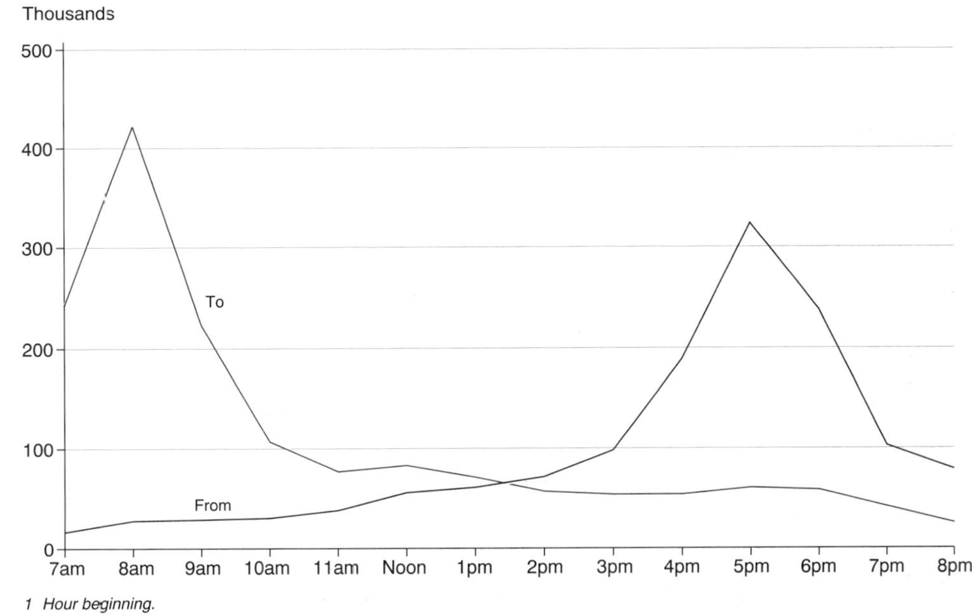

1 Hour beginning.

Source: Department of Transport

12.6

Transport used for trips in London: by ethnic group, 1991

Percentages

	White	Black Caribbean	Black African	Black Other	Indian	Pakistani	Bangladeshi	Chinese and other	All persons
Car driver	37	25	18	22	33	27	12	30	36
Walking	21	25	24	28	26	35	61	23	22
Car passenger	14	10	10	14	18	15	6	15	14
Public bus or coach	10	24	27	16	10	12	13	12	11
Underground	6	8	14	10	8	5	6	12	6
British Rail train	4	3	4	4	2	2	1	4	4
Van or lorry	4	3	1	1	3	3	1	1	3
Bicycle	2	1	1	2	1	0	1	1	2
Motorcycle	1	0	0	0	0	0	0	0	0
Taxi	2	1	1	2	0	1	0	1	1
All modes	100	100	100	100	100	100	100	100	100

Source: Department of Transport

12.7

Cars[1] and car ownership: by region, 1981 and 1992

United Kingdom Percentages

	Percentage of households with					
	One car only		Two or more cars		Cars per 1,000 population[2]	
	1981	1992	1981	1992	1981	1992
United Kingdom	45	45	15	24	277	367
North	41	42	10	17	227	306
Yorkshire & Humberside	43	43	12	19	245	334
East Midlands	47	47	15	26	273	358
East Anglia	51	47	18	27	321	419
South East	46	45	19	27	316	395
Greater London	42	44	15	19	287	347
Rest of South East	48	45	22	32	337	419
South West	51	48	18	30	329	417
West Midlands	46	46	16	24	290	397
North West	42	42	13	23	250	343
England	45	45	16	25	288	376
Wales	47	45	15	22	271	352
Scotland	40	42	11	15	217	311
Northern Ireland	46	47	14	19	238	298

1 Includes cars and vans normally available to the household.
2 See Appendix, Part 12: Car ownership.

Source: Department of Transport

Table 12.6 shows differences in the modes of transport used by London residents from different ethnic groups. People from the White ethnic group made a higher proportion of trips as car drivers than other groups. Bangladeshis, on the other hand, walked much more than other groups, and used cars much less. Black Africans were the group most likely to use public transport.

The survey also recorded the forms of transport used by people of differing employment status. People in employment were most likely to drive a car. Retired people were the group that relied most on buses, while school or college students were most likely to use the Underground. On weekdays, around a third of trips by Londoners were work-related, with shopping trips accounting for about another fifth. On Saturdays, in contrast, shopping trips accounted for over 40 per cent of trips compared with only 11 per cent for work.

Road

In 1992 only 57 per cent of households in Scotland had the regular use of a car (or van), the lowest figure in the United Kingdom; the comparable figure in the South West was 78 per cent (Table 12.7). Overall, the percentage with a car increased between 1981 and 1992, with the biggest increase in the East Midlands which showed a change of 11 percentage points. The percentage of households with only one car remained unchanged over this period, the increase taking place in those households with two or more cars. In 1992 almost a third of households in the South East outside Greater London had two or more cars - the biggest proportion in the United Kingdom.

The number of cars and vans per head of population of the United Kingdom increased by around 70 per cent between 1971 and 1992 (Table 12.8). Amongst the countries of the EC the smallest increase was recorded by Denmark, at just over a third, and the largest occurred in Greece, where the number of cars increased nearly fivefold over the same period. Of those countries in the table, the USA, regarded by some as the car capital of the world, had by far the largest number of cars per head of population - at 578 per 1,000 people in 1991.

The number of people licensed to drive a car in Great Britain increased by just over 10 million between 1975-76 and 1991-1993, to nearly 30 million (Table 12.9), or two in three of the population aged 17 and over. Over this period the number of women drivers doubled, whilst the number of male drivers increased by just under a third. In 1991-1993 around six in ten men aged 70 and over held a driving licence compared with two in ten women. In 1993 around 1.5 million driving tests were conducted in Great Britain with the pass rate for men some 8 percentage points higher than that for women. In the period 1993-94 the number of car driver licence holders in Northern Ireland stood at just over 1 million - an increase of over 10 per cent since 1990-91.

The growth in the number of cars causes problems in traffic management in many of our towns and cities, particularly at certain times of the year such as Christmas. One solution adopted by an increasing number of local authorities is the park and ride scheme, where the motorist is encouraged to park on the outskirts of town and is transported into the centre, generally by bus. The first park and ride scheme started around 20 years ago and in 1990 around half a dozen new schemes were implemented. When questioned by MORI in 1992, 25 per cent of

12.8

Car and van[1] ownership: international comparison

Per 1,000 population

	1971	1981	1992
USA[2]	448	538	578
Luxembourg[3,4]	251	363	515
Italy[2]	210	322	491
Germany[5]	247	339	464
France	261	367	419
Sweden	291	348	413
Belgium	223	325	401
United Kingdom[6]	224	281	380
Netherlands[4]	201	324	373
Spain	74	211	335
Japan[4]	154	211	313
Portugal[4]	54	135	310
Denmark	231	267	309
Irish Republic[3]	141	226	244
Greece	30	94	178

1 Includes taxis. See Appendix, Part 12: Cars and vans.
2 Data for 1992 relate to 1991.
3 Vehicles with a current licence only.
4 Data for 1971 relate to 1970.
5 As constituted since 3 October 1990.
6 Includes car-derived vans.

Source: Department of Transport

12.9

Full car driving licence holders: by gender and age, 1975-76 and 1991-1993

Great Britain — Percentages

	Males		Females		All adults	
	1975-76	1991-1993	1975-76	1991-1993	1975-76	1991-1993
Age						
17-20	*35*	*58*	*20*	*40*	*28*	*49*
21-29	*77*	*84*	*43*	*68*	*60*	*75*
30-39	*85*	*90*	*49*	*73*	*67*	*81*
40-49	*83*	*88*	*37*	*68*	*60*	*78*
50-59	*75*	*87*	*25*	*54*	*50*	*70*
60-69	*59*	*80*	*15*	*37*	*36*	*57*
70 and over	*33*	*59*	*4*	*17*	*15*	*34*
All aged 17 and over	*69*	*81*	*29*	*53*	*48*	*66*
Number of licence holders (millions)	13.3	17.3	6.1	12.2	19.4	29.5

Source: Department of Transport

12.10

Pedestrianisation[1], 1993

Great Britain	Percentages
	1993
Strongly in favour	*19*
In favour	*50*
Neither in favour nor against	*17*
Against	*7*
Strongly against	*3*
Can't choose	*2*
Not answered	*1*

1 Respondents were asked if many more streets in cities and towns should be reserved for pedestrians.

Source: Social & Community Planning Research

motorists in Great Britain indicated that they had used a park and ride scheme; this rose to 36 per cent in the South East and East Anglia.

Pedestrianisation of town and city centres has become increasingly common. Half of those questioned on the 1993 British Social Attitudes Survey were in favour of more pedestrianisation, with a further fifth being strongly in favour (Table 12.10).

The increase in the number of motor vehicles and the switch from public to private transport means that the volume of traffic on our roads has increased. Table 12.11 shows that the average daily flow on all roads in Great Britain increased by over 40 per cent between 1981 and 1993. Motorways experienced the greatest increase, 80 per cent, while the total length of motorways increased by around 19 per cent over the same period. Data for Northern Ireland have only been available since 1991. In the period 1991 to 1993 traffic on the motorways in the province increased by 7 per cent.

As part of the Citizen's Charter the Transport Secretary launched the *Cones hotline* in August 1992. It acts as a motorway information service for motorists advising them about the reasons for motorway works and lane closures and the period of time the work is expected to take. Advice is also given on diversionary routes to avoid the area of works. The hotline was relaunched at the end of 1993 on the telephone number 0345 504030, which allows callers throughout the United Kingdom to obtain information for the price of a local call.

Table 12.12 shows the average speeds recorded at free-flow sites on different classes of road in Great Britain in 1993. Not surprisingly the highest speeds were recorded on motorways, where the vehicles travelling the fastest were cars at an average of 70mph. Motorcycles on average travelled 7 miles an hour faster than cars on single carriageway 'A' roads, averaging 52mph; over a quarter exceeded the speed limit. More than half of car drivers exceeded

12.11

Average daily flow[1] of motor vehicles: by class of road

Great Britain				Thousands
	1981	1986	1991	1993
Motorways[2]	30.6	38.3	53.9	55.2
Built up roads				
Trunk	13.6	16.5	18.5	18.5
Principal	12.3	12.8	15.2	14.8
Non built-up roads				
Trunk	9.0	11.5	15.0	15.1
Principal	4.5	5.5	6.8	6.9
All minor roads	1.0	1.1	1.3	1.3
All roads	2.2	2.5	3.1	3.1

1 Flow at an average point on each class of road.
2 Includes principal road motorways.

Source: Department of Transport

the speed limit on motorways, but fewer than one in ten did so on single carriageway 'A' roads.

The M25 was designed partly to relieve congestion in London and partly to overcome the problem that, since Roman times, the road system in England and Wales had been centred on London, making journeys across London difficult. The final part (between the A405 and the A1), was completed in October 1986, by which time it had cost a total of nearly £1 billion to build. Traffic levels increased rapidly and today the M25 now carries more traffic than it was designed to transport. In July 1993 a programme of widening was announced by the Transport Secretary, which is continuing.

Chart 12.13 shows that in 1991 the heaviest weekday use of the M25 was made between 8am and 9am, when over 50 thousand cars were recorded joining the motorway. The number of cars peaked again between 5pm and 6pm when an almost identical number were recorded. There was a smaller peak in the middle of the day - 34 thousand between noon and 1 pm. The pattern of use by goods vehicles was different, with an almost constant level during the working day, a slight increase between midday and 1pm, and declining traffic after 5pm. Traffic volumes on the M25 vary considerably, depending where on the ring they are counted. The 1991 survey found that the quietest section was between junctions 30 and 31 in Essex, which recorded just a third of the traffic recorded on busiest section, between junctions 13 and 14 (near Heathrow Airport) and the junctions with the M3 and M4 motorways.

12.12

Traffic speeds: by class of road and type of vehicle, 1993

Great Britain

	Motorways		Dual carriageways		Single carriageway 'A' roads	
	Average speed (mph)	Percentage exceeding limit	Average speed (mph)	Percentage exceeding limit	Average speed (mph)	Percentage exceeding limit
Cars	70	*56*	67	*40*	45	7
Motorcycles	62	*37*	58	*30*	52	*28*
Buses and coaches	64	*21*	53	*29*	40	*14*

Source: Department of Transport

12.13

Weekday use of the M25: by hour[1] of day, 1991

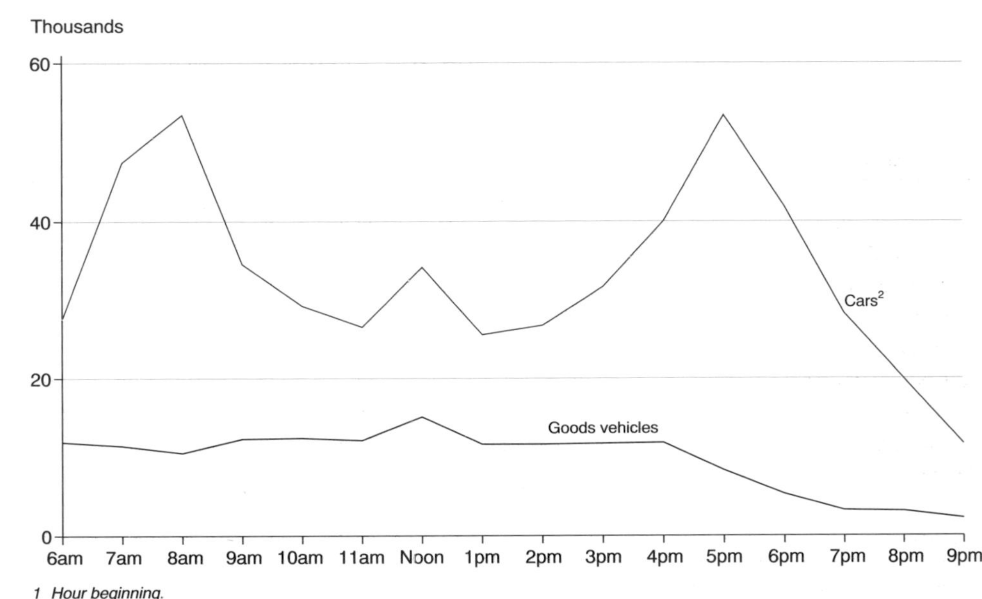

1 Hour beginning.
2 Includes taxis and vans.
Source: Department of Transport

12.14

Local bus travel

Great Britain

Indices (1981=100)

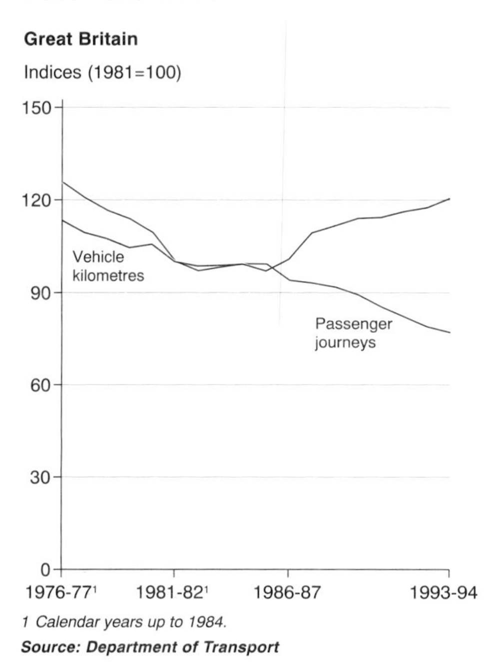

1 Calendar years up to 1984.

Source: Department of Transport

12.15

Goods moved[1] by road

Great Britain

Billion tonne kilometres

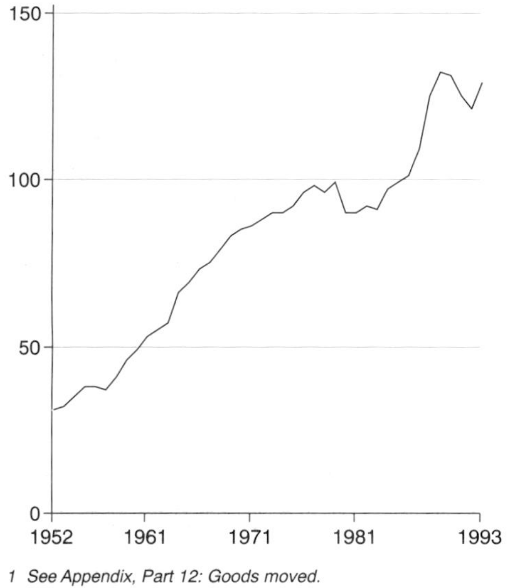

1 See Appendix, Part 12: Goods moved.

Source: Department of Transport

The number of passenger journeys made by local buses in Great Britain (journeys of under 15 miles) is illustrated in Chart 12.14. Whilst the number of local passenger journeys continues to fall, local bus mileage has increased since 1985-86. In 1950, 16.4 billion passenger journeys were made by local bus or tram, but by 1993-94 this had fallen to just 4.4 billion. Similarly, between 1950 and 1985-86 local bus mileage declined from 3.4 billion to 2.1 billion kilometres. However, between 1985-86 and 1993-94 it increased by nearly a quarter, to 2.6 billion kilometres, influenced by greater competition arising from the deregulation of buses outside London and by the trend towards higher frequency services using smaller buses.

Apart from private cars and public transport vehicles the road system is used to transport freight. The amount of freight carried by road doubled from 0.9 billion tonnes in 1952 to a peak of 1.8 billion tonnes in 1989. The amount then fell between 1989 and 1992, before rising to 1.6 billion tonnes in 1993. The amount carried on roads in 1993 represented more than 80 per cent of freight moved around the country. In 1993 nearly 130 billion tonne kilometres of goods were moved by road (Chart 12.15), an increase of 50 per cent since 1971 and over 300 per cent since 1952.

The other main methods of moving freight include water, pipeline and rail, though the railway system has become less attractive to hauliers and has declined in importance over the last 40 years. It is hoped that the opening of purpose built distribution centres, such as Trafford Park near Manchester, in connection with the Channel Tunnel, will transfer an increasing amount of freight back to rail.

In addition the movement of lorries through historic towns and villages has become an environmental issue. Chart 11.1 in the environment chapter shows the proportion of carbon dioxide emissions produced by road transport.

Rail

Over 1.5 billion passenger journeys were made by train in 1993-94. Under a half, or 713 million, of these journeys were made on British Rail trains, with a slightly greater number being made on London Underground (Chart 12.16). The number of journeys made on British Rail and London Underground trains declined with minor fluctuations from 1961, to a pronounced low in 1982. This low was at a time when there was a series of two-day strikes on British Rail and a fare rise of 91 per cent on London Underground, following the House of Lords decision on the 'Fares Fair' scheme. From 1982 passenger journeys were boosted on British Rail by improvements to services which were possible by electrification.

Other improvements included the introduction of new 'Sprinter' trains on many local and cross country services; Thameslink, which linked services north and south of the Thames; and the creation of sectors such as Regional Railways and Network SouthEast, which allowed services to be marketed more effectively.

From 1982 the number of passenger journeys increased on London Underground. They were boosted in 1983 by the introduction of the Travelcard (a ticket valid on London's buses and underground) and a 27 per cent reduction in fares. In 1985 the Capitalcard was introduced which added travel on British Rail to the Travelcard, with the result that in 1985-86 for the first time the number of journeys on the underground exceeded those on British Rail. In 1991 the London Area Transport Survey found that 11 per cent of Londoners owned a Travelcard.

In addition to the two main passenger railway systems there are an increasing number of other railways. These include lines transferred from British Rail and an expanding number of new light railway and tram systems, which often include converted old British Rail tracks. The first of these light railway systems was the Tyne and Wear Metro which opened in 1980. Systems opened subsequently, include the Docklands Light Railway in London in 1987, Manchester Metrolink in 1992 and the Sheffield Supertram in 1994.

Other schemes which have received Parliamentary authorisation include Midland Metro, Advanced Transport for Avon (Bristol) and the Leeds Supertram. Passenger figures for Manchester Metrolink were around 11 million for 1993-94 and surveys by Metrolink indicate that 40 per cent of passengers would have formerly used cars. The other rail system included in the figure is the Glasgow Underground, operated by Strathclyde PTE, which carried over 14 million passengers in 1993-94.

In order to improve standards and to make the railways more attractive to passengers, since 1986-87 overall targets have been agreed between the Government, British Rail and London Underground in respect of the quality of service that they should provide. Two aspects, namely reliability (percentage of the timetable operated) and punctuality (percentage of trains arriving on time), were incorporated in the targets, though in practice the targets differed in detail, both between the different sectors of British Rail and between British Rail and London Underground. Table 12.17 details the two performance indicators. In 1993-94 reliability on Network SouthEast and Intercity improved, but overall reliability targets were not met by any British Rail sector. Network SouthEast and Regional Railways met their punctuality targets, whereas Intercity failed again to meet its target.

12.16

Passenger journeys by rail

Great Britain

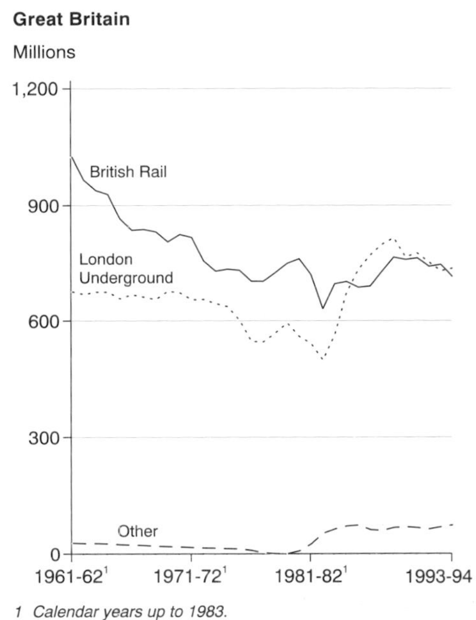

1 Calendar years up to 1983.

Source: Department of Transport

12.17

Railway performance indicators[1]

Great Britain Percentages

	Trains arriving within punctuality target				Trains cancelled[2]			
	1986-87	1991-92	1992-93	1993-94	1986-87	1991-92	1992-93	1993-94
British Rail								
InterCity	*85*	*84*	*85*	*89*	*0.8*	*2.3*	*1.7*	*1.1*
Network SouthEast	*91*	*91*	*91*	*92*	*1.6*	*1.2*	*1.5*	*1.1*
Regional								
Express and long rural	*91*	*92*	*91*	*92*	*0.5*	*1.3*	*1.1*	*2.7*
Urban and short rural		*89*	*91*	*91*		*1.6*	*1.6*	*1.9*
London Underground	*88*	*88*	*88*	*86*	*2.9*	*2.8*	*2.1*	*2.2*
Docklands Light Railway	..	..	..	..	..	*15.7*	*2.3*	*1.7*

1 See Appendix, Part 12: Railway performance indicators.
2 Percentage of scheduled services run for British Rail and scheduled kilometres operated for London Underground.

Source: Department of Transport

12.18

Passenger car arrivals at, and departures from, British ports: by overseas country

Thousands

	1981	1986	1991	1993
By ship				
France	1,402	1,944	3,329	4,058
Belgium	591	478	514	413
Netherlands	259	325	399	410
Germany	22	21	34	44
Irish Republic	378	345	611	621
Denmark	112	45	44	32
Scandinavia and Baltic	20	67	56	53
Spain and Portugal		27	47	70
All overseas routes	2,784	3,252	5,034	5,701
By hovercraft				
France	287	218	189	158
All overseas routes	3,071	3,470	5,223	5,859

Source: Department of Transport

12.19

International passenger movements: by mode

United Kingdom

Millions

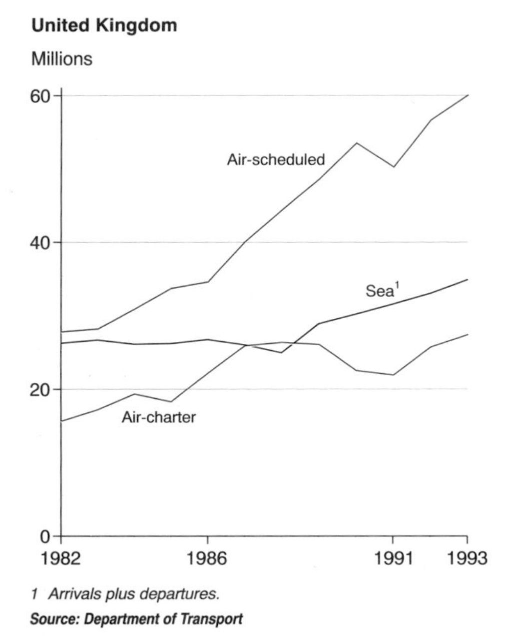

1 Arrivals plus departures.

Source: Department of Transport

In an attempt to make British Rail more accountable to its passengers the Government introduced the British Rail Passenger's Charter as part of its Citizen's Charter Initiative. This was published by British Rail in March 1992, and set individual targets for groups of lines, as well as announcing refunds to ticket holders if the service dropped below these targets. In 1993-94 British Rail paid out a total of nearly £5 million in season ticket discounts and compensation. The Passenger's Charter also included other things that the passenger should expect, such as clean stations and trains, a friendly and efficient service, clear and up to date information and a fair and satisfactory response when things go wrong.

Further major changes occurred to British Rail on 1st April 1994 when the Railways Bill on privatisation came into effect and new train operating companies were set up, which it is intended eventually to privatise. At the same time the Government set up a new organisation named Railtrack which assumed responsibility for the infrastructure.

Water and air

There are more passenger car arrivals at British ports from France, and departures to France, than for any other country. In 1993 over 4 million cars (and their passengers) crossed to and from France by ship and hovercraft (Table 12.18), more than double the number recorded in 1981. Routes to other destinations accounted for less than 30 per cent of cars carried, with the Irish Republic being the next largest. In addition to cars and goods vehicles, around 220 thousand buses and coaches were also carried in 1993. The number of vehicles using the ferries is set to change with the opening of the Channel Tunnel in 1994. The first vehicles to use the tunnel were goods vehicles. The full service for which commenced in October 1994. Subsequently Eurostar passenger carrying trains to the continent commenced on the 14 November 1994 with a limited "discovery" service. In 1992 MORI questioned drivers on whether they intended to use the Channel Tunnel, just 3 per cent said they were certain to, though a further 7 per cent said they were very likely to.

In 1993 there were nearly 35 million passenger movements by sea to, or from, Britain - an increase of nearly a third since 1982. International passenger movements by air have generally increased more dramatically, except for 1991 when the Gulf War caused a reduction in air transport activity. Since 1982 the number of passengers carried on charter flights has increased by three quarters, while the number carried on scheduled flights has more than doubled (Chart 12.19).

The number of passengers using air travel within the United Kingdom has also increased. Between 1972 and 1993 the number of domestic passengers handled at United Kingdom airports more than doubled (Table 12.20). Heathrow airport not only handled the most domestic passengers in the United Kingdom in 1993, but also handled the most international terminal passengers (40 million) of all airports worldwide for which statistics are available.

12.20

Domestic air passengers[1]: by selected airport

United Kingdom — Thousands

	1972	1981	1991	1993
Heathrow	2,947	3,867	6,714	6,753
Glasgow	1,411	1,426	2,289	2,399
Edinburgh	699	898	1,929	2,155
Manchester	707	983	1,906	2,042
Belfast	1,115	1,220	1,785	1,629
Aberdeen	188	1,037	1,317	1,460
Gatwick	588	1,011	1,012	1,398
Birmingham	303	378	720	778
Newcastle	320	378	544	629
Stansted	3	11	253	336
East Midlands	190	221	342	265
Luton	49	33	210	186
Bristol	58	44	141	185
Cardiff }	2,930	{ 62	56	69
Other }		{ 3,368	5,701	6,048
All airports	10,809	14,039	22,990	24,177

1 Passengers are recorded at both airport of departure and arrival. Includes British government/armed forces on official business and travel to/from oil rigs.

Source: Civil Aviation Authority

Transport casualties

Taking distance into account air travel is the safest form of transport, whilst travel by motorcycle carries the highest risk. Over the period 1982 to 1992 the average death rate for motor cyclists in Great Britain was over twice the rate for pedal cyclists and more than 20 times that for car users (Table 12.21). However, the intermittent occurrence of major disasters causes year to year fluctuations. In 1992, for example, eleven people were killed in

12.21

Passenger death rates[1]: by mode of transport

Great Britain — Rate per billion passenger kilometres

	1981	1986	1988	1989	1990	1991	1992	Average 1982-1992
Air[2]	0.2	0.5	0.0	0.4	0.0	0.0	0.1	0.2
Water[2]	0.4	0.5	0.5	23.2	0.5	0.0	0.5	9.3
Rail	1.0	0.8	1.7	0.8	0.9	1.4	0.7	1.0
Bus or coach	0.3	0.5	0.3	0.4	0.4	0.6	0.4	0.5
Car	6.1	5.1	4.2	4.4	4.2	3.7	3.6	4.6
Van	3.8	3.8	3.0	2.7	2.4	2.2	2.2	2.7
Motorcycles	115.8	100.3	103.4	107.0	110.1	94.4	97.0	104.0
Pedal cyclists	56.9	49.6	43.4	56.4	48.8	46.8	43.4	48.8
Foot	76.9	75.3	70.5	68.3	67.6	59.5	53.4	69.6

1 See Appendix, Part 12: Passenger death rates.
2 Data relate to United Kingdom.

Source: Department of Transport

12.22

Road deaths: EC[1] comparison, 1992

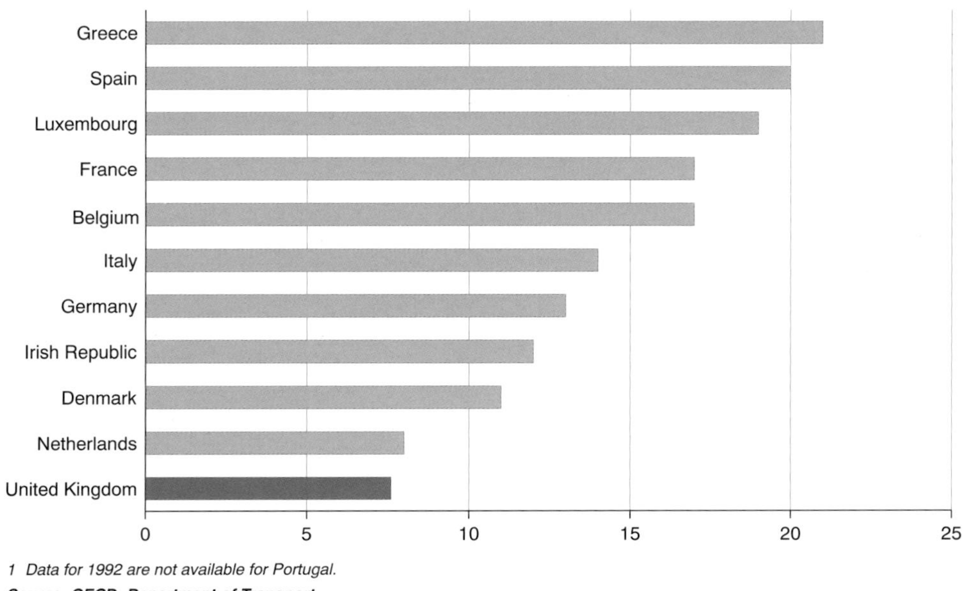

1 Data for 1992 are not available for Portugal.
Source: OECD; Department of Transport

a North Sea helicopter crash. However, a greater number of lives were lost in 1989 with the crash of a Boeing 737 aircraft at Kegworth (47 lives) and the sinking of the pleasure boat *Marchioness* (51 lives). Other major accidents include the 1988 multiple rail crash near Clapham Junction (35 lives) and the capsizing of the ferry *Herald of Free Enterprise* in 1987 (193 lives).

Chart 12.22 shows total road death rates per head of population for selected countries in 1992. In comparison with Europe and the other countries shown the United Kingdom has one of the lowest rates, at 8 per 100,000 population, with the Netherlands having a similar rate. Among those countries for which 1992 data are available the highest rate for road deaths was recorded in Greece where there were 21 deaths per 100,000 population.

12.23

Household expenditure on transport: by economic activity status of head of household, 1993

United Kingdom £ per week

	Employee	Self-employed	Unemployed and unoccupied	Retired	All households
Bus and coach fares	1.58	0.97	1.76	0.71	1.35
Rail fares	1.74	1.33	0.77	0.43	1.17
Air fares	1.39	..	..	..	1.16
Purchase of motor vehicles and spares	21.93	27.21	10.26	6.09	15.92
Maintenance of motor vehicles	6.62	6.58	3.33	3.07	5.02
Petrol and oil	12.98	14.96	6.73	3.93	9.55
Vehicle tax and insurance[1]	7.55	8.78	3.97	3.12	5.79
Other travel and transport	1.80	3.53	0.94	1.14	3.27
Total expenditure on transport	55.59	64.95	28.34	19.50	43.23
Expenditure on transport as a percentage of total expenditure	15.4	17.5	13.3	12.5	15.6

1 Less refunds.
Source: Central Statistical Office

Resources

In 1993 households on average spent nearly 16 per cent of their weekly budget, or around £43, on transport (Table 12.23). Most of this expenditure, about £36, was spent on the purchase, maintenance and running of motor vehicles. As would be expected those households where the head was working spent more on transport overall, with households with a self-employed head spending the most - £65 or 17.5 per cent of their weekly budget. However, households with an employee head spent the most on bus, coach and rail fares - just over £3 per week.

Between 1981 and 1994 bus and coach and rail fares increased by over 140 per cent, well above the rate of inflation, whilst motoring costs increased by under 100 per cent, less than the rate of inflation (Table 12.24). Changes in local bus fares have, however, shown wide regional variations. In English metropolitan areas, they were held well below inflation between 1982 and 1985-86, before substantial increases over the next two years brought them closer to those elsewhere. Fares in London fluctuated sharply during the 1980s, mainly because of the 'Fares Fair' policy and its subsequent reversal.

Around £2.5 billion was spent in 1993-94 in Great Britain on the construction and reconstruction of national roads (Table 12.25), an increase in real terms of around 35 per cent over the amount spent in 1971-72. National roads include motorways and the most important 'A' roads. The amount spent on other roads (including net expenditure on car parks) increased in real terms by only 2 per cent over the same period. Since 1987-88 some private capital has been used in the construction of roads. In 1993-94 this amounted to around £80 million and was mainly spent on the Second Severn River Crossing and the Skye Road Bridge projects.

Money is also spent to support public transport, particularly unprofitable but 'socially necessary' services as defined in *The Transport Act 1985* and to pay for local authority administrative costs and publicity associated with the tendering process for local bus services. In 1993-94 such payments amounted to £0.4 billion, a decrease in real terms of around a half from the amount spent in 1981-82.

12.24

Passenger transport prices[1]

United Kingdom — Indices

	1981	1986	1991	1994
Fares and other travel costs	100	135	186	219
Bus and coach fares	100	139	198	242
Rail fares	100	137	201	241
Other	100	107	136	155
Motoring costs	100	131	163	196
Purchase of vehicles	100	116	144	158
Maintenance of vehicles	100	138	195	239
Petrol and oil	100	145	156	191
Vehicle tax and insurance	100	146	220	320
Retail prices index (all items)	100	137	185	201

1 At January each year based on the retail prices index.

Source: Central Statistical Office

12.25

Public expenditure on transport: by type of expenditure

Great Britain — £ million at 1993-94 prices[1]

	1971-72	1981-82	1991-92	1993-94
National roads system				
Capital[2]	1,653	1,362	2,169	2,316
Current[3]	217	185	210	232
Total	1,870	1,548	2,379	2,548
Local transport				
Capital				
Roads and car parks	1,934	1,024	1,311	1,547
Public transport	283	486	140	152
Ports	..	30	12	14
Airports	..	68	153	75
Current				
Roads and car parks[4]	1,589	1,850	2,165	2,053
Revenue support to public transport	..	876	412	422
Concessionary fares	..	371	459	452
All local transport	3,805	4,705	4,651	4,715
Total[5]	6,089	6,253	7,030	7,263

1 Adjusted to real terms using the GDP deflator.
2 From 1981-82 includes new construction, reconstruction, new road surface, maintenance of bridges and other road structures and some VAT later reclaimed. Figures for Wales also include freight facilities grant.
3 From 1981-82 includes minor repairs, routine and winter maintenance.
4 Net of car park receipts.
5 In 1971-72 includes £58 million for administration not shown separately above.

Source: Department of Transport

References and further reading

The following list contains selected publications relevant to **Chapter 12: Transport**. Those published by HMSO are available from the addresses shown on the inside back cover of *Social Trends*.

Bus and Coach Statistics Great Britain, HMSO
Business Monitors MA6 & MQ6 (Overseas Travel and Tourism), HMSO
Car: Make and Model: Injury Accident and Casualty Rates Great Britain, HMSO
Cross Channel Passenger and Freight Traffic, HMSO
Family Spending 1993, HMSO
International Comparisons of Transport Statistics, Parts I, II and III, HMSO
International Passenger Transport, HMSO
International Road Haulage Survey, HMSO
London Area Transport Survey, London Research Centre; Department of Transport
London Journey Times Survey, Department of Transport
London Traffic Monitoring Report, HMSO
Merchant Fleet Statistics, HMSO
National Road Maintenance Condition Survey Report, HMSO
National Travel Survey, HMSO
New Motor Vehicle Registrations, Department of Transport
Overseas Travel and Tourism First Release, CSO
Ports Statistics, HMSO
Quarterly Road Casualties Great Britain, Department of Transport
Quarterly Transport Statistics, Department of Transport
Regional Trends, HMSO
Road Accidents Great Britain - The Casualty Report, HMSO
Road Accidents, Scotland, Scottish Office
Road Accidents Statistics English Regions, HMSO
Road Accidents: Wales, Welsh Office
Road Lengths in Great Britain, HMSO
Road Traffic Statistics Great Britain, HMSO
Road Travel Speeds in English Urban Areas, HMSO
Scottish Transport Statistics, Scottish Office
Statistics of Road Traffic Accidents in Europe, United Nations
Traffic in Great Britain, Department of Transport
Transport of Goods by Road in Great Britain HMSO
Transport Statistics for London, HMSO
Transport Statistics Great Britain, HMSO
UK Airports - Annual Statement of Movements, Passengers and Cargo, Civil Aviation Authority
Vehicle Licensing Statistics, HMSO
Vehicle Speeds in Great Britain, Department of Transport
Welsh Transport Statistics, Welsh Office

Contacts

Telephone contact points for further information relating to **Chapter 12: Transport.**

Department of Transport	0171 276 8513
Department of the Environment, Northern Ireland	01232 540808
Central Statistical Office	
Household expenditure	0171 217 4255/4245
Retail prices index	0171 217 4310

Chapter 13 Leisure

Home-based leisure activities

People in the United Kingdom watched on average 25 hours and 41 minutes of television a week in 1993, this was slightly less than in 1992. (Table 13.3)

Social, cultural and religious activities

Cinema admissions increased in 1993 for the ninth successive year, to 113 million. (Page 221)

People are most likely to visit a pub if they live in the North and least likely to if they live in London. (Page 221)

Sporting activities

After walking, the next most popular physical activity is swimming with a quarter of people participating in 1993-94. (Table 13.19)

Premier League attendances for the 1993/94 season were the highest since the 1980/81 season (for the old Football League Division One). (Page 225)

Holidays

In 1993, 23.5 million holidays abroad were taken by British residents, more than three times as many as in 1971. Holidays abroad now make up over 40 per cent of all holidays taken. (Chart 13.1)

In 1993, 16 per cent of Britons took two holidays, compared with just 12 per cent in 1971. (Page 226)

Six per cent of Britons said that they had had a holiday romance between 1989 and 1994; over half of them had not seen the person again. (Page 227)

13.1

Holidays taken by Great Britain residents: by destination

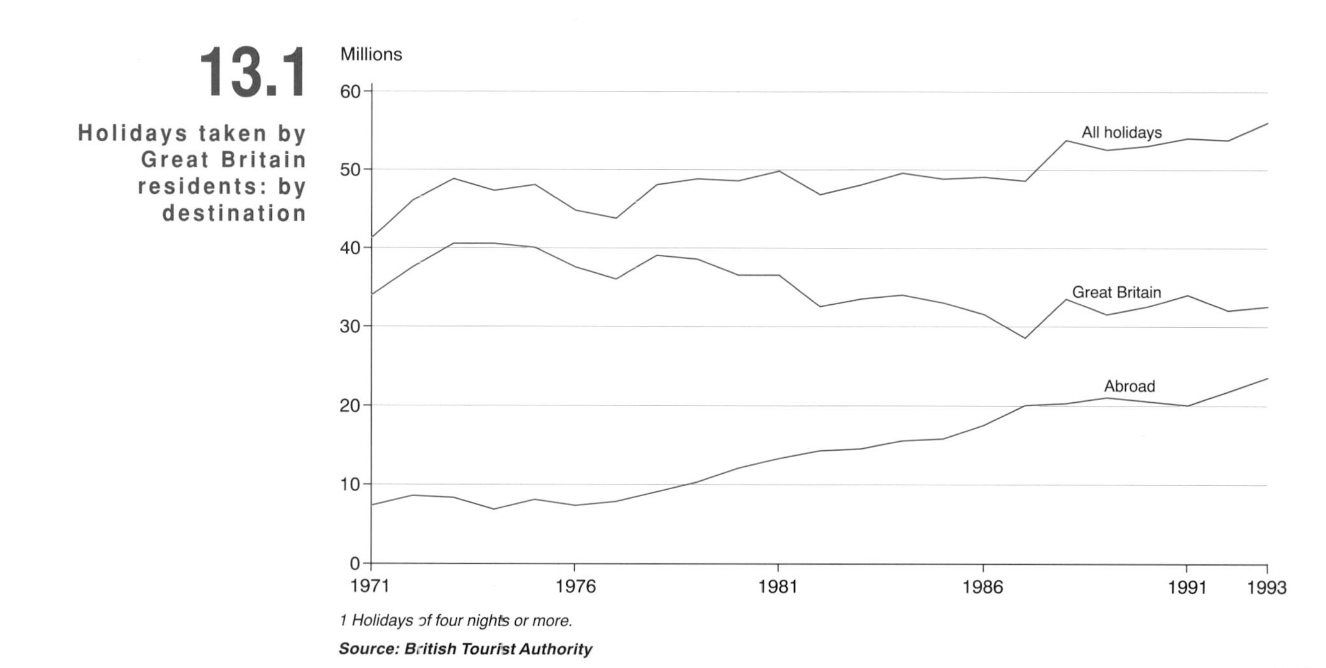

1 Holidays of four nights or more.

Source: British Tourist Authority

13.2

Participation[1] in selected home-based leisure activities: by social class[2], 1993-94[3]

Great Britain Hours per week

	AB	C1	C2	DE	All persons
Watching TV	13.5	15.4	17.5	20.2	17.1
Listening to the radio	9.2	8.7	11.6	10.9	10.3
Listening to CDs, tapes or records	4.3	4.0	3.4	4.4	4.0
Reading books	5.1	4.3	3.2	3.4	3.8
Reading newspapers	3.6	3.3	3.4	3.2	3.3
Caring for pets	2.6	3.1	3.2	3.5	3.1
Gardening	2.4	2.0	2.2	1.8	2.1
Cooking for pleasure	1.8	1.8	1.8	2.0	1.9
Watching videos of TV programmes	1.6	1.4	1.7	1.9	1.7
DIY or house repair	1.6	1.6	1.7	1.4	1.6
Sewing and knitting	0.9	1.3	1.4	1.5	1.3
Reading specialised magazines	1.2	1.1	1.0	0.8	1.0
Watching other videos	0.7	0.9	0.8	1.3	1.0
Reading other, magazines	0.6	0.8	0.7	0.8	0.7
Exercising at home	0.6	0.8	0.4	0.5	0.5
Using games computer or console	0.5	0.4	0.5	0.6	0.5
Car maintenance	0.4	0.4	0.9	0.3	0.5

1 Time spent in an average week in the 3 months prior to interview by persons aged 16 or over.
2 See Appendix, Part 13: Social class.
3 Data relate to the 12 month period ending September 1994.

Source: The Henley Centre

13.3

Television viewing: by age

United Kingdom Hours and minutes per week

	1986	1991	1993
Age groups			
4-15	21:06	18:20	19:12
16-34	21:38	22:20	22:42
35-64	27:56	27:38	26:24
65 and over	37:47	37:27	35:47
All persons	26:32	26:04	25:41
Reach[1] (percentages)			
Daily	*78*	*79*	*82*
Weekly	*94*	*94*	*95*

1 Percentage of the United Kingdom population aged 4 and over who viewed TV for at least three consecutive minutes.

Source: Broadcasters' Audience Research Board; British Broadcasting Corporation; AGB Limited; RSMB Limited

Leisure has become increasingly important as people retire earlier and live longer. This chapter looks at how we use our leisure time, both at home and away from home. It also looks at how people participate in religion, which was previously covered in the Participation chapter.

Home-based leisure activities

People in all social groups spent far longer watching the television in 1993-94, than they did on any other leisure activity (Table 13.2). Television viewing figures in this table are split up into watching TV, watching self-recorded videos of TV programmes and watching other videos. Table 10.4 later in the chapter gives a different coverage of television viewing. The second longest amount of time was spent listening to the radio; more information on radio listening is given in Table 13.4. For those in the non-manual groups the next most frequent activity was reading books, while those in the manual groups spent longer listening to CDs, tapes or records. Certain activities are more popular with women than men. These include watching TV, reading books, caring for pets, and sewing and knitting. The greatest difference between women and men was in sewing and knitting - 37 per cent of women, but only 2 per cent of men, had done some in an average week in the three months before they were interviewed.

The television viewing figures in Table 13.3 include satellite/cable viewing and timeshifted video recording (where a programme is recorded to watch later). Despite the increasing ownership of video recorders, satellite dishes and cable television, in 1993 people aged four or over in the United Kingdom watched over an hour less television than in the previous year - an average of around 25 and three quarter hours a week, which was the lowest figure since 1990. This fall in viewing reverses the recent trend where the time spent watching television had increased every year since 1990.

In 1993, people in the social classes A and B (managerial or professional) watched the least amount of television - under 20 hours a week, and more than a third less than those in social classes D and E. Perhaps surprisingly, the age group who watched the least amount of television were those aged 4 to 15; they watched around 19 and a quarter hours a week. The amount of viewing generally increases with age; those aged 65 and over watched nearly 36 hours a week which was around two hours less than in 1986. Despite the apparent fall in viewing in

1993, more than eight out of ten people watched television each day. This was the same proportion as in 1992 but around 4 percentage points more than in 1986.

In 1993, 73 per cent of households in Great Britain had a video recorder (see Table 6.7). In addition to taping television programmes, results from the Cinema Advertising Association's survey showed that, in an average month in 1993, 39 per cent of the population had watched a hired video, whereas 27 per cent watched videos they had bought. Using information from the British Video Association, the most popular rented video in 1993 was 'Sister Act', while the top bought video was 'Jungle Book' which became the first video ever to sell more than 4 million copies.

People aged 4 or over in the United Kingdom listened to the radio for an average of around 16 and a half hours per week in 1993 (Table 13.4), about two thirds of the time they spent watching television. The first local commercial station began broadcasting over 20 years ago in London in October 1973. Local commercial radio accounted for a third of listening time, while Radio 1 accounted for a fifth. People in social classes A and B listened to the least amount of radio, but spent longer listening to Radio 4 than those from the other social classes. BBC local and regional radio made up 10 per cent of listening time overall; people in social classes D and E spent a higher proportion of their listening time listening to these stations than those from other social classes. The most popular time for people to tune into the radio is around breakfast time; the number of listeners rapidly reaches a peak at around 8am and then generally declines throughout the rest of the day, with a much smaller peak around 4pm.

13.4

Radio listening[1]: by social class[2], 1993

United Kingdom — Hours and minutes per week

	AB	C1	C2	DE	All persons
Radio 1	2:13	3:09	4:10	3:05	3:16
Radio 2	1:58	2:03	2:05	1:57	2:01
Radio 3	0:29	0:14	0:07	0:06	0:12
Radio 4	3:44	1:55	1:01	0:55	1:40
Radio 5	0:21	0:21	0:17	0:18	0:19
BBC local/regiona	1:07	1:31	1:51	1:59	1:41
Atlantic 252	0:17	0:25	0:38	0:44	0:33
Classic FM	0:46	0:31	0:18	0:18	0:26
Virgin 1215	0:12	0:18	0:23	0:19	0:18
Local commercial	3:14	4:56	6:23	6:29	5:32
Other	0:20	0:28	0:30	0:34	0:29
Total listening time	14:41	15:51	17:43	16:44	16:27

1 Persons aged 4 or over.
2 See Appendix, Part 13: Social class.
Source: Radio Joint Audience Research; British Broadcasting Corporation

There have been dramatic improvements in the quality of sound reproduction in recent years, first with LP records, then cassette tapes and more recently with compact discs (CDs). Nearly 93 million CDs were sold in the United Kingdom in 1993, an increase of around a third on the number sold just a year earlier (Chart 13.5). LPs accounted for just 2 per cent of all cassettes, records and CDs sold in 1993, compared with more than half back in 1972.

A survey by Gallup in Great Britain in January 1993 asked people aged 16 or over about their purchase of LP, cassette and CD albums in the preceding six months. The results indicate that the most popular choice of music for both men and women is pop music: it accounted for the last album bought by 31 per cent of male and 40 per cent of female album buyers. Those people in social classes A and B were more likely to have bought a classical album, than people from any other social class.

13.5

Trade deliveries of LPs, cassettes, CDs and singles

United Kingdom

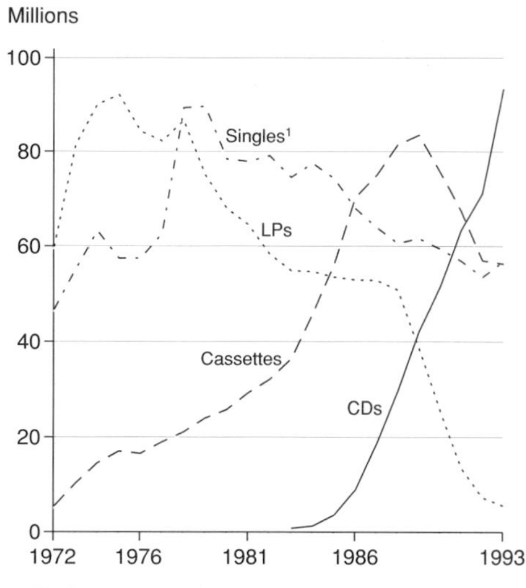

1 The figures include 7" and 12" singles as well as CD and cassette singles.
Source: British Phonographic Industry

13.6

Reading of national newspapers: by social class[1] and gender, 1993-94[2]

Great Britain Percentages

	Percentage reading each paper								
	AB	C1	C2	DE	Males	Females	All adults	Readership[3] (millions)	Readers per copy (numbers)
Daily newspapers									
The Sun	*7*	*18*	*29*	*30*	*25*	*19*	*22*	9.9	2.5
Daily Mirror	*7*	*13*	*22*	*20*	*18*	*14*	*16*	7.1	2.8
Daily Mail	*14*	*13*	*8*	*6*	*10*	*9*	*10*	4.5	2.5
Daily Express	*9*	*10*	*8*	*5*	*8*	*7*	*8*	3.5	2.5
The Daily Telegraph	*6*	*6*	*2*	*1*	*7*	*5*	*6*	2.6	2.6
Daily Star	*1*	*4*	*7*	*7*	*7*	*3*	*5*	2.2	2.9
Today	*3*	*4*	*5*	*3*	*4*	*3*	*4*	1.8	3.1
The Guardian	*8*	*3*	*1*	*1*	*3*	*3*	*3*	1.3	3.4
The Times	*8*	*3*	*1*	*1*	*4*	*2*	*3*	1.3	2.9
The Independent	*6*	*3*	*1*	*1*	*3*	*2*	*2*	1.1	3.5
Financial Times	*5*	*2*	-	-	*2*	*1*	*2*	7.4	4.2
Any national daily newspaper[4]	*61*	*58*	*64*	*59*	*65*	*56*	*60*	27.4	..
Sunday newspapers									
News of the World	*11*	*23*	*36*	*36*	*29*	*26*	*27*	12.4	2.6
Sunday Mirror	*9*	*16*	*24*	*21*	*19*	*17*	*18*	8.1	3.1
The Mail on Sunday	*18*	*17*	*11*	*6*	*13*	*13*	*13*	5.9	3.0
The People	*6*	*12*	*16*	*15*	*14*	*11*	*12*	5.6	2.8
Sunday Express	*13*	*13*	*9*	*5*	*11*	*10*	*10*	4.6	2.8
The Sunday Times	*21*	*8*	*3*	*2*	*9*	*7*	*8*	3.7	3.0
Sunday Telegraph	*11*	*4*	*2*	*1*	*5*	*4*	*4*	1.9	3.1
The Observer	*9*	*4*	*2*	*1*	*4*	*3*	*4*	1.6	3.2
Independent on Sunday	*7*	*3*	*1*	*1*	*3*	*2*	*3*	1.2	3.5
Sunday Sport	*1*	*2*	*3*	*3*	*3*	*1*	*2*	9.0	3.5
Any Sunday newspaper[5]	*69*	*68*	*72*	*65*	*70*	*66*	*68*	30.9	..

1 See Appendix, Part 13: Social class.
2 Data relates to the 12 month period ending June 1994.
3 Defined as the average issue readership and represents the number of people who claim to have read or looked at one or more copies of a given publication during a period equal to the interval at which the publication appears.
4 Includes the above newspapers plus the Daily Record, Sporting Life and Racing Post.
5 Includes the above newspapers plus the Sunday Post, Sunday Mail and Scotland on Sunday.

Source: National Readership Surveys Ltd

On average, over 27 million people read at least one daily newspaper in Great Britain in 1994; the most popular title was The Sun which was read by nearly 10 million people, almost one in four of the adult population (Table 13.6). Furthermore, it was the most popular daily paper for all but those in social classes A and B. Its long-time rival, the Daily Mirror, had just over 7 million readers. The increase of around 0.2 million in The Sun readership since 1992 is attributable, at least in part, to its recent low cover price policy. In all cases fewer women read each of the national dailies than men: The Sun with a readership of nearly 4.5 million was the most popular again.

Sunday newspapers are read by more people than daily newspapers, though readership has declined by over 350 thousand since 1992. The most popular

13.7

Reading of the most popular magazines: by age and gender, 1993-94[1]

Great Britain | Percentages

	Percentage reading each magazine								
	15-24	25-44	45-64	65 and over	Males	Females	All adults	Readership[2] (millions)	Readers per copy (numbers)
General magazines									
Weekly									
Radio Times	*13*	*10*	*14*	*11*	*12*	*11*	*11*	5.1	3.5
TV Times	*12*	*9*	*11*	*8*	*9*	*10*	*10*	4.4	4.3
What's on TV	*13*	*9*	*8*	*5*	*7*	*9*	*8*	3.6	2.3
TV Quick	*9*	*8*	*6*	*2*	*5*	*7*	*6*	2.7	..
Auto Trader	*9*	*6*	*5*	-	*7*	*2*	*5*	2.1	5.2
Other									
Reader's Digest	*8*	*12*	*18*	*15*	*14*	*13*	*14*	6.1	3.9
AA Magazine	*4*	*8*	*12*	*8*	*11*	*7*	*8*	3.8	..
Viz	*23*	*10*	*5*	-	*12*	*4*	*8*	3.6	5.1
Sky	*15*	*7*	*7*	*1*	*7*	*5*	*6*	2.8	21.1
National Geographic	*5*	*5*	*7*	*3*	*6*	*4*	*5*	2.2	..
Women's magazines[3]									
Take a Break	*16*	*13*	*12*	*6*	*5*	*16*	*11*	4.9	..
Bella	*10*	*10*	*11*	*7*	*4*	*14*	*9*	4.1	..
M & S Magazine	*5*	*9*	*12*	*4*	*4*	*11*	*8*	3.4	..
Woman's Own	*11*	*10*	*10*	*6*	*3*	*14*	*9*	3.9	4.9
Woman	*7*	*8*	*8*	*4*	*2*	*11*	*7*	3.0	3.9

1 Data relate to the 12 month period ending June 1994.
2 Defined as the average issue readership and represents the number of people who claim to have read or looked at one or more copies of a given publication during a period equal to the interval at which the publication appears.
3 The age analysis for women's magazines includes male readers.
Source: National Readership Surveys Ltd

Sunday newspaper remains the News of the World with over 12 million readers; four in ten people reading a Sunday newspaper read this paper. Many Sunday newspapers, and some daily papers, include colour magazines with the paper; the most popular of these magazines was the Sunday Magazine (included with the News of the World), which was read by nearly 12 million readers.

Four out of the top five weekly magazines in Great Britain in 1994 were connected with television, reflecting television viewing as the most popular home leisure activity. Of these magazines the most popular was the Radio Times with a readership of over 5 million (Table 13.7). Among all magazines however, the most popular title was Reader's Digest with a readership of over 6 million. Some magazines appeal to particular groups. Viz, for example, is read by nearly one in four 15 to 24 year olds, but is hardly read at all by the 65 or overs. In addition it is read by three times the proportion of men as women: 12 per cent of men compared with 4 per cent of women. The top women's magazine in 1994 was Take a Break; it was read by 16 per cent of women, but also by 5 per cent of men.

Reading books is one of the top five most popular home based leisure activities. Table 13.8 shows how the percentage of people reading books varies among the different ethnic groups. People from the European ethnic group were most likely to read books

13.8

Frequency of reading books: by ethnic origin, 1991

Great Britain | Percentages

	European	Afro-Caribbean	Asian
Regularly	*49*	*41*	*28*
Occasionally	*23*	*33*	*41*
Infrequently	*14*	*14*	*12*
Never	*14*	*10*	*18*
Don't know	*1*	*3*	*0*

Source: Policy Studies Institute

13.9

Library books issued: by type of book and area, 1992-93

Number per person per year

	Adult fiction	Adult non-fiction	Children's	All books
United Kingdom	5.39	2.37	9.67	9.68
London	4.12	2.74	10.35	8.90
Metropolitan districts	5.41	2.10	8.25	9.25
English counties	5.70	2.51	9.94	10.21
England	5.41	2.45	9.59	9.80
Wales	5.07	2.18	6.11	8.70
Scotland	6.12	1.98	13.36	10.00
Northern Ireland	3.11	1.46	11.54	6.71

Source: CIPFA

13.10

Participation[1] in selected leisure activities away from home: by social class, 1993-94[2]

Great Britain Percentages

	AB	C1	C2	DE	All persons
Visit a public house	*67*	*70*	*65*	*59*	*65*
Meal in a restaurant (not fast food)	*81*	*74*	*56*	*44*	*61*
Drive for pleasure	*50*	*53*	*45*	*39*	*46*
Meal in a fast food restaurant	*48*	*49*	*39*	*37*	*42*
Library	*57*	*46*	*32*	*31*	*39*
Cinema	*46*	*39*	*29*	*24*	*33*
Short break holiday	*41*	*34*	*28*	*19*	*29*
Disco or night club	*21*	*25*	*25*	*28*	*25*
Historic building	*41*	*29*	*19*	*12*	*23*
Spectator sports event	*25*	*24*	*23*	*18*	*22*
Theatre	*33*	*24*	*16*	*10*	*19*
Museum or art gallery	*34*	*23*	*14*	*10*	*19*
Fun fair	*12*	*13*	*15*	*16*	*14*
Exhibition	*24*	*17*	*10*	*8*	*14*
Theme park	*12*	*10*	*12*	*9*	*11*
Bingo	*3*	*6*	*11*	*17*	*10*
Visit a betting shop	*5*	*8*	*13*	*11*	*10*
Camping or caravanning	*9*	*9*	*10*	*7*	*9*
Pop or rock concert	*8*	*9*	*8*	*6*	*8*
Classical concert or the opera	*15*	*9*	*3*	*3*	*7*
Attend an evening class	*11*	*6*	*4*	*4*	*6*
Circus	*1*	*1*	*3*	*4*	*2*

1 Percentage aged 16 or over participating in each activity in the 3 months prior to interview.
2 See Appendix, Part 13: Social class.

Source: The Henley Centre

regularly; almost a half read books regularly. However, people from the Asian ethnic group were the least likely to read books regularly.

Nearly 0.6 billion library books were issued in the United Kingdom in 1992-93, and around 390 million visits were made to public libraries. People in the English Counties read just over ten library books each in 1992-93, compared with an average of just under seven in Northern Ireland (Table 13.9). Generally people read twice as many adult fiction books as non-fiction, with the highest figure being recorded in Scotland, at just over six adult fiction books per year. Scotland also had the highest figure in respect of children's books issued - over 13 per person per year.

In addition to books, libraries today provide an increasing range of material for reference, research and general interest. In 1992-93, for example, around 250 thousand copies of microfilm or microform were produced for readers in the United Kingdom, with around 55 million ordinary photocopies being produced. Some libraries now also hold audio and video tapes for lending; 29 thousand were issued in 1992-93. In addition, there were over 2 thousand computer terminals within libraries in the United Kingdom for use by, or on behalf of, the public.

Social, cultural and religious activities

The most popular leisure activity away from home among adults in Great Britain in 1993-94 was a visit to the pub (Table 13.10). However, among those in social classes AB and C1 a meal out at a restaurant was more popular; in the case of social class AB more than eight out of ten people had visited a restaurant in the last three months. People in social class AB participated more frequently in most of the activities shown in the table than those in the other social classes. The exceptions included visits to a disco or night club, betting shops, bingo and the circus. Certain activities were more popular with men than women: these included watching a sports event and going to a betting shop and the pub. Visiting the pub showed large variations by region; most people in the North visited the pub - around seven out of ten, while in London it was just five out of ten.

Cinema attendance varies according to social class, with those people in the non-manual social classes attending more often than those in other social classes. In 1993 three quarters of people in the non-manual social classes had ever visited the cinema, compared with just over half ten years ago (Table 13.11). Among these people, 8 per cent visited the cinema twice a month or more, which is double the proportion for those in the manual social classes.

Around seven out of ten people aged 7 or over visited the cinema in Great Britain in 1993 (Table 13.12), an increase of 7 percentage points on just one year earlier, and more than 3 million more than the projection made a year ago by the Cinema Advertising Association. The percentage of people visiting the cinema increased across all age ranges in 1993. The group which visited the cinema the most in 1993 were 7 to 14 year olds whilst the group which visited the least were those aged 45 or over. The total number of admissions, at 113 million, was the highest figure recorded since 1978 and the ninth successive year that the number of admissions has increased. The most popular films of 1993 were Jurassic Park, watched by over 14 million people, and The Bodyguard which was watched by over 7 million.

The number of people attending performances of opera in Great Britain has increased by a quarter since 1986-87 (Table 13.13), to 3 million in 1993-94. Despite this increase however, only 6.6 per cent of adults attended opera performances in 1993-94, making it less popular than ballet, which was attended by 6.8 per cent of adults and classical music performances which were attended by 12.2 per cent of adults. The most popular of the performing arts were plays, with an audience of 10.8 million; in 1993-94 they were watched by around a quarter of all adults.

13.11

Cinema attendance[1]: by social class[2] and frequency, 1983 and 1993

Great Britain — Percentages

	ABC1		C2DE	
	1983	1993	1983	1993
Twice a month or more	*3*	*8*	*2*	*4*
Once a month	*5*	*10*	*3*	*7*
Once every 2-3 months	*9*	*14*	*6*	*8*
2-3 times a year	*17*	*18*	*13*	*16*
Once a year	*17*	*11*	*16*	*11*
Less often		*16*		*16*
Ever go to the cinema	*51*	*77*	*40*	*62*

1 Persons aged 7 and over.
2 See Appendix, Part 13: Social class.
Source: Cinema Advertising Association; Cinema and Video Industry Audience Research

13.12

Cinema attendance[1]: by age

Great Britain — Percentages

	1984	1986	1991	1993
7-14	*73*	*87*	*80*	*93*
15-24	*59*	*82*	*88*	*90*
25-34	*49*	*65*	*70*	*82*
35-44	*45*	*60*	*70*	*73*
45 and over	*13*	*25*	*39*	*46*
All aged 7 and over	*38*	*53*	*61*	*69*

1 Percentage claiming to 'ever go' to the cinema.
Source: Cinema Advertising Association; Cinema and Video Industry Audience Research

13.13

Attendances at arts events

Great Britain — Indices

	1986-87	1991-92	1993-94
Opera	100	112	125
Ballet	100	111	120
Art galleries	100	102	105
Plays	100	102	105
Classical music	100	100	104
Jazz	100	82	87
Contemporary dance	100	77	86

Source: Arts Council of Great Britain

13.14

Church membership[1]

United Kingdom			Millions
	1970	1980	1992
Trinitarian Churches			
Anglican	2.55	2.18	1.81
Presbyterian	1.81	1.51	1.24
Methodist	0.69	0.54	0.46
Baptist	0.30	0.24	0.23
Other Free Churches	0.53	0.52	0.66
Roman Catholic	2.71	2.34	2.04
Orthodox	0.19	0.20	0.28
All Trinitarian churches	8.78	7.53	6.72
Non-Trinitarian Churches			
Mormons	0.09	0.11	0.15
Jehovah's Witnesses	0.06	0.08	0.13
Spiritualists	0.05	0.05	0.04
Other Non-Trinitarian	0.08	0.11	0.14
All Non-Trinitarian churches	0.28	0.35	0.46
Other Religions			
Muslims	0.25	0.31	0.52
Sikhs	0.08	0.15	0.27
Hindus	0.05	0.12	0.14
Jews	0.11	0.11	0.11
Others	0.05	0.05	0.08
All Other religions	0.54	0.74	1.12

1 Adult active members.

Source: Christian Research Association

Up to 31 March 1994 the main funding and development agency for the arts in Great Britain was the Arts Council of Great Britain. The Arts Council was established to develop and improve the knowledge, understanding and practice of the arts, to increase their accessibility to the public and to advise and co-operate with government departments, local authorities and other organisations. In 1993-94 the Arts Council received more than £200 million in government grants, over half of which went to drama and music projects. From April 1994 the Arts Councils of Scotland and Wales were made autonomous bodies alongside a new Arts Council for England and all inherited the responsibilities of the former organisation.

Many people devote a part of their leisure time to some form of religous activity. In 1992 6.7 million adults in the United Kingdom were members of the Trinitarian Churches (Table 13.14), a drop of nearly a quarter since 1970. The only Trinitarian church with over 2 million adult members in 1992 was the Roman Catholic church. However, this was 13 per cent lower than in 1980. Orthodox church membership continued to rise and in 1992 stood at 280 thousand. Membership of the non-Trinitarian churches increased by two thirds and membership of other religions more than doubled over the same period. The number of those belonging to Muslim religous bodies in 1992 was as large as the combined membership of Sikh, Hindu and Jewish religions.

Only just over one out of ten of those questioned on the 1993 British Social Attitudes Survey said that they attended their church, or meetings associated with their religion once a week or more (Table 13.15). Nearly a quarter said that they never, or practically never, attended.

13.15

Religious attendance[1]

Great Britain	Percentages
	1993
Once a week or more	*11.7*
Less often but at least once in two weeks	*2.0*
Less often but at least once a month	*5.6*
Less often but at least twice a year	*10.3*
Less often but at least once a year	*5.2*
Less often	*3.8*
Never or practically never	*22.7*
Varies too much to say	*0.6*
Not answered	*0.1*

1 Respondents were asked how often, apart from special occasions such as weddings, funerals and baptisms, did they attend services or meetings connected with their religion.

Source: Social & Community Planning Research

In 1993, 6.8 million people visited Blackpool Pleasure Beach (Table 13.16), making it the most popular free tourist attraction in the United Kingdom. The second most popular attraction, and the most popular museum, was the British Museum - 5.8 million visitors passed through its doors in 1993, more than double the number of visitors back in 1971.

The most popular historic property in Scotland in 1993 was Edinburgh Castle which was visited by around 1 million visitors. Another popular attraction in Edinburgh each year is the Military Tattoo; in 1993 it was watched by 210 thousand people. The most popular attraction in the United Kingdom which charges for admission was Alton Towers theme park; the number of visitors in 1993 was 4 per cent more than in 1992 and around two thirds higher than in 1981. In Northern Ireland the top attraction in 1993 was the Giant's Causeway, with 370 thousand visitors.

In 1993 adults in Great Britain made just over 2 billion leisure day visits in the months from April to September. Around two thirds of all trips, were to towns and cities (Chart 13.17). The second most popular destination was the countryside where the most popular activities were walks or rambles. On average most leisure day visits involved travelling no more than 15 miles away from home; the car was the main form of transport used, though trips by foot accounted for around three in ten of the total.

13.16

Attendances at selected tourist attractions

United Kingdom — Millions

	1981	1991	1993		1981	1991	1993
Museums and galleries				**Historic houses and monuments**			
British Museum	2.6	5.1	5.8	Tower of London	2.1	1.9	2.3
National Gallery	2.7	4.3	3.9	Edinburgh Castle	0.8	1.0	1.0
Tate Gallery	0.9	1.8	1.8	Roman Baths, Bath	0.6	0.8	0.9
Natural History Museum	3.7	1.6	1.7	Warwick Castle	0.4	0.7	0.8
Science Museum	3.8	1.3	1.3	Windsor Castle, State Apartments	0.7	0.6	0.8
Theme parks				**Wildlife parks and zoos**			
Blackpool Pleasure Beach	7.5	6.5	6.8	London Zoo	1.1	1.1	0.9
Alton Towers	1.6	2.0	2.6	Chester Zoo	..	0.9	0.8
Pleasure Beach, Great Yarmouth	..	2.5	2.4	Sea Life Centre, Blackpool	.	0.7	0.6
Pleasureland, Southport	..	1.8	2.0	Edinburgh Zoo	..	0.5	0.5
Chessington World of Adventures	0.5	1.4	1.5	Whipsnade Wild Animal Park	..	0.6	0.4

Source: British Tourist Authority; National Tourist Boards

13.17

Leisure day visits, 1993[1]

Great Britain

Percentages

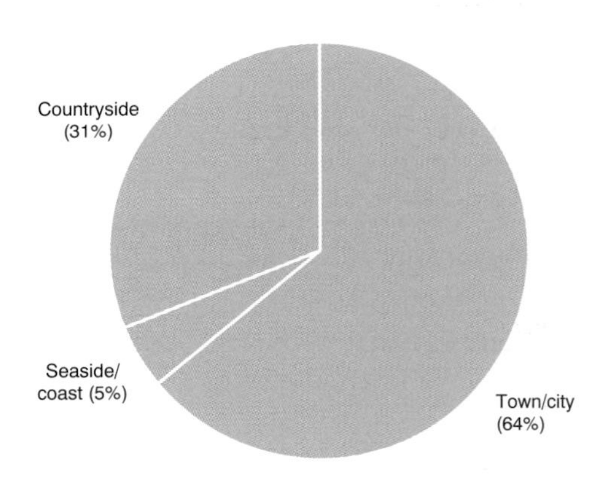

1 April to September 1993.

Source: Countryside Recreation Network News

13.18

Gambling: money staked in lotteries, casinos and bingo clubs

Great Britain		£ million at 1993-94 prices[1]	
	Lotteries[2]	Casinos[3]	Bingo clubs[4]
1976-77	..	2,317	1,118
1981-82	110	1,851	862
1986-87	31	2,319	795
1987-88	30	2,372	862
1988-89	27	2,236	768
1989-90	28	2,267	745
1990-91	30	2,120	726
1991-92	59	2,008	750
1992-93	48	2,097	801
1993-94	43	2,230	..

1 Adjusted to real terms using the retail prices index.
2 Excludes lotteries promoted under local authority registration.
3 Money exchanged for chips.
4 Licensed clubs only. Prior to 1988-89 includes dutiable bingo played at non-licensed clubs.
Source: Gaming Board for Great Britain

In 1993-94 people in Great Britain staked around £2.2 billion in casinos (Table 13.18), over 50 times the amount in lotteries. The amount of money staked in casinos was virtually the same in real terms as in 1976-77. The amount of money staked in bingo clubs in 1992-93 was less in real terms than in 1976-77, but has remained fairly constant since 1986-87. Lotteries however have not been so popular - in 1988-89 the amount staked was just under a quarter of the amount in 1981-82, but by 1993-94 this had partly recovered to around a third of the amount. This was set to change in 1994-95 with the introduction of the National Lottery.

It commenced in late 1994, with the first draw taking place on the 19 November, and subsequent draws taking place weekly. Almost 49 million tickets were purchased for the first draw. The proportion of money going to charitable causes is 28 per cent, distributed amongst the following: The Millennium Commission (which is to fund projects for the 21st century), National Heritage Memorial Fund, The Sports Council, The Arts Council and charities.

Gaming machines provide another form of gambling; in 1992-93 there were around 240 thousand licensed machines and around a further 30 thousand which did not require a licence. Around £9 billion was put in these machines in 1992-93. These machines are located in premises such as clubs and arcades with the majority being located in public houses.

Sporting activities

Walking was by far the most popular physical activity for people of all ages in 1993-94, with around half of adults participating in the three months before they were interviewed (Table 13.19). A quarter of adults had been swimming, the second most popular activity in the previous three months. However, participation drops sharply with age from the mid 40s on. Team sports are most popular among those adults aged 16 to 24 - three in ten adults of this age had taken part. Just under a third of adults had visited a sports centre in the last three months, although the proportion declined steeply by age; from 49 per cent of 16 to 24 year olds to only 11 per cent of people aged 60 or over.

Participation in physical and sporting activities also varies by social class. With the exception of fishing, people from the non-manual social classes were more likely to have participated in those activities shown in the table than those from the manual social classes. For example, people in social class AB were twice as likely to have gone swimming or played in team sports than those in social class E. Fishing is one of the few sporting activities that seems to be unaffected by social class, but men are much more likely to angle than

13.19

Participation[1] in and spectating at selected physical and sporting activities: by age, 1993-94[2]

Great Britain						Percentages
	16-24	25-34	35-44	45-59	60 and over	All persons
Participating						
Walking	*49*	*55*	*56*	*55*	*44*	*51*
Swimming	*31*	*39*	*34*	*19*	*8*	*25*
Team sports	*29*	*18*	*17*	*11*	*6*	*15*
Fishing	*8*	*7*	*7*	*4*	*1*	*5*
Other sports	*28*	*23*	*22*	*16*	*6*	*18*
Spectating						
Horse racing	*4*	*2*	*3*	*2*	*2*	*3*
Dog racing	*4*	*2*	*2*	*3*	*1*	*2*
Other sports	*32*	*25*	*27*	*21*	*10*	*22*
Visit to a sports centre	*49*	*42*	*37*	*22*	*11*	*30*

1 Percentage aged 16 or over participating in the 3 months prior to interview.
2 Data relate to the 12 month period ending September 1994.
Source: The Henley Centre

women. Spectating at racing was also more popular with men than women; the 'sport of kings' (horse racing), was most popular with those in social class AB, whereas dog racing was more popular with skilled manual workers.

The average attendance at Football Association Premier League and Football League Division One matches in the 1993/94 season both increased by around 10 per cent over the figure for the previous season to 23 thousand and just under 12 thousand respectively (Table 13.20). This increase in Premier League spectators halted the decline since 1990/91 and is the highest figure recorded since the 1980/81 season (for the old Football League Division One). However, it is still much lower than the attendances recorded back in the 1970s, since when capacities at most major grounds have been reduced as the traditional terraces have given way to seating accommodation. The capacity at Wembley, the home of the FA Cup final, for example, is now limited to 80 thousand spectators compared with 100 thousand in 1990. The average number of spectators watching Rugby Football League Premier Division matches declined for the second year running to around 6 thousand per match. However, the Rugby Silk Cup Challenge Final held at Wembley in April 1994 attracted 78 thousand people, almost a capacity crowd.

In 1994 there were around 38 thousand sports pitches in England to which the public had access to play sports such as football, rugby and hockey, etc. The region with the best provision of sports pitches was the East Midlands where there were over 12 pitches per 10 thousand people (Chart 13.21). The least provision was in Greater London with just over 5 per 10 thousand people.

13.20

Average attendances at football and rugby league matches

Great Britain Numbers

	Football Associaton[1] Premier League[2]	Football League[1] Division One[3]	Scottish Football League Premier Division[4]	Rugby Football League Premier Division
1971/72	31,352	14,652	5,228	.
1976/77	29,540	13,529	11,844	.
1981/82	22,556	10,282	9,467	.
1986/87	19,800	9,000	11,720	4,844
1989/90	20,800	12,500	15,576	6,450
1990/91	22,681	11,457	14,424	6,420
1991/92	21,622	10,525	11,970	6,511
1992/93	21,125	10,641	11,520	6,170
1993/94	23,040	11,752	12,351	5,683

1 League matches only until 1985/86. From 1986/87, Football League attendances include promotion and relegation play-off matches.
2 Prior to 1992/93, Football League Division One.
3 Prior to 1992/93, Football League Division Two.
4 Prior to 1976/77, Scottish League Division One.

Source: Football Association Premier League; Football League; Scottish Football League; Rugby Football League

13.21

Provision of sports pitches[1]: by region, 1994

Rate per 10,000 population

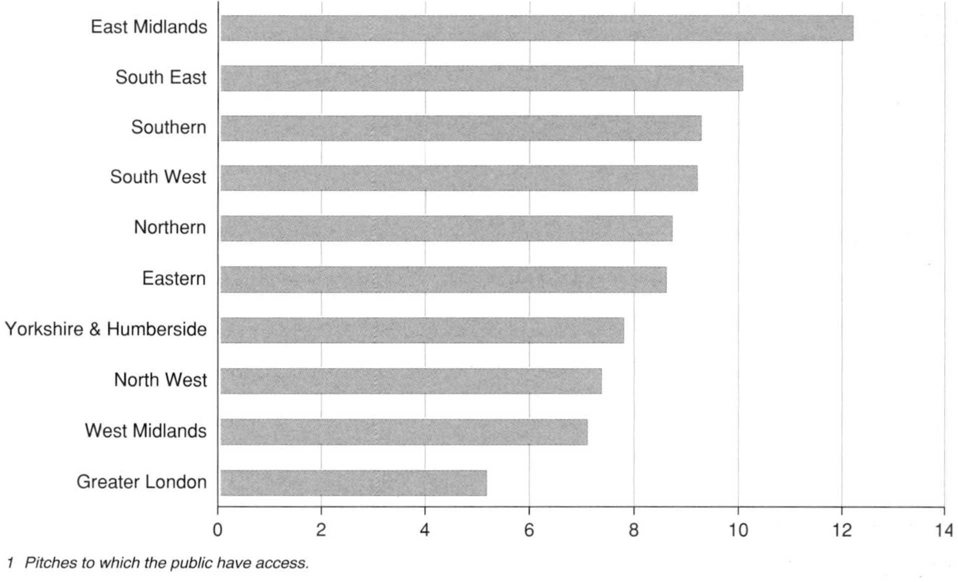

1 Pitches to which the public have access.

Source: The Sports Council

13.22

Holidays[1] taken at home by Great Britain residents: by destination, 1993

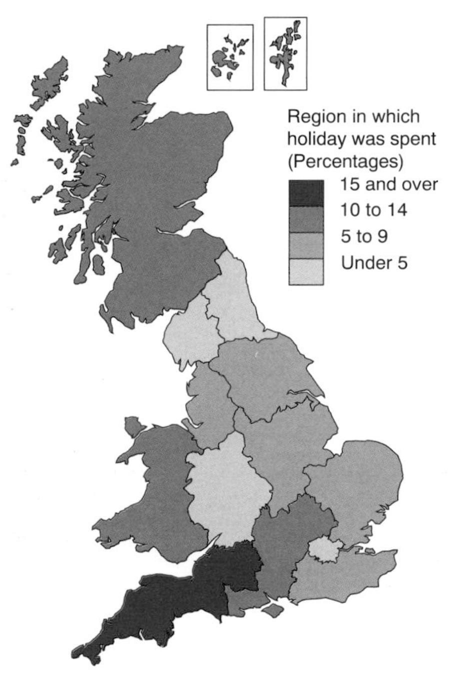

1 Holidays of four nights or more.

Source: British Tourist Authority

Holidays

The time we have to spend on leisure activities relies partly on the amount of holiday that we receive. In 1993 the average amount of paid holiday was 23 days for men and 25 days for women.

In 1993 three fifths of adults in Great Britain took one or more holidays a year, virtually the same proportion as in 1971. However in 1993, 16 per cent took two, while 9 per cent took three or more, compared with 12 and 3 per cent respectively in 1971. August is still the most popular month for Britons to take their main holiday in Great Britain; in 1993, 28 per cent of Britons holidaymaking in Great Britain started their holidays in this month.

Chart 13.1, at the beginning of this chapter, showed that Britons took a total of 56 million holidays in 1993, over 35 per cent more than the number taken in 1971. The number taken abroad tripled to 23.5 million, whereas the number of holidays taken in Great Britain, despite increasing in the 1970s and declining in the 1980s, was virtually the same in 1993 as in 1971. However, the number of visits to the United Kingdom by people from abroad has increased. In 1992 (the latest year for which figures are available), 18.5 million visits were made to the United Kingdom by people from abroad, an increase of around 60 per cent on the figure ten years earlier. Most visitors from abroad head for London, with just over half of all trips to the United Kingdom being based there.

In 1993 a quarter of all holidays of four nights or more taken in Great Britain by British residents were spent in the West Country (Chart 13.22), with Wales and Scotland being the next most popular destinations. Together these three destinations accounted for around a half of all holidays of this type. In 1993 around three quarters of people travelled to their destination by car, with just 13 and 7 per cent travelling by bus/coach and train respectively. The most popular type of holiday was the traditional beach holiday; around 40 per cent of people visited the seaside and a further quarter chose the countryside. In 1993, among those people taking their main holiday in Great Britain, around a quarter stayed in an hotel or guest house, with a fifth choosing either a caravan or a friends' or relatives' home.

13.23

Destination of holidays[1] abroad

Percentages

	1971	1981	1991	1992
France	*15.9*	*27.2*	*25.8*	*24.7*
Spain[2]	*34.3*	*21.7*	*21.3*	*22.0*
Greece	*4.5*	*6.7*	*7.6*	*7.8*
United States	*1.0*	*5.5*	*6.8*	*7.2*
Portugal	*2.6*	*2.8*	*4.8*	*4.8*
Cyprus	*1.0*	*0.7*	*2.4*	*3.8*
Italy	*9.2*	*5.8*	*3.5*	*3.4*
Netherlands	*3.6*	*2.4*	*3.5*	*3.1*
Irish Republic	..	*3.6*	*3.0*	*2.7*
Germany[3]	*3.4*	*2.6*	*2.7*	*2.4*
Austria	*5.5*	*2.5*	*2.4*	*2.3*
Belgium or Luxembourg	*3.6*	*2.2*	*2.2*	*1.8*
Other countries	*15.4*	*16.3*	*14.1*	*14.0*
Total (= 100%)(millions)	4.20	13.13	20.79	23.24

1 A visit of one or more nights made for holiday purposes. Business trips and visits to friends or relatives are excluded.
2 Prior to 1981 excludes the Canaries.
3 As constituted since 3 October 1990.

Source: Central Statistical Office

Among those United Kingdom residents who took a holiday abroad in 1992 France was the most popular destination (Table 13.23), with around a quarter of all people travelling abroad choosing this destination. Since 1971 the number of people holidaying in France has increased by around 10 percentage points. Spain is the second most popular destination with just over a fifth of people travelling there in 1992. Overall more than eight out of ten people holidaying abroad still chose a destination in Europe in 1992, with the United States being the most popular non-European destination.

Results from the British National Travel Survey in 1993 indicate that among those Britons who chose a holiday abroad in 1993, around a half chose to stay in an hotel or a pension (boarding house) with around a quarter choosing a rented villa or flat. Since 1983 the proportion who stay in an hotel or a pension has declined by 12 percentage points, while the proportion staying in a villa or flat increased by a similar proportion.

When asked by MORI in 1994 about the activities which they enjoyed doing most during all holidays taken over the past year around three quarters of Britons stated that they had enjoyed sightseeing (Table 13.24). Around a half said that they had enjoyed sunbathing, while a third had enjoyed reading. However, only an eighth stated that they had enjoyed the more energetic and dangerous activities such as skiing, parascending and water skiing, etc. The survey also recorded that only 6 per cent of Britons said that they had a holiday romance in the last five years, and of these people just over half had not seen the person since their holiday.

Resources

In 1993 households in the United Kingdom spent £43, or nearly 16 per cent of their average weekly budget, on leisure items (Table 13.25). Households consisting of one adult mainly dependent on the state retirement pension spent only around £1.70 a week on average on holidays, compared with £11.36 on average for households containing 2 adults with children. Among one retired adult households the second most popular items of leisure expenditure were purchases of books, newspapers and magazines. However, in the case of households consisting of two adults with children, more money was spent on going out, with around £16 a week spent on meals away from home and alcoholic drinks.

13.24

Holiday activities[1], 1994

Great Britain Percentages

	1994
Sight-seeing	*73*
Sunbathing	*46*
Reading	*32*
Family entertainment (eg theme parks)	*30*
Dancing/discos	*19*
Dangerous sports or activities[2]	*12*
Hobbies	*9*
Other forms of relaxing	*34*
Other forms of sport such as golf or tennis	*17*
Other activities	*18*

1 Respondents were asked to think about all the holidays that they had taken over the past 12 months at home and abroad, and to choose the activities that they enjoyed most doing on holiday.
2 Includes activities such as skiing, parascending, water or jet skiing and climbing.
Source: MORI

13.25

Household expenditure on selected leisure items: by household composition, 1993

United Kingdom £ per week

	One adult retired[1]	One man one woman retired[1]	One adult with children	Two adults with children	All households[2]
Holidays	1.66	4.09	4.92	11.36	10.75
Alcoholic drink consumed away from home	0.73	2.44	2.37	8.20	8.19
Meals consumed out[3]	1.25	2.76	2.42	7.46	6.83
Television, video, audio and home computers including rental	2.12	2.43	3.77	5.30	4.42
Books, newspapers, magazines, hobbies	1.74	3.16	2.13	4.78	4.29
DIY materials for home repairs, etc	0.31	3.57	0.99	5.68	4.03
Sports subscriptions and admission charges[4]	0.11	0.27	0.90	3.88	2.77
Cinema, theatre and other entertainment	0.16	0.38	1.02	2.43	1.82
Total weekly expenditure on above	8.08	19.09	18.52	49.09	43.09
Expenditure on above items as a percentage of total household expenditure	*10.9*	*13.6*	*10.9*	*13.4*	*15.6*

1 Households mainly dependent on state pensions.
2 Includes households of compositions not shown separately in the table.
3 Eaten on the premises, excluding state school meals and workplace meals.
4 Includes sports goods, but not clothes.
Source: Central Statistical Office

References and further reading

The following list contains selected publications relevant to **Chapter 13: Leisure**. Those published by HMSO are available from the addresses shown on the inside back cover of *Social Trends.*

Annual Reports of the Sports Council, Sports Council for Northern Ireland, Sports Council for Wales and the Scottish Sports Council, available from the individual Councils
Arts Council of England Annual Report and Accounts, Arts Council of England
Arts Council of Northern Ireland Annual Report and Accounts, Arts Council of Northern Ireland
BBC Handbook, BBC
BPI Statistical Handbook, British Phonographic Industry
Business Monitor MQ6 - Overseas Travel and Tourism, HMSO
Cinema and Video Industry Audience Research, CAA
CNC info, Centre National de la Cinématographie
Cultural Trends, Policy Studies Institute
Day visits in Great Britain 1991/92, HMSO
Digest of Tourist Statistics, British Tourist Authority
Employment Gazette, Harrington Kilbride
Family Spending - A report on the 1993 Family Expenditure Survey, HMSO
Film and Year Book, British Film Institute
General Household Survey, HMSO
Independent Broadcasting Authority Annual Report and Accounts, IBA
Leisure Futures, The Henley Centre
Social Focus on Children, HMSO
The UK Tourist, Tourist Boards of England, Northern Ireland, Scotland and Wales
Visits to Tourist Attractions, British Tourist Authority and National Tourist Boards

Contacts

Telephone contact points for further information relating to **Chapter 13: Leisure**.

Central Statistical Office	
Family Expenditure Survey	0171 217 4255
International Passenger Survey	0171 217 4328
Department of Finance and Personnel, Northern Ireland	01232 521154
Office of Population Censuses and Surveys	0171 396 2327
Arts Council of England	0171 333 0100
Centre for Leisure Research	0131 312 6895
Cinema Advertising Association	0171 439 9531
National Readership Surveys Ltd	0171 379 0344
The Gaming Board for Great Britain	0171 306 6200
The Henley Centre	0171 353 9961
The Institute of Public Finance Ltd	0181 667 1144
The Sports Council	0171 388 1277

Geographical areas of the United Kingdom used in Social Trends

Appendix: major surveys

	Frequency	Sampling frame	Type of respondent	Location	Set sample size (most recent survey included in *Social Trends*)	Response rate (percentages)
Agricultural Census	Annual	Agricultural lists	Occupiers of agricultural holdings	UK	242,000 individuals	87
Census of Population	Decennial	Detailed local	Household head	UK	Full count	98
British Social Attitudes Survey	Annual	Electoral Register/ Postcode Address File[1]	Adult in household	GB	4,752 addresses	67
British National Travel Survey - Yearly[2]	Annual	Electoral Register	Individual adult	GB	4,440 individuals[3]	55
British Crime Survey	Intermittent	Electoral Register	Adult in household	EW	11,400 addresses	77
Continuous Household Survey	Continuous	Rating valuation list	All adults in household	NI	4,500 addresses	71
Day Visits Survey[4]	Intermittent	Postcode Address File	All adults in household	GB	12,000	74
Family Expenditure Survey	Continuous	Postcode Address File	Household	UK	11,647 addresses[5]	69[6]
General Household Survey	Continuous	Postcode Address File	All adults in household	GB	11,787	82
Health Survey for England	Annual	Postcode Address File	All adults in household	E	3,016 addresses	82
International Passenger Survey	Continuous	International passengers at ports and airports	Individual traveller	UK	191,000 individuals	86
Labour Force Survey	Continuous	Postcode Address File	All adults in household[7]	GB	60,000 addresses	83[8]
National Food Survey	Continuous	Postcode Address File	Person responsible for domestic food arrangements	GB	12,309 addresses	61
National Readership Survey	Continuous	Electoral Register	Individual in home	GB	28,319 individuals	65
National Survey of Sexual Attitudes and Lifestyles	One off	Postcode Address File	Adult in household under the age of 60	GB	29,802[9]	65[10]
National Travel Survey	Continuous	Postcode Address File	Individual in household	GB	5,000 households per year	80
New Earnings Survey	Annual	Inland Revenue PAYE records	Employee[11]	GB	[11]	[11]
Survey of Personal Incomes	Annual	Inland Revenue	Individuals[12]	UK	80,000 individuals	98
Smoking among secondary school children	Biannual	DFE and SOED[13] records	School pupils (aged 11-15)	GB	9,728 pupils	87
Youth Cohort Study	Irregular	DFE schools records	Young people aged 16-19	EW	23,000 individuals	84

1 In 1991 half the British Social Attitudes sample was drawn from the Electoral Register and half from the Postcode Address File in order to investigate the effect of using different sampling frames. Prior to 1991 all sampling frames were drawn from the Electoral Register.
2 Previously known as the British Tourism Survey, yearly.
3 Basic sample only; in 1989 a further 4,302 individuals were contacted in connection with holidays abroad.
4 Trailer to the General Household Survey.
5 Effective sample only. Set sample includes ineligible households.
6 Response rate refers to GB.
7 Includes some proxy information.
8 Response rate to first wave interviews quoted. Response rate to second to fifth wave interviews 96% of those previously accepting.
9 Potentially eligible addresses. Set sample of 50,000 addresses included ineligible adults as those aged 60 and over were screened out.
10 Adjusted for the likely proportions of addresses with no eligible resident or addresses where no contact could be made.
11 In the New Earnings Survey employers supply data on a 1 per cent sample of employees who are members of PAYE schemes. 210 thousand were selected for the 1994 sample and there was a 94.1 per cent response but some 37 thousand returned questionnaires did not contain data.
12 In the Survey of Personal Incomes local tax offices supply data on individuals to a central point in Inland Revenue.
13 Department for Education and The Scottish Office Education Department.

Appendix: definitions and terms

Symbols and conventions

Reference years. Where, because of space constraints, a choice of years has to be made, the most recent year or a run of recent years is shown together with the past population census years (1991, 1981, 1971 etc) and sometimes the mid-points between census years (1986, etc). Other years may be added if they represent a peak or trough in the series.

Rounding of figures. In tables where figures have been rounded to the nearest final digit, there may be an apparent discrepancy between the sum of the constituent items and the total as shown.

Billion. This term is used to represent a thousand million.

Provisional and estimated data. Some data for the latest year (and occasionally for earlier years) are provisional or estimated. To keep footnotes to a minimum, these have not been indicated; source departments will be able to advise if revised data are available.

Non-calendar years.
Financial year - eg 1 April 1993-31 March 1994 would be shown as 1993-94
Academic year - eg September 1992/July 1993 would be shown as 1992/93
Data covering more than one year - eg 1990, 1991 and 1992 would be shown as 1990-1992

Units. The main unit used in each table is shown at the top of the table. Where a table also contains data in a different unit then this is labelled against the relevant row or column. Figures are shown in italics when they represent percentages.

Symbols. The following symbols have been used throughout *Social Trends*:

..	*not available*
.	*not applicable*
-	*negligible (less than half the final digit shown)*
0	*nil*

PART 1: POPULATION

Population and population projections

The estimated and projected populations of an area include all those usually resident in the area, whatever their nationality.
Members of HM forces stationed outside the United Kingdom are excluded. Students are taken to be resident at their term-time addresses. Figures for the United Kingdom do not include the population of the Channel Islands or the Isle of Man.

The population estimates for mid-1991 are final figures based on the 1991 Census of Population. Estimates for later years allow for subsequent births, deaths and migration. The estimates for 1982 to 1990 have been revised to make them consistent with both the 1981 and the 1991 figures based upon successive censuses.

Population projections for the United Kingdom are based on the estimates of the populations of England and Wales, Scotland and Northern Ireland at mid-1992.

The most recent set of national population projections are 1992-based. Further details of these were published in *National Population Projections: 1992-based Series PP2 No. 19* (HMSO). Subnational projections are also made.

Due to definitional changes, there are minor discontinuities for Scotland and Northern Ireland between the figures for 1971 and earlier years. At the United Kingdom level these discontinuities are negligible.

For summary presentation of population levels and changes, the Office of Population Censuses and Surveys uses a classification of local authority districts in England and Wales into three broad area types (Greater London, metropolitan and non-metropolitan) with a more detailed sub-division into ten types of area. The classification is based upon cluster analyses of 1971 and 1981 Census results for many variables at local authority district level. Full details of the classification are given in an appendix of 'Key Population and Vital Statistics: local and health authority areas (annual series VS/PPE, HMSO). This classification does not extend to local authority areas of Scotland or Northern Ireland.

International Passenger Survey migration estimates

The International Passenger Survey (IPS) data do not provide information on all migrants to the UK. Respondents to the survey state the length of time for which they intend to stay in the UK or abroad (the qualifying period is twelve or more months). Migrants to and from the Irish Republic are excluded as are diplomatic and military personnel. It is also highly likely that the IPS migration figures exclude persons seeking asylum after entering the country and short-term visitors granted extensions of stay, for example as students or on the basis of marriage. After taking account of persons leaving the United Kingdom for a short - term period who stayed overseas for longer than originally intended, the net adjustments needed range from about 10 thousand in 1981 to 50 thousand in 1992, i.e., an average of approximately 20 thousand a year.

Asylum

The basis for recognition as a refugee and hence the granting of asylum is the 1951 United Nations Convention relating to the Status of Refugees, extended in its application by the 1967 Protocol relating to the Status of Refugees. The United Kingdom is party to both. The Convention defines a refugee as a person who 'owing to a well-founded fear of being persecuted for reasons of race, religion, nationality, membership of a particular social group or political opinion, is outside the country of his nationality and unable or, owing to such fear, is unwilling to avail himself of the protection of that country'. In addition, the United Kingdom is prepared to grant, to applicants who do not meet the requirements of the

Convention, exceptional leave to stay here for an appropriate period, if it would be unreasonable or impracticable, in all the circumstances, to seek to enforce their return to their country of origin.

PART 2: HOUSEHOLDS AND FAMILIES

Households

A household: a person living alone or a group of people who have the address as their only or main residence and who either share one meal a day or share the living accommodation.

Size of household: is commonly refered to as household size and counts those people who are usually resident in the household irrespective of whether or not they are present on census night. In the General Household Survey the size of the household is the number of people who normally live there.

Families

A family: is a married couple, either with or without their never-married child or children (of any age), or a lone parent together with his or her never-married child or children. A lone parent (in the Census) is a married parent whose spouse does not reside in the same household, or any single, widowed, or divorced parent.

A lone parent family (in the General Household Survey): consists of a lone parent, living with his or her never-married dependent children, provided these children have no children of their own. Married lone mothers whose husbands are not defined as resident in the household are not classified as lone parents because evidence suggests the majority are separated from their husband either because he usually works away from home or for some other reason that does not imply the breakdown of the marriage (see OPCS's GHS Monitor 82/1). Couples describing themselves as married (or common-law married) but who are in fact co-habiting are coded and counted as married.

Children: are never-married people of any age who live with one or both parent(s). They also include stepchildren and adopted children (but not foster children) and also grandchildren (where the parents are absent).

Dependent children: in the 1961 Census, dependent children were defined as children under 15 years of age, and persons of any age in full-time education. In the 1971 Census, dependent children were defined as never-married children in families who were either under 15 years of age, or aged 15-24 and in full-time education. However, for direct comparison with the General Household Survey (GHS) data, the definition of dependent children used for 1971 in Table 2.6 has been changed to include only never-married in families who were either under 15 years of age, or aged 15-18 and in full-time education. In the 1991 Census and the GHS, dependent children are never married children in families who are aged under 16, or aged 16-18 and in full-time education.

PART 3: EDUCATION

Day care

Day nurseries: look after under 5s for the length of the adult working day. They may be provided by the local authorities under the *Children Act 1989*, by voluntary or private organisations who register them with local authorities or be exempt from registration (because they are on Crown property). Children will attend part-time or full-time depending on their parents' needs.

Childminders: look after children on domestic premises, usually their own home. They must be registered if they are paid for looking after children aged under 8 for more than two hours in any day and are not, for example, their parent, nanny, relative or foster parent. They generally offer a service all year round for all or part of the adult working day.

Playgroups: Playgroups provide sessional care for children aged between 3 and 5, though some may take children at two and a half. They aim to provide learning experiences through structured play opportunities in groups, and with involvement of the parents in all aspects of the operation of the group. Most playgroups are run on a self-help basis by groups of parents with one or two paid staff. Like day nurseries, they may be run by local authorities, registered with them or exempt from registration. Playgroup sessions last for a morning or afternoon, not all day.

Main categories of educational establishments

Educational establishments in the United Kingdom may be administered and financed in a number of ways:

Public sector: by local education authorities, which form part of the structure of local government;

Assisted: by governing bodies which have a substantial degree of autonomy from public authorities but which receive grants direct from central government sources;

Grant maintained: since 1988 all local education authority maintained secondary, middle and primary schools can apply for self governing (Grant Maintained) status and receive direct grants from the Department for Education and the Welsh Office. The governing body of such a school is responsible for all aspects of school management, including the deployment of funds, employment of staff and provision of most of the educational support services, staff and pupils. In January 1993 there were 75 primary and 266 secondary self governing schools in England and Wales;

Non-maintained: by the private sector, including individuals, companies, and charitable institutions;

Further Education Funding Councils (FEFCs): from 1993 all colleges in the FEFC sector and further education courses in other establishments have been funded by an FEFC;

Higher Education: since April 199x, publicly-funded HE courses in the United Kingdom have been funded by the HE Funding Councils, the FE Funding Councils of England and Wales, The Scottish Office Education Department, The Scottish Office Agriculture and Fisheries Department and the Department of Education, Northern Ireland;

Local Management of Schools (LMS): under LMS, which was introduced in Northern Ireland in 1991, all public sector and assisted secondary schools have delegated responsibility for managing their school budgets and staff numbers, and this delegation is being extended to primary schools in these sectors.

Pupil/teacher ratios

The pupil/teacher ratio within schools is the ratio of all pupils on the school register to all teachers employed in schools on the day of the annual count. Part-time teachers are included on a full-time equivalent basis, with part-time service calculated as a proportion of a full-time school week. Part-time pupils are counted as 0.5 (except in Scotland where they are counted on a full-time equivalent basis in nurseries and as 1.0 in other sectors).

Stages of education

There are three stages of education: primary (including nursery), secondary, and further (including higher) education. The first two stages are compulsory for all children between the ages of 5 and 16 years (15 before 1972/73). Both nursery and primary schools may include 'rising 5s', that is, pupils aged 4 at 31 August who will be 5 by 31 December. The transition from primary to secondary education is usually made between 10 and a half and 12 years but is sometimes made via middle schools (see below) after age 12. The third stage of eduction is voluntary and includes all education provided after full-time schooling ends.

Primary education: includes three age ranges: nursery, under 5 years of age; infant, 5 to 7 or 8 years; and junior, 7 or 8 to 11 or 12 years. The majority of public sector primary schools take both boys and girls in mixed classes. In Scotland the distinction between infant and primary schools is generally not made. The pattern for nursery and primary education in Northern Ireland is nursery education (age 3 to 4) and primary schools (age 4 to 11). Nursery education is provided in either nursery schools or nursery classes in primary schools. It is compulsory for children who attain the age of 4 on or before 1 July to commence primary school the following September. The usual age for transfer to secondary is 11 as in England and Wales. In Scotland it is 12.

Middle schools: in England and Wales middle schools take children from first schools and generally lead on, in turn, to comprehensive upper schools. They cover varying age ranges between 8 and 14. Depending on their individual age range they are deemed either primary or secondary.

Secondary education: provision of maintained secondary schools in an area may include any combination of types of school. The pattern is a reflection of historical circumstance and of the policy adopted by the local education authority. Comprehensive schools normally admit pupils without reference to ability and aptitude, and cater for all the children in a neighbourhood; but in some areas they co-exist with modern, grammar, and technical schools. In Northern Ireland secondary education normally begins when pupils reach the age of 11. Under current transfer arrangements from primary to secondary education parents have the choice as to whether or not their children take the Transfer Procedure tests which are compiled and marked by the Department of Education. The *Education Reform Order 1989* introduced new open enrolment arrangements whereby all secondary schools are required to admit pupils who have indicated a preference for the school provided there is room at the school. Where schools receive more applications for admission than places available then pupils must be admitted on the basis of published criteria prepared by the schools.

Special schools: either day or boarding, provide education exclusively for children who are so seriously handicapped, physically or mentally, that they cannot profit fully from education in normal schools.

Further education: the term 'further education' may be used in a general sense to cover all non-advanced education after the period of compulsory education. More commonly it excludes those staying on at secondary school, and those studying higher education at universities, polytechnics and some other colleges.

Higher education: the term 'higher education' as used in Table 3.18 covers all courses in universities, further and higher education colleges leading to qualifications above General Certificate of Education A level, Scottish Certificate of Education H grade and BTEC National Diploma/ Certificate or their equivalents.

School leaving qualifications
In England, Wales and Northern Ireland, the main examination for schools pupils at the minimum school leaving age is the General Certificate of Secondary Education (GCSE) which is taken in a wide range of subjects. This examination replaced the GCE O level and CSE examinations in 1987 (1988 in Northern Ireland). The GCSE examination is awarded at grades A to G. GCSE grades A to C are equivalent to O level grades A to C or CSE grade one.

The GCE is also offered at A level and usually taken after a further two years of study in a sixth-form, or equivalent. The results of candidates who have passed at A level are graded from A (the highest) to E (the lowest).

Secondary schooling in Scotland starts at age eleven and a half to twelve and a half years approximately. In 1986 the first phase of the Standard (S) grade examinations was introduced as the replacement for Ordinary (O) grade and by 1992 had superseded them. The courses begin in the third year and continue to the end of fourth year. Each subject has a number of elements, some of which are internally assessed in school. The award for the subject as a whole is given on a 7 point scale at three levels: Credit (1 and 2), General (3 and 4) and Foundation (5 and 6). An award of 7 means that the course has been completed. Pupils who do not complete the course or do not sit all parts of the examination get 'no award'. Standard grades 1-3 are broadly equivalent of the old Ordinary (O) garde pass. The examination of Higher (H) grade requires one further year of study and may be taken at the end of fifth or sixth year. For the more able H grade candidate the range of subjects may be as wide as at S grade and it is not unusual for candidates to study 5 or 6 subjects spanning both arts and science.

PART 4: EMPLOYMENT

Labour force
The civilian labour force includes people aged 16 and over who are either in employment (whether as an employee, self-employed, on work-related government employment and training programmes or doing unpaid family work, but excluding those in HM armed forces) or unemployed. The ILO definition of unemployment refers to people without a job who were available to start work within two weeks and had either looked for work in the previous four weeks or were waiting to start a job they had already obtained. Estimates on this basis are not available before 1984, as the Labour Force Survey did not then collect information on job search over a four week period. The former GB/UK Labour Force definition of unemployment, the only one available for estimates up to 1984, counted people not in employment and seeking work in a reference week (or prevented from seeking work by a temporary sickness or holiday, or waiting for the results of a job application, or waiting to start a job they had already obtained), whether or not they were available to start (except students not able to start because they had to complete their education).

Ethnic groupings
From the Spring 1992 survey, the Labour Force Survey data are based on an ethnic grouping which follows the classification developed for the 1991 Census of Population.

Occupational classification
From 1991 the Labour Force Survey has used the Standard Occupational Classification 1990 (SOC) which has replaced the old Classification of Occupations and Directory of Occupational Titles (CODOT).

Labour disputes
Statistics of stoppages of work caused by labour disputes in the United Kingdom relate to disputes connected with terms and

conditions of employment. Small stoppages involving fewer than ten workers or lasting less than one day are excluded from the statistics unless the aggregate number of working days lost in the dispute exceeds 100. Disputes not resulting in a stoppage of work are not included in the statistics.

Workers involved and working days lost relate to persons both directly and indirectly involved (unable to work although not parties to the dispute) at the establishments where the disputes occurred. People laid off and working days lost at establishments not in dispute, due for example to resulting shortages of supplies, are excluded.

There are difficulties in ensuring complete recording of stoppages, in particular near the margins of the definition; for example short disputes lasting only a day or so, or involving only a few workers. Any under-recording would affect the total number of stoppages much more than the number of working days lost.

Trade Union membership
Includes organisations described as staff associations. Thirty one organisations previously regarded as Trade Unions are excluded from 1975 onwards because they failed to satisfy the statutory definition of a Trade Union in section 1 of the *Trade Union and Labour Relations (Consolidation) Act, 1992.*

Definition of unemployment - claimant count
People claiming benefit (that is unemployment benefit, income support, or national insurance credits) at Employment Service local offices (formerly Unemployment Benefit Offices) on the day of the monthly count, who on that day state that they are unemployed and that they satisfy the conditions for claiming benefit. (Students claiming benefit during a vacation and who intend to return to full-time education are excluded.)

Unemployment rates - claimants
Unemployment rates, available down to the level of travel-to-work areas, are calculated by expressing the number of unemployed claimants as a percentage of the mid-year estimate of the total workforce (the sum of employees in employment (Employer survey-based measure), unemployed claimants, self employed, HM armed forces and participants on work-related government training programmes).

Narrower rates (as a percentage of employees in employment (Employer survey-based measure) and the claimant unemployed only) are also available down to the level of travel-to-work areas.

Definition of unemployment and unemployment rates - ILO/OECD concepts
The unemployment figures used in these standardised rates are estimated by the OECD to conform, as far as possible, with the definition of unemployment in the guidelines of the International Labour Organisation (ILO), and the rates are calculated as percentages of the total economically active, again as defined in the ILO guidelines. According to these guidelines the unemployed covers all persons of working age who, in a specified period, are without work, who are available for work in the next two weeks, and who were seeking employment for pay or profit in the last four weeks or are waiting to start a job already obtained. The total labour force consists of civilian employees, the self-employed, unpaid family workers, professional and conscripted members of the HM armed forces, and the ILO unemployed. The standardised rates will therefore differ from the unemployment rates published in national sources whenever the national definition of unemployment differs from that indicated above, or the denominator used to calculate the national rates is other than the total economically active.

PART 5: INCOME AND WEALTH

Equivalisation scales
Both HBAI and ROI use McClements equivalence scales to take into account variations in the size and composition of households. This reflects the common sense notion that a household of five adults will need a higher income than a single person living alone to enjoy a comparable standard of living. An overall equivalence value is calculated for each household by summing the appropriate scale values for each household member. Equivalised household income is then calculated by dividing household income by the household's equivalence value. The scales conventionally take a married couple as the reference point with an equivalence value of 1; equivalisation therefore tends to increase relatively the incomes of single person households and (since their incomes are divided by a value of less than 1) to reduce relatively incomes of households with three or more persons. For further information see *Households Below Average Income, A Statistical Analysis, HMSO.*

The HBAI analyses use both before and after housing costs scales, whilst ROI only use before housing costs scales.

McClements equivalence scales:

	Before housing costs	After housing costs
Household member		
First adult (head)	0.61	0.55
Spouse of head	0.39	0.45
Other second adult	0.46	0.45
Third adult	0.42	0.45
Subsequent adults	0.36	0.40
Each dependent aged:		
0-1	0.09	0.07
2-4	0.18	0.18
5-7	0.21	0.21
8-10	0.23	0.23
11-12	0.25	0.26
13-15	0.27	0.28
16 or over	0.36	0.38

The household sector
The household sector includes private trusts and individuals living in institutions as well as those living in households. It differs from the personal sector, as defined in the national accounts, in that it excludes unincorporated private businesses, private non-profit-making bodies serving persons, and the funds of life assurance and pension schemes. More information is given in an article in *Economic Trends*, September 1981.

Household disposable income is equal to the total current income of the household sector *less* payments of United Kingdom taxes on income, employees' national insurance contributions, and contributions of employees to occupational pension schemes. It is revalued at constant prices by the consumers' expenditure deflator.

Redistribution of income (ROI)
Estimates of the incidence of taxes and benefits on household income, based on the Family Expenditure Survey (FES), are published by the CSO in *Economic Trends*. The article covering 1993 appeared in the December 1994 issue, and contains details of the definitions and methods used.

Households Below Average Income (HBAI)
Information on the distribution of income is provided in the Department of Social Security (DSS) publication *Households Below Average Income: 1979 to 1988/89*. This gives a comprehensive statistical analysis of income relating principally to the lower half of the income distribution; and explains the methodology used to derive the figures from the FES.

Difference between Households Below Average Income and Redistribution Of Income series
There are two separate and distinct income series based on the FES, produced by two different government departments. Each series has been developed to serve the specific needs of that department. The DSS series, called 'Households Below Average Income' (HBAI), provides estimates of patterns of personal disposable income in the United Kingdom and of changes over time; as the name suggests, it concentrates on the lower part of the income distribution and shows disposable income before and after housing costs (where disposable income is after deduction of income tax and National Insurance). The CSO series, called 'Redistribution Of Income' (ROI), shows how Government intervention through the tax and benefit system affects the income of households; it covers the whole income distribution and includes the effects of indirect taxes like VAT and duty on beer, as well as estimating the cash value of benefits in kind (eg from state spending on education and health care). The ROI results are designed to show the position in a particular year rather than trends in income levels over time, although trends in the distribution of income are given. An important difference between the two series is that HBAI counts individuals (not households as in ROI).

Net wealth of the personal sector
Balance sheet estimates of the net wealth of the personal sector are published in the *United Kingdom National Accounts*, 1994 edition. These figures exclude the stock of consumer durables which are no longer available. Quarterly estimates of net financial wealth (excluding tangible and intangible assets) are published in *Financial Statistics*.

Distribution of personal wealth
The estimates of the distribution of the marketable wealth of individuals relate to all adults in the United Kingdom. They are produced by combining estimates of the distribution of wealth identified by the estate multiplier method with independent estimates of total personal wealth derived from the CSO personal sector balance sheets. The methods used were described in an article in *Economic Trends* (October 1990) entitled 'Estimates of the Distribution of Personal Wealth'. Net wealth of the personal sector differs from marketable wealth with the value of dwellings removed for the following reasons:

Difference in coverage: the CSO balance sheet of the personal sector includes the wealth of non-profit making bodies and unincorporated businesses, while the Inland Revenue estimates exclude non-profit making bodies and treat the bank deposits and debts of unincorporated businesses differently from CSO;

Differences in timing: the CSO balance sheet gives values at the end of the year, whereas IR figures are adjusted to mid-year;

IR figures: exclude the wealth of those under 18 and the very wealthy, to avoid producing misleading estimates.

Funded pensions: are included in the CSO figures but not in the IR marketable wealth. Also the CSO balance sheet excludes consumer durables and includes non-marketable tenancy rights, whereas the IR figures include consumer durables and exclude non-marketable tenancy rights;

Share ownership
Estimates of the value of shares held by individuals and others are obtained from the Share Register Survey, run by the CSO. Results of the most recent survey are published in *Share Ownership, The Share Register Survey Report*.

The survey results are based on an analysis of the ordinary share registers of a sample of UK companies listed on the London Stock Exchange. A sample of shareholdings on each register are analysed and allocated to one of the categories of beneficial ownership. Results are grossed to stock market totals.
Estimates of the number of individuals holding shares are obtained from a survey run by National Opinion Polls on behalf of HM Treasury.

PART 6: EXPENDITURE

Retail prices
The general index of retail prices measures the changes month by month in the level of the commodities and services purchased by all types of households in the United Kingdom, with the exception of certain higher income households and households of retired people mainly dependent on state benefits. These households are:

(a) the 4 per cent (approximately) where the total household recorded gross income exceeds a certain amount (£925 a week in 1991/92);

(b) those in which at least three quarters of the total income is derived from state pensions and benefits and which include at least 1 person over the national insurance retirement age.

The weights which are used to calculate the index are based on the pattern of household expenditure derived from the continuing Family Expenditure Survey. Since 1962 the weights have been revised in February of each year.

Expenditure patterns of one-person and two-person pensioner households differ from those of the households upon which the general index is based. Separate indices have been compiled for such pensioner households since 1968, and quarterly averages are published in the Central Statistical Office *Business Monitor MM23 (Retail Prices Index)*. They are chain indices constructed in the same way as the general index of retail prices. It should, however, be noted that the pensioner indices exclude housing costs.

A brief introduction to the RPI is given in the February 1993 issue of CSO *Business Monitor MM23 (Retail Prices Index)*, also available as a booklet from HMSO. Each month's edition of the RPI *Business Monitor* contains further articles of interest, covering topics such as reweighting, indicator items and the construction of the new foreign holidays index.

Household expenditure
The national accounts definition of household expenditure, within consumers' expenditure, consists of: personal expenditure on goods (durable and non-durable) and services, including the value of income in kind; imputed rent for owner-occupied dwellings; and the purchase of secondhand goods less the proceeds of sales of used goods.

Excluded are: interest and other transfer payments; all business expenditure; and the purchase of land and buildings (and associated costs).

In principle, expenditure is measured at the time of acquisition rather than actual disbursement of cash. The categories of expenditure include that of non-resident as well as resident households and individuals in the United Kingdom.

For further details see the article entitled 'Consumers' expenditure' in *Economic Trends*, September 1983.

Household saving
Household saving is the balance of income and expenditure on the current account of households, and is derived from the personal sector account, mainly by subtracting the income and the expenditure (and hence the saving) of the other parts of the personal sector.

The household savings ratio is household saving expressed as a percentage of household disposable income.

Household income comprises:
Wages and salaries, and forces' pay
Self-employment income
Rent, dividends, and interest
Income in kind
Pensions and benefits paid by life assurance and pension schemes
Social security benefits
Other current transfers

Household disposable income comprises:
Household income less
United Kingdom taxes on income
Social security contributions (excluding employers' contributions)
Employees' contributions to occupational pension schemes

Household expenditure comprises:
Interest payments
Community charge (until March 1993); Council tax (from April 1993);
Rates (Northern Ireland)
Expenditure on goods and services
Life assurance premiums etc paid by individuals
Other current transfers

(Note: this definition of household expenditure does not accord with that for national accounts purposes - see above.)

PART 7: HEALTH

Expectation of life
The expectation of life, shown in Table 7.2, is the average number of years which a person of that age could be expected to live, if the rates of mortality at each age were those experienced in that year.

The mortality rates which underlie the expectation of life figures are based, up to 1991, on total deaths occurring in each year and, in the case of subsequent years, on the mortality rates assumed for those years in the Government Actuary's mid-1992 based population projections.

Blood pressure level
On the basis of their blood pressure readings and whether they reported currently taking any drugs prescribed for high blood pressure, Health Survey informants were classified into one of the following four categories:

Normotensive untreated: systolic less than 160 mmHg and diastolic less than 95 mmHg, not currently taking drug(s) prescribed for high blood pressure

Normotensive treated: systolic less than 160 mmHg, and diastolic less than 95 mmHg, currently taking drug(s) prescribed for high blood pressure

Hypertensive treated: systolic greater than 159 mmHg and/or diastolic greater than 94 mmHg, currently taking drug(s) prescribed for high blood pressure

Hypertensive untreated: systolic greater than 159 mmHg and/or diastolic greater than 94 mmHg, not currently taking drug(s) prescribed for high blood pressure

Informants are described as having high blood pressure if they are hypertensive, or normotensive but are currently being treated for high blood pressure.

Blood pressure in the Health Survey was measured using an automatic machine, the Dinamap 8100 monitor. It should be noted that the results may not be directly comparable to readings taken using a standard mercury sphygmomanometer. Comparison of blood pressure levels from the Health Survey for England with other epidemiological studies which have used different measuring devices is problematic, and should only be done with caution.

Serum total cholesterol
Cholesterol is a lipid or fatty substance. Serum total cholesterol is known to be instrumental in the development of cardiovascular disease, particularly that associated with low-density lipoprotein (LDL). For example, a follow-up of subjects in the Regional Heart Study after a mean time lapse of 4.2 years showed that serum total cholesterol was an independent risk factor with the power to predict major ischaemic heart disease of a similar order to smoking and blood pressure.

The Renfrew and Paisley study found that men and women with plasma cholesterol levels in the top fifth of cholesterol values had a greater risk of coronary mortality than those in the lowest fifth; the relative risks were 1.77 for women and 1.56 for men, after allowing for age, cigarette smoking, diastolic blood pressure, body mass index and social class.

Cholesterol level is used to monitor health partly because it can be modified by changes in lifestyle or by treatment so that it is amenable to intervention. There is, however, some controversy about the wisdom of lowering cholesterol by drugs because some studies have suggested that this increases certain non-cardiovascular causes of mortality.

Conventional categories have been adopted for the analyses of cholesterol in this report and are as follows :

Level of total cholesterol millimoles per litre (mmol/l)	Description
Less than 5.2	desirable
5.2 - 6.4	mildly elevated
6.5 - 7.7	moderately elevated
7.8 or more	severely elevated

The table excludes adults who were on lipid-lowering drugs. The drugs affect the cholesterol levels of these individuals and their inclusion could therefore alter the apparent relationships between cholesterol level and other variables.

Physical activity level
The 'frequency-intensity activity' summary measure of physical activity used in the table to classify individuals according to the level of activity reported in the interview is based on the total number of occasions of moderate or vigorous intensity activity during the previous four weeks.

The summary measure follows the suggested guidelines (current at the time of the survey) for activity to have a protective effect against cardiovascular disease (CVD), and used a threshold of 20 minutes duration for an activity occasion. For non-sporting activities it was assumed in developing the summary measure that each occasion of moderate or vigorous activity reported was of at least twenty minutes duration. Sports occasions are only included if the average duration for an individual was at least 20 minutes.

The categories are as follows:

Level	Description
Level 5	Twelve or more occasions of vigorous activity
Level 4	Twelve or more occasions of a mix of moderate or vigorous activity
Level 3	Twelve or more occasions of moderate activity
Level 2	Five to eleven occasions of at least moderate activity
Level 1	One to four occasions of at least moderate activity
Level 0	No occasions of moderate or vigorous activity

Body mass index (BMI)
Obesity is linked to ill-health and results in an increased risk of a number of diseases. Body weight is a poor indicator of obesity on its own as it does not take account of skeletal size or body composition. A number of alternative measures of obesity have been developed. Body mass index (BMI) or Quetelet Index is the most widely used index of obesity which standardises weight for height and is calculated as weight (kg)/ height(m)^2. The index can only be calculated on cases where both height and weight measurements are considered to be valid: 3,114 men and 3,430 women in the Health Survey (1991 and 1992 combined).

While BMI is the most widely used measure of obesity it is not without faults. BMI does not take account of the relative distribution of fat on different parts of the body nor does it distinguish between body fat and muscle. It is known to give misleading measures of obesity on certain physiques, in particular, individuals with muscular physiques.

For the purposes of analysis, BMI is classified according to the following internationally accepted categories:

Level of index	Description
20 or less	Underweight
over 20 to 25	Desirable
over 25 to 30	Overweight
over 30	Obese

Diseases and conditions - ICD codes
The causes of death included in Table 7.12 correspond to the International Classification of Diseases as follows: lung cancer - 162; breast cancer - 174-175; malignant melanoma of the skin - 172; diabetes - 250; obesity - 278.0; neurotic disorders - 300; alcohol dependence - 303; drug dependence - 304; acute reaction to stress - 308; migraine - 346; hypertension - 401-405; ischaemic heart disease - 410-414; cerebrovascular disease (stroke) - 430-438; asthma - 493; dermatitis and eczema - 690-698; normal pregnancy - V22.

Standardised registration ratios (SRR)
The incidence of cancer varies greatly with age. The SRR is an index which enables ready comparison of incidence rates in populations with different age structures. It is calculated by denoting one set of age-specific rates as the standard. These are then applied to each of several index populations of known age structure to see how many registrations would have been expected in these index populations had they, at each age, experienced the cancer incidence of the standard population. The 'expected' incidence so found is then compared with the 'observed', their ratio being multiplied by 100 to give an index in which 100 is the value for the standard population.

Standardised death rates
The mortality rates are derived from the product of the UK rate and the Standardised Mortality Ratio (SMR) for each region. In turn, the SMR is the ratio of observed deaths to those expected by applying standard death rates to the regional population.

Accidental deaths
The data in Table 7.31 exclude deaths where it was not known whether the cause was accidentally or purposely inflicted, misadventure during medical care, abnormal reactions and late complications.

PART 8: SOCIAL PROTECTION

Unrestricted principals
An unrestricted principal is a medical practitioner who provides the full range of general medical services and whose list is not limited to any particular group or persons. In a few cases (about 20), he may be relieved of the liability to have patients assigned to him or be exempted from liability to emergency calls out-of-hours from patients other than his own. Doctors may also practise in the general medical services as restricted principals, assistants or trainees.

Clients of selected medical welfare organisations
Haemophilia Society:: Figures relate to members.
Leukaemia Care Society: Figures represent numbers of families.
National Back Pain Association: Excludes requests for 348 thousand leaflets and posters.
National Society for Epilepsy: Includes patients, long-term residents, outpatients and those seeking advice.
Terrence Higgins Trust: Figures relate to clients of community services in Greater London area only; they exclude around 20 thousand helpline users.

Selected advisory and counselling services
Al-Anon Family Groups: Includes Irish Republic.
Alcoholic Anonymous: Includes branches in the Channel Isles. The 1981 and 1990 figures exclude Northern Ireland.
Catholic Marriage Advisory Council: Figures relate to Great Britain.
Citizens Advice Bureaux: Figures given for 'Clients represent new enquiries in 1971, and new plus repeat enquiries thereafter.
Cruse: Cruse Bereavement Care. Figures given for clients exclude many short-term contracts.
Relate: Includes England, Wales, Northern Ireland, Channel Isles and Isle of Man. Marriage Guidance Scotland is excluded. Up to 1981, figures given for 'Clients' represented numbers of families (based on new cases during the year). From 1992 it represents all clients using Relate services.
Samaritans: Figures relate to the number of contacts.
Youth Access: Figures given are numbers of young people accessing information, advice and counselling services.

Groups of beneficiaries
Elderly people
Retirement pension
Non-contributory retirement pension
Christmas bonus paid with retirement pension and other non-disability benefits
Principal income-related benefits and social fund payments to people over 60[1]

Long-term sick and disabled people
Invalidity benefit
Attendanceallowance
Mobility allowance
Disability working allowance
Industrial disablement benefit
Other industrial injuries benefits
Severe disablement allowance
Invalid care allowance
War pensions
Independent living fund
Motability
Christmas bonus paid with disability benefits
Principal income-related benefits and social fund payments to disabled people and people sick for more than six months[1]

Short-term sick people
Statutory sick pay
Sickness benefit
Principal income related benefits and social fund payments to people who are sick up to six months and who do not receive a disability benefit1

Families
Child benefit
One parent benefit
Family credit
Family income support
Statutory maternity pay
Maternity allowance
Maternity grant
Social fund maternity payments
Principal income-related benefits and social fund payments to unemployed people and their families[1]
Housing and community charge benefits paid to people in work

Unemployed people
Unemployment benefit
Principal income-related benefits and payments from the social fund to lone-parent families[1]

Widows and other
Widow's benefits
War widow's pensions
Guardian's allowance and child's special allowance
Death grant
Industrial death benefit
Social fund funeral payments
Income support/supplementary benefit paid to people between 50 and 60 who have not had contact with the labour market for over 10 years

[1] Principal income-related benefits are income-support, housing benefit and community charge benefits.

Social security benefits
The National Insurance Fund provides insurance against loss of income in the event of unemployment, sickness and invalidity, widowhood or retirement. These are generally known as contributory benefits. Non-contributory benefits include income-related support to people or families with low income (income support and family credit). Payments, often in the form of loans, may also be made from the social fund to assist people with exceptional expenses which they would find difficult to pay out of their regular income. Non-income-related support is available through child benefit and, for the long-term sick or disabled, through severe disablement allowance, attendance allowance and disability living allowance and the various industrial injury benefits. A separate war pensions scheme pays benefit to people widowed or disabled as a result of wars, or service in HM armed forces, since 1914.

Housing benefit and rate rebate: figures for 1981/82 include Supplementary benefits recipients with rent assistance. All of these figures are average caseload throughout the year. Figures for 1991/92 and 1993/94 are taken from a point in time as at the end of February for each relevant year and include Income support recipients.

PART 9: CRIME AND JUSTICE

Drugs seizures
Drugs which are seized come in a variety of forms but for the purposes of Table 9.6, amounts have been converted to weights. Figures for LSD and MDMA (ecstasy) are not included in the table as they are measured in thousands of doses. Seizures can involve more than one drug and so figures for individual drugs cannot be added together to produce totals. Seizures of unspecified quantities are not included.

Type of area
Geographical areas as used in Table 9.8 come from the system used for the 1991 census - A Classification Of Residential Neighbourhoods (ACORN). Definitions are:
Thriving: wealthy suburban areas, rural and retirement areas
Expanding: affluent executives and well off workers in family areas
Rising: affluent professionals in towns and city areas
Settling: home owning areas with skilled workers and comfortable middle agers
Aspiring: new home owners, white collar workers, better off multi ethnic areas
Striving: less prosperous areas, council estates and low income multi ethnic areas

Offenders cautioned for burglary
Offenders cautioned for going equipped for stealing, etc were counted against 'Burglary offences' until 1986 and against 'Other offences' from 1987. Historical data provided in Table 9.17 have been amended to take account of this change. Drug offences were included under Other offences included for 1971.

Criminal courts in England and Wales
The courts of ordinary criminal jurisdiction in England and Wales are magistrates' courts, which try the less serious cases and the Crown Court which deals with the more serious cases. Prior to 1 October 1992, almost all offenders under 17 were dealt with in juvenile courts, which were a special form of magistrates' court. The *Criminal Justice Act 1991*, which came into effect on 1 October 1992, brought offenders aged 17 within their jurisdiction and renamed them youth courts. The Crown Court was established by the *Courts Act 1971*, which came into effect on 1 January 1972. From that date the former courts of assize and quarter sessions were abolished. Part III of the *Criminal Law Act 1977*, which came into effect on 17 July 1978, redefined offences according to three new modes of trial, namely:
(a) offences triable only on indictment
(b) offences triable either on indictment or summarily, but which are triable summarily only with the consent of the accused
(c) offences triable only summarily

For statistical purposes the figures for court proceedings and for police cautioning for 1979 onwards are shown in two groups; the first group is a combination of i. and ii. above which has been called 'indictable' and covers those offences which may be tried by jury in the Crown Court and the second group, 'summary' offences, covers iii. above and are usually only tried at magistrates' courts.

Criminal courts in Scotland
The courts exercising criminal jurisdiction in Scotland are the High Court of Justiciary, the Sheriff Court and the District Court.

The High Court is Scotland's supreme criminal court, and deals with the most serious cases and with all appeals. There is no appeal from it to the House of Lords. All cases in High Court are tried by a judge and jury (referred to as 'solemn procedure' or 'on indictment').

The Sheriff Court has both solemn and summary jurisdiction and deals with less serious cases. Most prosecutions are dealt with by summary procedure (ie before a sheriff and without a jury). The sentencing powers of the Sheriff Court are more limited than those of the High Court, but where a case merits more severe penalties the sheriff may remit it to the High Court for sentence.

The District Courts were established in 1975 by statute to replace the former Burgh Courts. The District Courts are presided over by lay justices or stipendiary magistrates who are professional lawyers appointed to the district courts and deal summarily with minor offences. The sentencing powers of the District Court are more limited than that of the Sheriff Court, except where it is presided over by a stipendiary magistrate, when it has the same jurisdiction and powers as a sheriff sitting summarily. Prosecutions in Scotland are brought by procurators fiscal who act in the public interest on behalf of the Lord Advocate. It is the procurator fiscal, advised in serious cases by Crown Counsel, who decides in each case whether to proceed, and if so, in which court to prosecute.

Criminal courts in Northern Ireland
Courts of criminal jurisdiction in Northern Ireland, like England and Wales, include magistrate's courts and Crown Courts with similar distinctions in treating offences of varying seriousness. However, since 1973 a special procedure has been developed for dealing with serious offences relating to terrorism. The majority of these offences are also tried in the Crown Court on indictment but they are tried by a judge without a jury, the judge alone deciding all issues of fact as well as law and passing sentence after conviction. The special non-jury Crown Courts are often referred to as 'Diplock' courts (as they are based on recommendations of a Commission under Lord Diplock). The offences triable in this way are listed in Schedule 1 of the *Northern Ireland Emergency Provisions Act 1991* and are referred to as scheduled offences. Some of the offences listed may be de-scheduled by the Attorney-General in particular cases. They should be de-scheduled if no element of terrorism was involved in their commission.

Sentences and orders
The following are the main sentences and orders which can be imposed upon those persons found guilty in 1991, 1992 and 1993. Some types of sentence or order can only be given to offenders in England and Wales in certain age groups. Under a new statutory framework for sentencing contained in the *Criminal Justice Acts 1991* and *1993*, the sentence must reflect the seriousness of the offence. A custodial sentence may also be justified by the need to protect the public from serious harm from a violent or sexual offender. Where custody is not justified, a court may pass a community sentence which may consist of one or more community orders, as well as a fine.

Absolute and conditional discharge
A court may make an order discharging a person absolutely or (except in Scotland) conditionally where it is inexpedient to inflict punishment and, before 1 October 1992, where a probation order was not appropriate. An order for conditional discharge runs for such period of not more than three years as the court specifies, the condition being that the offender does not commit another offence within the period so specified. In Scotland a court may also discharge a person with an admonition.

Attendance centre order
This sentence, available in England, Wales and Northern Ireland, involves deprivation of free time. The centres are mainly for boys between the ages of 10 and 16 found guilty of offences for which an adult could be sentenced to imprisonment. At the end of 1991, there were over 80 centres for boys aged 10 to 16, 18 of which also took girls in the same age group, as well as 26 centres for males aged 17 to 20. Attendance is on Saturday mornings or afternoons for up to three hours on any one occasion and for a total of not more than 36 hours and (normally) not less than 12. The activities include physical training and instruction in useful skills (eg first aid).

Probation
The *Criminal Justice Act 1991* states that a court may make a probation order where this is desirable in the interests of securing the rehabilitation of the offender or protecting the public from harm or preventing further offending. An offender sentenced to a probation order is under the supervision of a probation officer (social worker in Scotland), whose duty it is to advise, assist, and befriend him. A cardinal feature of the order is that it relies on the co-operation of the offender. In England and Wales probation orders may only be made on people aged 16 or over (17 or over prior to 1 October 1992).

The *Criminal Justice Act 1991* also extended the use of supervision orders, previously limited to juveniles aged under 17, to include those aged 17. There is no age limit in Scotland, but children under 16 would normally be dealt with outside the criminal justice system. Probation orders may be given for any period between 6 months and 3 years inclusive.

Community service
An offender aged 16 or over who is convicted of an offence punishable with imprisonment may be sentenced to perform unpaid work for not more than 240 hours, and not less than 40 hours. Prior to 1 October 1992 those aged 16 could be required to perform a maximum of 120 hours. In Scotland the *Law Reform (Miscellaneous Provisions) (Scotland) Act 1990* requires that community service can only be ordered where the court would otherwise have imposed imprisonment or detention. Probation and community service may be combined in a single order in Scotland.

Combination order
The *Criminal Justice Act 1991* introduced the combination order, which combines elements of both probation supervision and community service, and may be given to offenders aged 16 or over. The order may require the offender to perform between 40 and 100 hours unpaid work and to be supervised by a probation officer for a period between 12 months and 3 years.

Imprisonment
The custodial sentence for adult offenders is imprisonment or, in the case of mentally abnormal offenders, hospital orders which may include a restriction order such that Home Office consent is needed for release or transfer. Prior to 1 October 1992 in England and Wales a third of a prisoner's sentence, or one half for those serving sentences of 12 months or less, was remitted subject to good conduct and industry. Those serving sentences of over 9 months (18 months in Scotland) could be released under the parole scheme after serving 6 months (12 months in Scotland) or a third of the sentence, whichever was the longer. The *Criminal Justice Act 1991* abolished remission and substantially changed the parole scheme in England and Wales. Those serving sentences of under 4 years, imposed on or after 1 October 1992, are subject to Automatic Conditional Release and are released, subject to certain criteria, halfway through their sentence. Those serving sentences of four years or longer are considered for Discretionary Conditional Release after having served half their sentence, but are automatically released at the two-thirds point of sentence. All offenders serving a sentence of 12 months or more are supervised in the community until the three-quarter point of sentence. Additional days imposed for breaches of prison discipline can delay a prisoner's early release. A life sentence prisoner may be released on licence subject to supervision and is always liable to recall. The *Prisoners and Criminal Proceedings (Scotland) Act 1993* effected similar changes in Scotland as from 1 October 1993.

Fully suspended sentences
The *Criminal Justice Act 1991* provides that fully suspended sentences may only be passed in exceptional circumstances. In England, Wales and Northern Ireland, sentences of imprisonment of two years or

less may be fully suspended. A court should not pass a suspended sentence unless a sentence of imprisonment would be appropriate in the absence of a power to suspend. The result of suspending a sentence is that it will not take effect unless during the period specified the offender is convicted of another offence punishable with imprisonment.

The *Criminal Justice Act 1972*, which came into force on 1 January 1973, gave the courts power, on passing a suspended sentence of over 6 months, to impose a 'suspended sentence with supervision order' placing the offender under the supervision of a probation officer for a specified period not longer than the period of suspension.

Partly suspended and extended sentences of imprisonment
Section 5 of the *Criminal Justice Act 1991* abolished the courts' power to pass a partly suspended sentence of imprisonment or to pass an extended sentence of imprisonment on a persistent offender, with effect from 1 October 1992.

Young offenders institutions
The *Criminal Justice Act 1991* made a number of changes to the custodial sentencing arrangements for young offenders in England and Wales. A common minimum age of 15 for boys and girls was set for the imposition of a sentence of detention in a young offender institution, thus removing boys aged 14 from the scope of this sentence.

From 1 October 1992 the minimum period for which those aged 15 to 17 may be detained is 2 months (previously 21 days for boys and 4 months for girls) and the maximum is 12 months. For offenders aged 18 and under 21 the minimum is 21 days and the maximum is the same as the adult maximum for the offence. A sentence of custody for life is mandatory for offenders convicted of murder aged 18 and under 21, and is also available for other grave offences. Young offenders serving determinate sentences are eligible for early release (see above).

In Scotland the system is somewhat different. Children under 16 are dealt with by the children's hearings system, which is not part of the criminal justice system. For young offenders (aged 16-21) Borstal training was abolished in Scotland by the *Criminal Justice (Scotland) Act 1980*, and detention centres were abolished by the *Criminal Justice Act 1988* and replaced by detention in a young offenders institution.

Young Offenders Centres: Northern Ireland
On 1 June 1979 provisions in the *Treatment of Offenders (Northern Ireland) Act 1968* were brought into operation so that those under 21 years of age would no longer be sent to prison unless the court wished to impose a sentence of 3 years or more, but would be detained in a Young Offenders Centre.

Fines
The *Criminal Justice Act 1993* introduced new arrangements on 20 September 1993 whereby courts should take account of an offender's means in setting fines. This system replaced the more formal unit fines scheme, included in the *Criminal justice Act 1991*. The Act also introduced the power for courts to arrange deduction of fines from income benefit for those offenders receiving such benefits. Fines may be imposed with or without time to pay the fine. If the fine is not paid in the time allowed imprisonment or detention may result. In Scotland the *Law Reform (Miscellaneous Provision) (Scotland) Act 1990* introduced supervised attendance orders for use by selected courts. These orders are intended to provide an alternative to custody for fine defaulters. The minimum number of hours is 10 and the maximum 60. Orders will comprise work of benefit to the community and/or sessions devoted to topics such as debt counselling and advice on alcohol abuse.

Compensation Orders
The *Powers of Criminal Courts Act 1973* and *Criminal Justice (Scotland) Act 1980* enable criminal courts to help the victims of crime, imposing compensation orders on those found guilty. The *Children Act 1989* abolished the courts' power to make care orders in criminal proceedings, with effect from 14 October 1991.

Ombudsmen
All ombudsmen listed in Table 9.33 are the members of the British and Irish Ombudsmen's Association and there are differences in the procedures for recording and dealing with complaints.
As such, the figures are not comparable between different Ombudsmen - some figures include complaints or cases from the previous year, some include cases which are later found to be outside the terms of reference of the office. Also, the reporting year varies; some are based on the financial year while others use calendar years.

Civil courts in England and Wales
The main civil courts in England and Wales are the High Court and the county courts. Magistrates' courts have a very limited civil jurisdiction, for example, in some family proceedings. Most appeals in civil cases go to the Court of Appeal (Civil Division) and may go from there to the House of Lords.

Since July 1991, county courts have been able to deal with all contract and tort cases and actions for recovery of land, regardless of value. Cases are presided over by a judge who almost always sits without a jury. Jury trials are limited to specified cases, for example, actions for libel. Other types of matter dealt with by these courts include Equity (such as trusts and mortgages), bankruptcy and insolvency, and family proceedings (including divorce and adoption). Some courts will have jurisdiction to deal with all these types of work; others are designated to deal with only some.

Civil courts in Scotland
The Court of Session is the supreme civil court in Scotland. As a general rule it has the original jurisdiction in all civil cases and appellate jurisdiction (that is the power to hear and give decisions on appeals) over all civil courts, unless such jurisdiction, original or appellate, is expressly excluded by statute. The Court is divided into two parts, the Inner House and the Outer House. The Inner House exercises appellate jurisdiction on reclaiming motions from the Outer House and on appeals from the inferior courts. Appeals from the Court of Session may go to the House of Lords. The Sheriff court is the principal local court of civil, as well as criminal, jurisdiction in Scotland. Its civil jurisdiction is comparable with that of the county courts in England and Wales but is more extensive in certain directions. These is no limit to the sum which may be sued for in the Sheriff court. The Sheriff's jurisdiction now includes actions of divorce, but does not extend to actions of declarator of marriage, or to certain other actions; but, with these exceptions, the civil jurisdiction of the court is generally similar in scope to that of the Court of Session. In addition, the Sheriff deals with a mass of quasi-judicial and administrative business, some of which is similar to that dealt with in county courts in England and Wales, but of which a large part is particular to the Scottish system.

Legal aid
Advice and assistance provided by a solicitor, short of actual representation in court or tribunal proceedings, may be obtained free by those whose capital and income are within certain financial limits. Assistance by way of representation covers the cost of a solicitor preparing a case and representing a client in court. It is available (either free or on payment of a contribution

to those who are financially eligible) for some civil cases in the magistrates' court, for proceedings before Mental Health Review Tribunals', discretionary life prisoners before the parole board and disciplinary hearings before a prison governor, and for certain proceedings relating to the care of children and young people.

Legal aid in civil cases covers all work up to and including court proceedings and representing by a solicitor and a counsel, if necessary. Legal aid in these cases is available free or on a contributory basis to those whose capital and income are within certain financial limits. Applicants must show that they have reasonable grounds for asserting or disputing a claim. Certain types of action, including libel and slander, are excluded from this type of legal aid.

In the criminal courts in England and Wales a legal aid order may be made if this appears desirable in the interest of justice and the defendant's means are such that he requires financial help in meeting the costs of the proceedings in which he is involved. No limit of income or capital above which a person is ineligible for legal aid is specified, but the court must order a legally-aided person to contribute towards the costs of his case where his resources are such that he can afford to do so.

Civil Legal Aid in Scotland operates on a similar basis to that in England and Wales. Advice and assistance has similar scope in Scotland but is available to those who are financially eligible either or on payment of a contribution. Assistance by way of representation (ABWOR) is granted mainly for summary criminal cases where a plea of guilty is made, though it also covers proceedings before Mental Health Review Tribunals, discretionary life prisoners before the parole board and disciplinary hearings before a prison governor, and certain civil proceedings. Criminal Legal Aid, which is granted by the Scottish Legal Aid Board for summary cases and for all appeals, and by the courts for solemn cases, is not subject to a contribution.

Support for victims of crime

The Criminal Injuries Compensation Tariff Scheme was introduced on 1 April 1994 to provide lump sum compensation for victims of violent crime in Great Britain. Injuries of comparable severity have been grouped or banded together in a tariff of awards with 25 tariff bands ranging from £1000 to £250,000. The scheme applies to anyone criminally injured within Great Britain or on a British aircraft, hovercraft or ship.

PART 10: HOUSING

Dwellings

Great Britain

Estimates of the stock of dwellings are based on data from the censuses of Population, with adjustments for enumeration errors and for definitional changes. The figures include vacant dwellings and temporary dwellings occupied as a normal place of residence. Privately rented dwellings include those rented from housing associations, private owners and other tenures; including dwellings rented with farm or business premises and those occupied by virtue of employment.

Northern Ireland

Estimates of the stock of dwellings are based on data from the Valuation and Lands Agency listings, with adjustments for enumeration errors and for definitional changes. The figures include vacant dwellings and temporary dwellings occupied as a normal place of residence. Privately rented dwellings include those rented from private owners and other tenures; including dwellings rented with farm or business premises and those occupied by virtue of employment.

Housing Market Package

In his 1992 Autumn Statement, the Chancellor of the Exchequer announced that he had allocated £577 million to housing associations, to enable them to purchase homes from private vendors. The aim was to restore confidence in the depressed owner-occupied market by boosting sales without pushing up prices. The properties had to be ready for occupation and funds were targeted mostly in the south east where the decline in housing prices had been most marked. This initiative subsequently became known as the Housing Market Package.

Bedroom standard

This concept is used to estimate occupation density by allocating a standard number of bedrooms to each household in accordance with its age/sex/marital status composition and the relationship of the members to one another. A separate bedroom is allocated to each married couple, any other person aged 21 or over, each pair of adolescents aged 10 to 20 of the same sex, and each pair of children under 10. Any unpaired person aged 10 to 20 is paired, if possible with a child under 10 of the same sex, if that is not possible, is given a separate bedroom, as is an unpaired child under 10. This standard is then compared with the actual number of bedrooms (including bedsitters) available for the sole use of the household, and deficiencies or excesses are tabulated. Bedrooms converted to other uses are not counted as available unless they have been noted as bedrooms by the informant; bedrooms not actually in use are counted unless uninhabitable.

Homeless households

Great Britain: households for whom local authorities accepted responsibility to secure accommodation under the *Housing (Homeless Persons) Act 1977* and the *Housing Act 1985* which defines 'proiroity need'.

Northern Ireland: households for whom Northern Ireland Housing Executive has accepted responsibility to secure permanent accommodation, not neccesarily those for whom permanent accommodation has been found.

Unfit dwellings

The 1989 *Local government and Housing Act* states that a dwelling-house is fit for human habitation unless in the opinion of the local housing authority it fails to meet one or more of the requirements below and by reason of that failure is not reasonably suitable for occupation.

Requirements of the standard: it is free from serious disrepair; it is structurally stable; it is free from dampness prejudicial to health of the occupants (if any); it has adequate provision for lighting, heating and ventilation; it has an adequate supply of wholesome water; it has an effective system for the draining of foul, waste and surface water; it has a suitably located WC for exclusive use of occupants; it has for the exclusive use of the occupants (if any) a suitably located bath or shower and wash-hand basin, each of which is provided with a satisfactory supply of hot and cold water; there are satisfactory facilities in the dwelling home for the preparation and cooking of food including a sink with a satisfactory supply of hot and cold water.

Mix-adjusted series

Simple average house prices and the mix-adjusted house price index are based on the DOE/CML 5 per cent sample survey of mortgage completions. House price changes are measured by the mix-adjusted index. The mix (type, size, location and age of dwelling) changes through time, a house price series that account of this provides a better measure of true house price movements than an index based on the simple average price where variations in mix are not taken into account.

Household type
the classification of household type uses the following categories:
1 adult aged 16 to 59
2 adults aged 16-59
Small family: 1 or 2 persons aged under 16 or over and 3 or more persons aged 16, or 3 or more persons aged 16 or over and 2 persons aged under 16.
Large adult household: 3 or more persons aged 16 or over with or without 1 person aged under 16.
2 adults, 1 or both aged 60 or over
1 adult aged 60 or over

Households found accommodation
Households for whom local authorities accepted responsibility to secure permanent accommodation under the *Housing Act 1985* and the *Housing (Scotland) Act 1987, Part II* which defines 'priority need'. Data for Wales include some households given advice and assistance only. Includes actions where priority need category is not known.

PART 11: ENVIRONMENT

Quality of bathing water
Directive 76/160/EEC concerning the quality of bathing water sets inter alia the following mandatory values for the coliform parameters:

- for total coliforms 10,000 per 100 ml; and
- for faecal coliforms 2,000 per 100 ml.

The Directive requires that at least 95 per cent of samples taken for each of these parameters over the bathing season must meet the mandatory values. In practice this has been interpreted in the following manner: where 20 samples are taken a maximum of only one sample for each parameter may exceed the mandatory values for the water to pass the coliform standards; where less than 20 samples are taken none may exceed the mandatory values for the water to pass the coliform standards.

CHAPTER 12: TRANSPORT

Journey purpose
The purpose of a journey is taken to be the activity at the destination, unless that destination is 'home' in which case the purpose is defined by the origin of the journey. A journey is defined as a one-way course of travel having a single main purpose.

To and from work: journeys to a usual place of work, or from work to home.

In course of work: personal journeys in course of work. This includes all work journeys by people with no usual place of work (eg site

workers) and those who work at or from home.

Education: journeys to school or college etc, excluding part-time non-vocational courses.

Escort for work/education: used when the traveller has no purpose of his own, other than to escort or accompany another person to a place of work or education. All other escort purposes are included with the purpose of the person being escorted.

Shopping: all journeys to shops or from shops to home.

Personal business: visits to services eg hairdressers, launderettes, solicitors, churches etc and for medical consultations/ treatment, and eating and drinking unless the main purpose was entertainment/social.

Social and entertainment: meeting friends etc, travelling to all types of entertainment, voluntary work, non-vocational evening classes etc.

Holidays and day trips: journeys (within Great Britain) to or from any holiday (including stays of 4 nights or more with friends or relatives) or journeys for pleasure (not otherwise classified as social or entertainment) within a single day.

Car ownership
Car: the figures for household ownership include four wheeled and three wheeled cars, Land Rovers, Jeeps, minbuses, motorcaravans and dormobiles.

Cars per 1,000 population: body type cars regardless of taxation class includes two, three, four and five doored saloons, convertible coupés, estate, sports, tourers, hearses and limousines. Does not include vans or any light goods vehicles.

Cars and vans: road motor vehicle other than a motorcycle, intended for the carriage of passengers and designed to seat no more than nine people (including the driver). The term 'passenger car' therefore covers microcars (need no permit to be driven), taxis and hired passenger cars, provided that they have fewer than ten seats. This category may also include pick-ups. The above definition is primarily used for international comparisons.

Goods moved
By all goods vehicles including those under 3.5 tonnes gross vehicle weight.

Railway performance indicators
The following punctuality and reliability targets are used in Table 12.17:

Percentage of trains arriving within time shown[1]	Percentage of scheduled services to run[2]
Intercity	
90%/ 10 mins	99
Regional Railways	
Express & long rural	
90%/ 10 mins	99
Urban & short rural	
90%/10 mins	99
Network SouthEast[3]	
92%/ 5 mins	99

1 Monday to Saturday measured at the end of the route.
2 Intercity and Regional Railways Express & long rural target was 99.5 per cent until 1992-93.
3 Punctuality target was 90 per cent until 1990-91.

London Underground has a number of performance targets including 'trains in peak hour service' for which the 1993-94 target was 98 per cent. There is no target based on 'kilometres run' as used in Table 12.17.

Passenger death rates
The following rates are used in Table 12.21:

Air: world passenger carrying services of United Kingdom airlines for fixed and rotary winged craft over 2,300 kilograms. Passenger kilometres relate to revenue passengers only.

Sea: domestic and international passenger services of United Kingdom registered vessels.

CHAPTER 13: LEISURE

Social class: Institute of Practitioners in Advertising (IPA) definition
Social class categories are based on the head of household's occupation as follows:

Class A: Higher managerial, administrative, or professional
Class B: Intermediate managerial, administrative,or professional
Class C1: Supervisory or clerical, and junior managerial, administrative, or professional
Class C2: Skilled manual workers
Class D: Semi and unskilled manual workers
Class E: State pensioners or widows (no other earners), casual or lowest grade workers, or long term unemployed

Index

The references in this index refer to table and chart numbers, or entries in the Appendix.

Published for the Central Statistical Office by HMSO

ISBN 0 11 620653 5

SNAPSHOT OF BRITAIN

Do you need economic and social statistics on different parts of the United Kingdom? If so, Regional Trends is the most comprehensive source of regional statistics.

Here's what the press have said about this famous publication ...

'... the Government's annual 'snapshot' of the nation's regions...' - *The Birmingham Post*

'... reveals a remarkable insight into the way the British live, work, rest & play...' - *Courier & Advertiser (Dundee)*

'... essential to Government planners, scientific researchers or businessmen seeking a profile of an area in which to test their market...' - *Daily Telegraph*

'... myths exploded by the latest statistics from Regional Trends...' - *The Guardian*

'...The regional dimension has been crucial to the story of Britain's economy over the last 10 years...' - *The Independent*

'...The latest *Regional Trends*...shows where to go - and where to stay clear of...'- *The Times*

'...includes district statistics...providing an intriguing insight into small pockets of the country'- *Daily Express*

'...contains some information to confirm stereotyped images of lifestyle around Britain's regions-but also some to challenge them...' - *Financial Times*

From HMSO and through good booksellers.

Published for the Central Statistical Office by HMSO.
Price £27 net
ISBN 0 11 620 649 7

Articles published in previous issues of *Social Trends*

No. 1 1970
Some general developments in social statistics Professor C A Moser, CSO
Public expenditure on the social services Professor B Abel-Smith, London School of Economics and Political Science
The growth of the population to the end of the century Jean Thompson, OPCS
A forecast of effective demand for housing in Great Britain in the 1970s A E Holmans, MHLG

No. 2 1971
Social services manpower Dr S Rosenbaum, CSO
Trends in certificated sickness absence F E Whitehead, DHSS
Some aspects of model building in the social and environmental fields B Benjamin, CSC
Social indicators - health A J Culyer, R J Lavers and A Williams, University of York

No. 3 1972
Social commentary: change in social conditions CSO
Statistics about immigrants: objectives, methods, sources and problems Professor C A Moser, CSO
Central manpower planning in Scottish secondary education A W Brodie, SED
Social malaise research: a study in Liverpool M Flynn, P Flynn and N Mellor, Liverpool City Planning Department
Crimes of violence against the person in England and Wales S Klein, HO

No. 4 1973
Social commentary: certain aspects of the life cycle CSO
The elderly D C L Wroe, CSO
Subjective social indicators M Abrams, SSRC
Mental illness and the psychiatric services E R Bransby, DHSS
Cultural accounting A Peacock and C Godfrey, University of York
Road accidents and casualties in Great Britain J A Rushbrook, DOE

No. 5 1974
Social commentary: men and women CSO
Social security: the European experiment E James and A Laurent, EC Commission
Time budgets B M Hedges, SCPR
Time budgets and models of urban activity patterns N Bullock, P Dickens, M Shapcott and P Steadman, Cambridge University of Architecture
Road traffic and the environment F D Sando and V Batty, DOE

No. 6 1975
Social commentary: social class CSO
Areas of urban deprivation in Great Britain: an analysis of 1971 Census data S Holtermann, DOE
Note: Subjective social indicators Mark Abrams, SSRC

No. 7 1976
Social commentary: social change in Britain 1970-1975 CSO
Crime in England and Wales Dr C Glennie, HO
Crime in Scotland Dr Bruce, SHHD
Subjective measures of quality of life in Britain: 1971 to 1975 J Hall, SSRC

No. 8 1977
Social commentary: fifteen to twenty-five: a decade of transition CSO
The characteristics of low income households R Van Slooten and A G Coverdale, DHSS

No. 9 1979
Housing tenure in England and Wales: the present situation and recent trends A E Holmans, DOE
Social forecasting in Lucas B R Jones, Lucas Industries

No. 10 1980
Social commentary: changes in living standards since the 1950s CSO
Inner cities in England D Allnutt and A Gelardi, DOE
Scotland's schools D Wishart, SED

No. 14 1984
Changes in the Life-styles of the Elderly 1959-1982 M Abrams

No. 15 1985
British Social Attitudes R Jowell and C Aire SCPR

No. 16 1986
Income after retirement G C Fiegehen, DHSS

No 17 1987
Social Trends since World War II Professor H Halsey, University of Oxford
Household Formation and Dissolution and Housing Tenure: a Longitudinal Perspective A E Holmans and S Nandy, DOE; A C Brown, OPCS

No. 18 1988
Major Epidemics of the 20th Century: from Coronary Thrombosis to AIDS Sir Richard Doll, University of Oxford

No. 19 1989
Recent Trends in Social Attitudes L Brook, R Jowell and S Witherspoon, SCPR

No. 20 1990
Social Trends, the next 20 years T Griffin, CSO

No. 21 1991
The 1991 Census of Great Britain: Plans for Content and Output B Mahon and D Pearce OPCS

No. 22 1992
Crime statistics: their use and misuse C Lewis, HO

No. 24 1994
Characteristics of the bottom 20 per cent of the income distribution N Adkin, DSS

Printed in the United Kingdom for HMSO.
Dd.0300316, 1/95, C100, 3400, 5673, 310649.